A Theory of Medical Ethics

A THEORY
OF MEDICAL
ETHICS

ROBERT M. VEATCH

Basic Books, Inc., Publishers   New York

ACKNOWLEDGMENTS

The following previously published material by Robert M. Veatch, used by permission, has been adapted by the author and incorporated into *A Theory of Medical Ethics:*

Case 7, The Homosexual Husband. From the *Hastings Center Report* April 7, 1977, pp. 15–17.

Case 9, Active Killing with Parental Consent. From the *Hastings Center Report* October 9, 1979, p. 19.

Case 10, Justice and Efficiency in Care for the Mentally Retarded. From *Case Studies in Medical Ethics* (Harvard University Press: Cambridge, Mass., 1977). By permission of the publisher. Copyright © 1977 by Robert M. Veatch.

"The Hippocratic Ethic: Consequentialism, Individualism, and Paternalism." From *No Rush to Judgment: Essays on Medical Ethics*, pp. 238–64, edited by David H. Smith and Linda M. Bernstein (Bloomington, Ind.: The Poynter Center, 1978). Copyright © 1978 by the Indiana University Foundation.

"From Cases to Rules: The Challenge in Contemporary Medical Ethics." From *Frontiers in Medical Ethics: Applications in a Medical Setting*, pp. 43–61, edited by Virginia Abernethy (Cambridge, Mass.: Ballinger Publishing Co., 1980).

"Professional Medical Ethics: The Grounding of Its Principles." From *Journal of Medicine and Philosophy* March 4, 1979, pp. 1–19.

Library of Congress Cataloging in Publication Data

Veatch, Robert M.
    A theory of medical ethics.

Bibliography: p. 358
    Includes index.
    1. Medical ethics.   I. Title.
    R724.V42   174'.2   81-66106
    ISBN 0-465-08437-0   AACR2

Cases

Contents

PART II
The Basis of Medical Ethics

PART III
The Principles of Medical Ethics

PART IV
Relating Cases and Principles

Preface

The seeds of *A Theory of Medical Ethics* began to germinate many years ago. In the early 1970s I served as coordinator of the newly created Program in Medical Ethics at Columbia University's College of Physicians and Surgeons as part of my responsibilities as a staff member of the Hastings Center, the research center in Hastings-on-Hudson, New York, devoted to problems of ethics and the life sciences. The first human heart had just been transplanted. Kidney machines were a scarce resource whose distribution was based on the subjective judgments of physician administrators across the country or of equally subjective committees holding the life-or-death power of selection. Abortion, not yet legalized by the Supreme Court's 1973 decision, was increasingly being tolerated by physicians, other health professionals, and society at large, while both practical and moral problems of the issue troubled many people.

We began an integrated program giving medical students opportunities to deal with real life medical ethical problems they would face on the wards of their hospitals and in their private offices. We often encountered what seemed at the time to be difficult moral problems: a dying woman whose physician would not tell her of her tumor; a psychiatric patient whose therapy, purportedly for her own good, was brutal electroshock; a research project involving manipulation of fertilized human egg cells. We would ponder the vast ethical, philosophical, and religious issues these provoked and then often would turn to the codes and oaths of mainstream Western medicine to try to resolve our dilemmas. We would consult the Hippocratic Oath or the Declaration of Geneva or the AMA's "Principles of Medical Ethics" that were in effect at the time.

Increasingly, I became frustrated with that method of attempting to resolve our medical ethical quandaries. Sometimes the real moral question did not seem to turn so much on what action the young physician should take in a particular case as on the action that others—patients, administrators, nurses, judges, or good citizens—should take. The focus of traditional codes of medical ethics, however, was on what physicians of a particular group—whether the Hippocratic medical sect of ancient

Greece, the physicians of the worldwide modern medical community, or the members of the AMA—should do in order to be members in good standing of their professional group. More troubling, even when a problem faced on the hospital wards really did seem to demand deciding what a physician ought to do to be ethical, simply looking up the answer in a code somehow seemed inadequate. That would tell us what a particular group of physicians in a particular time and place in history believed to be their ethical mandate, but was not really satisfying. We would occasionally encounter cases where we were not sure a code was giving us the right answer. "The Oath says this is the right course," we would want to say, "but is it really right?" Especially when various codes and oaths conflicted, as is their wont, both instructors and students would be left singularly dissatisfied.

The foundations of medical ethics, it seemed, had to be something deeper than mere consensus of the members of a professional organization at a particular time and place. It had to be possible to say that a code or oath had it wrong, that the AMA "Principles," for example, could be changed in order to make them conform more closely to what is really required in a physician–patient relationship. The recent revision by the AMA of its "Principles" seems to suggest that its members share this conviction. But for us to say that the codes and oaths were not definitive, not final sources of moral answers, meant that we needed a moral vantage point, a fulcrum from which to gain critical leverage. I was left with the question: What is the foundation and the normative content of a medical ethic?

What began in those debates with Columbia medical students became an intellectual puzzle that would not go away. It was carried throughout the years at Columbia and into my research endeavors at the Hastings Center during the rest of the 1970s. It was brought with me to the Kennedy Institute of Ethics at Georgetown University when I accepted a research professorship there in 1979. These centers, the richest, most fertile soils in which to nurture such ideas, provided an ideal climate for doing medical ethical theory. My debt to my colleagues at both institutions is enormous. At Hastings, Daniel Callahan and Willard Gaylin, the director and president, respectively, not only provided the environment so rich in intellectual nutrients but were personally supportive of my research interests and acted as constant stimulants to my thinking. The staff and fellows of the Center—especially those related to the Research Group on Ethics and Health Policy—tolerated my testing of ideas over the years. The results have found their way into the theory of medical ethics presented here.

Preface

Since coming to the Kennedy Institute of Ethics the luxury of time has been available to me in which to complete drafting the portions of the volume which were not completed at Hastings. I have had the research and intellectual support of a group of colleagues that is any researcher's dream. I am grateful to Eunice and Sargent Shriver for their support through the Kennedy Foundation which allowed this project to grow to fruition. Their dedication to the study of these issues and their never-ceasing, thought-provoking prodding on these issues has made possible more than they could ever know. Thomas King and LeRoy Walters, directors respectively of the Institute and its Center of Bioethics, have been enormously helpful. My faculty colleagues—Tom Beauchamp, Tristram Engelhardt, Ruth Faden, Isaac Franck, William May, Richard McCormick, Lawrence McCullough, and Warren Reich—have all read drafts of portions of the manuscript. Their comments and criticisms have helped me to avoid confusions, oversights, and outright mistakes. Sara Fry has spent countless hours in research and debate with me regarding the issues addressed here; Emilie Dolge and Cecily Hilleary have both worked on manuscript preparation and countless other critical tasks. To all of them, my special gratitude is expressed.

In addition many others have read and helped me in the construction of the volume. They include Virginia Abernethy of Vanderbilt University; David Smith of Indiana University; James Todd, the chairman of the AMA's Ad Hoc Committee responsible for the 1980 revision of its "Principles of Medical Ethics"; Rihito Kimura of the Law School at Waseda University, Tokyo, and a Visiting Scholar at the Kennedy Institute; and Paul Menzel of Pacific Lutheran University, also a Visiting Scholar. They have each provided substantial help with various portions of the manuscript. Of course, I remain responsible for errors of fact or of concept that remain. My family, Laurie, Paul, and Carl, have also contributed to the volume in many ways. In places they will recognize their ideas, elsewhere only the personal sacrifices they made.

A Theory of Medical Ethics

Introduction

Medical ethics has come of age once again. Scores of volumes, hundreds of journal articles, and thousands of courses—hardly a philosopher, ethicist, or physician dares to admit that medical ethics is not a crucial part of his or her profession. It is not the first time that an outpouring of medical ethics has come upon us. The ethical ideal of the Hippocratic cult remains with us as a vision of that ancient Golden Age. A seventeenth- and eighteenth-century flurry of activity in medical ethics in Britain and the United States culminated in Percival's code of medical ethics, which he described ambitiously as "a general system of medical ethics."

In spite of the current infatuation and its historical precedents, we are still far from anything resembling a general theory of medical ethics. The contemporary round of activity, much like its predecessors, seems to have grown out of serious clashes of interests, theories of medicine, and schools of thought. These clashes have given rise to role conflicts. In classical Greek medical ethics, Pythagorean concepts of the physician's role conflicted with those of the empiricists and methodists. In Percival's Manchester Hospital, the physician's role conflicted with the roles of surgeon and apothecary. Today, traditional professional medical ethics, as transmitted by physicians from generation to generation, is being challenged by a number of nonprofessional competitors. The most dominant of these seems to be the secular libertarian tradition, which has ruled political philosophy since our country's founding and has reached new levels of passion in the liberation movements of the past decade. Not only civil libertarians and consumer activists, but physicians themselves have begun to realize that doing what will benefit the patient may not be the same as preserving patient autonomy and dignity.

A number of other competing schools of ethical thought have forced themselves through to the physician's consciousness. The evolution of birth control and abortion technologies has left every student of medical ethics with an awareness of the tradition of Catholic moral theology and its rich history of medical ethics. An emerging ethic of the technological imperative, which medical students are likely to absorb in their basic science days, conflicts with the more conservative ethic of the traditional principle, 'do no harm'. Whether or not they have studied the Hippocratic Oath and sealed that pledge with a public swearing of loyalty to the professional group (and in the traditional Oath, its gods), physicians and other students of medical ethics give ample evidence that they indeed have been socialized into an ethical tradition. It is a tradition that stretches from the Hippocratic cult through Maimonides and Percival up to the founding fathers of the AMA and the early twentieth-century efforts at code writing, and on through the latest revision of the AMA's Principles of Ethics. The result is a folk ethic of the health professional.

The sources of data on the folk ethic—the letters appearing in the national and state medical journals, the casual value messages passed from the clinical teacher standing at the bedside to neophytes being initiated into the profession, the apparently platitudinous preambles to health policy debate—reveal the depths of the socialization of the tradition into the ethic of the profession. When challenged to justify the ethics of their actions, physicians and other health professionals invariably appeal to one of the summarizing ethical principles meant to define the professional ethic: the physician's duty is to do what he thinks will benefit the patient, *primum non nocere* (the 'do no harm' principle that is the negative of the Hippocratic dictum), or simply to do good and avoid evil. The conveyors of these traditions often do not realize that these traditional slogans are potentially in conflict. Doing no harm to the patient may not mean precisely the same thing as doing what will benefit. Benefiting the patient is often not the same as doing good in general. Moreover, any of these traditional professional summarizing ethical principles may be in conflict with the ethical traditions that impinge upon citizens of the twentieth-century West from outside the sphere of medicine.

It is not surprising that at the historical intersection of these many conflicting traditions there should once again be a clash in deciding what counts as good medical ethics. What is surprising is that the authors of the glut of printed and spoken words on the subject have been

4

so reluctant to step back and carry out the debate in terms of the basic ethical principles themselves. The focus has been on specific ethical issues—abortion, euthanasia, transplants, confidentiality, behavioral control—or, more recently, on health policy questions, such as resource allocation, compromises of freedom in the name of efficiency or justice, and the ethics of human experimentation. What is still lacking is a discussion of the ethics. The time has come for a debate about what could be called "theories of medical ethics."

To be realistic about it, "theories of medical ethics" is too pretentious. What we really have before us is a series of unsystematic, unreflective, ethical stances, or traditions. What we need is some ordering of that chaos we term a tradition, some systematic structuring of medical ethics so that physicians, other health professionals, government health planners, and consumers of medical care—all those who are important medical decision makers—can have some grasp of where they stand and why they may be in conflict with others with whom they interact. Physicians should be able to grasp that if they opt for the Hippocratic formula (to do what each thinks is for the benefit of the patient) they are standing in a very peculiar, and very particularistic, tradition. It is one that at times is compatible with, but at its root is alien to, the ethics central to our culture. It is a tradition often at odds with the Judeo-Christian ethic, the Kantian ethic, the utilitarianism of contemporary economists and health planners, the libertarianism of American pluralism, and the natural law traditions of the Stoics, Catholics, Calvinists, and their modern representatives. Lay people have always made and continue to make the vast majority of medical decisions. They should understand why their decisions may seem incompatible with the views of the mainstream of health professionals. They will, after all, find it necessary to interact with those health professionals from time to time, and they should be able to recognize that the professionals, whether full-fledged Hippocratists or not, may make medical judgments on the basis of quite different systems of beliefs, values, and ethics.

This is a book that attempts to map the turf of medical ethics. Its first goal is to state explicitly what the issues of a medical ethical theory are and what the classical answers to them have been, whether given by physicians, philosophers, political leaders, or lay people (who are the most pervasive and critical medical ethical decision makers). It will go beyond this mapping, however, and attempt to show that many positions of medical ethics tend to lie in uninteresting, out-of-the-way places—dead ends where no reasonable travelers of the terrain of medical ethics would enjoy finding themselves.

This critical phase of ethical analysis—where one attempts to show that another's positions are untenable—is the easy part. I hope I can move beyond to begin construction of a theory of medical ethics that is more plausible than the traditional Hippocratism of the medical profession. I shall attempt to work out what might be called a contract or covenant theory of medical ethics.

There are several kinds of questions in medical ethics, or in any theory of ethics for that matter. Thus, part I of this book attempts to trace the incredible diversity and richness—including the outright contradictions—of medical ethical positions taken in history. The critical analysis begins in part II, where I ask the question: What is the source of our ethical norms and what do we mean when we say something is right? Sometimes medical ethics is viewed as a branch of what is called professional ethics. Many meanings, some contradictory, can be implied by the term. Professional ethics can mean nothing more than the set of ethical principles to which all human beings, professionals or not, can or should subscribe as appropriate for a professional acting in a professional role. On the other hand it can mean the set of ethical principles perceived only by the professionals themselves to be appropriate for their professional behavior. In its extreme form, professional ethics can be seen as a highly particularistic ethic about which, *in principle*, only members of the profession can have knowledge. I shall examine the place we should give to such a special professional ethic articulated by members of the profession and fully revealed only to those members.

The only solution, I suggest, is to abandon the idea that an ethic for medicine can be based on a professionally articulated code. Medical ethics can no longer be seen as a set of principles or commitments generated from within a profession and transmitted to new members during their socialization into it. In its place, I claim, an ethic for a profession in its relationship to lay people and society in general must be the result of a process far more fundamental. It must be the result of a complex set of understandings between the professional and society; thus the contract or covenant theory of medical ethics that I am proposing. For some, this contract or covenant will be generated by a moral community, a society made up of lay people and professionals reaching an agreement under some critical specified conditions about what ought to be the normative ethical principles governing social relationships, including social relationships involving medical decisions. Others will insist on going still deeper, seeing the contract or covenant reached among members of the moral community as an agreement on what they discover to be the even more fundamental ethical principles—whether they be viewed as created by God, required by reason, or simply present empirically as laws of nature. In this sense, the contract is an epistemological device, a way of knowing what is morally required.

In fact, a school of thought that might be called contractarianism is beginning to emerge as a major alternative to the traditional professional medical ethics that has dominated Western physicians' thought from the day of Hippocrates. The social contract or social covenant has long been with us; it is fundamental to Judeo-Christian thought in terms of the covenants made between God and His people. Its secular derivative is manifested in what has come to be known as the social contract perspective.[1] For many years I have been attracted to the social covenant or contract as a basis of medical ethics.[2] Over the past decade both physicians (especially Edmund Pellegrino, Richard Magraw, and Howard Brody[3]) and medical lay people (especially William May and Richard Epstein[4]) have contributed to an emerging view that medical ethics fundamentally involves social relationships among lay people and health professionals built upon complex layers of mutual loyalty, fidelity, respect, and support.

Some have tried to distinguish sharply between contract and covenant, believing the contract metaphor to be irretrievably tainted by the legal and business connotations of the term, and arguing that it necessarily implies a legalistic and individualistic relationship. I have not followed their use of the language, although I share the linguistic concern that medical ethics in a contract perspective might be taken as limited only to legal relationships occurring between two isolated individuals. I see *contract* as closely interrelated with the notion of *covenant*, while admitting that the terms can cause confusion. For example, the latter is used in "real estate restrictive covenant" (which can be very legalistic and totally lacking in the spirit of fidelity). Conversely, *contract* can be used more broadly as in "marriage contract" which implies a rich mix of religious communal faithfulness as well as an element of legal requiredness. I shall speak of *contract* in medical ethics in the sense that it is used in "marriage contract."

Covenant is a particular kind of contract—one emphasizing the moral bonds and the spirit of fidelity. I shall continue to refer to the perspective developed here as both contractual and covenantal, hoping to imply neither the legalism and individualism of *contract* nor the overly pietistic quality that *covenant* can convey. The contractual or covenantal foundation of medical ethics implies real flesh-and-blood relationships in a moral community. It, rather than mere professional consensus, is fundamental to knowing what is required in a medical ethic.

Some will inevitably take this reformulation of the foundations of medical ethics to be a challenge to those who are health professionals within our moral community. That will be an unfortunate and mistaken conclusion. A covenant or contract ethic is one built fundamentally on trust and fidelity. The point is not that health professionals cannot or should not be trusted. Quite to the contrary. They seem to be among the most dedicated and trustworthy members of the human community. To be sure, there are members of the various health profession groups who occasionally do evil. There are even scoundrels, if we are to believe the exposés that appear now and then of corruption in Medicaid, of graft by means of unnecessary surgery, and of violation of the public trust by the selling of narcotics. The numbers engaged in such violations of the public trust, however, are extremely small. I have never known a health care professional who I considered to be an evil person, one who could not be trusted to act out of motivation that was at least up to a morally acceptable level. Most are dedicated, morally motivated, and possessed of the highest intentions.

To suggest that a contract theory of medical ethics implies a mistrust of health care professionals misses the point. The point is that for certain kinds of knowledge—in this case, knowledge about what is morally appropriate human behavior insofar as it involves questions with a medical dimension—it makes no sense to assume that good will, dedication, and moral motivation together with requisite medical skill are in any way related to what we want to know. It makes no more sense to depend upon a health professional to provide knowledge of what is morally appropriate behavior in medicine than to trust a friend who is a rabbi to help select a good ham for a Sunday dinner. It is not that the rabbi is not worthy of our utmost trust and confidence. It is simply that the question posed is not one about which it is appropriate to turn to the rabbi. Physicians, like rabbis, tend to be worthy of our trust. Yet there are some questions, such as what should be the moral foundation for medical decisions and for relationships between lay people and professionals, where other sources may be more appropriate. We encounter one such case in determining the source of medical ethical norms.

It is in part for this reason that there is no fully articulated theory of virtue in the chapters that follow. It cannot be denied that the virtues (the 'faith, hope, and love' of Christian ethics, the justice, prudence, temperance, and fortitude of classical Greek thought) are important in evaluating the moral motivation of medical decision makers, whether they be lay people or physicians. Physician ethics in the time of Percival emphasized the character traits of tenderness, steadiness, authority, and condescension—all taken to be essential to the character of a "gentleman." Chinese medical manuscripts stress humaneness and compassion. The modern patient's rights movement speaks of dignity. These virtues or character traits describe the moral motivation of an actor, the attitude with which one approaches a moral decision.

While these attitudes are important, it should be clear that they are fundamentally independent of the moral rightness of an action itself. It is not enough for a physician to be morally motivated—loving, compassionate, or condescending. Though well-intentioned, he or she may make a horrendous moral mistake. Furthermore, different groups among different cultures (and different subgroups within a culture) favor, probably with adequate justification, different traits of character even for those in a particular role—for example, mother, lawyer, or physician. It may turn out, then, that no single definitely correct set of character traits exists for either lay person or physician. In any case, the issue of character traits for a theory of medical ethics is separate from the theory of right actions. Different lay–professional relationships are likely to include different ideal character traits. They will, for the most part, be agreed upon at what I shall come to refer to as the third contract, the one between individual patients and individual physicians (or at most, small groups of patients and physicians). There is a place for a theory of virtue in a medical ethic. At some point those of us interested in a theory of medical ethics will have to address the question of the virtues. I have made a conscious decision, however, to suspend that discussion, turning first to what I take to be a more public, a more universal task—the development of medical ethical norms for lay and professional action, and the establishment of some understanding of the appropriate source and justification for such norms.

Once we have some sense of the source of medical ethical norms and the place of professional activity in determining what is ethical in medical decision making, we must turn to the substantive question for a normative theory of medical ethics: What is right and wrong behavior in the medical sphere? Traditionally, professional articulations of medical ethics have shared one common focus, that of consequences.

The duty of the physician has been to do what he or she thinks will benefit the patient or at least to do the patient "no harm." This principle I take to be the core of traditional physician ethics in Western medicine. It is stated twice in the Hippocratic Oath and appears in virtually the same form in professional codes and oaths up through the middle of the twentieth century. I shall refer to these formulations of duty as the Hippocratic principle. I am not suggesting, of course, that all physicians have operated precisely in the same moral framework from the time of Hippocrates until the present. The Hippocratic writings themselves are complex. The author of the Hippocratic Oath almost certainly was not the same person who wrote the essays in the Hippocratic Corpus, which are filled more with scientific than moral content. Moreover, the physicians on the Isle of Cos in ancient Greece who subscribed to the Hippocratic Oath as a commitment to benefiting their patients had a distinctive interpretation of what counted as a benefit. They also had a unique system of beliefs and values that influenced their judgments. Not only were Hippocratic physicians pledged to secrecy, they followed a unique tripartite division of medicine into dietetics, pharmacology, and surgery. "Love of the art" was central; the virtues were of purity and holiness. Thus the physician of the historical Hippocratic cult functioned in a rather different context of values and virtues than exists today. What has remained consistent, however, is the physician's commitment to a moral mission that directs him to use his judgment to benefit the patient, however benefit is defined. Thus, when I refer to the Hippocratic tradition I am not focusing exclusively or even primarily on the actual historical group gathered in ancient Greece, but on all those who see themselves as committed to what I am calling the Hippocratic principle: the directive to benefit the patient according to the physician's ability and judgment.[5] My criticism, such as it is, will apply only to those, whether of old or modern day, who are committed to that concept, for the Hippocratic principle will turn out to be far more controversial than it at first appears. As we explore the normative principles of a medical ethic we shall have to ask if the consequences are what count. Further, is it toward benefit in general that the physician is working, regardless of whether it accrues to the physician's patient or, as is implied in the Hippocratic principle, is it only the *patient's* benefit that is supposed to be morally relevant, or do the rights of the patient count as well? It may be that the goal is not to benefit the patient, but to do what is right by the patient even if it is not the most beneficial course. Turning physicians loose on society to do what they think may benefit their patients can lead to moral outrage. That, at least, is what I shall try to show. If the potential benefit to the patient is all that is morally relevant, then research on healthy subjects for the good of science is categorically immoral. At least it is immoral where the projected benefits to the individual subject are not as great as the projected risks, even where the total benefits envisioned far exceed the subject-risk. The Hippocratic principle does not say that the physician's duty is to benefit the patient according to his ability and judgment *unless* the patient waives the right to be benefited. Rather it is to benefit, pure and simple. There is no notion of consent in that tradition, no overriding justification of risk taking with one's patient for the benefit of mankind.

On the other hand, if benefits to society, calculated by some utilitarian calculus of net benefits over harms, are to replace the hyperindividualism of the Hippocratic tradition, how does one avoid the crassness of trading off the welfare of, let us say, one innocent infant for the economic or social benefit of the world's citizenry? This tension in medical ethics between benefit to the patient and benefit to the society will be the focus of chapter 6.

The problem, I shall claim, revolves again around covenant or contract loyalty. Contract loyalty is an often neglected category in ethics. Fidelity to a covenant, or as we shall see a series of covenants, may provide a way out of the twin evils of hyperindividualism, on the one hand, and crass subordination of the individual's welfare to society, on the other hand. The solution may be radically different from that of the Hippocratic tradition. A contract theory pushes medical ethics beyond good consequences. It deals with promise keeping, autonomy, truth telling, avoiding killing, and just distribution of benefits and burdens. This is the meat of any normative theory of ethics. If the normative principles of ethics are articulated by reasonable people—lay and professional, contracting together in mutual loyalty and fidelity—then no reasonable person would be foolish enough, I shall argue, to contract with medical professionals authorizing them to do simply whatever they think will benefit patients. Instead what is needed is a new constructive synthesis.

The synthesis will be an effort to return medical ethics to the main roads of Western ethical thought: to the traditions that speak of natural laws, of covenants and contracts, of moral agents who are autonomous ends in themselves. The covenant or contract developed here will provide a radically different sort of basis for a theory of medical ethics than traditional, professional, Hippocratic ethics. It will recall the covenant of Yahweh with His people, the social contract of the founders of modern political philosophy (recaptured from oblivion by John Rawls), and it will echo the contemporary notions of contract. This is the moral basis for relations between parties who are unequal in skill and resources, but come together in a mutual pledging to fulfill an agreement. The result, I hope, will avoid the problems that come when medical relations are viewed as individual, private agreements outside of a social context. It will also offer an alternative to the individualism, the consequentialism, and the paternalism of the Hippocratic tradition. It will provide a basis for medical decision making that will apply to lay people and health professionals alike, one that extends beyond the ethnocentrism of the codes of traditional physician ethics.

Traditional professional ethics has been committed to the necessity of focusing on individual, real case problems. It is a slogan of the medical ethical tradition that every case in medical ethics is unique, that no general rules can produce answers. General ethical rules are widely viewed as nothing more than rules of thumb, guidelines in clinical decision making that should direct its focus to each particular case. That the case is crucial to medical ethics is beyond dispute. Can moral rules, though, take us beyond the case and provide a moral instruction more definitive than just a rule of thumb? That will be the focus of chapter 13.

As evidence of the seriousness with which I take cases, throughout this volume case studies will be the focal point for the theory of medical ethics that I develop. They will vary somewhat in style, but (with one clearly identified exception) all will be based on real-life situations. Some are matters of public record, taken from court cases or disciplinary proceedings. I have used real names and accurate details from those cases. Others are not publicly documented. While based in fact, names and details in those cases have been modified to provide both anonymity and clarity. The purpose of the case discussions is to move beyond their particularities to see the kinds of questions they pose and what those questions mean for a theory of medical ethics. The results may not be conventional, at least not in terms of professional ethics, but, as Raphael tells Thomas More prior to describing his island of Utopia, "If we're never to say anything that might be thought unconventional, for fear of its sounding ridiculous, we'll have to hush up."

PART I

Hippocrates, the Popes,
Ahimsa, and Patient's Rights:
A History of Diversity

Chapter 1

The Hippocratic Tradition

Case 1: The Humane Murder of a Helpless Infant

Ms. R. arrived at the physician's office simultaneously depressed and agitated. She had been under Dr. T.'s care for a little over a year, but today was especially traumatic for her. Her breast cancer was developing rapidly. Since the birth of her daughter a few months ago, she had been rapidly losing strength. She feared that soon she would have to give up her baby in order that someone or some institution could care for her. She had no family, no husband, no one to turn to for help except Dr. T.

In the privacy of his office, she reviewed her tragic story. None of the obvious options would work. Adoption would not meet the baby's needs adequately, and given the baby's problem with a malformed hip, probably no one would want to adopt her anyway. As for the institutions that care for the moneyless orphans of the street, Ms. R. said they could not possibly give her baby the care she needed. There were no friends or neighbors she could rely on. The city was large and anonymous.

She proposed to Dr. T. that she fulfill her responsibility to her child by doing what she considered the most loving, the most caring thing. She wanted to bring about the death of the infant—humanely—so as to spare her the inevitable misery of her existence. She asked Dr. T. for information about how to carry out the fateful deed in a way that would be quick, sure, and peaceful. She was willing to take responsibility for her act. But given her own condition, time was short.

What the state might do to her, a dying woman, could be no worse than the death she faced soon in any case and the agony she would feel at failing in her responsibility to her child. She turned to Dr. T. for help.

THE NOTION OF THEORIES OF MEDICAL ETHICS

Before examining why key decision makers in this case reached the conclusion that the woman's plan was justified, it is necessary to have some framework for analyzing this problem and others of medical ethics. Here there are at least two central problems. The first, the most crucial, is certainly the moral judgment reached by Ms. R. Many decisions of a moral nature are made in the medical sphere by lay people every day. Parents choose types of care for their children, cancer patients decide to turn away from orthodox medical treatment, public policymakers withhold health service funding for the poor, a judge authorizes a kidney transplantation from a mentally retarded boy to his mentally normal brother. These examples suggest that matters of medical ethical controversy are unlikely to be resolved simply by turning to professional codes of ethics, which express a particular group's consensus about what ethical physicians should do.

For this reason, it is helpful to distinguish between medical ethics and physician ethics. I shall use the term *medical ethics* to refer to a more general application of ethics to problems in the medical sphere, whether those problems are faced by lay people, public officials, physicians, or other health professionals. *Physician ethics* is a much more specific body of applied ethics. As I use the term, it will be limited to theories, principles, rules, and specific case-problem solutions dealing with what physicians ought to do to be considered ethical in their professional practice.

Physician ethics can be formulated by professional groups of physicians, such as those who gathered around Hippocrates on the island of Cos or those who attend annual meetings of the American Medical Association's House of Delegates. It can be formulated also by others who are not professionally involved in medicine, much less physicians: by church groups, by consumer groups, by philosophers working in applied ethics, or by any other group with its own cultural perspective. When it is formulated by members of a professional group, I shall refer to it as a professionally articulated ethic or simply a professional ethic.

By the same token, medical ethics can be formulated for or by other health professions. Nursing ethics, by this usage, is the branch of medical ethics pertaining to ethical conduct for nurses. Professional nursing ethics is nursing ethics formulated by professional groups of nurses. Social worker ethics, physician assistant ethics, and chaplain ethics are, by the same usage, other branches of medical ethics (as would be ethics for patients, parents, and guardians when they are involved in medical ethical decisions). Given this range of possible formulations of a medical ethic, why should Ms. R. be bound irretrievably by the consensus of a professional group of physicians of which she is not a member, even if she should happen to have knowledge of that group's code of ethics?

The professional code does offer somewhat more promise in resolving the second ethical dilemma raised by the case; that is, how Dr. T. ought to respond to Ms. R.'s request. But even here there is a problem. The physician, like the patient, is a member of many social groups, some of which have ethical frameworks that may not be consistent with the professional medical ethical consensus.

In order to carry out the moral analysis necessary to resolve the two ethical questions posed by this case, both patient and physician must have an ethical framework, a theory of medical ethics, if you like. It would be nice if they shared the same theory, but that may not be possible. A theory of medical ethics might provide specific answers to apply in particularly difficult situations, like the one involving Ms. R. It will provide much more, however. An ethical theory is a complex, integrated approach, articulating an ethical framework coherently and systematically. The components of a complete theory of ethics will answer such questions as what moral rules apply to specific ethical cases, what ethical principles stand behind the rules, how seriously the rules should be taken, and what constitutes the fundamental meaning and justification of the ethical principles.

General works in the theory of ethics address these issues in great detail.[1] In fact, whole volumes are written debating some of the subpoints under each of these core questions in ethical theory. Logically, if one is to resolve a problem in medical ethics, something resembling an ethical theory will be required. At the least, implicit answers to each of these questions will have to be given. Of course, the woman making a life decision for her daughter, like the patient deciding to accept or refuse surgery for cancer, does not work systematically through these questions to formulate a medical ethical theory de novo. It is unnecessary to do so because such questions have been answered in fragmentary ways throughout the person's life. She or he is a member of religious, cultural, and ethnic groups that have developed general frameworks for answering such questions. Physicians also do not go through this exercise from scratch when they meet an ethically difficult case. They too belong to nonprofessional groups that provide ethical frameworks. Moreover, the profession to which they do belong has a long history of ethical reflection about what is right and wrong in the practice of medicine. Physicians can, if they so choose, turn to that tradition—to the Hippocratic Oath, to the codes that follow in that tradition, and to the informal consensus that has developed within the profession about the right way to practice medicine.

In short, there are a number of theories or prototheories from which persons may choose. Many of these work out in some detail appropriate behavior for particular medical contexts—in this case, for Ms. R., who faces the primary decision, and for Dr. T. and other health care professionals, who find themselves in a medical ethical dilemma that requires subsidiary decisions about whether to cooperate in the patient's plan.

Many guidelines for action in such cases are mere fragments of theory. They have not been formulated in any systematic way. In order to understand how decisions can and should be reached in Ms. R.'s case, and in countless others like it, we need to have a map of the potential theories—the portions of medical ethical theories that exist and those that could exist. Before turning to the construction of a theory that will be more adequate to the task of decision making in a pluralistic secular society, let us look at the range of positions from which we may choose. In this way, we shall see what we can do to analyze and understand the fate of that baby put to death by her mother with the support and collaboration of her physician.

THE HIPPOCRATIC OATH

To see whether Ms. R. would want to turn for an answer to the Hippocratic tradition of professional physician ethics, it is necessary to explore its rich and complex history in some detail. If the Hippocratic tradition does not provide Ms. R. with an adequate resolution of her problem, then she will have to look elsewhere, to some other tradition, to some other implicit theory of medical ethics (in the broader sense in which I am using the term).

The Hippocratic Oath is only the focal piece of a long tradition, but it remains as the central document, the single most often-cited summary of the physician's own understanding of what is morally required to be a good medical doctor. Scores of later codes and oaths have reformulated the Hippocratic Oath for application to different times and cultures. They have gradually become part of what I am calling the Hippocratic tradition. Like many deeply ingrained ethical world views, the tradition is often transmitted informally. The attending physician—standing at the bedside with a group of medical students gathered round— smiles approvingly, or scorns, or raises an eyebrow as students reflect, or fail to reflect, the tradition their teacher has absorbed. Commencement exercises are filled with platitudinous references to the characteristics of the good physician. Medical journals constantly reflect the tradition in editorials, in pious closing paragraphs, in scientific articles, and—most conspicuously—in the letters to editors.

As with any tradition, there are subtle variants within it, and description necessarily involves oversimplification. What I am about to do, then, is construct an admittedly oversimplified ideal type, a construct of a pure form to which individual physicians within the tradition conform in varying degrees. The picture that results, however, is one that I feel clearly constitutes the main core of ethical thinking to which the Western physician has subscribed, at least until very recently.

The Hippocratic Oath can be analyzed in two ways: What did it mean for the physicians on the island of Cos who originated it some twenty-three hundred years ago, and what does it mean today for physicians who, although they may never have read the Oath, have some vague sense of loyalty to it as a summary of the highest goals to which they can aspire? I am much more interested in the latter question, in the modern formulations made by physicians who believe they are reflecting the ethical standards of a long tradition. Thus, what goes on in this volume under the rubric of the Hippocratic tradition is not primarily a synthesis of historical scholarship about the Oath and its authors. We shall discover, in fact, that this Hippocratic tradition in some ways distorts the stance of the first Hippocratic group in ancient Greece that originally formulated the Oath. In many other ways, however, the modern formulation of the tradition reflects ethical commitments and moral maneuvers that are closer to the intent of the Oath's originators—or so at least I shall contend.

The "Oath" is the shortest and most widely known of a group of Hippocratic writings collectively termed the deontological or ethical works. These also include the "Law," "Decorum," "Precepts," and "Physician."[2] While these and many others are attributed to Hippocrates, in reality their authorship is unknown. (For many centuries, Hippocrates' name was attached rather indiscriminately to medical works. Some, dating from as late as the fifteenth century, are clearly spurious.[3]) Of the ancient works, those that are scientific and technical are now recognized as distinct from the ethical ones. Together they are referred to as the Hippocratic corpus. This term identifies a school of thought, or at least a collection of manuscripts, while leaving open the question of authorship.[4]

Hippocrates does seem to have been an actual historical figure, a fifth-century B.C. physician born in Cos. W.H.S. Jones, translator of the definitive English edition of the Hippocratic corpus, identifies him as a member of a guild of physicians called Asclepiadae.[5] The Oath, however, is from a later period. Ludwig Edelstein, the classicist and medical historian, dates it from the late fourth century B.C.,[6] although some scholars conclude it was formulated as late as the first century A.D., when the first documented reference to it was made by Scribonius Largus.

The ethical precepts contained in the Oath and the related literature are rather distinctive. While some scholars associate them with the popular ethics of the time,[7] many elements in the writings have a unique character. Edelstein, whose influential studies of the Hippocratic literature are widely respected, identifies the Oath as reflecting Pythagorean thought.

Even a quick reading makes it obvious that the Oath contains two parts: a vow of allegiance to the physician's teacher and a pledge to follow some rather strange rules of medical ethics and etiquette. The evidence for Edelstein's Pythagorean thesis comes from both the vow and the rules. The vow, or oath itself, pledges the physician to hold his teacher as:

> equal to my parents and to live my life in partnership with him, and if he is in need of money to give him a share of mine, and to regard his offspring as equal to my brothers in male lineage and to teach them this art—if they desire to learn it—without fee and covenant; to give a share of precepts and oral instruction and all the other learning to my sons and to the sons of him who has instructed me and to pupils who have signed the covenant and have taken an oath according to the medical law, but to no one else.[8]

This kind of pledge to secrecy and to loyalty to one's teacher is patently offensive to the modern rational, scientific mind; yet in the fourth century B.C. it must have seemed an acceptable social practice. Some have argued that the Oath was designed to meet the needs of a time when the transmission of a craft from father to son was being replaced by the transmission of learning from the teacher to his "adopted" son, the student. The oath would in that case be part of the adoption ritual. Edelstein rejects this hypothesis, however, claiming there is no evidence that the adoption of pupils by their teachers was a common characteristic of archaic education.

He does identify, however, one particular historical setting where this practice can be found: "The Pythagoreans of the fourth century apparently were wont to honor those by whom they had been instructed as their fathers by adoption."[9]

Pythagoras, like Hippocrates, was an Ionian Greek who gave rise to a society—a cult, if you like—with religious, political, and philosophical interests. It elevated pursuit of knowledge to the level of a religious quest. The knowledge, viewed as cultic, was protected by bonds of secrecy.

Edelstein shows that the moral rules of the Hippocratic Oath are also in accord with Pythagoreanism. The Oath prohibits the giving of a "deadly drug," even to those who ask for it—a prohibition taken to preclude assisting suicide (or possibly homicide)—in spite of the fact that many Greek schools of thought held suicide permissible in at least some cases. It also prohibits giving a woman an "abortive remedy," another provision reflective of Pythagoreanism.[10] Treatment of diseases in the Oath falls into three areas—dietetics, pharmacology, and surgery—again reflecting Pythagorean thought. Edelstein concludes:

> The provisions concerning the application of poison and of abortive remedies, in their inflexibility, intimated that the second part of the Oath is influenced by Pythagorean ideas. The interpretation of the other medical and ethical stipulations showed that they, too, are tinged by Pythagorean theories. All statements can be understood only, or at any rate, they can be understood best as adaptations of Pythagorean teaching to the specific task of the physician. Even from a formal point of view, these rules are reminiscent of Pythagoreanism: just as in the Oath the doctor is told what to do and what not to do, so the Pythagorean oral instruction indicated what to do and what not to do. Far from being the expression of the common Greek attitude toward medicine or of the natural duties of the physician, the ethical code rather reflects opinions which were peculiarly those of a small and isolated group.[11]

THE HIPPOCRATIC TRADITION

While some specific, often archaic, features of the Oath were abandoned, many of its essential elements remained as the Oath began to find its place in Western culture. Specific views on surgery, the tripartite division of medicine, and the swearing by Apollo disappeared, but among the significant features retained throughout the history of the Hippocratic tradition is the view that the practice of the physician's art is a calling, something having a quasi-religious overtone. This concept carries with it a sense of loyalty to one's teachers that, by the late Middle Ages, came to mean loyalty to one's professional group.

Even more central to this common tradition is a moral perspective that dominates the Oath. At two points, a fundamental moral principle—what I shall call the Hippocratic principle—is stated. It comes first in the section related to dietetics, but many modern interpreters have generalized it so that it applies to all treatments. The taker of the Oath says, "I will apply . . . measures for the benefit of the sick according to my ability and judgment; I will keep them from harm and injustice." Later, when the Oath refers to visiting the sick, the same theme is repeated: "Whatever houses I may visit, I will come for the benefit of the sick, remaining free of all intentional injustice. . . ."[12]

This I take to be the core of professional physician ethics, the core of the Hippocratic tradition. Those who have stood in that tradition are committed to producing good for their patient and to protecting that patient from harm. (To be sure, this consequentialism was originally given a very peculiar turn in the Hippocratic cult; medicine was viewed as "the art," and special cultic values like purity and holiness heavily influenced the interpretation of what would count as benefit.) Love of the art was a central value. Modern proponents of the tradition loosely related to the Oath still retain, in varying degrees, this special vision of the good. The principle in its core has thus remained, although sometimes there are variants. Avoiding harm may be given priority over benefiting the patient, for example. This version has been given the dignity of latinization into the formula *primum non nocere,* "first do no harm," but this is not Hippocratic. "The Epidemics," the Hippocratic work to which this formula is sometimes attributed, does not really give a priority to avoiding harm. "As to diseases," the author of "The Epidemics" wrote, "make a habit of two things—to help, or at least to do no harm."[13]

Sometimes, especially in contemporary physician "folk" ethics, the formula is converted into the principle of preventing harm by preserving life. That is a variant without classical roots,[14] and it has received only minority support even in the decades of heroic medical interventionism in the mid-twentieth century. Only one important twentieth-century code commits the physician to the preservation of life, the

World Medical Association's International Code of Medical Ethics, and that seems highly qualified with exceptions and seems targeted at the abortion issue rather than at contemporary problems in the care of the terminally ill. The Hippocratic formula, its variants, and the ethical problems it raises will be the subject of chapter 6. For now, it is important merely to identify the Hippocratic principle and to relate it to the Hippocratic deontological writings. Only gradually will we begin to see how bizarre and controversial this Hippocratic ethic is and how strange it would be if modern, rational people, whether operating out of the religious or secular moral frameworks, were to revive the ethic of the Pythagorean-Hippocratic cult.

From its position as a minority document for an isolated group of physicians, the Oath, together with related ethical documents from the Hippocratic corpus, gradually emerged as the dominant summary of the physician's own understanding of his ethical responsibility. The works were known to Plato, and many were commented upon by Galen (although apparently not the Oath specifically or the other deontological writings).[15] Erotian, writing at the time of Nero, knew of the Oath and apparently considered it genuinely Hippocratic.[16] One interpretation of the rise to prominence of the Hippocratic ethic has been that it was deemed compatible with Christianity and was elevated to a more central status as the religion grew in influence.[17] However, I have found little concrete evidence for this view of close ties between early Christian thought and the Hippocratic tradition. Some church fathers did know of the Hippocratic tradition, but the evidence is that their knowledge was superficial at best and often disapproving.[18]

The most impressive argument for a link between Christian ethics and the Hippocratic tradition is the existence, in a tenth- or eleventh-century manuscript, of a Christian version of the Hippocratic Oath entitled, "From the Oath according to Hippocrates in so far as a Christian May Swear It."[19] The title itself reveals that there are tensions between the two traditions. Of course, the pagan deities are deleted, replaced by Christian references. More substantive changes have also been made. The pledge of secrecy is deleted, replaced by a pledge to teach the art "to those who require to learn it." The indenture of the student to his teacher in the pagan version of the Oath is explicitly rejected, as is the prohibition on surgery. Still present, however, is the Hippocratic core—the pledge to use treatments to help the sick according to the physician's ability and judgment. Thus, for our purposes, the Christian revision is in many ways still a true part of the Hippocratic tradition. The question is whether this medieval pledge represents the mainstream Christian view about the physician's role or whether it is merely a strand of thought among some physicians who are in only marginal contact with Christian theology. What evidence there is suggests the latter.

The interest in Hippocratic ideas that endured among physicians through the Middle Ages drew from Hippocratic rather than from biblical and clerical authorities on the subject.[20] Some Hippocratic texts were not introduced into Latin scholarship until as late as the fifteenth century, and those that came earlier were of greater interest to humanists and physicians participating in the revival of ancient Greek writings than they were to Christian theologians and scholars. Some of the texts focused on interests, such as numerology and astronomy, that were decidedly contrary to those of Christianity.[21] In fact, in the twelfth century, John of Salisbury complained about young physicians who returned from Salerno or Montpellier boasting of their acquaintance with Galen and Hippocrates, and St. Bernard of Clairvaux criticized those who followed the advice of Hippocrates and his followers, to the detriment of their more spiritual welfare.[22] Thus, the several new translations of the Hippocratic corpus (including the Oath) that were made by fifteenth- and sixteenth-century humanists appear to reflect interest in medical scholarship and classical Greek antiquity rather than to demonstrate any real convergence with Christian thought.

Whatever its source, though, interest in the Hippocratic tradition continued and flourished into the modern period of medical practice. In Elizabethan England, for example, we find four versions of the Hippocratic Oath, all containing variants of what I have identified as the core of the Hippocratic ethic.[23] The major Anglo-American event signaling the emergence of the Hippocratic tradition in the modern period, however, came at the end of the eighteenth century, when a feud broke out at the Manchester Infirmary.[24] In 1789, an epidemic of typhoid or typhus struck, taxing the infirmary staff. At the time, medical practitioners were divided into three groups: physicians, surgeons, and apothecaries. Tensions among these groups were exacerbated when staff changes were made to respond to the epidemic. Some of the staff resigned, taking the changes to be a negative reflection on their efforts. In order to keep the peace, the trustees of the infirmary approached Thomas Percival, a physician who had been on the infirmary staff but had resigned years earlier because of physical disabilities. He had maintained close relationships with the infirmary and its staff and was asked to draw up a "scheme of professional conduct relative to hospitals and other medical charities."[25] The result was Percival's famous

"Medical Ethics; or, a Code of Institutes and Precepts Adapted to the Professional Conduct of Physicians and Surgeons. . . . " Out of these meager beginnings, in a local dispute over intraprofessional division of labor, was to emerge the foundation of Anglo-American medical ethics.[26]

American medical ethics took its lead from Percival. In 1847, at the founding meeting of the American Medical Association in Philadelphia, a code of ethics, which drew heavily upon Percival's pragmatic, problem-solving approach to professional squabbles, was approved. Like its predecessor, it reflected the core of the Hippocratic ethic, pledging physicians to "minister to the sick with due impressions of the importance of their office; reflecting that the ease, the health, and the lives of those committed to their charge, depend on their skill, attention and fidelity."[27]

That code has been revised from time to time over the past century, most significantly in 1957 and 1980. The 1957 revision replaced the detailed compilation of rules and interpretations of the earlier versions with a set of ten principles stating in more general terms the ethical mandate of the physician, and the 1980 update introduced for the first time a rights perspective into professional physician ethics. Only in these very recent versions, as we shall see in due course, did the Hippocratic commitment to benefit exclusively the patient, according to the physician's judgment, begin to give way to other ethical commitments—those that take into account the interests of the rest of society; those that take into account physicians' rights and duties as well as benefits and harms; and those that take into account the judgment of the patients and others beyond the physician.

While the Hippocratic ethic has started to give way in the mainstream of American medical ethics, the commitment of the World Medical Association to the traditional ethic is nearly intact. In 1948, its General Assembly adopted what has become known as the Declaration of Geneva. A conscious effort to update the Hippocratic Oath, its commitment to Hippocratic tradition is bold. "The health of my patient," it reads, "will be my first consideration." Colleagues are to be treated as brothers, and the physician is to maintain "by all means in my power, the honor and the noble traditions of the medical profession." In 1949, the same group, meeting in London, adopted its International Code of Medical Ethics, containing again, in the following words, the patient-centered commitment: "Any act, or advice which could weaken physical or mental resistance of a human being may be used only in his interest."

CONCLUSION

If Ms. R., then, wanted to turn to the Hippocratic tradition for a resolution of her ethical dilemma about how to treat her soon-to-be-orphaned child, she would learn very little. The tradition lays out some
principles for guiding physician conduct but says nothing at all to this
mother, a lay person, about deciding how to care for her child. Even
her physician, Dr. T., receives much less help than we might have
expected. Should he choose his Greek ethics out of the Pythagorean
tradition rather than that of the Platonists, Cynics, or Stoics, he would
learn that he should not give a deadly drug if a patient asks for it. But it
appears that Ms. R. did not ask him for a deadly drug, only for some
information about how to kill humanely. Unless Dr. T. follows the
modern deviation (discussed in detail in chapter 6) that commits the
physician to preserving life, he gets no help here. His guidance would
have to come from that core element of the Hippocratic tradition, the
commitment to do what he thinks will benefit his patient according to
his ability and judgment. That is pretty vague moral advice. In this
case, it is not even clear who his patient is. If Dr. T. broadens his
horizon to include the baby as well as the mother, he would have to
ask whether his participation in the baby's death, by giving information, can be justified as benefiting the baby according to his ability and
judgment. That, of course, would be a subjective judgment, one that
can in no way be implied from the Hippocratic Oath or its successors.
According to this Hippocratic principle, Dr. T. is on his own in judging
whether death would, on balance, benefit the baby. Apparently, the
views of others inside or outside the profession would at best serve
only as supporting evidence and counsel. And the existence of laws
prohibiting murder is not, according to the principle, taken into
account.

The results of applying the Hippocratic principle are not very satisfactory in this case. It could justify a decision by Dr. T. to participate in
the murder by providing information and it tells us nothing about Ms.
R.'s responsibility. In order to get a sense of the alternative systems of
medical ethics available to him and to Ms. R., then, it is necessary to
examine other options, the more or less coherent medical ethical theories outside of Western professional physician ethics.

Chapter 2

The Dominant Western Competitors

THE JUDEO-CHRISTIAN TRADITION

The Hippocratic ethic is a consistent tradition, but one that must be teased out of oral tradition, codes, and the writings of medical professionals. It is implicit in a variety of formulations, but not formally organized into a body of doctrine. The Hippocratic tradition is not the only ethical tradition in Western thought, however. There are some competitors. There are several other bodies of Western thought that focus specifically on the ethics of medical practice. Some of these are more straightforward, more organized, and more explicit than those expounded by the followers of Hippocrates. Both Judaism and Christianity, for example, have embedded within them what can be called a medical ethic. While some of their tenets are probably compatible with the Hippocratic ethic (there are passing references to Hippocrates as a "saint" in Hebrew sources), others are so radically different that it may seem impossible for someone to be simultaneously a loyal follower of Hippocrates and of a major branch of the Judeo-Christian tradition. I am not concerned simply with the obvious, explicit religious content of the original Hippocratic pledge—the one sworn "by Apollo Physician and Asclepius and Hygieia and Panaceia and all the gods and goddesses." Those words were deleted in all attempts to Christianize and modernize the Oath. Rather, I mean more basic elements that seem at odds with the dominant religious traditions of the modern West.

JUDAISM

Since passage of its Anatomy and Pathology Law in 1953, modern Israel has been torn by a medical ethics controversy. It is not over euthanasia, psychosurgery, or abortion, but autopsy. A battle fought in the Christian world in sixteenth-century England and Scotland is being waged with equal religious fervor in contemporary Israel. The fight is between Israeli physicians, who have modern, secular interests and seek knowledge from autopsy and dissection, and Israel's Orthodox Rabbinate, which is the only body governmentally recognized in religious Judaism in that country and seeks to uphold its interpretation of the traditional Jewish commitment to respect the corpse. Orthodox rabbis demonstrated over the issue in cities throughout Israel, and 356 of them signed an opinion written by Israel's chief rabbi. It states that "autopsy in any form whatsoever is prohibited by the law of the Torah . . . there is no way to allow it except in a matter of immediate danger to life, and then only with the approval of an eminent rabbi."[1]

Who would have thought, given knowledge of the Hippocratic ethic, that the medical issue bringing demonstrations to the streets would be autopsy of the human body? Yet it is not at all surprising if one considers the tradition of Orthodox Jewish medical ethics.

That tradition is complicated as well as rich, perhaps more so in Israel today because so many Jews, including some Israeli physicians, are not orthodox. Though Reformed and Conservative branches of the tradition draw heavily on the values and doctrines of the Orthodox, rabbinic tradition, they allow variants, some of which make accommodation to contemporary secular and professional medical ethics. Many modern (ethnic) Jews are completely secular in their ethics. There is a core of Orthodox Talmudic medical ethics, however, that is unmistakable and is often in dramatic contrast to Hippocratic ethics.

The first, most obvious, difference is exemplified by the role of the rabbis in the autopsy dispute. While the ethic of the Hippocratic physician is articulated by the profession with little outside involvement, the Jewish medical ethic is integrated into the full, rich tradition of Jewish law, which is conveyed and interpreted by the rabbi. Indeed, many of the most important scholars in contemporary Jewish medical ethics are rabbis: David Bleich,[2] Immanuel Jakobovits,[3] Moses Tendler,[4] David Feldman,[5] and Seymour Siegel.[6] And of the physicians writing in the area (such as Fred Rosner,[7] and many writing in the Israeli journal, *Assia*) many are thoroughly trained scholars in *Halakah*, or rabbinical law and ethics. In fact, traditionally, the physician was often first a rabbi. It has been estimated that over half of the best known rabbinical scholars and authors in medieval times were physicians. These included Moses Maimonides (1135–1204), to whom is attributed, probably wrongly, a well-known prayer that summarizes Jewish views on the practice of medicine.[8] Moreover, the physician in Jewish law is treated as a quasi-religious official.[9]

As the Hippocratic tradition finds its roots in the deontological (ethical) writing of the Hippocratic corpus, so the rabbinic tradition is grounded in the Jewish Bible, the Talmud, in the twelfth-century codification by Maimonides, *Yad Ha-Hazakah* or *Mishneh* Torah, and in both the older and more recent *Responsa*. As early as the sixth century, we have evidence of a distinctly Jewish medical oath of Asaph Horafe (Asaph the physician). While sometimes referred to as the Jewish Hippocratic Oath, there is really no continuity between them, either historically or intellectually.[10] The form is reminiscent of the Ten Commandments, complete with a list of "thou shalt nots." Cast as an oath taken by the physician Asaph ben Berachyahu, it begins with a series of commandments: Thou shall not kill; thou shall not lust after beautiful women; thou shall not disclose secrets; thou shall not covet; thou shall not harden your hearts against the poor and needy, but heal them. This last "commandment" we shall also find in ancient Chinese medical ethics and in socialist perspectives, but it is absent from the Hippocratic tradition. The Jewish oath also strongly prohibits sorcery and, a proscription so dominant in the Hebrew tradition, idol worship.

The Jewish medical ethic is thus integrally linked to a religious tradition with a moral law extending well beyond the medical enterprise. It is accessible to those without medical training, and indeed is often given interpretation and definitive opinion by a medical lay person, namely a rabbi, steeped in the religious tradition.

The content of the law as applied to medicine can be summarized in a set of principles that are in some cases quite different from the Hippocratic principle of subjective benefit to the patient. Jakobovits, citing biblical foundations, articulates the core principles of the medical ethic: the sanctity and dignity of human life, the duty to preserve health, an uncompromising opposition to superstition and irrational cures—including faith healing—a rigid code of dietary restraints and sexual morality, and many other basic formulations of moral imperatives including strict instructions on the rights of the dead.[11]

While many wrongly interpret the central core of the Hippocratic tradition as committing the physician to preserve life, this is a central precept of the Jewish medical ethic. Jews, whether they be physicians or lay persons, are the original advocates of the right to life at almost any cost. More precisely, Jews, to the extent that they are committed to rabbinic law, feel a duty to unequivocally preserve life.

It is impossible to overstate the emphasis that Judaism places on the value and sanctity of life. It rejects Hippocratic as well as Christian and Anglo-American secular compromises. It reflects nothing of the distinctions made in those ethics between natural and artificial, ordinary and extraordinary, and heroic or nonheroic measures to preserve life.[12] The rabbinic sources are consistent. Bleich cites the Talmudic passage regarding the creation of Adam: "Therefore only a single human being was created in the world, to teach that if any person has caused a single soul of Israel to perish, Scripture regards him as if he had caused an entire world to perish; and if any human being saves a single soul of Israel, Scripture regards him as if he had saved an entire world."[13]

This duty to preserve life takes precedence over virtually all Jewish ritual commandments, including dietary laws and observance of the Sabbath and Holy Days. It is even *obligatory* to disregard ritual laws when they conflict with immediate claims of life or health.[14] The only prohibitions that remain inviolate are those against idolatry, incest, adultery, and murder. Violations of any other laws in order to preserve life are not even in need of atonement. According to *'Orah Hayim*, "It is religious precept to desecrate the Sabbath for any person afflicted with an illness. . . ."[15] The most rigorous formulations of the life-saving principle permit violations even if a person is moments away from inevitable death. The Talmud, as summarized by Jakobovits, says that if someone were to kill a child who was falling from a tall building, he would be guilty of a capital offense just like any ordinary murderer. The fact that the death was hastened by only a few minutes would not be relevant.[16]

On the other hand, Roman Catholic moral theology and some recent versions of professional physician ethics condone the withdrawal of treatment from a patient whose condition seems hopeless or whose treatment demands heroic or extraordinary efforts. Rabbinical medical ethics makes no such exception, as illustrated by Bleich in this story about the nineteenth-century Polish scholar popularly known as Reb Eisel Charif:

> The venerable Rabbi was afflicted with a severe illness and was attended by an eminent specialist. As the disease progressed beyond hope of cure, the physician informed the Rabbi's family of the gravity of the situation. He also

informed them that he therefore felt justified in withdrawing from the case. The doctor's grave prognosis notwithstanding, Reb Eisel Charif recovered completely. Some time later, the physician chanced to come upon the Rabbi in the street. The doctor stopped in his tracks in astonishment and exclaimed, "Rabbi, have you come back from the other world?" The Rabbi responded, "You are indeed correct. I *have* returned from the other world. Moreover, I did you a great favor while I was there. An angel ushered me in to a large chamber. At the far end of the room was a door and lined up in front of the door were a large number of well-dressed, dignified and intelligent-looking men. These men were proceeding through the doorway in a single file. I asked the angel who these men were and where the door led. He informed me that the door was the entrance to the netherworld and that the men passing through those portals were those of whom the Mishnah says, "The best of physicians merits Gehinnom." Much to my surprise I noticed that you too were standing in the line about to proceed through the door. I immediately approached the angel and told him: "Remove that man immediately! He is no doctor. He does not treat patients; he abandons them!"[17]

If rabbinic ethics can be said to tolerate any withdrawals of treatment, it does so on the basis of a distinction unique to Jewish tradition. It recognizes a state called *gesisah*, that is, a stage in which the patient has become moribund and death is "imminent,"[18] which is sometimes defined as within three days. Active killing of a patient at this or any point is still considered plain murder, and withdrawal of treatment is morally the same. But in *gesisah* it is permitted to withdraw an impediment to dying. A traditional example given is the withdrawal of a noise like the chopping of wood which is said to keep the soul from departing. There is some question, however, as to whether removal of hindrances to dying applies to removal of medical therapies that prolong the dying.[19]

Aside from this one possible exception, the duty to preserve life is a most stringent obligation. It is imposed on the physician in a way never considered in either ancient Greek medicine or in its liberal, individualistic counterpart, the AMA position where the physician is given substantial discretion in choosing whom he will serve. The Jewish pro-life imperative is also imposed on the patient himself. And if a patient refuses lifesaving medical treatment, a right that is now widely advocated in the patient's rights movement and that has the imprimatur of Anglo-American common law, it does not justify nontreatment, according to rabbinic law. The patient has an obligation to preserve his own life and, according to some sources, treatment should be forced upon him even against his will if it will preserve his life.[20] The contrast with the liberal, rights-oriented approach is dramatic.

A rabbinic approach to the case of Ms. R. and Dr. T. is by now obvious. Unlike the Hippocratic tradition, which is silent with respect to Ms. R.'s duty, Jewish medical ethics would clearly and decisively reject her plan to kill her daughter for mercy. While the Hippocratic tradition can be interpreted as justifying Dr. T.'s collaboration (providing he judges it to be in the daughter's or perhaps the mother's interest), Judaism would allow no such rationale. Neither the daughter not the mother is *goses*, in a moribund state, so not even withdrawal of treatment would be justified, even if there were a treatment to be withdrawn. Certainly, merciful killing would be unthinkable.

The duty to heal in Judaism is often seen as an outgrowth of the duty to preserve life, but upon occasion, the two diverge. According to Bleich, the duty to heal "encompasses not only situations posing a threat to life or limb or demanding restoration of impaired health, but also situations of lesser gravity warranting medical attention for relief of pain and promotion of well-being."[21] Nahmanides bases the duty to heal on the commandment, "Thou shalt love thy neighbor as thyself." Although liberals might interpret this to allow "beneficent nontreatment" of one's neighbor as a way to end his prolonged suffering because self-love would lead to nontreatment, Nahmanides gives no such twist to the principle.

The Jewish dietary laws and sexual morality are well known, as are the prohibitions against idol worship. As already stated, and in contrast to much of Christianity, Judaism strongly condemns magic, incantations, and faith healing. There is a minority opinion within Judaism that condemns human medical intervention as a faithless act in opposition to reliance on divine power for healing. But the mainstream is overwhelming in its rejection of this radical dualism. While the idea that man should not intervene in divine providence dominates much early Christian thinking, Judaism has rejected this. The Jewish view of the healer is given biblical authority in the passage requiring that if a man injures another in a fight he must "cause him to be thoroughly healed."[22] Although the text refers more directly to financial liability, it has been interpreted as giving license and, indeed, responsibility for human medical intervention.[23]

Perhaps most unique in Jewish medical ethics is the emphasis placed on duties related to the care of the newly dead. As signaled in the autopsy dispute between the rabbis and Israeli physicians, the Jew is obliged to give proper respect to the body and to observe important rabbinical law and ritual. The body is considered divine property, not merely the bodily remains from which the soul has escaped, as in the

Gnostic view. Thus, neither the state, the medical profession, nor another human agent has the right to use the body except as prescribed.[24]

The implications for autopsy, medical research, anatomical dissection, and transplantation of organs are enormous. Except when necessary to save the life of an identifiable patient in need (under Jewish law's general exemption in order to save a life), the body cannot be violated. This explains why rabbis are guardedly open to lifesaving cadaver transplantations of organs while at the same time opposed to autopsy that the secular world generally deems less controversial. Even in the exceptional lifesaving case where autopsy is condoned, tradition demands that removed parts be returned for burial with the body. Thus, routine practices in secular hospitals (and even some with vague Jewish roots) may constitute a violation of some patients' religious and ethical obligations. Similarly objectionable may be routine pathological practices including standard autopsy requests for the purpose of satisfying medical curiosity or of verifying diagnosis.

Despite the many unique features of rabbinical law, there are points of contact with the Hippocratic traditions. These include the commitment to healing and the relative unimportance of "rights" as commonly outlined in the "patient's rights" movement (see chapter 1). But Hippocratic, patient-centered beneficence is supplemented in Judaism with a rich tradition of law that governs the care of the living, the dying, and the dead. Jewish medical ethics is rooted in an ethic of a people and is meant to be known, understood, and required for all, medical lay people as well as physicians. In fact, as has been stated, rabbis are ordained with an expertise in understanding an interpretation of the law that places them in a superior position to the physician without rabbinical training. This viewpoint is totally incomprehensible to the mainstream of Hippocratic physician ethics as we have come to know it.

CATHOLIC MORAL THEOLOGY

Catholic moral theology, like Judaism, approaches problems in medical ethics from a long tradition of coherent, systematic thought. The subject evolves as a subcategory of a class of moral problems to be resolved by the systematic application of techniques and principles rooted in a theological framework and system of authority. Through many centuries of continuity, the Roman Catholic medical ethic has been handed down and interpreted to the laity primarily by a priesthood whose members have not, for the most part, been medically trained. Thus a potential conflict looms between them and a group of medical professionals whom some have called the new priesthood, a group made up almost exclusively of physicians who lack theological training.

Like Judaism, Catholicism has historical points of contact with the Hippocratic tradition, but the contact has at times been abrasive. Early Christianity showed little awareness of the Hippocratic cult. The neo-Pythagorean mystery cults were often explicitly rejected by early Christians. But with the convergence of Christianity and Greek thought that reached its apex in the Constantinian period beginning early in the fourth century, interaction between Christian and Hippocratic thinking became more common. Jerome, the fourth-century Latin church father, refers to Hippocrates but shows little knowledge of the contents of the Hippocratic Oath.[25] He sees provision of medical care as part of the priest's clerical duties but makes clear that the Christian priest's obligations are greater than those prescribed for students of Hippocrates.

The practice of medicine that emerged in the Middle Ages is sometimes referred to as monastic medicine. It was dominated by monks for whom medical practice was a religious duty, but whose framework was of course theocentric and ecclesiastical.[26] There is still much controversy and uncertainty, however, over the extent to which ecclesiastical authorities exerted significant influence on medical history.[27] In late medieval monastic medical manuscripts there are some efforts to reconcile the Hippocratic and Christian traditions, but the two primarily retained separate identities.

The religiously based medicine of the early Middle Ages sets the stage for the integration of medical morality into a general moral theology. All that was needed was the advent of the great theological systematizers, the scholastics, of the thirteenth century. They developed a comprehensive theory of morality that became integral to systematic theology. Following the framework set by Thomas Aquinas and other great systematic theologians of the high Middle Ages, discussions of physicians' obligations began to appear in confessors' manuals and in summaries of moral theology.[28] A particularly well developed model is the *Summa moralis* of Antoninus of Florence in 1477. He comments upon both the honors due to the physician and the vices and sins that can befall him.[29] What is important to note is that the framework of the discussion is thoroughly Christian. The physician's role model is Christ, not Hippocrates.[30] The discussion of morality in medicine is buried in a section on the obligations of various states of life that is contained in a broad treatise on morality.

The framework was thus established for a modern Catholic medical ethic deeply embedded in a general Catholic moral theology. Even after lay physicians began to reappear as a division of labor emerged between priest and physician, the Church continued to exert a strong influence on certain religiously oriented strands of professional medicine and on ethical judgments relating to medical practices.[31] The Catholic medical ethic of today is built on a rich theological tradition. Hundreds of volumes on medical ethics have appeared since Antoninus which take systematic Catholic moral theology as their framework. David F. Kelly, professor of moral theology at St. Bernard's Seminary in Rochester, New York, has written a comprehensive history of Roman Catholic medical ethics in North America.[32] He lists no fewer than eighty-three North American works or editions from the last century alone. Kelly and virtually all the authors he cites are theological scholars, not physicians, as is appropriate for analyses of the application of a moral theology. At the same time, this points out the distance that must crop up between the experts on this tradition's medical morality and the clinicians who often see themselves as the crucial medical decision makers. It is ironic, and somewhat tragic, that medical ethicists rooted in Catholic moral theology and physicians oriented to the Hippocratic tradition meet separately and do research, often in geographical proximity, with neither group aware of the enormous efforts of the other. It is a tragedy that one of the great systems of medical ethics is so often isolated from the medical professionals who sometimes seem to be struggling to reinvent the medical ethical wheel.

A real system of medical ethics does exist with Catholic moral theology. Its two primary components are: a set of principles derived from the more general ethical theory of Catholic theology and a more problem-oriented set of rules and insights to help people make decisions about specific ethical problems. This second component is often called casuistry. Some say that it has been overformalized to the point that Catholic medical ethics is reduced to nothing but minutiae and technical distinctions. For example: It is acceptable to remove a cancerous uterus jeopardizing the life of a pregnant woman even though it happens to contain a living fetus who will surely die because of the removal, but it is unacceptable to remove a living fetus in order to save the life of a woman when the pregnancy itself jeopardizes her life. The subtleties of the casuistry, however, have an elegance about them, derived from its integral link to the principles of the Catholic system of moral theology. And the complex theoretical justifications for casuistry often (though not always) produce conclusions that concur remarkably with common sense, moral intuition, and reason.

The principles themselves resonate at times with the principles of other systems of ethics, but they usually maintain a unique character. Anyone who wants to make medical decisions about his or her own care within an orthodox Catholic context will have to understand the principles. So too will physicians who adhere to the orthodox Catholic view or who want to treat patients of such views without violating their religious–ethical convictions. Physicians must understand the implications of the Catholic ethic on the practice of medicine and, what may be troublesome, may have to abandon some of the elements of good Hippocratic medicine in order to follow Catholic teaching. What should physicians do, for example, when they are convinced that a Catholic paitent needs to be sterilized in the interests of health, if they know that in such circumstances sterilization is condemned in Catholic thought? They could follow their Hippocratic convictions and sterilize the patient, even if it requires using deception to obtain consent, or even perform the surgery without consent. Both would be good Hippocratic medicine, but bad Catholic moral theology. On the other hand, they could permit the patient to make the sterilization decision and yield to that decision. That would be good liberal affirmation of the principle of self-determination, but bad Catholic moral theology and bad Hippocratic medicine. Finally, they could also refuse even to mention the procedure and its potential benefits to the patient, searching instead for the next best way to prevent the feared harms. This last course might be what Catholic moral theology requires.

In order to grasp the coherence of the positions taken in Catholic medical ethics, one must understand its basic principles and its theological framework. The core of that framework has been, especially until recently, a particular kind of natural-law thinking in which God is seen as imprinting certain purposes or ends on the human's nature.[33] The natural law, in theory, can be known by all through the use of reason. But, the system says, human reason is corrupted so knowledge is never perfect. Natural law is understood within Catholic moral theology then, as a law of reason (not just biological nature). It can be known from reason by understanding inclinations (to live, to procreate, and so forth). The natural law also is said to be confirmed by divine revelation and can be summarized, as Thomas Aquinas has argued, by the formula "good is to be done and promoted, and evil is to be avoided."[34]

To modern philosophers steeped in Kant and the ethics of human rights, this may sound strangely oriented to consequences, but the casuistry of Catholic moral theology spares us any worry that Catholic medical ethics will be confused with the ethics of a John Stuart Mill or a Jeremy Bentham. Contrasted to the Hippocratic principle, however, the absence of an exclusive focus on the benefits and harms to the individual is conspicuous.

The generalities of natural law—doing good and avoiding evil—do begin to work themselves out in principles that lead to specific answers to medical ethical dilemmas. These dominate the core literature in Catholic medical ethics.[35] But the principles always emanate from the affirmation of a divinely authored natural law, which determines the end of man and which subordinates man to the deity.

Here are the five basic principles of Catholic medical ethics as I see them:

The Principle of Stewardship. Since human life comes from God, says the ethic, no person is the master of his or her own body. Humans are merely stewards with responsibility to protect and cultivate spiritual and bodily functions.[36] From this derives the obligations to seek appropriate medical care and care for the body to ensure that it functions properly.

The Principle of the Inviolability of Human Life. Since life is God's and the human is only a steward, it is understandable that life might be viewed as sacred or inviolable.[37] In a more recent debate, this principle has been expressed as the *right* to life. That expresses the meaning but may lead to confusion, since the term *right* may be read as giving sufficient discretion for a decision to end one's life by suicide. Rights, however, both in modern secular political philosophy and in Catholic thought, are inalienable, which means that, while they cannot be confiscated, they cannot be surrendered either.[38] In this sense, one can use the expression *right to life*, but what is really conveyed is a duty of custodianship. From this, the ethics of abortion, euthanasia, and other life and death matters eventually flow. Edwin F. Healy outlines the range of infringements if life is deliberately taken by suicide.[39] First, of course, it violates God's right over determining human life. But society's right to public peace and order is also violated, much as suicide was viewed in English common law as taking property belonging to the king. Finally, deliberate taking of life deprives friends and relatives of the deceased's love and service.

There are, according to Catholic moral theology, limits to this inviolability of life; many within the tradition see the taking of life as justifiable in cases of self-defense or in a 'just war', a term that itself has generated an enormous moral casuistry.[40] Accidental killings are also excusable. Some even justify capital punishment on the grounds that the life taken is no longer innocent. But as summarized by Charles E. Curran, professor of moral theology at the Catholic University of America, "The direct killing of an innocent person on one's own authority is always wrong."[41]

The Principle of Totality. Since the human body is God's and is only "on loan" to the individual, some justification is demanded for surgical procedures in which bodies are cut up and sometimes even mutilated. The principle of totality does the job.[42] According to this principle, a part exists for the good of the whole and may be sacrificed when necessary to serve a proportionate good for the whole. This justifies sacrificing tissues and organs for alleviating great pain or removing pathological organs necessary to preserve the whole.

The principle is one that applies only when a part of the body jeopardizes the interest of the whole body. It does not extend to sacrificing the individual for the sake of the total society, which could permit research on human subjects "for the good of society" or the taking of an organ from one person for transplantation into another. It also does not apply to the destruction of the fetus to serve the interests of the mother, that, according to the tradition within which we are working, would be sacrificing one human life for the sake of another. Some have tried to use the principle of totality to justify sterilizations and other mutilations of sexual function. The reason that that is rejected within this system is made clear by the next principle.

The Principle of Sexuality and Procreation. Since the time of Paul's lukewarm endorsement of marriage ("It is better to marry than to burn," I Cor. 7:9), Christianity has struggled over the morality of sexual relations. Augustine, whose early sexual life was quite adventuresome, struggled in his Christian period with a justification of marriage and procreation, defending it against the ascetic opposition of the Manicheans on the one hand and the permissiveness of the libertines on the other. In order for human sexuality to be legitimate, it had to be embedded in an end far deeper than the mere satisfaction of sexual desire. The sexual function, as all human functions, had to be given meaning in the context of God's purposes and in the natural ends of these functions. Catholic moral theology has identified two purposes of the sexual function. The first, procreation and nurturing of children, has until recently been identified frequently as the primary end of marriage.[43] The second purpose of the sexual function is to express the loving union or companionship within the marital bond.

Catholic moral theologians have tended to separate reproductive functions from nonreproductive ones.[44] The nonreproductive functions exist for the good of the individual, but the reproductive power, in Gerald Kelly's words, "is primarily for the good of the species, not for the individual; and this function is not directly subordinated to the individual's well-being."[45] The prohibition on sterilization and even contraception thus follows inevitably. The principle of totality alone cannot justify the sacrifice of reproductive powers. But it means that Catholics are faced with difficulties in cases such as the previously mentioned cancerous uterus which, if not removed, would surely kill the patient. As stated, perhaps surprisingly, removal of the uterus might be justified, even if at the time it bears a fetus. To see why, we must study the next principle.

The Principle of Double Effect. The principle of double effect is one intuited by many ordinary citizens who feel that giving a potentially lethal dose of a narcotic to a cancer patient in order to relieve pain is morally different somehow from deliberately setting out to kill that patient on grounds of mercy. It is again perceived by those who feel that accidentally killing a bystander in a military encounter when prudent precautions have been taken is morally different somehow from setting out to kill innocent civilians on purpose in order to demoralize an enemy. Only Catholic moral theology, however, has taken this intuition to a point of scholarly precision and elegance.[46] The principle of double effect justifies certain actions that produce "indirectly" certain evil consequences, provided at least four conditions are met: the action, by itself and independently of its effect, must not be morally evil; the evil effect must not be a means to producing the good effect; the evil effect is sincerely not intended, but merely tolerated; and there is a proportionate reason for performing the action, in spite of its evil consequences.[47]

The principle explains Catholic justification of such acts as the removal of the cancerous fetus-bearing uterus, the administration of a pain-relieving narcotic that may produce respiratory depression, and other equally subtle but sophisticated positions taken in Catholic medical ethics.

These principles, together with others that deal with cooperation in sinful acts and tempting or inciting others to sinful acts,[48] combine within a richly developed Catholic theory of conscience to provide a framework for answering the entire range of issues in medical ethics.

The casuistry from which the ethic developed, however, of course leaves many areas open for potential dispute. It is here that the uniquely Catholic theory of the authority of the Church provides a context for resolving the dispute. Like Jewish medical ethics, but very much unlike secular professional physician ethics, Catholic moral theology provides a religious basis for moral authority. Contrary to some stereotypes, the areas in which a pope speaks infallibly are quite limited. Authority has at various times and on various issues rested with popes as well as with other bishops, church councils, and even the individual conscience. Medical ethics has not traditionally been an area in which infallible pronouncements are made. Thus, in the deliberations of the papal commission on birth control, there was considerable jockeying for position among theologians, with much effort to establish that the Church's teaching was in doubt. In 1950, however, the encyclical *Humani Generis* of Pope Pius XII declared that when a pope speaks explicitly on a controverted subject it is no longer in doubt. In 1968, in *Humanae Vitae*, Pope Paul VI spoke directly on birth control, foreclosing for many the possible legitimacy of so-called artificial contraception within Catholic thought. In spite of this, there remains considerable dispute even among Catholic theologians over the exact structure of moral authority within Catholic moral theology. The potential for tension in modes of establishing what is ethical remains, as do the tensions over substantive issues in medical ethics. There is complete agreement, however, as there is within Judaism, that the issues are religious and theological and that the Church, through one or more of its official voices, retains authority that cannot be yielded to other groups, even medical professionals.

Should Ms. R. and Dr. T., the mother and physician contemplating the merciful killing of Ms. R.'s daughter, look to the long and rich tradition of Catholic moral theology, there can be little doubt how the casuistry and the basic principles would be applied. The principle of double effect permits standing aside in certain cases of terminal illness where the treatments offered to extend life would be gravely burdensome or simply useless. In this regard, the tradition of Catholic moral theology differs from Jewish thought. That is not what is being proposed in Ms. R.'s case, however. The proposal is one of outright, direct, if merciful, murder. The principle of the inviolability of human life certainly would make such a scheme intolerable, and no amount of merciful motive would excuse the killing. No amount of benefit to the infant girl, as judged by the physician or anyone else, would make moral the killing of the innocent child. Contrary to the mainstream of Hippocratic ethics, the prohibition on killing is an independent moral principle in Catholic moral theology.

PROTESTANTISM

Protestant theological ethics offers a much less sharply formulated alternative to Hippocratic medical ethics than do Jewish and Roman Catholic thought. It has nothing like their consistent, rich tradition with a fully developed literature attempting out of which to draw a medical ethics. However, Protestant thinkers trained in ethics have probably done more work in medical ethics in the last decade than any other group, including physicians representing organized medicine.

In principle, Protestant theologians ought to hold, as their Catholic and Jewish brethren do, that the subject of medical ethics is but a subcategory of applied ethics derived from their systematic theology. A few systematic theologians such as Karl Barth[49] and Helmut Thielicke[50] do work in this mode. But many contemporary Protestants trained in ethics work much closer to the core topics in medical ethics and much more remotely from the dominant themes of systematic theology. They tend to address such topics as abortion, euthanasia, genetics, confidentiality, and perhaps justice in health care delivery. (For a discussion of justice in health care delivery, see chapter 11.) Sometimes they use an explicit theological framework, but more often this remains implicit only.[51]

Still, at some points, important Protestant theological themes emerge as central to the medical ethical theories of all the authors. For example, Paul Ramsey, Harrington Spear Paine, professor of religion at Princeton, claims in *The Patient as Person*, one of the most important Protestant medical ethical treatises of the decade, that he is writing as a Christian ethicist.[52] His medical ethics is based on a covenant theory, viewing relations between physician and patient as a manifestation of covenant relations between persons generally. He acknowledges his links with Barth and could as easily have traced those roots back to reformation theology, especially to Calvinist theology and ultimately to Jewish notions of the covenant. He affirms as a basic principle "the Biblical norm of fidelity to covenant."[53]

The contrasts with Hippocratic medicine and professional medical ethics are dramatic, although Ramsey sometimes does not grasp the tension. He sometimes assumes without explanation and contrary to reason that the content of the covenant is merely a unilateral pledge that the physician will benefit the patient according to his judgment.[54] The Hippocratic Oath is a kind of covenant, to be sure. It is sworn by the gods and binds physician to his fellow physician, but nowhere in the mainstream of Hippocratic medicine, from the Oath to the AMA's "Principles of Medical Ethics," is there an ethic of covenant fidelity morally binds physician and patient reciprocally. There is no generation of a moral community by mutual pledges of loyalty between professional and lay person.

Covenant is rooted in faithfulness or loyalty, in an ethic of keeping promises. Covenant loyalty stands behind Jewish medical ethics, and is at the root of all Jewish notions of obligation. It also emerges in secular social contract theory, but a covenant between lay person and professional is alien to professional ethics as we have received it.

In Protestant theological ethics, broad theological themes such as the covenant tend to replace the more sharply formulated principles of Catholic moral theology.[55] A second, strong Protestant theme is what is sometimes referred to as one of the Christian virtues, *agape*, or love. Ramsey refers to it as "a moral quality of attitude and of action owed to all men by any man who steps into a covenant with another man. . . ."[56] Joseph Fletcher, as different as he is from Ramsey in much of his thinking, concurs in making agape, or neighbor love, his central ethical category, at least in his more theoretical work.[57] His concept, though, equates the loving act to the one that will produce the best consequences.[58] It is this calculation of consequences that dominates his more explicit medical ethics work. In this way, he is closer to the concern of Aquinas for doing good and avoiding evil than most followers of either Aquinas or Fletcher would like to admit.

The trick, or course, is knowing what is the loving thing to do when one is in the crisis of a situation. Take our first case, for example, the handicapped infant whose fatally ill mother believes that the infant would be better off dead. Protestant theological ethics has been skeptical of appeals to natural law to determine whether, for example, the physician should collaborate with the mother in bringing about the death of the baby. Ramsey calls natural law a "sub-Christian source of insight."[59] Fletcher concurs, viewing it as Catholic legalistic reasoning.[60]

There are two separate problems here. Fletcher is concerned about legalism, the resolution of ethical dilemmas by the application of excessively rigid rules. He suspects Catholic casuistry here. So his appeal to love combined with Protestant notions of individual responsibility for interpreting the Scripture make Protestantism ripe to conspire with professional physician ethics in emphasizing case-by-case approaches. If physicians are wont to say that every case is so unique that no rigid rules apply, some branches of Protestant ethics are eager to provide a theoretical underpinning for that situationalism. Small wonder that

Fletcher finds such a warm bed in the chambers of the medical school and the medical profession.

On the other hand, Protestant thought has within it a critique of this extreme emphasis on individual cases. Mainstream Protestant theology sees the human as a fallible, sinful creature who lacks the capacity to reason through a problem while in the line of fire. This leads some (see chapter 13) to urge that physicians approach the bedside with at least a few strong guidelines, and perhaps even with rules that will bind them against impulses that seem fit in the heat of the moment.

The second problem raised by the Protestant attack on natural law as a basis for applied ethics is not so much a concern over the ethic of rules as a concern over man's ability to determine those moral rules using unaided reason. Protestant thought has often, but not always, driven a sharp wedge between what can be known by naked, fallible reason and what is revealed in Scripture. Only recently has there been a resurgence of interest in natural-law thinking among Protestant theoreticians, but its form is quite different from that informing Catholic theological ethics. Still, there is, or ought to be, complete agreement that the foundations of ethical authority are theological, since the Protestant notion of authority links the individual more directly to Scripture than does the Catholic.

In Protestantism, the line of authority to the cleric is short-circuited because there is a priesthood of all believers. But there is no more a place in Protestant thought than in Catholic or Jewish for a professionally based authority for medical ethics. Protestantism sometimes sees physicians as having a "calling," with the almost religious overtones that word conveys,[61] but that calling does not give them authority over those who medically are lay people.

THE MODERN SECULAR WEST

The major religious traditions of the West all have at least incipient theories of medical ethics. Some are richly developed; others, especially in Protestantism, less so. Sectarian religion offers still other variants. Jehovah's Witnesses are well known for their refusal of blood transfusions based on a rather peculiar interpretation of Scriptural prohibitions against eating of blood.[62] Christian Science has a fuller theory of the relationship of secular organic medicine to healing based on its own spiritual principles. It is clear that these religiously based theories of what is ethically required in medical decisions can at times come head-on into conflict with traditional Hippocratic medicine and what I am calling Hippocratic tradition. What is the poor physician to do? What if he or she is a good Catholic and still trying to remain loyal to the ethical canons of the profession of medicine? What is a patient to do who is devoutly committed to a religious tradition, but who still feels that medical care is needed from those with the skill and knowledge reserved to those within the medical profession? Does an ordinary visit to the doctor's office require a suspension of the patient's, and even the physician's, religious convictions? It may not happen often, but it is required frequently in routine encounters between physician and patient when the physician "practicing good medicine" makes decisions based on the codes of ethics of the profession. To complicate matters, Western society has developed a somewhat coherent and plausible political philosophy that is not totally dependent upon any of the religious ethics affirmed by various of its members. That secular Western political philosophy is deeply embedded in the belief system of individual citizens and is reflected in the legal decisions made by our legislature and courts. Thus, if physician and patient are in dispute over the legitimacy of killing a baby whose parent is about to die, the dispute will be resolved neither by the Hippocratic ethic nor by the ethic of the religious group to which physician or patient may happen adhere to.

WESTERN LIBERAL POLITICAL PHILOSOPHY

The core elements of modern Western liberal political philosophy can be found in some religious traditions, especially those associated with the evolution of the modern period. Western individualism can be seen in the more mystical and individualistic branches of the left wing of the Protestant Reformation, as exemplified by such sixteenth-century mystics as Hans Denck, Thomas Münzer, and even Martin Luther's one-time compatriot Andreas Bodenstein von Karlstadt. Notions of separation of church and state can be seen emerging in the ideas of sectarians such as the Zurich Anabaptists in the early sixteenth century, George Blaurock and Conrad Grebel. Religious tolerance that anticipated modern liberal pluralism was seen in Philipp of Hesse (1504–1567), who refused to order the death penalty for the Anabaptist dissenters.

But the real emergence of modern liberal political philosophy does not come until more than a century later, with John Locke in the late seventeenth century and with the weaving together of Rousseau's interpretation of the social contract and Kantian ethical commitment to the respect of persons in the eighteenth. The result has been a political philosophy, a social ethic if you like, that has within it an incipient medical ethic, one with elements that stand in radical contrast to both the Hippocratic tradition and the mainstream religiously based medical ethics. One of its central elements is a love of liberty that has come to dominate mid- and late-twentieth-century American court decisions on medical issues. As late as the end of the nineteenth century, Pope Leo XIII was able to paint liberalism with the same black brush as socialism, rationalism, and "naturalism."[63] Yet the courts, in adjudicating disputes about the adequacy of informed consent, elevate the liberals' principle of self-determination to the highest and most decisive principle. Justice Schroeder, in *Natanson v. Kline,* a 1960 landmark case in the development of the American legal doctrine of informed consent, is able to say that "Anglo-American law starts with the premise of thoroughgoing self-determination. It follows that each man is considered to be master of his own body and he may, if he be of sound mind, expressly prohibit the performance of life-saving surgery, or other medical treatment."[64] This glowing affirmation of the principle of self-determination as the starting point of medical decision making is never found in the Hippocratic tradition. To be sure, more modern professional ethical codes have references to freedom of choice for patients in selecting their physicians and to freedom of choice for physicians in selecting their patients, but even here the liberal principle plays no significant role for decisions made within the physician–patient relationship. Neither is it found in any central way in religious medical ethics, at least not until the contemporary times, primarily among Protestants who have become modern in the full sense of the word, absorbing the liberal perspective only nascent in early Reformation thought.

In addition to a liberal affirmation of self-determination and tolerance, modern secular political philosophy, especially as expressed in the American ethos, affirms a principle of equality. Liberty and equality are often cojoined as they were in the French Revolution in virtually every crucial American political document. "All men are created equal" and they are "endowed by their Creator with certain inalienable Rights," including liberty.

In the most recent and fullest expression of the secular American medical ethic (1978), the National Commission for the Protection of

Human Subjects of Biomedical and Behavioral Research presented in its *Belmont Report* a scheme involving three fundamental ethical principles.[65] Its foundation was not the notion of physicians doing what they thought would benefit patients. It certainly was not the principles of stewardship and totality, nor was it the doctrine of double effect. Rather, it was a broadly formulated principle of beneficence (not limited to benefit to the patient) carefully hedged in by principles of justice and respect for persons. It is under the latter Kantian notion of respect for persons that autonomy and self-determination are developed. It is under the principle of justice that crucial ethical concerns with distribution of health care are handled. Once again, it is a dimension wholly absent from the Hippocratic tradition, where such distribution is apparently seen as outside the scope of the physician's concern.

The language of modern secular political philosophy is quite different from that of either Hippocratic or religious ethics, and this has had its impact on secular nonprofessional medical ethics. The natural law tradition of the Stoics and of Catholic moral theology has shifted into a secular natural rights perspective. It says that man is endowed with rights, not duties, obligations, or interests. I am not aware of a single document in the history of professional physician ethics before 1980 that so much as mentions rights; rights talk has been as fundamentally alien to the Hippocratic tradition as it was to most religious ethical discussion, at least until the modern period. Rights talk is a modern phenomenon; it has arrived with a vengeance in the more public versions of contemporary medical ethics. We now talk about a woman's right to control her own body, the patient's right to consent to medical treatment, and the citizen's right to health care, whatever that might mean. Some of the scholarly work on these various medical rights is being articulated explicitly in the context of our modern political forefathers.[66]

In April 1980, an international meeting was held in Messina, Sicily, on the subject of the teaching of human rights in schools of medicine. Held in collaboration with UNESCO, participants included members of the medical profession and staff from the United Nations Division on Human Rights. Those without extensive exposure to the medical profession took human rights to be something beyond controversy, only to discover that, within medicine, rights talk is something that is at least new, and often quite threatening. Some of the medical professionals expressed great concern about problems that can emerge when benefits to the patient conflict with the protection of the patient's rights.

THE PATIENT'S RIGHTS MOVEMENT

In the United Sates, the most important expression of this liberal Western political philosophy in medicine has evolved into what is now sometimes referred to as the patient's rights movement. The term encompasses a broad coalition of those unhappy with the paternalism and emphasis on good consequences of traditional medicine. The movement, if it can be called that, includes abortion rights activists, critics of professional domination of medical research, and advocates of freedom of choice for or against treatments for the terminally ill. These and others reflect the basic American natural rights heritage. As formerly unpopular ethical positions on some of these topics have become part of the mainstream of American thought, opponents of abortion, contraception, euthanasia, and other controversial medical ethical decisions have found themselves increasingly talking rights language in order to protect their newly deviant positions.

In 1973, under the auspices of the American Hospital Association, *A Patient's Bill of Rights* was formulated, incorporating many of the basic ethical commitments of this secular ethical tradition.[67] It has been criticized as redundantly bestowing on Americans many of the legal and moral rights they have long possessed.[68] It has been attacked, as well, for being the product of an organization of health professionals, even though the committee that drafted the bill included lay people as well as health care professionals. Overall, though, it has captured the attention of the American public and summarizes many of the deeply held convictions of both lay people and some physicians who are beginning to question their Hippocratic heritage.

The bill of rights, a document developed by a private association of hospitals, of course has no legal standing. Soon after its appearance, however, governmental bodies began adopting legally binding bills of rights for patients. The Minnesota legislature was the first, and others have followed. The New York State Department of Health compiled a bill for the rights of patients that was adopted in 1976. The federal Department of Health, Education, and Welfare adopted a set of regulations in 1974 on rights for patients in skilled nursing facilities, and another set in 1976 for Medicaid residents of intermediate care facilities.

Comparable secular reformulations of medical ethics in rights terms have occurred recently in Europe as well. In January 1976, the Parliamentary Assembly of the Council of Europe adopted Recommendation 779, entitled "On Rights of the Sick and Dying."[69] The action, affirming the patient's right to refuse medical treatment, was grounded in "the right to personal dignity and integrity." Similar rights appeals appear in the UN Declaration of Human Rights, which includes an affirmation that everyone has "the right to a standard of living adequate for the health and well-being of himself," including the necessary medical care.

The patient's rights movement has focused primarily on the liberty side of Western social ethics. The cry has been for freedom from constraint to make decisions of one kind or another: for abortion, against cancer surgery, for or against participation in medical research. These are what philosophers sometimes call liberty rights, the right to choose to conduct one's life in one's own way provided it does not infringe upon the rights of others.[70] The concern for equity or justice, which is the essential complementary principle in Western political thought, is being heard, however, in close relation to another appeal for what philosophers call entitlement rights, that is, claims that extend beyond the mere right to be let alone to those that generate an obligation on someone else to provide the resources necessary to exercise an option. Thus, the claim for the right to health care extends far beyond the mere right to choose a health service if someone is willing to provide it and if the individual can pay the necessary price. The entitlement right claim calls for actual delivery of certain health services: primary medical care through a national health insurance or health service, catastrophic health care at government expense, or even abortions paid for by Medicaid. The rights language of the modern secular thinker accommodates the range of concerns in modern liberal political philosophy. That language provides a dramatic alternative to the more traditional way of talking about problems in medical ethics.

If Ms. R. and Dr. T. saw themselves as standing in this modern, secular, liberal tradition of natural rights, they might turn to the basic documents of that tradition for guidance in helping make their decisions about whether to participate in the merciful killing of Ms. R.'s daughter. They probably would not get as much help as they would like. Whereas the Hippocratic tradition would couch its moral advice in terms of benefits to the patient, the new natural rights give Dr. T. no easy justification for collaborating in the killing by claiming his belief that it was in his patient's interests. On the other hand, secular liberal political philosophy, with its rights talk, does not clearly condemn their proposed scheme.

Certainly, Western political and legal thought can be read as condemning such killings. In most jurisdictions, including the United States, mercy is not a defense against homicide. The *Patient's Bill of*

Rights favors primarily liberty rights such as the right of individuals to refuse medical treatment. It certainly does not extend to the entitlement right of one person to kill another. Even libertarian defenses of 'rational suicide' stop at nonvoluntary mercy killings. In short, the modern, liberal, rights-oriented West seems to condemn Ms. R.'s plan, but not so forcefully and directly as the Jewish and Roman Catholic systems of medical ethics. In order to understand the full range of moral options in the case, however, it is necessary to push beyond the Anglo-American West; there are other incipient systems of medical ethics that pose alternatives to the Hippocratic tradition.

Chapter 3

Medical Ethical Theories Outside the Anglo-American West

It would be hard enough to choose a medical ethic from among the implicit and explicit theories of the Hippocratic tradition, the Judeo-Christian tradition, and the ethics of the modern West. They seem to differ so widely in their understanding of ethics, in their substantive ethical positions, in the language they use in talking about ethics, and in their theories of moral authority. Unfortunately, these are not the limit of options available. It would be parochial and narrowly conceived, indeed, to focus exclusively on choices only within our own heritage. Once we move beyond the confines of the modern liberal West, a much wider range of medical ethical theories is available.

Anyone who has arrived at the emergency room of a municipal hospital in any large American city may have faced the confusion of suddenly being thrust into a physician-patient relationship with a physician who is not only a stranger to the particular patient but also a stranger to the entire Anglo-American tradition. Much of the difficulty in communicating with the foreign physician comes from a conflict in cultures. This conflict is dramatically highlighted in the microcosm of the medical crisis that brought the patient to the emergency room. The physician may bring with him a belief system, possibly an entire metaphysics, that is fundamentally alien to the patient. The physician may stand outside the mainstream of American values. Unless we understand the alternative ethical frameworks behind the decision making that will take place in the emergency room, we shall never be able to bridge the gap between physician and patient.

SOCIALIST MEDICAL ETHICS

Had Ms. R. and Dr. T. faced their medical ethical dilemma in a socialist country of Eastern Europe, or China, or perhaps in Cuba, they probably would have met up with a somewhat different set of norms. Just as in the liberal West, these socialist nations have shown a recent resurgence of interest in medical ethics. A literature on the teaching of medical ethics (deontology, as the Europeans call it) began to appear in the Soviet Union and other socialist countries around the start of the 1970s, just as it did in the Anglo-American West.[1] There is no obvious historical connection for the convergence, beyond the obvious impact of modern medical technology on citizens throughout the world, whether in New York or Moscow.

Much of the socialist literature, as in the United States, is devoted to debate over remarkably mundane, pedagogical issues such as how many lectures should be given, where they should come in the medical school curriculum, and whether the subject of ethics should be integrated into scientific and clinical studies or should stand alone as a separate course.[2] It is accompanied, however, by an even larger literature on the substantive issues. Z. Ander, of the Tirgu Mures Medical Pharmaceutical Institute in Romania, says he counted 123 articles on medical ethics in Romania in the twenty-five-year period ending in 1970—more, he says, if one counts chapters in books.[3]

The most important institutional event in socialist medical ethics during this period was the formal adoption of a definitive text called "The Oath of Soviet Physicians" by the presidium of the Supreme Soviet in March 1971.[4] It has the feel, almost the rhythm, of its Hippocratic forefather. It could be taken as almost a straightforward updating, until one grasps the content. The pledge of loyalty is hardly made "by Apollo and all the gods and goddesses." It is a pledge "to keep and to develop the beneficial traditions of medicine in my country, to conduct all my actions according to the principles of the Communistic morality, to always keep in mind the high calling of the Soviet physician, and the high responsibility I have to my people and to the Soviet government."[5] The Soviet Oath commits the physician to service to the people, even to the extent of working "conscientiously wherever the interests of society will require it." This principled commitment to serve in a broader societal perspective rather than solely in the interests of the individual is very un-Hippocratic. The only other professional code with anything like this kind of a commitment is the semisocialist principles of the American Medical Association. The tenth AMA principle of medical ethics of the 1957 version says that the "responsibilities of the physician extend not only to the individual, but also to society where these responsibilities deserve his interest and participation in activities which have the purpose of improving both the health and the well-being of the individual and the community."[6] The commitment to serve society, though, is most often identified, especially by Western commentators,[7] as the fundamental characteristic of socialist medical ethics.

The Soviet Oath, like most other professional codes, is quite general. Dr. T., were he a Soviet physician, would have a difficult time getting a precise answer to his problem of whether to disclose methods of killing a baby humanely. Presumably, the broad commitment of loyalty to society would direct him to existing public laws and tradition for an answer.

Ms. R. gets even less help with her problem. Exactly what the legal system of a socialist country would do with her scheme to cut short what she feels will be her baby's miserable existence is difficult to say. There is a general rejection of infanticide as morally unacceptable, even though it is practiced upon rare occasions.[8] And I am aware of no evidence that merciful infanticide even in cases such as this one is officially condoned. Arguments in medical ethics in socialist societies are often cast in terms of the prior obligation of the society to provide for the basic needs of the people. In the socialist state, so the argument goes, a baby would not be left in the helpless condition Ms. R. foresees. Several other core problems in Western medical ethics—how to handle population planning, for example—are seen in Marxist theory as being the result of the capitalist economic system and therefore nonexistent in a socialist society. It is safe to assume Ms. R.'s problem would be analyzed in the same way.

In the sphere of health services, the constitutions and legal systems of the socialist state often grant an explicit right to health care, differing dramatically from liberal Western states where legal affirmation of such a right is still quite controversial.[9] The Cuban constitution, to pick an example patterned very much on the Eastern European model, guarantees in Article 49 that "Everybody has the right to health protection and care." It even goes so far as to spell out that this includes free medical and hospital care, free dental care, health publicity campaigns, and prevention of communicable disease. Based on my own, admittedly brief, on-site study of the Cuban health care system in 1979 and on several published studies,[10] I am convinced that the government takes its societal moral and legal commitment very seriously, given the country's serious financial constraints.

Given this public, legal basis for the right to health care and the clear affirmation of the physician's responsibility to society, the authority for medical ethical decision making is no doubt quite different from that in Hippocratic and religiously based theories. Sometimes the authority of the state, or at least of communistic principles, is taken for granted.[11] For the most part, in fact, physicians in socialist countries are salaried agents of the state. The Soviet Oath affirms the physician's commitment to "communistic principles of morality." Ander summarizes the teaching of medical ethics in Romania as being taught "according to the standards of socialist medical ethics."[12] A fascinating article from the Revolutionary Committee of the Hua Shan Hospital, Shanghai First Medical College, claims that its teachings are based on "Marxism-Leninism-Mao Tse-tung Thought."[13] (It then goes on to present discussions of teaching strategies, such as integrating teaching into clinical work, that sound as if they came straight out of an early 1970s debate in an American medical school curriculum committee.) With this focus on grounding professional ethics in the ethics of the broader culture, one gets a sense of the subordination of all professions to the society. In fact, Cubans talk of the principle of double subordination, by which they mean that the practice of medicine is subordinated professionally to the state professional health bureaucracy (the Ministry of Public Health) and subordinated politically to the will of the people, the *Poder Popular*, or local citizens' councils. These councils have the remarkable power, seldom used but always available, to hire and fire at local polyclinics (health and welfare clinics).

Still, a closer look at some socialist nations reveals a lingering ambivalence among many professionals about their roles; at least that is the conclusion I reached based on studies of health-care delivery systems that I made in Cuba and Poland, and supplemented by strong evidence from literature elsewhere.

The most dramatic battle for testing the relationship between the professional sense of obligation and the obligation to the state is the struggle in the Soviet Union over what has been called the political uses of psychiatry. Western critics and dissidents within the Soviet

Union have argued that the state has used psychiatry to label, discredit, and even constrain political troublemakers. The most well-known case has been that of the famous Soviet biochemist Zhores Medvedev.[14] In a volume he coauthored with his brother, Roy, Medvedev describes the terror of the night of May 29, 1970, when three Soviet policemen and two psychiatrists broke into his house, forced him into a minibus, and took him to a mental hospital. He was committed as an "incipient schizophrenic" with "paranoid delusions of reforming society." While most have taken the episode and others like it to be a clear-cut case of subordination of the profession of psychiatry to the interests of the state, the Medvedevs' own account suggests ambiguity. They report that a supporter of Zhores's case, whom they refer to only as Old Bolshevik Lert, was able to interview Galina Petrovna Bondareva, the psychiatrist in charge of the wing of the Kaluga Psychiatric Hospital where Zhores was held. The exchange begins with Lert pressing the psychiatrist, Bondareva, for an explanation of Medvedev's commitment:

L: And how did a psychiatrist come to be in the Chairman's office when she was having a talk with one of her constituents?

B: Well, I really don't know. Apparently someone from the City Soviet had some dealings with Medvedev, was struck by the oddness of his behavior and called in a psychiatrist.

L: Then am I to understand that the Chairman of the City Soviet is responsible for beginning this whole affair?

B: I don't know whether it was Antonenko or somebody else who works there.

L: But as the doctor in charge of the case, I assume you know exactly what these anonymous officials from the City Soviet found so odd in Medvedev's behaviour?

B: That's a medical secret.

L: But if officials from the City Soviet can know, why is it being kept secret from Zhores's wife and brother? A patient is not told he has cancer, but his family is warned. . . . By what you say, you are giving the impression that the reasons for committal are clearly not a medical secret but some other kind.

B: Our sole concern is the welfare of the patient.

L: If we are to talk about the welfare of the patient, to use your term for a moment—although Zhores is in fact perfectly well—then what was the reason for compulsory hospitalisation? As far as I know, it is not applied to all patients, but only to those who are a public danger. Perhaps you can tell me what deeds or actions of Zhores Medvedev were a threat to those around him?

B: He is mainly a danger to himself.

L: Do you really believe that it is within the competence of medicine to decide whether particular views are harmful or beneficial?

B: We judge Medvedev's mental state only on medical evidence. . . .[15]

The puzzle in all this is why Soviet psychiatrists, pledged to serve the interests of society, have to try so hard to convince Lert that they were acting in good Hippocratic fashion to serve only the interests of their patient. Nowhere in the Soviet Oath is that traditional ethic of benefit to the individual patient given that kind of priority.

Later in their volume, the Medvedevs reprint a moving letter written by Alexander Solzhenitsyn on behalf of Zhores. They say that within a day of the appearance, the letter, entitled "This Is How We Live," had become widely known not only among the Moscow intelligentsia but also abroad. It refers to Bondareva and her colleagues as "servile psychiatrists who break their Hippocratic oath and are able to describe concern for social problems as 'mental illness,' "[16] thus accusing them of serving state interests in spite of their protestations to the contrary. The charge certainly accuses the doctors of subordinating their duty to the patient to their duty to society, but whoever said that Soviet physicians were supposed to be good Hippocratic, patient-centered practitioners? Apparently, there is still some residuum of Hippocratism in medical ethics behind the Iron Curtain.

As mentioned above, I sensed the same ambiguity among the physicians I interviewed in Cuba and in Poland. These physicians, especially in Cuba, appeared to be dedicated to the principles of the revolution. Cuba was blessed, from its point of view, with a mass exodus of 3,000 of its 6,000 prerevolutionary physicians immediately after Fidel Castro came to power, producing an instantaneous ethical and ideological purging. Still, among the apparently dedicated physicians who remained, a sense of commitment to their profession as the real authority on matters of complexity and controversy could be detected.

In the independent Communist nation of Yugoslavia, physicians had apparently become uncomfortable with the state's authority in determining social and nonmedical indications for abortion. In 1968 they convened the second Congress of Slovene Physicians in Ljubljana to struggle with the problem. The resulting statement sounds like an American Medical Association defensive attack on the government for treading upon professional autonomy:

> The legalization of abortion without medical indications or with nonmedical indications is an exceptional case of the state interfering by force of

law in the right of treatment which constitutes . . . the exclusive domain of the physician and his full responsibility. . . . When the State interferes in the physician's domain, this does not only affect the gynecologists, but must encourage every physician to do his best in his own sphere of work in order to make this intervention unnecessary as soon as possible, or at least to limit it to its really inevitable scope. This would enable us to enforce entirely the wording of the code of ethics of medical workers of SFRJ (Socialist Federal Republic of Yugoslavia).[17]

The intervention of the state is inevitable, but the goal is to limit it as much as possible so that the professional code, which seems once again to be the highest authority, can reign supreme. It appears that the physicians of the socialist countries are still trying to hold on to their professional authority, fearing that unbridled commitment to the interests of the state will result in an intolerable sacrifice of the individual. Later, when we discuss the principle of justice in chapter 11, we shall see if the way out of the bind in which socialist physicians find themselves is to open the door to society, the same door opened by the AMA in 1957 when it legitimated the interests of the community as well as those of the patient.

ISLAMIC MEDICAL ETHICS

The socialist perspective presents only one integrated alternative to the Hippocratic and other medical ethical systems of the modern secular West. In the Near East, Islam provides another moral framework to which the woman of our case study and her physician with the perplexed conscience might turn for moral guidance. Were they Muslims, they would have inherited a long and complex moral tradition influenced by Greek, Jewish, Christian, Persian, and Indian thought. The Babylonian Code of Hammurabi, dating from the eighteenth century B.C., is the earliest recorded attempt to formulate a code that governs conduct, including that of physicians. For example, it states that if a physician injured a nobleman in surgery to the extent that his patient died, his hand is to be cut off.[18] The code set fees according to the social status of the patient. It was not, however, a professionally generated code; rather, the professional's obligations were specified by the social authorities as part of a more comprehensive system of law.

The Code of Hammurabi tells us little about whether infanticide for humane purposes would be tolerated or approved. It is generally known, however, that suicide and the taking of life, even for humane motives, were disapproved. Suicide was considered cutting oneself off from the gods.[19] In Assyria, according to the Middle Assyrian Law dating from about the fifteenth century B.C., a woman who had an abortion by her own hand was to be impaled on a stake and left unburied. During the Aryan period in Persia, according to the *Avesta* (the holy book of Zoroaster), to destroy life was to destroy the highest form of creation.[20] Abortion was forbidden. There was strict rules for the care of pregnant women and even pregnant animals. Special care of children was required during the first seven years. In this context, it is hard to imagine that a scheme to collaborate in the killing of a soon-to-be-orphaned child would be considered, much less approved.

In the seventh century A.D., with Muhammad's conquest of the Near East, the great Islamic systhesis followed. By the ninth and tenth centuries, Arab scholarship in medicine was at its zenith. Influenced by Greek and Indian as well as Judeo-Christian thought, the medical literature reflects clear influence of Galen and the Hippocratic corpus.[21]

In the ninth century, Ishāq ibn Alī al-Ruhāwī wrote *Adab al-tabib* [*Practical ethics of the physician*], the only work known to have considered the aspects of ethics on a broad scale in Arabic medicine.[22] It exudes Greek neo-Platonic and Hippocratic influence. In fact, al-Ruhāwī was apparently a Christian, although he incorporated much of the Muslim belief system into his thought.[23] The Hippocratic influence continued through the period of high Islamic culture. In the thirteenth century, an Arabic version of the Hippocratic Oath is found in *Lives of Physicians*, written by Ibn abi Usaybia.[24] The opening references to the deities are changed, making them consistent with Islamic monotheism, but the core Hippocratic ethic remains, in these words: "In all my treatment I will strive so far as lies in my power for the benefit of the patients." This mixture of Greek, Christian, and Islamic influence produces an ethical framework that only vaguely resembles the medical ethical system of contemporary Islam. Modern Islamic ethics replaces the concern that the physician use his powers to benefit the patient with a much more theocentric affirmation of Allah and the moral law as recorded in the Qur'an and the *hadith*, the tradition based on Muhammad's words and deeds.

The core of the Islamic medical ethics can be said to be derived from 'the word', the crucial summary of the Muslim's faith: "There is no god but Allah, and Muhammad is Allah's apostle."[25] From this affirmation of a radical monotheism comes a sense of the transcendence and omnipotence of the deity. In matters of health and medicine, as in all other spheres, "Allah's will be done." There is a reverence for Allah as the all-powerful one. All human effort, including the physician's, will fail if restoration of health is contrary to Allah's preordained decree.[26]

This theocentrism has often been expressed, especially in more popular renditions of Islam, as a kind of fatalism. It can be perceived in the serious objections that have arisen over anatomical dissection and organ transplantation (in part because of their potential impact on life after death). Artificial prolongation of the life of a dying person might offend Islamic sensibilities in the same way that hastening a death would do so.[27] Birth control has created serious moral problems, at least in more popular or folk expressions of Muslim thought, not because of explicit theological objections as in, say, Catholicism, but because fertility has often been viewed by Muslims as something in the hands of Allah that ought not be tampered with.[28]

Even more strongly, this antiinterventionistic attitude has expressed itself in a prohibition against killing. "Whoever killeth a human being for other than manslaughter or corruption in the earth," the Qur'an says, "it shall be as if he had killed all mankind, and whoso saveth the life of one, it shall be as if he had saved the life of all mankind."[29] In the context, it is not surprising that infanticide in all forms is forbidden in Islamic thought. Presumably, the dispensing of information to help someone commit infanticide would also be forbidden.

If there is any doubt, however, the Muslim does not rely, as the Hippocratic tradition does, on the physician's assessment of what would be in the patient's interest. Nothing could be further from the reality.

In the matters of dispute, a *fatwa*, a religious ruling on the meaning of Islamic law, will be rendered by religious authorities. As in Protestantism, the primary basis for the ruling will be interpretation of a holy text, in this case, the Qur'an. As in Catholicism, that interpretation of the text will be aided by the tradition, the *hadith*. And as in both branches of Christian thought, Islam has its mysticism, especially in Sufism, a movement dating from the eleventh century. If disputes arise about the ethics of decisions within the medical sphere, whether they be actions taken by lay person or professional, the religious structure within Islam will be the final authority.

HINDU MEDICAL ETHICS

While the Christian has the Bible and the Muslim the Qur'an as a foundation of a medical ethic, the physician and patient in India approach the subject from a very different history. They too have a text, or more accurately, texts, but the form and content of the writings are very different. The most important medical sources in India are in three collections: the *Caraka Samhita*, the *Susruta Samhita*, and the *Vagbhata*.[30] These collections comprise, in part, a complex medical system known as the *Ayurveda*, which began developing as early as the first millennium B.C. The *Caraka* and the *Susruta* each contain oaths of initiation taken by students of medicine as they begin their training.[31]

The oath of the *Caraka Samhita*, the oldest of the three, dates from about the first century A.D. but contains material that is certainly much older. It has certain structural similarities with the Hippocratic Oath, but it requires the student at his initiation to make an even more grandiose and subservient commitment to his teacher than the Hippocratic Oath does. The teacher of the *Caraka* demands that the poor student agree to the following: "There is nothing that thou should not do at my behest except hating the king, causing another's death, or committing an act of great unrighteousness or acts leading to calamity." The teacher's instructions continue: "Thou shalt dedicate thyself to me and regard me as thy chief. Thou shalt be subject to me and conduct thyself forever for my welfare and pleasure. Thou shalt serve and dwell with me like a son or a slave or a supplicant." The teacher then has the nerve to demand of the student that he act "without arrogance." Suffice it to say that, like the Hippocratic Oath, the *Caraka* hints at an analog of a father-son adoptive bond in the relationship between student and teacher.

Also like the Hippocratic Oath, this Hindu oath of initiation follows with standards of moral conduct. Some of the content resembles the Greek oath. For example, the instruction, "Thou shalt endeavor for the relief of patients with all thy heart and soul; thou shalt not desert or injure thy patient for the sake of thy life or thy living" resembles the Hippocratic core commitment: "I will apply measures for the benefit of the sick. . . ; I will keep them from harm and injustice." There are prohibitions against adultery with patients, a proscription against treating females "unattended by their husbands or guardians," and a vague commitment to confidentiality—all reminiscent of the Hippocratic Oath.

But there are also remarkable differences in the two oaths. The first moral instruction in the *Caraka* is to "pray for the welfare of all creatures beginning with the cows and Brahmanas." There is an intriguing list of people who should not be treated, including those "who are hated by the king or who are haters of the king," those who are "extremely abnormal, wicked, and of miserable character and conduct," and, most provocatively, "those who are on the point of death." The last group brings to mind the Judaic insight that proscribes the wood-chopper from disturbing the moribund patient who cannot die because of the noise. But it is certainly not Hippocratic.

Some commentators are disturbed by this unusual view of the physician's duty to the dying. M. B. Etziony, a compiler of physician's oaths, is troubled by it, claiming it is "not in accord with the ethical conduct of the physician."[32] He says, "We now know better." He is comforted by the fact that the oath in the *Susruta Samhita*, presumably a later document, contains no such exclusion of the moribund. It does, however, contain other exclusions: for hunters and fowlers and people "who have lost their caste through immoral conduct."[33] This last exclusion reveals the caste-based discrimination in the history of Indian thought. It shows the direct implications for medicine of a theory of karma, the law whereby every action produces an appropriate result or "fruit" according to its moral quality.[34] Its requirement to exclude evil-doers and those who have lost their caste through immoral conduct derives from a strongly held theory that one reaps what one has sown. The physician is not to treat these people "lest you be defiled by contact with them and fail in treating them, for their sufferings are the natural consequences of their failure to obey the moral code."[35] The *Susruta*'s view of class-based distribution of a physician's services, with class in turn linked to moral conduct in a previous life, will be important when we turn to questions of justice in the distribution of health care in chapter 11. It contrasts dramatically with the Chinese interpretation of the duty of the physician, which we shall examine shortly.

In the *Caraka*, the paternalistic commitment of the physician to withhold potentially disturbing information from a dying patient is canonized. "Even knowing that the patient's span of life has come to its close, it shall not be mentioned by thee there, where if so done, it would cause shock to the patient or to others." Although this compassionate paternalism has crept into modern physician ethics, it is at best only implied in the Hippocratic Oath itself under the general commitment to protect the patient from harm.

The modern Indian physician is, of course, no more a blind follower of the *Caraka* than the modern physician is of the Hippocratic Oath. Many layers of thought have influenced Indian culture since the classic texts became dominant. Buddhist impact in the middle of the first millennium A.D. was followed by Greco-Arab influence beginning around the thirteenth century.[36] The result of the latter was the development of *Yūnānī* medicine, based on ancient Greek philosophy and Hippocratic principles adapted to the Asian environment. The code of conduct for the *Yūnānī* physician was similar to the Hippocratic Oath. It seems to have been little influenced by earlier Indian customs, beliefs, and traditions.

Modern medical ethics in India combines these influences from Western thought with more traditional Indian themes. Several are important for comparing approaches to medical ethics and for compiling a catalog from which the elements of a systematic theory might be built. One of the most prominent features of Hindu thought is the doctrine of karma. Karma controls the round of rebirths determined by the actions individuals take in each successive incarnation. The medical implications are provocative. If one's present condition is the inevitable result of behavior in a previous life, the moral claim of the one needing medical services is quite different from what it would be in the modern Western scientific medical model, in which one is in no way responsible for his medical fate. Under this view, it becomes understandable that the *Caraka* excluded from care the "extremely abnormal" as well as the wicked.

A second theme important in the Indian tradition is the proscription against killing.[37] While treatment at the point of death is perhaps wrong, there is a deep-seated respect for life—hence, a traditional prohibition against killing. Arjuna, in the Bhagavad Gita, recognizes that the killing of one's own kinsmen, even for a righteous cause, is morally untenable.[38] With such a forceful prohibition on killing, the conclusion about the ethics of killing one's child or collaborating in the killing would seem clear.

A third theme of Indian thought may turn out to be the most important for our study. The principle of ahimsa occupies a central place in Hindu thought and, in fact, derives from it. It incorporates the notion of noninjury or nonviolence and extends to the concept of nonhatred.[39] It is applied especially to the noninjury of other creatures. While some have seen it linked to Hindu notions of transmigration and thus to the risk of eating one's own kind, others argue that it reflects a more primitive respect or awe for life in all its forms.[40] Prohibition of the eating of flesh can be traced in part to the fact that life is destroyed through injury to animals.

In later Hindu thought, ahimsa became the first rule of life for those who renounced the world.[41] While at first the doctrine was not central to Indian thought, it became prominent with the influence of Buddhism, and has dominated the moral framework of many modern figures, from Gandhi to Westerners who have turned eastward in search of an antiinterventionist ethic. Marc Lappé, a California health department official who is an expert on genetics (as well as a student of Eastern thought), argues that in the field of genetic counseling we may have to admit that all we can ever do is minimize the bad. Explicitly rejecting Christian ethical formulations, he turns to "acceptance of Ahimsa," which, he says, "leads to a continuous obligation to minimize the potential suffering that one can perceive in human actions."[42]

It is in the context of this radical separation of the commitment to do good from the commitment to avoid harm that we can begin to understand the controversial nature of the contemporary Western folk ethics summary of the Hippocratic tradition—*primum non nocere* [first of all do no harm]. While many spouters of the slogan have nothing so nuanced in mind, some Western physicians interpret this much as the Indian tradition does, committing the physician to place a higher priority on avoiding suffering than on doing good. The Indian model makes clear that nonviolence or noninjury requires nonintervention even when potential benefit may come from intervening. From this perspective, it is clear that mercy killing, even if it were to relieve great suffering, would not be tolerated. One must simply not partake in the violence of the killing, regardless of the consequences.

CHINESE MEDICAL ETHICS

Chinese medical ethics is at least as complex as that based in Indian thought. It reflects a convergence of three major Eastern traditions: Confucianism, Taoism, and Buddhism.[43] We have the good fortune of the recent publication in English of historical anthropologist Paul U. Unschuld's important and fascinating study, *Medical Ethics in Imperial China*,[44] which contains the full translation of the crucial Chinese medical ethical texts. They reveal a rich, complicated history with ample evidence of a tradition of intense interest in some of the central issues of medical ethics. It will be impossible to trace that history here or even to identify the patterns of argument among the key figures in the historical debate. However, several important themes can be cataloged.

As Unschuld traces the history of Chinese medical ethics, its dominant theme is the struggle over the professionalization of medicine and over control of medical resources.[45] The explicit aim of Chinese medical

ethics, he contends, is to affirm the responsibility of medical practitioners in order to legitimate their control over the skills and knowledge of
medicine and over the material and nonmaterial rewards of practice. If
he is right, the history of Chinese medical ethics evolves into the history of the relationship between professionals and lay people in specifying appropriate behavior for medical professionals. This makes this
history excitingly relevant to the most contemporary American contro-
versies in medical ethics.

Unschuld identifies one school of Chinese thought as orthodox Confucian. Lu Chih (754–805) was a Confucian scholar, civil servant, and
advisor to the emperor. For him, medicine derived its ethical content
directly from the primary virtues of Confucianism—humaneness and
compassion. If Unschuld's interpretation is correct, Lu Chih held the
view that "medicine should be a matter of course for everyone who is
endowed with 'an attitude of humaneness' . . . . The logical conse-
quence of this thought is that the 'primary' resources of medicine [that
is, the knowledge, skill, drugs, equipment, and technology] have to be
distributed evenly among the population."[46] This could be identified as
a major characteristic of classical Chinese medical ethics.

This indeed is the position of orthodox Confucianism. Medical
knowledge was to be the responsibility of every family, with every
educated man possessing sufficient medical knowledge to be able to
care for his relatives.[47] Ho Ch'i-pin, writing in 1895 but reflecting this
ancient Confucian vision, exclaimed, "Whoever intends to protect his
body and wants to serve his relatives has to have medical knowledge!"[48] Medicine was not to be practiced as an occupation, but as an
act of humaneness and familial responsibility or piety. Medicine was at
its most noble height when practiced without fee.[49]

On the other hand, the increasing complexities of medical knowledge and the self-interest of practitioners necessitated an increasing
professionalization and a need to produce a rationale for restricting
access to medical practice. Freestanding practitioners, including Buddhists and Taoists, thus began a revision of the orthodox Confucian
understanding of medicine leading to a different ethic.[50] Unschuld
identifies the seventh-century figure Sun Szu-miao as the first Chinese
author to articulate this perspective. Often identified as a Taoist, but
influenced by Buddhist thought, he included in his work, *Ch'ien-chin
fang*, a long section on "the absolute sincerity of the Great Physicians."[51] Thus is introduced the notion of the "Great Physician," whom
Sun contrasted with ordinary physicians. The Great Physicians are
given the special status of an inner core, an elite with special knowl-

edge and responsibility. The transfer of this special responsibility to the elite, Unschuld says, is legitimated by an ethical mandate in order to gain a much higher potential of trust and to obtain rewards not accessible to persons merely interested in individual profit.[52] Along with this transfer came some of the ethical trappings we have seen in Western Hippocratic ethics: the duty to keep professional secrets,[53] the conviction that it is unethical to criticize one's professional colleagues,[54] and even the prohibition on soliciting patients.[55]

A second theme clearly evident in Chinese sources is an emphasis on the ethics of virtue. Defined as traits of good character or attitudinal considerations, virtues dominate the concern of the Chinese physician just as they dominate more general Chinese ethical concern. The traditional Confucian virtues are cited over and over again: humaneness (jen), compassion (tz'u), and filial piety (hsiao).[56] The emphasis is on virtue over and above producing the right actions or good consequences, and it is similar in structure if not in content to some strands of professional physician ethics in the Hippocratic tradition. It recalls Percival's insistence that the physician act as a gentleman displaying "tenderness with steadiness" and "condescension with authority,"[57] though the Confucian list of virtues is perhaps more attractive. Many today would prefer humaneness and compassion to condescension in their physicians. In both cases, however, good character seems in some ways as important as right actions.

Filial piety is appropriate where medicine is practiced in a family context. In this sense, the Confucian-derived medical virtues are more general than the Hippocratic ones; they come from a general theory of moral conduct applicable to all. This is a third characteristic of Chinese medical ethics. In the Chinese system, the gap between general ethical theories—religious or secular—and those of health professionals is not nearly so great as in Western medical ethics, where the Hippocratic tradition seems so distant from religious ethics and political philosophy.

One of the themes from the general ethics of Chinese culture that penetrates deeply into its articulated medical ethics is the concern for equal treatment. While the Hindu physician absorbs the caste-based patterns of his culture, the Chinese physician over and over again has emphasized opposition to discrimination in rendering medical care. The physician should "pledge himself to relieve suffering among all classes. Aristocrat or commoner, poor or rich, aged or young, beautiful or ugly, enemy or friend, native or foreigner, and educated and uneducated, all are to be treated equally."[58] Chu Hui-ming, at the end of the sixteenth century, reported that, "In antiquity it was said: 'There are no two kinds of drugs for the lofty and the common; the poor and the rich receive the same medicine.' "[59] Kung T'ing-hsien, in 1615, attacked those who have reduced medicine to a profession, arguing, "When they visit the rich, they are conscientious; when they deal with the poor, they act carelessly. This is the eternal peculiarity of those who practice medicine as a profession, and not as applied humaneness! . . . How could I be generous on one occasion and petty on the other, just because some are rich and the others are poor? . . . We should not divide the poor and the rich; likewise they are all living people!"[60]

Hsü Yen-tso (1895) bemoaned the fact that "I have come to know those [physicians] who consider rich and high-ranking people important and tremble with fear [when they confront them]. . . . Then I have met those [physicians] who despise the poor and lowly and conduct themselves pompously in addition. . . . Both types of conduct are not only wanting in every respect; the question comes to mind, what sort of conscience can such people have? In the Buddhist classics we read: 'The whole world is equal.' "[61]

This is not to say, of course, that prerepublican China always practiced nondiscrimination and treated people as equals. The current government in China has been most critical of the aristocratic tendencies of the Confucian past.[62] But there is an interesting and important ideal in that past. It is perhaps like the American rhetoric of liberty and equality for all, which occasionally rears its head (as in the 1860s and 1960s), and becomes temporarily a serious guide for action. The Hippocratic tradition, by contrast, does not have in its history even a token of a principle of justice or equality that could prick the conscience of the physician in history's more introspective moments. The Hippocratic commitment is simply to the individual patient; no problems of distribution need be addressed.

If the Chinese see the virtue of humaneness as working itself out into a principle of equal treatment ("applied humaneness," according to Ch'en Shih-kung), they also see it as requiring honesty with patients. Chu Hui-ming was particularly critical of withholding information and of professional secrecy. In antiquity he said, at the turn of the seventeenth century, physicians were rewarded for accurately disclosing the hopelessness of a fatal condition. By contrast, "Today however physicians are afraid to tell an unpleasant fact to a patient. . . . Truth seems to be ready on their tongue, but, in view of the circumstances, in the end they do not dare utter it. Then suddenly their struggle will be lost, and they will have to accept rebukes."[63]

The tensions of Chinese culture are at times reflected in disagreements about ethical stances in medicine. It is seen not only in disputes over professionalization, but also in attitudes toward the treatment of the dying and the prolongation of life. There was a constant tension between the love of life that led to efforts to preserve it and the wisdom that recognized that inevitable death should not be combated. Certain versions of Taoism tended toward commitment to pursue aggressively the prolongation of life.[64] On the other hand, Confucian influences advised acceptance of the implications of human finitude. The result was a commitment to the preservation of life, particularly strong in Taoism[65] but also present in other strands of thought,[66] as well as a general sense that the life struggle should not be prolonged in a hopeless case.[67] Huai Yüan, an advocate of Confucian medical values, observed in 1808 that there were only two reasons to continue treatment in hopeless cases: emotional ties with relatives and "the hope of great profit."[68]

What does come through in the tradition is a prohibition on killing. Sun Szu-miao's five exhortations began, "First: not to kill."[69] This is expanded later in the text to "not to kill, nor injure anyone," perhaps reminiscent of the notion of ahimsa and the Hippocratic *primum non nocere*. This implies that this tradition would not look with favor on the decision to kill. Confucian thought in prerepublican China contains some record of tolerating abortion and the killing of congenitally malformed infants.[70] Intentional abortion and infanticide were not a traditional concern in Chinese law.[71] But the dominant trend seems to have been toward condemnation of both abortion and infanticide. They were strongly opposed as early as the second century in the Taoist text *T'ai-p'ing ching*;[72] and as late as 1909 in the penal code (Da Qing xianxing xinglü), which said life could no longer be at the mercy of the parent or of any other agent.[73]

JAPANESE MEDICAL ETHICS

We have come far in our search for an account of the ethical foundations for the choice to be made by Ms. R. and Dr. T. In the process, we have seen that a wide range of views exists on what is ethical in the medical sphere. Each of these views constitutes at least an incipient theory of medical ethics. Some, such as Catholic moral theology, count as richly developed and articulated theories. Others, such as the Indian and Protestant positions, are little more than speculative applications of a general world view to medical problems. Still others, such as the Hippocratic and Chinese perspectives, are somewhere in between. They are more specific and more developed than general philosophical world views; yet they are not full-blown medical ethical theories either.

Thus far, we have found relatively few theories or world views that would tolerate a decision made by our physician and his patient to collaborate in the killing of the soon-to-be-orphaned infant. An utterly libertarian, modern, secular westerner might justify such a decision by combining the principle of liberty with a theory of personhood that grants no independent moral standing to an infant. Ancient Chinese thinking might be open to the woman's decision and possibly even to the physician's collaboration. Other than these, only modern Hippocratic physician ethics seems to provide a conceivable rationale for a physician to decide to provide the needed information on how to end the baby's life. If his task is to do what he thinks will benefit his patient and he thinks that the death, on balance, would be beneficial, it follows that he may—he must—provide the information.

Before turning to the intriguing problem of how Ms. R. and Dr. T. might choose among these alternatives for resolving their problems, we must acknowledge that there are many other traditions we might have explored: African, American Indian, ancient European, and Eastern Orthodox Christianity, among others. There are also modern religious sectarian movements, such as Christian Science, Seventh-Day Adventists, and Jehovah's Witnesses, all of which offer coherent accounts of what is morally required in the medical sphere, and some of which (for example, African) have been open to various kinds of infanticide.[74] Space simply does not permit full accounts of each of these. There is good reason to believe, however, that most of the essential elements for the construction of a systematic theory of medical ethics are before us. Before discussing the thinking that led Ms. R. and Dr. T. to their moral conclusion, though, one final cultural group must be examined. The fact is that our case took place in Japan—something I have not previously disclosed—and we can hardly understand the participants' moral positions without examining the Japanese traditions in medical ethics.

Japanese views on medicine are a complex synthesis of Buddhist and Confucian influences from China and Korea with an indigenous world view.[75] This traditional Japanese religious viewpoint is known as *kami no michi* (the way of Kami), or Shinto, according to the Chinese.[76] It was based on a belief in numerous spirits (*kami*), who possessed men and caused sickness.[77] At this point, there was no rational system of law and ethics. Tribal rules, customs, and taboos governed personal problems, including the medical.

In the fifth and sixth centuries A.D., with the penetration into its culture of Chinese civilization, Japan's rulers adopted what has been called a "multivalue system,"[78] synthesizing Shinto with Confucian and Buddhist beliefs. As in medieval Europe, there was no distinct ethic or code of ethics for practitioners of the healing art. The basic ethic was derived from the culture.[79] Chinese influences, however, especially in the *Taihō*, or Code of Laws dating from 701 A.D., called for a comprehensive educational program in medicine that admitted only the sons of nobility and high-ranking court officials. Japanese medicine, instead of being the province of the shamans, magicians, and traditional healers who followed the way of *kami*, was to become a profession restricted to privileged classes. A special curriculum was developed for students in medical literature, including the *Ko-Kyo* (the book of filial piety) and the *Rongo* (a collection of Confucian writings).[80]

Chinese influence remained great in Japanese medicine. By the sixteenth century, an approach to disease commonly known as the *Ri-shū* was introduced and disseminated throughout Japan.[81] The medical practitioners drew up a code or set of rules for their students that has remarkable parallels with that of the Hippocratic group of physicians in ancient Greece.

The code, known as the Seventeen Rules of Enjuin, begins with the injunction that all disciples of the school must follow the path of the Buddha. It then requires that the practitioner should always be kind to people and devoted to loving people. This is vaguely reminiscent of the Hippocratic ethic, which is even more clearly parallelled in other Japanese texts. An important one, *Yojokun* [*How to Live Well*, by Kaibara Ekiken (1630–1714)], includes the statement, "Medicine is the practice of humanitarianism. Its purpose should be to help others with benevolence and love. One must not think of one's own interests but should save and help the people who were created by Heaven and Earth."[82] This same emphasis on benefit to patients was expressed by Shingu Ryotei (1787–1854), who is said to have taught his pupils that benevolence is the essence of the medical profession.[83] The hyperindividualism of the Hippocratic tradition is not dominant, however. As with the

Chinese, service was to the people, not just to the isolated patient. No long list of right and wrong behavior was superimposed on this general notion of benefit, however, and certainly, no notion of rights of patients over and above benefits to the patients is expressed. While the Japanese traditional medical ethical texts are not so explicitly paternalistic as the Hippocratic tradition, the sentiment of "doctor knows best" seems to pervade the literature. Shingu Ryotei views the physician as the general of the army facing the enemy in "medical combat," a notion strikingly similar to the paternalistic Hippocratic idea of the physician as the captain of the team.

After the Seventeen Rules of Enjuin express these basic commitments to serving the patient, some very Hippocratic requirements follow that could be viewed as an effort to protect the purity of the physician's knowledge (or, less kindly, as a conspiracy in restraint of trade to protect the practitioner's monopoly in the practice of the art). Students of the school are not to tell others what they are taught without permission. As a later rule states, "Proper or not, you should not tell others what you have learned in lectures, or what you have learned about prescribing medicine."[84] Other rules dictate: The teaching of medicine should be restricted to selected persons; if any disciples cease to practice and successors are not found at the death of the disciple, all the medical books of the school should be returned to the medical school; and no member is to speak ill of other physicians. The Federal Trade Commission would have a case against the School of Enjuin that would make the AMA's current behavior look like the epitome of free enterprise. It has not been until recently, under modern, secular influences, that a much more public model with an important role for lay people began to be recovered. In the late 1960s, for example, under a court mandate, the concept of a contract between the patient and the physician was developed. The patient asks for a medical explanation of his ill health and proposes a course of action (presumably in conjunction with the advice of the physician). The physician who concurs with the contract begins the medical treatment.[85] The model, an attractive alternative to the Hippocratic and Enjuin approaches, will serve as a basis for developing a contract theory of medical ethics when we turn to the more systematic building of a theory in chapter 5.

Before examining the specific moral foundations of the contract made between Dr. T. and Ms. R., it is important to have a brief understanding of the historical roots of the more general public morality, especially the morality of Buddhism, which remains an important influence in Japanese thought.

Our patient and her physician seemed to have focused on the potential suffering to the infant after the death of the mother. Suffering and its prevention are central to Buddhist ethics. The first of the four noble truths of Buddhism is that life is *dukkha,* or suffering. The ethical precepts of Buddism are oriented to the relief of suffering, a therapy for which is prescribed in the other three truths: The cause of suffering is *tanha* or desire; its cure lies in the overcoming of desire; the way to overcome it is through the eightfold path.[86] The eightfold path includes as one of its points the principle of right behavior, which in turn includes five (sometimes more) precepts providing rules for the morally good life: Do not kill, do not steal, do not lie, do not be unchaste, and do not drink intoxicants.

These basic moral precepts are at times in conflict with Western professional physician ethics. Hippocratic medicine contains no direct prohibition against killing except insofar as benefiting the patient would preclude it. (In the case before us, it is precisely whether killing would be of benefit that is the issue.) The Hippocratic tradition is also silent on lying. In fact, the telling of falsehoods seems sometimes to be required when it would benefit the patient. The Hippocratic literature *is* sympathetic to the concern about chastity; it warns against taking liberties with one's female patients. The Western code is silent on stealing (presumably because it is not central to the physician's primary moral problems). And it says nothing also about drinking intoxicants. (Modern professional physicians' meetings seem not very Buddhist in this respect.)

The moral precepts are not only in tension with Western professional physician ethics but at places also clash with Japan's own professionally articulated rules. For example, the School of Enjuin's strictures on open disclosure apparently have their counterpart today in contemporary medical practice in Japan. Rikuo Ninomiya, director of the Ninomiya-Naika Clinic in Tokyo and a commentator on contemporary Japanese professional physician ethics, claims that as a rule terminal illness, such as cancer, is not reported to the patient.[87] It is a pattern that at least until recently dominated Western Hippocratic physician ethics, but it seems in sharp contrast to the precepts of the eightfold path.

We are left with a complicated problem. Dr. T. and Ms. R. seem to share the concern over suffering that is common to so much of Eastern thought. Yet if they were to follow the eightfold path that Buddhism prescribes as the answer to suffering, they soon encounter the precept that killing is apparently prohibited. Of course, our physician and his patient may no more be good Buddhists than Western physicians are necessarily good followers of Hippocrates or Western liberalism or one of the religiously based medical ethics. But it is interesting to account for their conclusion that killing of the child was the morally appropriate course, given the ethical principles of Eastern thought.

The Buddhist precept against killing extends to all living beings, from insects to man. It affirms man's close relationship with all living things,[88] and it has been expressed in Japanese medical ethics as a passion for preserving life. Hirata Atsutane (1776–1843), a medical scholar of the Tokugawa period, made the point in a medical philosophy similar to that of Sun Szu-miao of China. Both placed great emphasis on the passion with which the physician should struggle to preserve life.[89]

Much of the Buddhist-inspired literature, however, assumes that preserving life is synonymous with preventing suffering and benefiting the patient. As with the Hippocratic tradition, it is vague regarding the rare case such as ours, in which killing the patient seems the best way to prevent suffering. Hippocratic medicine never rules out killing in such cases; it simply shouts over and over again that the physician's only duty is to do what he thinks will be beneficial. In these rare cases that might logically entail killing.

The arguments for the prohibition against killing in Buddhist thought seem to be open to the same maneuver. According to ancient texts, the Buddha taught the prohibition against killing by advising that one compare one's own life with that of other beings. "Everyone fears violence, everyone likes life," he says. "Comparing oneself with others one would never slay or cause to slay."[90] It seems, however, that not everyone necessarily agrees with the Buddha, especially in cases where killing seems to be the only alternative to intractable suffering. Both physicians and lay people who have killed for mercy, including apparently Dr. T. and Ms. R., must have given higher priority to the prevention of suffering than to a prohibition against killing. There are documented reports from Japan of compassion winning out in this tension and justifying euthanasia.[91]

Even a superficial knowledge of Japanese culture makes clear that suicides are at least tolerated, and even considered morally commendable, in certain difficult situations.[92] Others in the culture neither admire nor condemn it but consider it meaningless (since karma accompanies a person even after death).[93]

The killing of the infant would, of course, be homicide, not suicide. But even collaboration in homicide has been tolerated under certain special conditions in Japanese society. Two perspectives deserve attention. First, Dr. T. might have judged that he was not actually partner to the homicide, but was only assisting by providing knowledge. H. Saddhatissa, a Buddhist monk and a scholar of Buddhist ethics, outlines six means of killing. They include killing by one's own hand and causing another to kill by giving an order, but do not seem to extend to the mere providing of information.[94] All this is the kind of reasoning, however, that has given casuistry in Western ethics a bad name. There is no evidence that the Japanese physician sought to exculpate himself from the mother's homicide plan by arguing that he was merely providing information. In fact, in terms reminiscent of the Hippocratic Oath, Rules of Enjuin explicitly prohibit teaching about poisons, receiving instruction about poisons, or giving abortives.[95] If there is an account to justify the decision made by the Japanese physician and the mother, it must come from something deeper in Japanese culture.

The decision in our case should not be viewed as an ordinary example of suicide or homicide. In Japan, there is a long history of love suicide (jyoshi) and group suicide (shinjyū), especially within families. Such acts are supposed to be a means of showing "the real state of the heart."[96] "When a man and woman in love could not live together and were troubled in affection and duty, or were in economic difficulty, they committed jyōshi."[97] These same terms are used to refer to parental love killing of family members, often by the male head of the household, followed by suicide. If the man is absent, the mother will kill first her children and then herself.[98] The general reason given is that the family has reached a state that it cannot endure. It is striking that, for the most part, the Japanese literature on shinjyū does not distinguish between the love murder-suicide of adults and the killing of a child by the parent followed by the parent's own suicide. Some of the literature speaks specifically of "parent-child suicide."[99]

The practice of love murder-suicide was found before the Edo era (the Tokugawa period, 1600–1868). It was prohibited by Yoshimune, the eighth shogun (1716–1745), who condemned infanticide and suicide.[100] Since the overthrow of the shogunate, however, the practice has not died out and in fact has increased. It is still found today.[101]

For a westerner it may be impossible to grasp the basic cultural and psychological dynamic of such homicide–suicide love killings. Several authors identify its source in religious roots, such as the belief in an afterlife and reunion in that next life.[102] Some have observed that many cultures give a parent the right to destroy a newborn infant.[103] Even in

72

the context of the Buddhist prohibition on killing there is apparently some tendency to provide a religious basis for the relative tolerance of killing an infant. Saddhatissa says, "The Karmic results of killing a man and killing a child vary in proportion to the physical and mental development of the two."[104] Thus, to the extent that the ethics of the killing is related to the karma of the deed, there is culpability "to a lesser degree."

This may provide some very tentative cultural context for the mother's plan. The literature on the social psychology of the Japanese adds further insight. It suggests that love suicides must be understood in terms of the Japanese attitude toward primary relationships.[105] The primary, single, one-to-one bond has been identified as the most distinctive social psychological feature of Japanese social structure.[106] The parent-child bond, especially between mother and child, is so crucial that it is viewed as archetypical of the basic scheme of Japanese social organization.[107] The family bond is also extraordinarily enduring. Once it has been established, it is expected to be maintained. This intense mother-child bond, according to psychiatrist Takeo Doi, is the origin of a psychological phenomenon, called *amae*, which is the dominant characteristic of the Japanese personality.[108]

Amae is not easily translated, but conveys a dependency and willingness to presume upon another's benevolence. It describes a child's attitude or behavior towards its parents, especially its mother. It is a desire to be loved, an "unwillingness to be separated from the warm mother-child circle and cast into a world of objective 'reality.' "[109] According to Doi, the Japanese never give up their basic emotional desire to show *amae* and dependence.

Doi relates the increase in the number of children who are killed by their parents in Japan to the emotion of *amae*. The exact link is not obvious, but two theories seem plausible and can be applied to our own case study. According to one view, Ms. R., herself having experienced *amae* and continuing to experience it, could empathize with her daughter who is about to lose the one on whom she is dependent. When that relationship is lost, it will take away the sense of meaning from life.[110] Moreover, the one who has lost this relationship of the intimate familial bond is treated as an outsider by society and even if finally accepted, probably would be placed at the bottom of the hierarchy without being given the full rights of group membership.[111] If this is the future of the orphan, then perhaps the mother, with the sympathy of a physician who shares this social psychology, is led to the conclusion that her child would be better off dead than as a suffering orphan, especially one with a medical abnormality.

The second view of *amae*, on the other hand, focuses primarily on the parental affect of *amae* and the potential for collapse of the clear boundary lines of personal identity between the mother and the child. According to Doi, the *amae* relationship "implies a considerable blurring of the distinction between subject and object; as such it is not necessarily governed by what might be considered strict rational or moral standards, and may often seem selfish to the outsider."[112] This accords well with some westerners' observations that this case reveals such a strong desire by the mother to be reunited with her child after her own death that she was willing to take the child's life.

Either of these explanations provides at least a psychological account of Ms. R.'s decision. A kind of moral account also is given in the concern shown for the welfare of an infant abandoned in the world without a mother to play her role in the crucial dependency relationship. What the actual explanation of Dr. R.'s and Ms. T.'s reasoning is we shall probably never know, but the principle of preventing suffering and acting for the welfare of the dependent one provide a normative explanation that is moral in form. Whether the conclusion to kill the child was morally correct, is, of course, another matter.

This case and its prolonged analysis reveal, I hope, that it is impossible to understand the morality of a specific medical ethical problem without knowing something of its cultural setting. Knowing that setting does not by itself explain what ought to be done. No one but a pure social relativist would say that. But it does tell us a great deal about the kind of actions contemplated. I am hopeful that the analysis also shows that it is no longer enough to appeal to some parochial set of ethical rules or code of ethics to decide what is morally right in any medical ethical dilemma. It should now seem absurd to think we can resolve problems of this nature by appealing simplistically to the Hippocratic ethic. It offers little guidance to a Japanese physician who is working out of a psychology and ethic very different from that of the Western physician. Even if the Hippocratic ethic were applied, it could be read to justify the physician's collaboration based on his judgment that death was in the interests of the mother or the infant, compared to the alternatives. He would be doing what he thought was in the interest of the patient according to his ability and judgment. In no case, though, does the Hippocratic ethic tell us what the primary actor in the case, the mother, ought to do. Even if one were to hold that the Hippocratic ethic, rather than the one of this Japanese patient and physician, should provide the decisive answer at least for the physician, there is no way that any of the actors in this case could or should be persuaded to accept its moral framework as binding.

If we are to have a systematic theory of medical ethics, it should in principle be applicable to all and accessible to all. We are left with the problem of whether some foundation for a medical ethic can be salvaged from this hodgepodge of competing views about what is ethical in medicine.

PART II

The Basis of Medical Ethics

Chapter 4

The Problems with Professional Physician Ethics

Case 2   *Physician Advertising and the FTC*

Urologist offers complete medical service for VD, prostatitis, NSU venereal warts and diseases of the kidney and bladder.

You may not need surgery—new medical techniques.

Exclusive, prestigious physician.

Special student discount.

No extra charges.

These advertising blurbs are taken from the pages of a single issue of a weekly newspaper. They signal that physician advertising is well on its way. Professional medical associations are upset. Some are urging that traditional professional sanctions be involved against advertising claims like those above.

On October 13, 1979, the Federal Trade Commission ordered three medical societies—the American Medical Association, the Connecticut State Medical Society, and the New Haven County Medical Association—to "cease and desist from restricting, regulating, impeding, declaring unethical, interfering with, or advising against the advertising . . . of physicians' services."[1]

Thus the FTC, acting in the public interest, has attempted to impose regulations on professional physician organizations that have traditionally regulated their own ethical standards.

The AMA, in response to the FTC order, has argued that its major reason for banning advertising is to avoid consumer deception.[2] To this it adds the desire to maintain every patient's confidence and to avoid adverse effects on the quality of medical services. It further claims to want to avoid the risk "that unlimited advertising will be used to lure people to unqualified or unscrupulous practitioners who cannot attract or retain patients on the basis of their medical skills."[3]

Raymond T. Holden, chairman of the AMA's board of trustees, and Max H. Parrott, its president, claim that "advertising by a profession is the very antithesis of professionalism. Physicians should not solicit patients. A patient should go to a doctor on the basis of need, not on the basis of advertising."[4]

Writing in 1971, Russell B. Roth, then speaker of the AMA's house of delegates, laid a moral basis for the professional limitation on advertising. He called it unethical for physicians "to promote a system of medical service which would not be in the best interests of the public."[5]

We are left with several questions: Is advertising in the interest of the public, as the FTC claims, or contrary to public interest, as Roth claims? Is public interest an appropriate standard for judging the problem or should some other standard be used, such as the traditional Hippocratic norm of patient benefit or the Anglo-American legal standard of the individual's right of freedom of speech? And before answering either of these questions we need to decide whether a government agency or a professional association is the more appropriate authority to pick the principle for deciding the case. What person or group should pick the principle for deciding the case, and what person or group should decide whether advertising conforms to the principle selected?

There was a day when it was fashionable to lump together the issues of advertising, fee splitting, and professional courtesy as matters of mere medical etiquette not worthy of serious discussion in contemporary medical ethics. History has a way of making strange turns, however. The ethics of advertising may turn out to be one of the most crucial problems in the current incarnation of medical ethics. It is over advertising that the fight over basic principles apparently will take place. It is over advertising that the even more crucial metaquestion of who has ethical authority in professional ethical controversy may be resolved. The familiar ethical questions once again become the most critical and timely.

The ethics of advertising is a central issue of traditional American professional ethics. Although the Hippocratic Oath and Percival's Code are silent on advertising, the AMA's 1847 Code of Medical Ethics cites as the third duty "of physicians to each other and to the profession at large" a condemnation of "public advertisements."[6] Solicitation of patients has been viewed as unprofessional conduct since then. In 1971, prior to the current public debate over the legality of professional ethical prohibitions on advertising, the AMA Judicial Council stated boldly that "solicitation of patients, directly or indirectly, by a physician, or by groups of physicians, is unethical."[7] Such prohibitions have also appeared in the Principles of Ethics of the American Dental Association as amended in 1974, the Ethical Standards for Psychologists as amended in 1972, the Code of Ethics of the American Osteopathic Association for 1965, and the American Pharmaceutical Association's Code of Ethics adopted in 1969. Outside the medical field, professional groups with codes dealing with advertising include the American Arbitration Association, the Music Teachers National Association, and the Motion Picture Association of America. In fact, public debate about strictures on advertising arose over the codes of the American and International Bar Associations before the issue was brought up regarding the medical profession. In the recent Bates case,[8] the U.S. Supreme Court ruled that constitutionally lawyers cannot be prohibited from advertising by the ABA's Code of Professional Responsibility.

If there is such a professional consensus that advertising is a matter for professional regulation within codes of ethics, does that not settle the matter? The answer is important, for what is at stake in the FTC's challenge is something far more basic than the interpretation of a professional code of ethics. What is being questioned is the authority of a professional group to set its own ethical standards and to adjudicate disputes about the conduct of its members.

Once a professional code of ethics has received such a direct challenge, it is obvious that the traditional solution to a problem in professional ethics will not work. Traditionally, if we wanted to know whether advertising or breaking confidences or stopping treatment on a patient was ethical, we would turn to the professional code and look up the answer. The AMA's "Principles of Medical Ethics," for example, includes not only the statement of its principles, but also detailed interpretations of them, creating a kind of case law based on previous cases the group's Judicial Council has resolved to its satisfaction. The newest British physicians' code has similar detail; it is the length of a small book.[9] But when the principles of medical ethics themselves are questioned and the authority of professional associations to adjudicate disputes is rejected, as it has been by the FTC, then we have to find a justification for continuing to use professional associations to resolve any medical ethical dispute.

The fundamental question raised by the FTC challenge is why the general public should be bound in any way by the opinion of a council of a private professional organization, such as the AMA. Members of the public have never joined the AMA. They have never authorized the AMA to establish principles of medical ethics governing relationships between physicians and patients. They have never designated any professional organization to speak on their behalf in matters ethical. What, then, are the characteristics of a professional ethic and what are the alternatives to letting a professional group resolve matters of ethical public policy? How shall society decide matters as fundamental as whether it is in the public interest to advertise or, to take a familiar case, whether it is acceptable to try to kill one's baby humanely out of fear for its seemingly inevitable future of misery as an orphan?

PROFESSIONAL ETHICS AND ROLE-SPECIFIC DUTIES

Any medical ethics includes a set of ethical standards, principles, rules, or codes for physicians or other health care professionals. In many cases these are articulated by professional groups themselves for their members. When groups do this, we have what I referred to in chapter 1 as a professional ethic. Such professional ethics normally have special characteristics. For an ethic to be a professional ethic in the sense I am using the term, the group must make the claim that the professional group generates the norms, principles, or correct professional conduct or at least that it is the only body having knowledge of what is ethically required for members of the profession. A true professional ethic also includes the claim that only the profession itself is capable of adjudicating ethical disputes related to professional conduct and, moreover, that it bears a responsibility for imposing ethical discipline on its members.

The sociology of the professions is a field that has examined characteristics distinguishing professions from mere occupations or businesses.[10] Among the characteristics of a true profession that sociologists identify is the fact that the professional group articulates its own set of ethical standards—usually in the form of a code—and disciplines its own members for violation of those standards. The existence of a code or set of standards is seen as so essential a characteristic that it can be used to resolve disputes over whether those in an occupational group, such as accountants or appraisers or archivists, can be termed real professionals. Of course, members of occupational groups sometimes try to elevate their status by generating a code of ethics, attempting to prove that they belong to true professions. Thus the Comics Magazine Association of America, the National Hearing Aid Society, and the Society for Clinical and Experimental Hypnosis have all produced codes, hoping that the prestige of professional status will follow.[11]

Some groups, such as lawyers and physicians, have successfully made the claim that they merit self-regulation based on internally generated codes of ethics. Other groups with some promise of gaining real professional status, such as pharmacists and physicians' assistants, have written codes also in an attempt to acquire the same kind of legitimation.

A true profession, to fit my requirements, has had both its code of ethics and its authority to adjudicate ethical disputes accepted by the broader society. It is this kind of ethic that I am calling a professional ethic. To avoid confusion, it is important to distinguish a professional ethic in this sense from other articulations of moral duties that attach to specific roles in society, including professional roles.

Many of the major schemes of medical ethics—Catholic moral theology, the secular political philosophy of the West, socialist ethics, for example—include notions of proper moral conduct for physicians and other health professionals. These are not, however, professional ethics because they are not expressions of professional consensus articulated by members of the profession. They also do not require that disputes be adjudicated exclusively by mechanisms set up within the profession.

All of these major schemes of ethics, rooted in more general systems of ethics, do recognize duties for some individuals that are not applicable to others in society. In particular, there are duties for health professionals, some of which may not even apply when the health professional is functioning in other roles.

Advertising is an issue often approached as requiring special norms for those in certain professional roles. It is not something generally regarded as immoral. Plumbers, painters, and piano tuners advertise; why not pediatricians? Yet true professional groups claim that there is something wrong with a pediatrician advertising his professional services, even though they would have no objection to his placing a want ad to sell his car or to proclaim his ability as a concert singer.

Of course, there are those who would argue that all advertising is immoral, that it systematically diverts people from rational decision making by using tactics that are essentially nonrational. That argument is difficult to sustain, and is rejected by all but the most vehement critics of capitalism. Even this group, however, would recognize that the professional physicians' associations are not making any such claim. Rather, they say that advertising is wrong for someone in the role of physician.

How can it be that certain people have duties (and presumably rights) in one role that others do not have and that they do not have when they are not acting in the special role? Philosophers and others working on this problem have talked about role-specific duties, sometimes using the technical term *duties of station.* [12]

Analysts working on the problem begin by observing that some moral duties seem to apply to everyone while others are acquired only by certain people. [13] For example, certain duties related to the keeping of promises apply to everyone, regardless of position in life. But once a promise is made, the one doing the promising normally acquires a new duty in addition to the general one of keeping promises. He has to do what he promised. If I injure someone it is generally held that I have a duty to make amends, to help the injured party. This acquired duty to help in a specific case is quite different in character from the general duty people have to help injured persons.

If special duties come automatically when one assumes a role, then in this technical sense, these duties are acquired. In fact, taking on a role is sometimes appropriately viewed as a kind of promising. The process of assuming a professional role often illustrates this. Many professional groups have rituals of initiation that include oaths of allegiance. The Hippocratic Oath is only the most famous example. It begins with a pledge of loyalty to the cult group.

Acquired duties are more complicated, however, than merely making a promise or assuming a role. An individual cannot necessarily of his own free choice pledge loyalty to a group and thereby assume the responsibilities and privileges of membership. Certainly professional and fraternal associations do not allow this choice. What a person taking on a role may consider to be his duty, these groups may see as not even his right, and if someone is to have a duty to engage in a certain behavior, then he also must have the right to engage in it. If the Japanese physician in our first case study analyzed his problem about providing information to help the dying woman kill her daughter, he might reach the conclusion that the basic values and commitments of his professional group gave him the duty to provide the information. Others outside his group may question whether he even has the right, much less the duty. In order for a pledge of rights and duties to be complete and binding, much more than taking on a new role must occur—assumption of the role and those rights and duties must be legitimated.

Two different kinds of ligitimation are common. One depends on acceptance by other parties involved. The other is independent of such acceptance, but it demands meeting other special conditions.

The first method that sometimes can legitimate the assumption of duties and rights of a role is for all the other parties involved to accept one's assumption of the new role and its responsibilities. It is strange to speak of assuming the duties of membership in, say, the fraternal order of Elks or of Masons or of the Knights of Columbus, unless one has the right to consider oneself a member. In the case of fraternal organizations this means that the promise made and the role assumed must be acknowledged by the group as a prerequisite to membership.

So one way for a duty to be legitimated is to have the right to act as a member affirmed. It follows that one way to gain the right to assume the characteristics of the role is to have other interested parties accept the pledge that one has made. At that point, duty corresponds to the right of the role that has been assumed.

We see, then, that self-selection into a role is not always enough to justify actions related to that role; that rights and duties are fully legitimated only when something else happens. In fraternal orders, where initiation into membership brings with it new duties, this something else may simply be acceptance of the initiate by members of the order according to rules and procedures (some of which may be arcane and totally incomprehensible to outsiders).

The same legitimation process would appear to be true for professional groups. The act of assuming the physician's role might generate new duties, but the role might not be legitimated until members of the professional group accept the new member by whatever ritual and procedure they have established for themselves.

There is a problem, however. In the case of the professional, virtually all decisions made will have direct bearing on people who are not members of the profession—on patients, their families, and others. We have said that the right to act on role-specific duties requires acceptance of the initiate by other relevant parties directly affected. But those affected by a physician's act often extend well beyond the other members of the profession. If the duty were limited to taking care of the medical needs of other members of the professional group, as is required in the Hippocratic Oath, then possibly only members of the profession would be directly involved. But to the extent that non-professionals are directly affected when someone takes on the duties of a professional role, mere acceptance by others within the profession cannot do the job.

Consider the hypothetical dilemma of a pledge to college fraternity Alpha Beta Gamma. The pledge may be told that all pledges, in order to become full members of Alpha Beta Gamma, must steal an object from the dean's office and present it to one of the senior fraternity members. The pledge might even promise to commit the theft, thereby feeling he has a duty to steal based on loyalty to the group and to the promise made. The seniors of the fraternity might accept the promise providing that dimension of legitimation. Clearly, however, not everyone has accepted the promise. The dean might justifiably argue that the pledge has neither a duty nor even the right to steal. A promise does not generate a duty of station, a role-specific duty, for the pledge unless all involved accept the duty as legitimate.

Yet some physicians appear to ground their ethical obligations in a pledge and group loyalty similar to those of our hypothetical pledge. H. Thomas Ballantine, a physician and professor at Harvard University, and a member of an AMA committee to revise the group's "Principles of Medical Ethics," claims that physicians are a privileged group given "high rank" and, under the ancient principle of noblesse oblige, having a special duty to promote the welfare of others.[14] He even claims that society has bestowed this special status on the profession, thus adding the social legitimation of which we speak. The evidence for societal concurrence is not given, however.

In the case at the start of chapter 1, the physician faced the possibility that he might help the infant's mother with the murder. Certainly a promise that he might have to commit or help commit the murder does not give the physician the right to engage in these actions. Suppose, however, that all physicians of his particular professional group affirmed that his acceptance into membership gave him the right and the duty to kill infants facing the fate of the inevitable misery of being an orphan. It seems that would not settle the matter either. At the very least, the dying mother, who is not a member of the professional group, should have some voice of veto. Most people would go further. They would say that even complete acceptance by the physician, his professional group, and the mother, of the principle that he has a right and duty to kill in this particular case is not enough to give him that right or make it morally acceptable.

This means that acceptance or nonacceptance of a person's commitment by those affected by his actions may not necessarily settle matters. Even if everyone affected were to accept the action of the one assuming a role, certain actions may not be morally or legally acceptable. This would be the case where some more basic moral or legal infringements take place, one not subject to modification by the mere approval of those directly involved.

We turn then to a second way in which duties accompanying a role may sometimes be legitimated. This method does not depend on concurrence by all persons directly affected. Consider the special duties and rights of one in the role of policeman. Most of us agree that a person in that role has the authority to engage in actions that others cannot rightfully engage in. Police officers may use weapons, or at least restrain people, in certain circumstances that would be assault and battery or illegal imprisonment if done by others. Furthermore, some of the people most directly affected by a policeman's action do not necessarily concur in what he is doing, or even with the principles behind what he is doing. Are physicians sometimes like the police in the sense that they can act on special role-related notions of right and duty even though patients may not accept the special formulation of those notions? For example, does a psychiatrist have the duty, and the right, to commit someone to a mental hospital even though the person being committed does not concur?

Policemen, judges, teachers, and possibly even physicians apparently do have special role-related duties and rights of this kind. But they can never legitimately defend their special ethical characteristics by appealing to the fact that other members of their professional group agree that they should have such duties and rights. If that were the case, police would probably behave very differently. They might favor greater violence or less due process than the public is willing to accept, for example.

Military generals, too, have special duties and rights by virtue of the fact that they too are in special roles. But they also cannot justify those special rights and duties simply by appealing to the fact that their fellow military officers agree that they should have them. (We know that the ethics of war is too important to be left to the generals.) The moral justification for the generals and others comes by a very different kind of appeal. In principle, it is a mandate from society at large through established political and legal procedures. Society recognizes that generals have special rights and duties, but it does so because the structure of those rights and duties is specified in terms of a frame of reference relevant to the population as a whole. In principle, all ought to be able to understand and affirm the special duties and rights given to generals or policemen.

If physicians have special moral obligations or rights by virtue of their assumed roles, those rights and duties can gain legitimation only if one of the two characteristics we outlined have been obtained. If no basic moral or legal requirements (or both) are violated, the acceptance of the person into the role by all those affected will be sufficient. Exactly who has to accept depends on who is affected by the duties assumed by the individual. The duties can be related strictly to intraprofessional relationships affecting only fellow professionals who have accepted the unique obligations of their role. This would justify peculiar cultic relationships that might exist among group members provided no one outside the group is affected and no more basic societal norms are violated. If, however, the duties generate actions that bear directly on those outside the profession, on patients, for example, then outsiders would have to be involved in approving the assumption of role-specific duties, if approval is to be the method of legitimation.

If, however, duties are to be legitimated without acceptance by all involved, then they will have to be grounded in basic premises or perspectives that are in principle accessible to all. That is how the duties of not only the policeman and general, but also of the parent, are legitimated, all roles in which those directly affected do not actively concur in the assumption of the duties. Parents have special obligations to serve the interests of their children. Others in society, whether they be parents or not, presumably understand and recognize the validity of this special role-related duty.[15]

All medical ethical systems accept the necessity of role-related duties for health professionals. Whether the system be that of Islam or the patient's rights movement, role-related duties are affirmed. Profession-

al physician ethics, however, affirms role-related duties in a very special way, by the member's acceptance of a code or set of standards
generated within or articulated by the professional group itself. '

Codes of professional ethics are not generated by the broader population which is affected by their content. They are not even grounded
in philosophical or ethical thought accessible to the broader population. The Hippocratic Oath itself contains a pledge of secrecy. The physician pledges to transmit the precepts and oral instruction "to my sons
and the sons of him who has instructed me and to pupils who have
signed the covenant and have taken an oath according to the medical
law, but to no one else." Jones points out that likewise the other deontological writings share this characteristic of requiring secrecy. The
"Precepts" and the "Decorum," he maintains, are very much like ad-
dresses to secret societies.[16] The "Law" concludes with the sentences,
"But holy things are shown to holy men. The profane may not be
shown them until they have been initiated into the rites of science." As
part of the research for this volume, I wrote the British Medical Association requesting a copy of its *Ethical Handbook*. I was told that it was not
available to nonmembers of the association.[17]

A code of ethics, even if released for public study, is essentially a
professionally generated document. As such it differs greatly from the
basic ethical sources used by theologians, philosophers, lawyers, and
others who may be working with other systems of medical ethics. William May, in his "Code, Covenant, Contract, or Philanthropy," reveals
how code ethics differs from other approaches to moral problems in
society.[18] The essay, one of the most important in contemporary medical ethics, emphasizes the difference between ethics rooted in codes
and those rooted in promising or covenanting or contracting. May argues that the rules of a code are categorical, or universal, in the sense
that they do not receive their authority from particular events. They
remain valid for all similar occasions. Universal does not mean, however, that the rules are in principle accessible and applicable to all
people. May points out that Hammurabi's code was obligatory only for
particular peoples. Codes of ethics are summaries of behavioral norms
for particular groups, such as members of a profession.

May suggests that a code conveys not only the rules for action but
also the style of action, an ideal of professional virtue. The ideal of the
codes of the medical profession, May argues, is philanthropy. The Hippocratic physician takes upon himself the burden of serving his patient. But it is a gratuitous, rather than a responsive and reciprocal, act.

The ideal "succumbs to what might be called the conceit of philanthropy."[19] He contrasts the ethic of the professional code with that of an ethic based on covenant or contract. *Covenant*, a term with essentially religious and political roots (which I shall discuss in much greater detail in chapter 5), is rooted in historical events, according to May. It is based on an actual or anticipated specific exchange between "partners"; an exchange of gifts, labor, or services. It is reciprocal. The lives of both parties are shaped by the promising.

The Hippocratic ethical tradition, by contrast, has never involved pledges or promises made with or accepted by those outside the professional group. To be sure, the Hippocratic Oath is a pledge sworn "by Apollo Physician and Asclepius and Hygieia and Panaceia and all the gods and goddesses, making them my witnesses." But it is not a pledge made to or with patients. It is to one's colleagues who are members of the cult. It is a pledge to hold one's teacher "as equal to my parents and to live my life in partnership with him." It goes so far as to pledge money to him if he is ever in need; to regard his offspring as "equal to my brothers"; to teach them the craft of medicine without fee or covenant. It is a classical oath of initiation into a cult or mystery religion.

The Oath also contains, however, a list of obligations that the physician owes to his patients including the paternalistic, philanthropic obligation to do what the physician believes will best benefit the patient. In no sense, however, is this a promise made to the patient. It is not negotiated with, or reciprocated by, the patient. The medical ethics of Percival begins with the following famous instruction to the physicians and surgeons (originally of the Manchester Infirmary, but later applied to all those of the Anglo-American world):

> Hospital physicians and surgeons should minister to the sick, with due impressions of the importance of their office, reflecting that the ease, the health, and the lives of those committed to their charge depend on their skill, attention and fidelity. They should study, also, in their deportment, so to unite *tenderness* with *steadiness*, and *condescension* with *authority*, as to inspire the minds of their patients with gratitude, respect and confidence.[20]

It is, of course, the code of the British gentleman, philanthropically and with proper condescension bestowing benefits on patients who ought to show appropriate gratitude. It was not a set of duties negotiated mutually between the physicians and surgeons of Manchester, on the one hand, and the patients and the citizens of the town who used the infirmary, on the other.

90

The same spirit is seen in the AMA Code of 1847, which was rooted in the work of Percival: "A physician should not only be ever ready to obey the calls of the sick, but his mind ought also to be imbued with the greatness of his mission, and of the responsibility he habitually incurs in its discharge."[21] The paragraph ends with the words taken directly from Percival: "They should study, also, in their deportment, so to unite *tenderness* with *firmness*, and *condescension* with *authority*, as to inspire the minds of their patients with gratitude, respect and confidence."

The 1847 Code was adopted as a unilateral action at the AMA's meeting in Philadelphia and was approved the same year by the New York Academy of Medicine. The lay persons of Philadelphia and New York were not consulted. To the extent that the codes constitute pledges or promises at all, they are pledges to the profession, that is, they justify behavior vis-à-vis the profession only. As with the Hippocratic Oath, the Code of 1847 distinguishes between duties of physicians to their patients and duties of physicians to each other and to the profession at large. Additionally, a third section of the code is entitled, "Of the duties of the profession to the public, and of the obligations of the public to the profession." As a unilateral document, however, the moral status of pledges made by physicians to each other and to the profession at large must be different from the status of gratuitous gestures of philanthropy made by the profession to the patient and the public. A pledge made by a member of the profession to the profession cannot be binding on third parties. It cannot justify behavior to patients or to society if the patients and society are not party to the original pledging. The claim of obligations of patients and the public to the physician and the profession is ethically even more precarious. It is strange that an individual or group can articulate a claim of obligation on another and expect it to be binding. It is particularly strange when the party making the claim believes that the other parties cannot have knowledge of the basis of the obligation. Yet this is precisely what articulators of classical professional ethics claim. To be a true professional ethic (rather than merely an articulation of role-specific duties), these characteristics must be present: the ethic must include either the claim that only members of the profession can know what is ethically required of them or that the professional ethic ultimately has a different grounding than ordinary ethics. It also includes the claim that the profession itself has the responsibility for its members' ethical discipline and for adjudication of ethical disputes.

THE CONSENSUS OF PROFESSIONALS AS THE FOUNDATION FOR PROFESSIONAL ETHICS

The most radical professional ethic is the one that depicts professional obligation as nothing more than what the profession says it is. This is ethical positivism run amok in professional conceit. What is ethically required of the professional is literally nothing more than what is agreed to by consensus of the members of the profession. There is no way that those outside the profession can comprehend the rationale for the stands taken. In fact, there may be no rationale. There is, in any case, no more fundamental moral foundation than agreement among the members of the group.

Regarding the AMA's prohibition on physician advertising, Roth, writing in 1971 as speaker of the group's house of delegates (he was later to become its president), proclaimed that the profession "has imposed upon itself certain proscriptions which are often poorly understood by the public, such as the avoidance of any semblance of professional advertising which is all right for almost everyone except physicians."[22]

Roth is making a claim about a role-specific duty. The prohibition applies to almost no one but physicians. That is not a controversial claim. What is controversial is his suggestion that the profession has imposed this prohibition upon itself. No wonder that it is often poorly understood by the public.

His view gives a very peculiar account of what it means for something to be ethical. It implies that what is ethically required of physicians is nothing more than what they as a group, by custom, deliberation, and common agreement, have decided should be required. The judicial council says that it uses the term *ethical* to refer in part to "customs and usages of the medical profession," and the term *unethical* to refer to conduct which fails to conform to these professional standards, customs and usages, or policies, as interpreted by the American Medical Association."[23]

Some professional responsibilities are plausibly viewed as nothing more than mere custom or self-imposed obligations—hence a section in the Code of 1847 entitled "Of the Duties of Physicians to Each Other and to the Profession at Large" begins with the statement that the physician who enters the profession incurs an obligation to "maintain its dignity and honor, to exalt its standing, and to extend the bounds of its usefulness." The profession has instituted laws "for the government of its members." The relationship is analogous to that of an individual who pledges at the time of initiation into a private club or fraternity to observe the group's special rules of conduct, rules not applicable to those outside the group. Likewise the member of a religious group may pledge to engage in certain sacramental, educational, and ritualistic behavior, or the fraternity member may pledge to use a secret hand-shake and not reveal it to nonmembers. Those outside the group can-not be expected to understand the special rules of behavior, much less to follow such practices. The rules are incomprehensible to those out-side because they have their origin with the group and its members.

Codes of professional ethics are similar if they are merely self-im-posed. The medical ethics of Percival is, in part, a code of ethics for the gentleman of England. In the preface to his "little Manual of Medical Ethics," Percival says, "The study of professional ethics, therefore, can-not fail to invigorate and enlarge your understanding; whilst the ob-servance of the duties which they enjoin, will soften your manners, expand your affections, and form you to that propriety and dignity of conduct, which are essential to the character of a GENTLEMAN." (Perci-val's capitalization)[24]

The Hippocratic Oath forbids surgery for gallstones. Some have in-terpreted this prohibition to reflect a division of labor. Such a division, however, would not be grounded in any special sense of obligation. Some have seen it as consistent with the general Pythagorean skepti-cism over the value of surgery. But the Oath says that the Hippocratic physician will "withdraw in favor of such men as are engaged in this work," hardly compatible with the thesis that the value of surgery was rejected completely. Edelstein interprets the prohibition as a kind of special ethical rule applicable only to the Pythagorean cult. "The stipu-lation against operating is valid only for him who has dedicated him-self to a holy life."[25] It is a special ethic analogous to the requirements of chastity for the priest or of the dietary laws for the observant Jew.

In the analogous cases, however, those who recognize a special mor-al obligation for themselves do not transfer the obligation to others outside the group and do not expect outsiders to understand or be affected by the special duties. The priest does not preach the virtue of celibacy for the layman. The rabbi does not insist that gentiles main-tain the dietary laws, or even expect them to understand them. In pro-fessional physician ethics, however, the special requirements are only partially limited to interactions within the group. The 1847 AMA code states that "there is no profession, from the members of which greater purity of character and a higher standard of moral excellence are re-quired, than the medical." This is followed by a list of duties the professional "owes to his profession." Included are fraternal courtesy; gratuitous care of other practitioners of medicine, their wives, and children while under paternal care; rules for consultation; and a prohibition on "meddling inquiries" into the work of another physician.

But the same section claims that this duty of purity of character is owed also to patients.[26] It becomes clear that many of the special rules that are supposed to govern conduct among members of the gentlemanly profession also have major impact on patients. It is in the next paragraph that advertising is proscribed:

> It is derogatory to the dignity of the profession, to resort to public advertisements or private cards or handbills, inviting the attention of individuals affected with particular diseases—publicly offering advice and medicine to the poor gratis, or promising radical cures; or to publish cases and operations in the daily prints, or suffer such publications to be made....[27]

The possibility that a medical ethics can be founded on custom or self-imposed standards without reference to any higher authority so stretches the meaning of the term *ethics* that one wonders whether it has not been simply misused. There is a school of thought in the analysis of the meaning of ethical terms that claims such terms refer only to what is customary or what is approved by the relevant social group whose members use the terms. This position is a particular kind of relativism, in that ethical claims are viewed as referring to nothing beyond a speaker's own social group or culture. It is a kind of *metaethical* relativism, a relativism in the meaning of ethical terms. While those within the relevant group grasp and understand that a particular behavior is or is not ethical, those outside the group may not reach the same conclusion. There is no reason why they should, since the foundation of the ethical judgment is nothing more than the consensus of the social group.[28] In fact, according to this account, it is logically consistent for some other group to hold some other view about what behavior is morally required in a particular situation or for a particular role without there being any contradiction. In our case, those outside the professional group of physicians may hold some other view of what is ethically required in the physician's role. And proponents of particular systems of medical ethics, such as those discussed in part I, may reach still other conclusions. If what is ethical for members of a group is merely what various groups state is ethical, then it is to be expected that in some cases different groups will reach different conclusions.

This kind of social relativism has been quite popular in periods of human history when apparent cross-cultural differences in ethical judgments and practices were being discovered—in the time of the Stoics, for example, and in the anthropological discoveries of cultures with practices alien to Western beliefs and values during the early twentieth century.[29] Possibly the recent realization that professionals and nonprofessionals sometimes diverge in their views of ethically appropriate medical practice may generate this same kind of relativistic interpretation. The FTC and the AMA may simply have different views about what principle is appropriate to apply regarding physician advertising and about what the correct decision based on that principle should be.

The reasons for doubting this interpretation of disagreements in medical ethics are, however, overwhelming. In the first place, there are good reasons to doubt the empirical claim that there is no common ground for establishing ethical agreement. Much of the evidence for this kind of social relativism rests on an empirical claim that people in different social groups disagree in fundamental ways over issues that are ethical. However, it may be that the dispute over physician advertising depends not on fundamental differences over the ethical principles, but rather on questions of fact. It may be, for example, that both the FTC and the AMA agree that the goal is to serve the common good, as they both claim. They may simply disagree over the consequences of advertising. Either group may have a distorted appraisal of the predicted consequences because of very different self-interests. They may have access to different data. In short, efforts to establish that cross-cultural differences in ethical judgment exist and reduce to fundamental differences in ethical frameworks have met with great difficulty. Many have concluded that such efforts have indeed failed.[30]

The more fundamental attack on social relativism is not empirical but conceptual. Do defenders of professional ethics really believe that ethical obligation is grounded in nothing more than common agreement among professionals? Does Russell Roth really believe that physicians have a duty not to advertise simply because the professional group has imposed such a restriction upon itself? It seems that even members of the profession would want to base their sense of what is morally required as physicians on something more basic than mere common custom. Do they not base their duty to benefit their patients on some more fundamental, far-reaching grounding of morality?

If professional ethics means nothing more than those behaviors required by the professional group, then it is logically impossible to say that one's professional group has taken a morally incorrect stand. If advertising is by custom forbidden by physicians' groups and what is ethical is nothing more than what custom dictates, then it follows that, for physicians, advertising must be wrong and must continue to be wrong until custom changes. Why custom in this matter would change is not clear under these conditions.

But it must make sense linguistically (if not ethically) for a physician to say that even though his professional group condemns advertising, it is still an open question whether advertising is morally acceptable. If that is the case, then what is ethical for the physician cannot possibly be simply what custom dictates. This is what philosophers call the open question test.[31] Whatever the validity of the test for certain more sophisticated efforts to equate the ethical with some empirical reality,[32] the effort to equate it with the beliefs or pronouncements of some organization surely fails.

Even if this social relativism can be defended, however, as an accurate account of what defenders of professional ethics mean when they say that physicians have such and such a duty, it leaves professionals in a very awkward position. There is in principle no common ground for ethical discussion with those outside the group. The FTC, being made up of nonprofessionals, would have no basis for understanding the professional stance on the question of advertising. Its members certainly would have no reason to adopt the professional association's position unless by chance their own social groups adopt a similar opinion, an outcome that seems unlikely.

If there is no common ground of moral discourse between those within and those outside the professional group, matters of ethical dispute, insofar as ethical dispute makes sense, will be resolved by psychological manipulation, inducement, or sheer force. It is in the interest of the professional group at least to behave as if there were some common ground for resolving the dispute. Otherwise, given the power relations between the contending parties, the professional group will certainly lose everything it stands for.

What is necessary is some more universal underpinning for ethical discussion. By universal, there is no implication of rigidity in the application of moral rules. That is a separate question to be discussed later. Rather, what is being sought is some common basis for carrying on the conversation over what is ethically required in a particular role. What is sought is a more universal leverage point for discussing role-specific duties. Exactly what that leverage point is will depend on many variables. It might be the will of a deity, the laws of nature, the common consent of all affected parties, the reason shared by all people, or some other source of morality that extends beyond the mere custom of one of the affected parties. Any idea that the professional group on its own generates or establishes the ethical norms will lack this more universal underpinning. That is why it is so unfortunate that, even after the FTC decision, James Sammons, executive vice president of the AMA held on to the idea that his organization should establish the standards. "We shall continue," he says in 1980, "through whatever channels are appropriate, to work to overturn this decision so that the medical profession can continue to serve the public *by establishing ethical standards* for its members."[33] (Italics mine.)

It may turn out that some of the rules governing conduct within a profession can be maintained without such a common basis shared with nonprofessionals. These, however, will turn out to be viewed as mere custom, practices agreed upon by members of the group. As long as they have no impact on others, the practices will be tolerated or ignored. Falling into this category in physicians' groups will be agreements about annual fees for membership or about care of fellow members at no charge; in fraternal groups, they would be about handshakes, passwords, and the like. Matters that really count, though, including those that have impact on outsiders, surely cannot be left to consensus among the group. That, at least, cannot be the grounding for ethical judgments and practices. No public agency like the FTC would have any rational basis for yielding to such professionally self-generated obligations.

THE CONSENSUS OF PROFESSIONALS AS THE WAY OF KNOWING PROFESSIONAL ETHICS

Our conclusion is that a professional ethics grounded in nothing more than agreement, custom, or vote by a group's members can have no ethical bite. No one outside the group would have any reason for conforming to the professional ethical judgments. They would have no basis for accepting the rights and duties that the professionals and their group may want to claim for themselves.

Sometimes this leads to a shift in the definition of what a professional ethic is. Facing the bleak future of moral chaos and powerlessness that would come from a professional ethic based only on consensus of members, some defenders of such an ethic search for a firmer foundation. They recognize that for a practice to be considered ethical by those outside as well as within the profession, the ethic must have some more universalizable source. That does not necessarily mean, however, that nonprofessionals will have a role in the formulation and articulation of role-specific duties for professionals. The alternative that manages to keep the articulation of these duties within the profession is the claim that only professionals have the experience or skill or knowledge necessary to understand what the duties are. This view holds that the duties of the professional are indeed more universally grounded, but that knowledge of what is required is limited to those within the profession.

The claim that makes the ethic *professional*, as I am using the term, is an epistemological one; that is, a claim about the way ethical obligation can be known. Lord Brock, engaged in a heated debate in Britain over the ethics of what was called euthanasia, made the epistemological claim: "As an ordinary citizen I must accept that the killing of the unwanted could be legalized by an Act of Parliament, but as a doctor I must know that there are certain things which are part of the ethics of our profession that an Act of Parliament cannot justify or make acceptable."[34]

Lord Brock's claim was not just that physicians have a special responsibility to preserve life, entailing a unique role-specific duty that prohibits euthanasia. That is an interesting claim, perhaps even a morally appropriate one, about how physicians should act in their role, but it is not what Lord Brock was arguing. Rather he was saying that as a physician he knew something about the physician's role that others, such as members of Parliament, did not know. This makes the appeal one of professional ethics and not merely one about duties of physicians, which anyone might be able to debate in principle.

It may be that those engaged in the dispute over advertising have this same notion of a professional ethics in mind. They may be saying that only by being a physician can one know that it is unethical for physicians to advertise. When Russell Roth says the profession has imposed upon itself certain proscriptions that the public poorly understands, he really may have meant that the profession has knowledge of certain requirements about physician advertising that the public poorly understands. Perhaps other modes of knowing exist, or other people without the requisite skills can have some knowledge of what is appropriate for physicians' behavior, but, lacking the special skills, training, and temperament of the profession, according to this view, they can know only dimly.

That at least implies there is some common ground for the debate.

Both lay person and professional may be attempting to learn the moral obligations of the physician from a source that is in principle relevant for both their groups. They may be appealing to reason, to a common religious heritage, or to some contractarian framework.

The problem then is how systems of medical ethics, other than the Hippocratic, handle claims about special ways of knowing. Some of them do accept that certain individuals have special skills or special faculties for knowing moral requirements. But none of them identify medical skills as particularly relevant. Jewish and Roman Catholic traditions recognize rabbis and priests as having skills in knowing moral truths. Catholicism even has taken it to the point of some rather well worked-out notions of papal and conciliar authority. Neither, however, recognizes medical professional skills as important in knowing matters of ethics within their own systems. Protestant and sectarian religious traditions include within their ranks mystics and evangelicals who have accepted the idea that certain people can possess special knowledge: the mystic through direct spiritual revelation and the evangelical through scriptural revelation as interpreted by those within the tradition. However, these groups, also, give no special place to the skills of the medical professional.

It may turn out that the very process of socialization involved in becoming a physician does provide unique ways of knowing that can be possessed only by those within the profession. If that is the case, however, and if matters of ethical conduct toward those outside the profession are based on this special knowledge, the professional is in no better position than he was under the claim that ethical requirements actually originate within the profession. If the claim is that in principle outsiders cannot know the ethics (even though they are affected by them), then why should the outsiders take such a claim seriously? Why should they take the claim of the physicians any more seriously than people without mystical powers take the mystic or than those outside of Christianity take revelation?

If members of a profession want to have their interpretations of moral requirements for their roles taken seriously by others, they must claim not only that their moral framework is applicable to outsiders, but also that it is comprehensible to outsiders.

There actually may be limited situations where it would be rational for outsiders to accept, for pragmatic reasons, limited pronouncements by a profession about what is morally required in a professional role. If an evangelical Protestant thought that the professional group could read the relevant source of morals as well as he and his group could, then nothing would be lost in letting the profession do the work. In general, if the professional group is going to be using the same source of norms, and there is reason to believe that the group can know and understand well what that source says for the role-specific duties of the profession, then the profession could reasonably be vested with the task. Normally, however, there will be doubts.

Even those working with secular systems of ethics based on reason or intuition or knowledge of the moral laws of nature may have good reason to be hesitant about ceding epistemological authority for mere purposes of convenience.

Another pragmatic reason why nonprofessionals might be willing to accept a professional's word for what is required in the professional role is that what is at stake is too trivial to worry about. When advertising and fee splitting were viewed as trivial (both by those inside and outside the profession) no one really cared whether the profession was articulating the physician's duty properly. However, now that we realize how important these matters are in providing fairly priced care of good quality we realize the issues are not trivial. Like war left to the generals, these issues are too important to be left to others in cases where behavior based on their conclusions will have a direct impact on us.

In the end, the epistemological claim for a professional ethic—that only professionals can know what is required in the professional role—makes no more sense than the metaethical claim, which says that what is required in a professional role is grounded in nothing more fundamental than the consensus of the profession.

THE ROLE OF THE PROFESSION IN FORMING CODES AND ADJUDICATING ETHICAL DISPUTES

In the light of this it seems strange that lay people and professionals alike assume that it is correct for professions to form their own codes of ethics and adjudicate ethical disputes arising out of the application of those codes. Yet in both lay and professional literature, if a question arises over ethical issues such as killing a baby or advertising, it is often assumed that the question can be resolved by turning to the professional code of ethics. If a possible violation has been committed, it is assumed the codes will resolve the problem. This sometimes happens in public processes (court cases, licensure hearings, and so forth) as well as professional ones.

During the Vietnam war Captain Howard B. Levy, a physician, was charged with violating a lawful command from his superior officer, Colonel Henry F. Fancy, to train Green Berets in dermatology.[35] The medical skills would be used, among other things, to treat local Vietnamese and win their support for the American cause.

In his court-martial defense Levy offered three arguments. The first was that the order was illegal because it would require him to participate in war crimes. The second was that the order was illegal because it was motivated primarily by a desire to increase punishment. These are structurally plausible defenses since it is illegal both to participate in war crimes and to give orders motivated by a desire for punishment. But his third argument is problematic; Levy said the order forced him, as a physician, to violate medical ethics. By this he meant professional ethics as articulated by the profession. He cited the Hippocratic Oath in his defense, pointing to the passage that says, "I swear . . . that by my precept, lecture and every other mode of instruction, I will impart a knowledge of the art to . . . disciples bound by a stipulation and oath, according to the law of medicine but to no others. . . ."[36]

The puzzling thing is not Captain Levy's judgment that the order was unethical and illegal. It is that he felt the court would and should honor his argument that the order would make him violate his professionally imposed ethical duty. How can it be considered that an oath sworn by someone to his professional colleagues to teach in only a certain manner would be accepted by the courts as justification for refusing to obey a command? The first two arguments appeal to the laws of the state which are binding on the superior officer, the court, and Captain Levy. They provide a common framework for discourse. Captain Levy also might have appealed to a higher law, assuming that both he and his accusers would recognize such a law. But why should he appeal to his professional commitment and have any reason to expect the broader society, represented by the court, to be influenced by the appeal?

A fascinating and popular journal, *Medical Economics*, advises physicians on nonclinical matters of importance, including how to invest their money, how to avoid malpractice suits, and, from time to time, what is ethical in their professional practice. In July 1973 the magazine posed a series of ethics case problems and included boxes where readers could check off whether the physician's conduct seemed ethical or unethical. These were then scored by what must have been taken as the definitive standard, the rulings of the AMA's Judicial Council.[37]

The problem of appeals to professional authority is no less great in Britain. In 1970 the British Medical Association published a booklet,

Medical Ethics, which outlined its policies effective then. It said that the Association had devised "ethical machinery" for "the resolution of disputes between members of the profession."[38] Though there are problems in trying to envision what ethical machinery might be, there are no difficulties in understanding that an organization would want to develop methods for adjudicating disputes among its members. But the British booklet goes further. It says that one of the medical association's most important functions is to advise and assist members on ethical problems, including those that arise in relation to official bodies and to the general public. Still, this might not be a problem. If a private group wants to advise its members, it is hard for outsiders to complain. But the British courts have apparently accepted this role of advisor for the professional association as well. The General Medical Council is a British hybrid of professional and public representatives charged with disciplinary authority over British physicians in cases involving "serious professional misconduct." It defines "serious professional misconduct" (which it equates with "infamous conduct") in its official pamphlet, *Professional Discipline,* by quoting two justices. Lord Justice Scrutton delivered a judgment in 1934 that stated, "Infamous conduct in a professional respect means no more than serious misconduct judged according to the rules, written or unwritten, governing the profession."[39] Thus the deciding feature is the rules governing the profession. That may, however, leave open the possibility that the rules governing the profession are articulated by some body other than the profession. The second quote from the General Medical Council pamphlet clarifies the matter. It cites Lord Justice Lopes, who wrote in 1894, "If a medical man in the pursuit of his profession has done something with respect to it which will be reasonably regarded as disgraceful or dishonourable by his professional brethren of good repute and competency, then it is open to the GMC, if that is shown, to say he has been guilty of infamous conduct in a professional respect."[40]

For some reason he considers the judgment of "professional brethren of good repute and competency" that a colleague has acted disgracefully or dishonorably as the triggering mechanism for quasi-public judicial review.

I say "quasi-public" because while the General Medical Council is established by British law (The Medical Act of 1858), it includes membership positions reserved for members of the British Medical Association and other professional bodies. Thus, public judicial activity in Britain is conducted by a body in which some of the members are appointed by a professional group in which the definition of misconduct is left to the profession.

The situation is even worse in the United States. In most states, "professional misconduct" is illegal. It is a violation of state licensing laws and can lead to public penalties, including revocation of a physician's license to practice medicine. Yet the definition of professional misconduct is often made by the profession itself. The adjudication of the charges of professional misconduct varies from state to state. In some jurisdictions, such as Maryland, the state medical society is required by law to investigate all reports of professional misconduct.[41] It may initiate action by virtue of information coming from its own members, referrals from the State Commission on Medical Discipline, or through any other source.[42] Even a Maryland physician who is not a member of the medical society must have charges against him investigated by the professional organization. Only when action against a physician's license is deemed necessary does the medical society then send the results of its investigation and recommendations to the State Commission for further action.

Prior to 1969, a Board of Medical Examiners made up of eight physicians elected by the Maryland state medical society had full disciplinary powers in the *name of the state*. In 1969 the law was revised on the recommendation of the professional organizations, and the state Commission on Medical Discipline assumed responsibility for disciplining physicians. This appears to have been a shift in the direction of public control, but since the commission does not act until after the medical society it has very little independent authority. Furthermore, the commission is made up of eleven members, nine of whom are physicians. Two, by law, are the president of the state medical society and the chairman of its council; two more are nominated by the medical society; two are appointed by the state secretary of health; and three more are nominated by the Board of Medical Examiners, which in turn is elected by the medical society. Only two are lay members appointed by the governor and are not part of professional medicine. As the chairman of the state medical society's peer review committee concludes : "
. . . the effect of this new law has been to greatly enhance the Medical Society's role in physician discipline."[43] The state has thus ceded to a private professional organization not only the definition of the standards governing grounds for suspension of the publicly granted license, but also the authority to judge whether those standards have been violated.

In some other states, there is titular governmental control over the adjudication process, but in practice the critical decision-making authority is left to members of the profession. In New York, for example, licensure is controlled by the state Board of Regents, a governmental body responsible for educational standards as well as licensing of some twenty-nine different professions. The crucial authority for reviewing cases of professional misconduct, however, rests with the state Board for Professional Medical Conduct, which is made up primarily of physicians—forty-seven of its fifty-six members in 1979. Furthermore, although board members are appointed by the governor, the physicians are recommended by county medical societies, the state medical society, and the Academy of Medicine, thus lodging crucial control over the vast majority of the board in professional organizations. Each case involving a charge of professional misconduct must pass through the state commissioner of health, who is normally a physician, and through a hearing committee made up of five people, four of whom are physicians.[44] Only after a physician has been found guilty at these earlier, professionally controlled stages does the Board of Regents have a chance to review the decision. Thus, even in this apparently public review, members of the profession exercise substantial control.

This same close collaboration between the public board and the professional medical association is seen in California. Its public Board of Medical Quality Assurance (a body with some lay members but a majority of physicians) has published a joint statement, *Physician Responsibility*, with the California Medical Association. The two groups urge that any physician who is concerned about another's hospital practice discuss the matter first with a hospital or other institutional department head or chief of staff and then "if the problem has community-wide ramifications, refer the information to the county medical society."[45] Only if, in the concerned physician's opinion, satisfactory action is not taken by the hospital and the county medical society, should the Board of Medical Quality Assurance "be considered." The model is one of peer review—peers, that is, of the accused physician and not of the patient who may have been wronged or whose rights may have been violated. The writers of the joint statement assume that physicians, not a patient or another lay person, will bring the complaint. The close collaboration between the public state body and the private professional group revealed by the statement calls into serious question the public body's degree of impartiality in adjudicating disputes between the professional and the lay person or in selecting principles for deciding what conduct is unprofessional.

Many assume that professional monitoring and adjudication of charges of members' misconduct is a problem because physicians, like other human beings, have a tendency to protect their own, to look out for the self-interest of themselves and the profession as a whole. If this is the case, then the profession will act only in cases where the violation has been so extreme that the reputation of the profession as a whole is in jeopardy.

Thus New York State authorities were slow to bring action in the case first publicized in 1972 of Dr. Max Jacobson, a New York City physician who prescribed amphetamines for the various psychological and physical complaints of his patients (including such famous ones as John F. Kennedy and playwright Tennessee Williams).[46] Only after a sensational exposé, including front page stories in *The New York Times*, did the state Division of Professional Conduct act to suspend Jacobson's license. The doctor, some of whose patients did not know what they were receiving, argued that the question of whether his behavior was blameworthy was a matter of "professional judgment."

The professional society's own mechanisms for adjudicating the charges of professional misconduct were even more lethargic than the state's. While the Division of Professional Conduct had finally begun an investigation of Jacobson by the time of *The New York Times*'s exposé, the county medical society had not. Though the matter had been brought up years before, the professional group did not take action until three days after the appearance of the story in the newspaper.[47] Very few cases reach any medical professional society for review. Though American records are not open to scrutiny (the professional associations claim this is a matter of professional confidentiality), actions of the British General Medical Council are available to the public. A one-year search of these records in 1972 revealed eighteen cases, fourteen of which were included in published reports.[48] Twelve of the cases involved physicians who had been charged with gross violations of traditional personal and moral standards. Complaints included filing of false claims for services not rendered, drug and alcohol abuse, violation of abortion laws, canvassing for patients by paying taxi drivers for abortion referrals, and adultery with patients. In most of these cases, the physicians had already been prosecuted by civil authorities and found guilty. The two other cases involved more subtle problems of ethical relationships with patients. One dealt with a physician who refused to visit two patients in critical condition, in spite of pleas for help. His case was postponed. The other was a breaking-of-confidentiality case in which a physician told a sixteen-year-old girl's parents that she had received birth control pills from a clinic. This case, which will be discussed in detail in chapter 6, resulted in acquittal of the physician on the grounds that "[the] Committee do[es] not regard your action in disclosing the information referred to in the charge as improper."

The problem has apparently been with us for a long time. W. H. S. Jones, one of the leading modern scholars of the Hippocratic Oath, claims it is fairly certain that the physician who did not follow the Oath was not punished unless he sinned against the law of the state.[49] Otherwise, the only penalty was the dishonor of having violated one's pledge.

Accusations that professional groups are not very aggressive in their self-regulation of professional misconduct imply, however, that in principle they could do the job adequately if only they took their responsibility seriously. The implication is that organized members of a profession should be able to adjudicate claims of professional misconduct.

If the earlier discussion of the problems of professional ethics is correct, however, this conclusion is not warranted. The real problem does not seem to be the failure of the professions to live up to an ideal of self-responsibility, but rather their tendency to apply internally generated ethical standards without reference to other medical ethics systems, which could be brought to bear on many issues.

The advertising case is an interesting example. Some claim that physicians have not applied their own moral standards well, have allowed their self-interest in restricting advertising to cloud their judgment of what is ethical. The evidence for this is not very convincing, however. In this area, at least, it appears that the profession has done an outstanding job of communicating and enforcing its understanding of what it thinks is ethical in the professional role. Physicians really do seem to believe that advertising hurts the patient and the public welfare by demeaning the role of the professional and by lowering the standards of physician practice.

The real question is whether the ethical and empirical judgment of doctors is a morally accurate one and whether it is in accord with the values of those outside the medical role. From this point of view, the real problem is the use of professional ethical standards rather than those rooted in some more universally accessible source of morality. One is forced to conclude that the use of a professionally generated ethic, at least for conduct that has an impact on those outside the profession, makes no sense in theory or in practice. There are in fact, some extreme cases where the profession has done its job and eliminated practices that are harmful to patients and physicians alike. But the theoretical underpinning of reliance on professional modes of coping with ethical dimensions of relations between professionals and lay people is lacking. It does not bear the scrutiny of analysis.

To repeat, an ethic that professionals base on their own consensus of what their role entails has no ethical force, at least with nonprofessionals. It is doubtful such a standard can be called an ethic at all. It is really more a set of customs or mores governing behavior of members of a private group. Even a medical ethic that rests on more universal foundations but which it is claimed can be known only by professionals provides little basis for application to nonprofessionals. Nonprofessionals would have no reason for assuming on faith that the profession has interpreted these ethical foundations properly in their application to the physician's role. Because of this, it makes no sense to rely on professional ethics and professional organizations to adjudicate ethical disputes.

At best, an ethic articulated by physicians handles only a small fraction of the ethical problems in medicine, those involving the physician. In principle, it leaves out the ethical problems of nurses, pharmacists, social workers, hospital administrators, and other health professionals. It can handle neither the problems of interrelationships among these professionals nor the vast majority of ethical decisions made every day by lay people in the ordinary course of living. What is needed is some other foundation for a medical ethic.

Chapter 5

The Triple Contract:
A New Foundation
for Medical Ethics

Case 3 *The Health Professional's Duty to Warn a Potential Murder Victim*

Prosenjit Poddar was a student at the University of California at Berkeley. He participated in folk dancing classes at the school, where he met and fell in love with Tatiana Tarasoff. Rejected by Ms. Tarasoff, Poddar fell into a deep depression resulting in declining health and neglect of his studies. In August 1969 he sought treatment as a voluntary outpatient at Cowell Memorial Hospital, a university-affiliated facility. According to the eventual legal complaint against him, it is alleged that he confided to Dr. Lawrence Moore, a psychologist at the hospital, that he was going to kill an unnamed girl, readily identifiable as Tatiana, when she returned from spending a summer in Brazil. Dr. Moore, with the concurrence of two psychiatrists, decided that Poddar should be committed for observation to a mental hospital.

He wrote a letter of diagnosis to the campus police requesting that they detain Poddar for emergency psychiatric evaluation. They did so, but released Poddar when he appeared rational and promised to stay away from Tatiana. On October 27, 1969, Poddar killed Tatiana Tarasoff, two months after confiding his intention to do so to Dr. Moore.

The central issue in the court case was whether a health professional, a psychiatrist or psychotherapist, has a duty to warn an intended victim in cases such as this. The American Psychiatric Association entered the case as an amicus arguing against such a duty. It offered three defenses against the duty of warning.

First, it argued that the standard of warning is unworkable since prediction by therapists of violence has a low level of accuracy. The court acknowledged that prediction can be difficult and that no health professional should be liable when he or she conforms to the standards of skill possessed by the profession. In this case, however, it pointed out that there was no doubt about the therapist's ability to predict that Poddar was a serious danger. In fact, the psychotherapist and his colleagues had made the judgment that Poddar should be detained.

The second argument of the APA was that warning a potential victim is a breach of confidentiality inconsistent with the therapeutic relationship. The third argument contended that a duty to warn untenably puts therapists between their duty to the patient to keep confidence and their duty to protect public safety.

The tension is a familiar one. Breaking confidence, so the argument goes, may turn out to jeopardize the quality of the therapy either because patients will be reluctant to discuss their problems openly or because the warning itself will interrupt the therapy.

Whether the people who are in danger will be benefited more by the keeping or breaking of a confidence is an empirical question. There is also a question of principle, however. If it turns out that the patient would benefit more by keeping the confidence, but others would benefit more by breaking it, should the therapist break the confidence or keep it? Is he or she to compromise the commitment to the patient in order to serve society? This is the issue over which the court and the professional society disagreed. Our question is: To what extent should the court let a professional group's commitment to patient confidentiality influence its decision on the duty of the therapist?[1]

By now it should be clear that a professional person's judgment about what is required in cases of conflict of principle should not automatically decide the issue. The fact that a professional or his or her group believes that a confidence should be kept, a patient killed, or an advertisement proscribed cannot definitively resolve the question of whether each of these acts is ethically or legally right. If the answer is to be persuasive for those outside the profession, there must be some more far-reaching basis on which to decide what is right in difficult medical ethical situations. I think we can find a firmer foundation for a medical ethic in what I shall call the triple contract—a three-level social contract or covenant that begins by establishing the most basic social principles for human interaction, progresses to establish a social contract between society and the professional group, and finally, provides a basis for individual contractual relationships between the professional and the lay person.

THE BASIC SOCIAL CONTRACT

Some medical ethical decisions may be entirely private: The decision to commit suicide is a conceivable example. Even here, however, others are almost always affected, if only indirectly. Most medical ethical decisions are social decisions in that they involve direct human interaction. The parent of a child whose head aches following a head injury decides either to give aspirin or to take the child to the hospital for X rays. A physician decides to collaborate in his patient's plan to kill her child. A therapist decides to withhold from a potential victim information about a plan to murder. In most cases, the social relationships are very complex and involve not just the physician and patient as isolated individuals, but also those to whom physician and patient are linked. Thus is constituted what can be referred to as the professional and the lay teams.[2] Some decisions are more social than others, such as those involving health planners who make resource allocation decisions that affect whole populations.

Again and again we have seen that people disagree over what the basic ethical principles ought to be and how they should be applied to particular case problems. If the problems involved in making medical ethical decisions are ever to be resolved, some commonly acceptable basis for their resolution must be found. At the crudest level, decisions could be enforced by the sheer power and strength of the decision makers, but surely it is better to reach some kind of agreement or acceptance based on the legitimacy of a common framework.

The bare minimum would be a private agreement in which two people, let us say provider and patient, agree that it is mutually advantageous to pursue a common course. Morally, though, it is rather unsatisfying as a basis because our primary concern often is not merely what we can do, but what we ought to do. We want a common framework for the morality of the decision, not just a pact of mutual self-interest. If we despair of finding some ground on which to base universal common assent, we may at least move toward small-scale moral communities where those involved agree on a moral framework for medical ethical decisions. The result would be what I shall call sectarian medicine.

Seventh Day Adventists, knowing they have a system of beliefs and values about medicine that are not widely held and acted upon by the wider community, set out to train physicians of their own kind. These doctors appreciate the intricate connections between religious beliefs and medical practice, just as a Park Avenue, secular humanist physician may share the work view of his Park Avenue, secular humanist patient. Similar, shared attitudes may exist between the Catholic patient and the Catholic physician trained at a Catholic school and practicing at a Catholic hospital. A moral community is created with a shared morality and a shared bond of loyalty.

From the standpoint of making the professional–lay relationship work by providing a common moral framework, this bond solves the problem. Both professional and lay persons share a common religious, moral, and cultural perspective enabling them to tackle the medical ethical problems from a common conceptual ground. Sectarian medicine, medical decision making based on shared perspectives, makes sense in a pluralistic world. Seeking out professionals who share one's views is prudent when one has reason to believe that the holding of those views will affect decisions made in the professional relationship. Since it no longer seems doubtful that medical decisions are influenced by one's world view, it makes sense for lay people to seek out, actively and aggressively, professionals who share their most deeply held beliefs and values. Often people seem embarrassed to use a lay referral network or to question a professional's religious, political, and ethical convictions when selecting a medical adviser, but such strategies are wiser than many take them to be.

Some time ago I studied the pairings of physicians and patients in one community with respect to the morally sensitive questions of birth control, childbirth, and potential sterilization and abortion. I found no evidence of a link between patients and physicians based on their beliefs.[3] This meant that a patient hostile to family planning was possibly getting her medical counseling from a physician who did all the local abortions, while the woman eager for what she considered "responsible" family planning may have been seeing a physician whose religious views gave him a notion of "responsibility" quite different from hers. One wonders whether medicine practiced at Methodist Hospital is different in any way from that practiced at City Hospital down the street. If it is, why is so little notice of that fact taken by potential patients and staff? If it is not, why do religious and private groups expend such resources doing what can, and should, be done in the public and nonsectarian institutions?

Sectarian medical ethics with patients and providers pairing up on the basis of attitudes and beliefs solves some problems, but not others. It provides the common framework morally acceptable to patient and professional alike, but it is of relatively little use in more complex social situations involving people of differing moral, religious, and philosophical convictions. It would be more satisfying if we found a broader basic agreement for medical ethics than pluralistic sectarianism.

There is another reason why a more fundamental common agreement would be desirable. Most people, even those functioning within a sectarian framework, tend to hold that the important questions—in the realm of science or in the realm of values—are ones which, in principle, we should all be able to agree upon. Such issues are viewed as questions of truth or, at least, questions about which reasonable people ought to be able to agree. It may turn out that we are unable to reach such an agreement so that we have to return to more sectarian, smaller groups. It is worth trying for a more universal foundation of morality, however.

Thus for both practical and theoretical reasons we strive for a common, universally applicable framework in which to resolve important social questions. In both science and ethics, the common working assumption is that a framework is universal in the sense that it applies to everyone. In science, certain common premises are taken on faith: the existence of external reality and the laws of cause and effect, for example. These are universal in that they are seen by those working within the scientific world view as applying to everyone, independent of cultural milieu. If I say it is a scientific fact that digitalis slows and strengthens the heart when taken precisely as stipulated by a particular patient, I am saying that any observer, regardless of cultural or religious affiliation, should be able to determine that effect on the heartbeat in that person. Scientific statements are universal or absolute in this sense. Everyone ought *in principle* reach the same conclusion if exposed to the same evidence.

I am here using *absolute* or *universal* in a very special and technical sense, in the same way *absolutism* has been used by Roderick Firth and many others.[4] It has nothing to do with legalism or the rigid application of rules. Rather it is the notion that some statements have a truth or falsity to them such that if one person affirms such a statement and another rejects it, a contradiction exists. This is not the case, for example, if one person says he likes chocolate ice cream and another person says he does not; that is a matter of taste, hardly absolutist in this sense. If, however, one person says that the dose of digitalis just given does slow a patient's heart and another says it does not (in the same patient, at the same time), everyone recognizes a contradiction that begs for resolution. All presume that one or the other must be wrong.

If we are going to cut through the apparent cultural relativism of the endless list of possible principles for medical ethics, we are going to have to seek a universal or absolutist basis for a medical ethics. It will not do to have one set of basic principles about what the physician should do in a particular case held by one religious or professional group and another set of principles held by another group about what the same physician should do in the same situation. Above all, we need a common framework, acceptable to both lay people and professional, within which to decide what is ethically acceptable medical practice.

This condition of universal applicability is so central to ethics that it is often incorporated into the very notion of what ethics means. When someone claims that a particular behavior in a particular circumstance is unethical, he is making a claim that he believes should be accepted in principle by everybody. To the extent that people do not accept it, they either have misunderstood the facts, are thinking of a somewhat different circumstance, or have made an error in moral judgment. A claim that a particular behavior is ethical thus comes to more than a matter of mere taste or preference. We think it is a matter worth fighting about when we talk of whether a particular physician in Japan ought to collaborate in a murder or whether a particular psychotherapist ought to disclose a confidence to an identified potential victim. On the other hand, we tend not to care whether the Japanese prefer raw fish to pizza; that is a matter of taste. Ethical questions are basic. If we label the claim ethical, rather than merely preferential, we are making a judgment within a framework that we take to be applicable to all.

I am not claiming that all confidences should or should not be broken or that all kinds of advertising should or should not be permitted. It may turn out that some moral rules can be stated in rigid legalistic fashion so as to apply in any situation (a separate problem I shall consider in chapter 13), but that is not my concern now. Rather I am claiming now that when reflecting upon a particular case with all its idiosyncratic facts, if we consider the judgment one of ethics we believe that others ought to reach the same judgment about the rightness of the action that we have reached. We would like to be able to say that Dr. Moore in the Tarasoff case was either right or wrong morally, not merely that the psychiatric profession approved of his action while some other groups or individuals did not. To the extent this is possible, we can be said to be rendering an ethical judgment rather than merely expressing a preference.

DISCOVERING A UNIVERSAL BASE FOR MEDICAL ETHICS

It remains to be seen whether a universal base for making medical ethical decisions can be discovered or even invented. Those approaching medical ethics in a theological context should feel comfortable with the quest for a universally applicable framework in which to evaluate ethical judgments. At least in Western theological systems, which are monotheistic and tend to be universal, God is the ultimate test of morality. The action of a physician, for example, is in accord with God's decree or meets with God's approval or adheres to God's law. The standard is viewed as relevant to all, professional and lay person, private individual and public official. To say that Dr. Moore ought to disclose information because it is in accord with God's law to do so is a far more fundamental statement than merely encouraging him to disclose because the disclosure is approved by Dr. Moore or his professional group. This fundamental statement appeals to a moral frame of reference that embraces everyone and that is binding on all parties in a way that the agreement among members of a professional group is not.

If there is such a divinely created or approved moral order, then it remains only for us finite human beings to have it revealed to us or to develop a way to discover it. Fortunately, Judaism and Christianity come equipped with a theory of revelation that makes the fundamental order available even to the finite and limited believer. Moreover, some strands within this tradition hold that the moral order also can be discovered through the use of human reason. Of course, since the human is a finite and fallible creature, the reason is corrupt and will provide only a clouded picture of the truths of the moral order. Nevertheless, the twin epistemological resources of revelation and reason make knowledge of morality possible for the believer.

Many people in many different cultures have held that there is a natural moral order, sometimes referred to as a natural moral law, inherent in the structure of the universe. Presumably if there is a natural moral law that determines what is morally right in a particular situation, it applies to everyone and would therefore be absolute, in the way I am using the term. Some theories of natural law are theologically based. If there is a divine source of morality, then it can be said that the moral order is in the nature of things. Theologically based theories of natural law sometimes take a teleological form, as in the views of St. Thomas Aquinas and of post-Aquinian Catholic moral theology. All things, according to Aquinas, partake in the eternal law by having imprinted on them an inclination to their proper end.[5] Protestant theologians also have accepted the existence of a divinely generated natural moral law. It has been affirmed in various forms, by John Calvin especially and by contemporary theologians such as Brunner[6] and Tillich.[7] There are other Protestants, ranging from Martin Luther in the sixteenth century to Karl Barth in our own time, who have expressed pessimism about man's ability to know the natural law either by reason or observation without the aid of revelation. Even they, however, concur in the existence of a moral order.

Protestants differ from Catholics in another way. Even those who are more optimistic about man's ability to know the natural law often have divorced that law from the Catholic's more teleological notion that things possess a natural end. According to this view, there exists a natural moral order, a structure of moral requiredness. It is not that things have a natural end, but rather that there are moral principles, moral relationships, inherent in reality. Like the laws of gravity, certain moral obligations exist as part of nature—the golden rule, the law of love, principles of justice, truthfulness, beneficence, and the like. This view of natural law, unlike the more teleological view, does not rely on any notion of beings having a natural end, or a tendency toward it, from which morality can be deduced. Moral requiredness is rather a part of the universe just as certain physical relationships are.

Not all, of course, count themselves part of a religious community that affirms a center of ultimate reality called a god. It is not essential, though, to affirm a divine source of a moral order in order to believe that a moral order exists. It is possible that a universally applicable moral framework can be discovered even if a theological source is denied.

Although many natural law thinkers have held that God is the source of the natural law, even natural law theories need not be theological. In fact, several natural law positions, from those of the Stoics to modern secular natural law and natural rights theories, do not have their origins in explicit theological positions.[8] Many thinkers in political philosophy—Hobbes, Locke, and Rousseau, for example—have natural law positions existing side-by-side with theological commitments.[9] The theologically committed person, believing that the natural moral order exists, should not be surprised if some secular thinkers catch a glimpse of the order without grasping its origin.

For those who hold that there is some universally applicable, discoverable basis for moral judgment, the way of knowing that order constitutes the only remaining problem. For some, it is accessible by the use of reason, or 'practical reason', to use Kant's term. For him, reason can discover that there are certain rules of behavior, or maxims, that one can will and, at the same time, will that the maxim become what he called a universal law of nature. These maxims, he maintained, are the maxims of morality.

Others have held that the basis for moral judgment is discoverable not so much by reason as by observation. According to this view, man is equipped with a moral capacity to sense what the laws of nature are. This theory of moral sense, which can be traced back at least as far as Francis Hutcheson and David Hume in the eighteenth century, has had more recent expression in the naturalistic theories of morality of Ralph Barton Perry and Roderick Firth. According to Firth, for example, morality is absolutist (in our sense of being independent of the observer). An action is right if it would tend to produce a feeling of approval in an ideal observer. An ideal observer is defined as having characteristics very similar to those we would attribute to an ideal scientist. He or she is omniscient with respect to nonethical facts: impeccably sensitive, impartial, dispassionate, consistent, but in other respects normal. In short, the ideal observer is like a person, but without the limitation and biases of an ordinary human being.

The beauty of the theory is that Firth and others at no point insist upon or assume the existence of such a person. They concede that they have given "a partial description of God,"[10] but claim merely that if such an observer did exist, we would regard as moral anything accorded his or her approval. This is comparable to saying that a true statement of scientific fact is one that would be made by an ideal scientist, free of the biases and limitations of a real, finite scientist. The fact that no such ideal scientist exists in no way jeopardizes our conviction that if one did exist, he or she would be able to give a relatively unequivocal account of nonmoral facts. Many (including some who would consider themselves empirical naturalists) hold that in the realm of morality there is also a natural order that an ideal observer could give an account of if such an observer existed.

The holders of any of these positions have identified and accepted a common basis for a universally applicable framework for making ethical judgments and, therefore, medical ethical judgments. They regard morality as absolute and believe that ethical propositions have a truth value about which people ought to agree. For those who hold that some universal basis of morality is discoverable, a common reference point for making medical ethical judgments can be found.

If we accept some version of the position that a universal base can be discovered, we can approach the problem confronting Dr. Moore. If we want to know whether he should disclose the potentially lifesaving confidential information that his client is considering a murder, we should look not directly at Dr. Moore's conscience or at Prosenjit Poddar's conscience or at anyone else's conscience. Neither should we look to the principles of ethics of the American Medical Association, the American Psychiatric Association, or any other association. We should turn instead to some framework that is more universally relevant to the problem at hand: to God's will, or to the natural law as known through man's reason or the moral senses. In so doing, we can avail ourselves of general principles or practices that will help us fit the specific case into a universal framework. Many of these systems will provide us with more specific moral rules that show the application of the principles to the specific case. These principles and rules will be the subject matter of the next chapters. But an enormous task remains before we can discuss the content of a normative medical ethic.

Unfortunately not all agree that a universal basis is discoverable, is existing objectively for us to find by revelation, awareness of the natural law, reason, or our moral senses. This does not mean that an endless relativism is the only alternative, however. We may be able to bring many of the doubters into a common community of moral discourse. They may be persuaded that it is possible to invent a universal base, or at least a base large enough to accommodate everyone involved in medical ethical decisions. If the base they invent is identical with the one purportedly discovered by others, or at least largely compatible with it, then the two groups may share enough of a moral framework to make common discourse and medical ethical evaluation possible.

INVENTING A UNIVERSAL BASE FOR MEDICAL ETHICS

If, without the benefit of having discovered a universal base for a common moral framework, one finds oneself in the unfortunate position of having to interact with physicians, nurses, health planning bureaucrats, parents, and others who make social medical ethical decisions, what is one to do? This is a world that, in Hobbes's terms, is nasty, brutish, and short. If one is to avoid the terror of a struggle of brute force pitting all against all, it would be prudent to strike a bargain for inventing, if possible, some framework that provides at least a minimal basis for communal interaction.

The first and most obvious maneuver might be to reach an agreement that renounces force and accords to everyone certain basic freedoms: freedom of thought and freedom of action insofar as one's actions do not impinge upon the liberty of others. We would accept what Robert Nozick, in an important, sophisticated elaboration of this view, calls the "libertarian side constraint."[11] We would set about structuring our moral community by contracting together, with the proviso that force be eschewed and freedom be respected.

Those who hold that morality can be discovered would be dissatisfied, of course, with this arrangement. They would argue that private agreements made in self-interest within the constraint of respect for freedom have nothing to do with morality. But also those who despair of discovering a universal framework for morality could have reason to be dissatisfied with this initial proposed agreement. Strictly from the point of view of mutual self-interest, it seems clear that the inequalities of talent and ability deriving from the natural lottery would eventually lead to a situation in which some particular group would become dominant and make life miserable for those technically free to bargain, but lacking sufficient psychological, economic, political, and/or physical resources to strike an attractive bargain. The masses in this situation would be technically free, in the sense that they are permitted to make bargains; but psychologically, economically, politically, and perhaps physically, they would have no freedom in the sense of having options open to them in making bargains that would be at all attractive. This larger, disadvantaged group might reasonably be expected to resort to using force against oppression by the dominant group. If someone or some group used natural talents or good fortune to parlay bargaining into a position of domination, the masses could not be expected to restrain themselves and remain content with whatever bargains they could make. The result would be little better than the brutish state of nature.

This need not happen, however. One could agree to respect other constraints in addition to freedom, and collectively, these constraints could be termed "the moral point of view."[12] The moral point of view would include, in all probability, the condition that liberty be respected, but it would have to extend beyond this limitation to include the crucial constraints that self-interest be abandoned and that the welfare of each person be counted equally in contracting or bargaining. That, of course, is a high price to pay, at least for the relatively powerful and talented. In the Nozickian world their interests count heavily because their power, talent, or good fortune assure them a very good bargaining position. But if their bargains threaten a stable moral order because of widespread dissatisfaction, then it might be prudent to add more conditions.

The principle that each person's welfare should count equally is crucial if the community generated is to be a moral community. The moral community is one of impartiality. If the community employed an impartial perspective to draw up the basic principles or practices for the society, the principles would be generated without reference to individual talents, skills, abilities, or good fortune. Another way of formulating this condition is to say that the basic principles or practices established must meet the test of reversibility. That is, they must be acceptable to one standing on either the giving or the receiving end of a transaction.[13] The general notion is that the contractors must take equal account of all persons. It is only by such an abandonment of an egoistic perspective that common social intercourse is possible. As Plato wrote in Book I of the Republic, "the unjust are incapable of common action . . . and [the] utterly unjust, they would have been utterly incapable of action."

The most intriguing contractual theory of ethics that makes this commitment to impartiality or reversibility is that espoused by John Rawls.[14] In his version of social contract theory, Rawls asks us to envision ourselves in what he calls the original position. He does not pretend that such a position exists or ever could exist. Rather, it is a device for making "vivid to ourselves the restrictions that it seems reasonable to impose on arguments for principles of justice, and therefore on these principles themselves."[15] The restrictions on the original position are that no one should be advantaged or disadvantaged in the choice of principles either by natural fortune or social circumstances. Persons in the original position are equal. To help us imagine such a situation, he asks us to impose what he calls a "veil of ignorance," under which "no one knows his place in society, his class position or social status, nor does any one know his fortune in the distribution of natural assets and abilities, his intelligence, strength, and the like."[16]

From that position one can derive impartially a set of principles or practices that provide the moral foundations for a society. Even if we cannot discover a universal basis for ethical decisions, perhaps we can create a community that accepts rules such as respect for freedom and the impartial consideration of interests; that is, one that adopts the moral point of view and thereby provides a common foundation for deciding what is ethical. Those who take this view believe it possible to generate some commonly agreed upon principles or practices for a society. The creation of a contractual framework could then provide a basis for making medical ethical decisions that would be commonly recognized as legitimate.

A SYNTHESIS CONTRACT THEORY

We now face the most critical problem. Can those who want to discover a foundation for resolving a problem such as Dr. Moore's reconcile their approach with those who want to invent a framework by creating a social contract? Trying to invent a fundamental framework for medical ethical and other ethical decisions may seem radically different from trying to discover one. Rationally pursuing enlightened self-interest (by adopting the moral point of view) seems very different from trying to sense the natural law. I am not sure we need be that pessimistic, however.

An affinity clearly exists between objective, universal understandings of morality, such as the ideal-observer approach, and the models that pursue enlightened self-interest, such as the Rawlsian social contract with its veil of ignorance. In thinking about how the two approaches would be used to resolve ethical dilemmas, the affinity becomes even greater. The approach of the discoverer of the moral principles might be seen as following the scientific model. If one, in seeking a fact, is unavoidably limited by the condition that all possible observers are finite and fallible, one might gather together the best observers available, knowing them to be less than ideal. After encouraging them to be as objective and unbiased as possible, we might ask them to try to reach a consensus in which unsuppressible biases will tend to neutralize one another. In determining the moral law, however, who are the best observers? Who can be identified as knowing divine will or as being uniquely skilled in rational pursuit of the moral principles? There is little evidence that training in the science of ethics improves one's ability to know what is moral. There is also little evidence that training in the nonmoral components of a decision-making area gives one expertise in the morality of the problem. As I have noted, war is too important to be left to the generals—they are not experts in the morality of war simply because they excel in the nonmoral sphere of fighting a war.

In fact, developing expertise in a particular area may imply that one has developed a unique and biased commitment to that area or perhaps has valued it uniquely before entering the field. After all, experts are unique in considering their area of specialization sufficiently fascinating or important to warrant developing the expertise. Especially because many significant moral problems hinge on the relative importance of one sphere of goods in relation to another, there may be extraordinary risks in assuming that people with expertise in the nonmoral facts in any given area would be equally expert dealing in the moral components as well.[17] They may give special weight to the value of their sphere of expertise. This implies that were we to try to gather together observers to discover the fundamental moral principles for structuring the society, we would have no basis for giving preference to any particular observer. Thus, we would want to include all, knowing that each observer is deficient in some respects and holds biases that distort perception, but hoping that the biases will neutralize one another. We would then have an entire moral community coming together in an attempt to perceive the fundamental moral structure from the moral point of view in as objective and unbiased a manner as possible. This is a picture strikingly similar to the image Rawls asks us to hold of rational people coming together under a veil of ignorance such that they possess no knowledge of their peculiar biases and interests.

The potential compatibility between those who want to discover an objective basis for morality and those who think it must be invented by some sort of social contract increases when we realize that the contract is fundamental to many religious traditions. The Judeo-Christian tradition, in fact, is fundamentally contractarian. The people of Israel were created by a contract (or covenant, to use the more traditional religious term). More accurately, they were created by a series of covenants.

The priestly account of the Hebrew story conveys that at the end of the flood, because Noah alone was found righteous, God made a covenant with him and all living creatures that he would never again destroy the earth.[18] To be sure, it was a rather one-sided contract by modern standards. God, as all-powerful, conceived the agreement and bound Himself to it. He granted a new privilege to humans: They were permitted to eat animal meat provided it was bloodless. The privilege, though, was accompanied by a new obligation—a prohibition against the wanton shedding of blood of any creature, especially man. Thus, although there was an enormous power differential, the parties of the covenant were bound by their mutual acceptance of obligation.

This was followed, according to the Hebrew story, by the covenant with Abraham.[19] This involved a pledge by God that Abraham would be the father of many nations and that his descendants would be given the land of Canaan. The covenant was sealed with the commandment requiring circumcision.

These two covenants are preliminary to the Sinai covenant, which provides the moral foundation for the people of Israel. Contemporary biblical scholarship makes clear that the Sinai covenant was regarded as the decisive constitutive event in the history of Israel.[20] Israel is called through Moses to be a holy community. The Decalogue is "the stipulation of the obligations to the deity which the community accepted as binding. . . . It is . . . the source of community policy in law."[21]

There is some question as to whether the covenant is historically the foundation of the Israelite community or whether it functions merely as a myth of origin. Evidence seems to point in the direction of a real historical covenantal relationship. It is now known that there existed at the time in the Near East both suzerainty treaties by which a king bound his vassals to him and more democratic covenants binding vassals into relationship with one another as peers. In the words of the biblical scholar, George Mendenhall, "We now know that covenant relationships were the very foundation of relations between originally separate groups, and the legal responsibilities took place most naturally by covenant."[22] He goes on to summarize contemporary scholarship, stating:

> The existence of a covenant-bond community of tribes as a religious federation can hardly be doubted on rational grounds so far as the period of the Judges is concerned. The major question is whether or not that federation of tribes had a precursor in the nomadic period before the entry into Canaan. The present writer believes that the federation of tribes can be understood and explained only on the assumption that it is a conscious continuation and re-adaption of an earlier tradition which goes back to the time of Moses. The covenant at Sinai was the formal means by which the seminomadic clans, recently emerged from state slavery in Egypt, were bound together in a religious and political community.[23]

Anyone working in the history of Judeo-Christian ethics must recognize that covenant or contract is the fundamental foundation of moral obligation within that tradition. Those within the Calvinist tradition, especially, have continued to see the covenant as central. More striking is the compatibility of the theocentric perspective with the thinking of those considered to have laid the foundation for modern theories of social contract. Locke and Hobbes both affirmed the existence of a God-given law of nature, and the social contract, so central to their thought, must function for them within that framework.[24] For these classical contract theorists, the contractors come together not merely to invent the basic principles and practices for a society, but to discover together what the structure of a compatible moral community must be. As with the ideal observer theory, we once again face the problem of how finite, fallible human beings can know the natural moral law.

One solution seems possible for all those who favor the idea that a universally applicable moral framework can be discovered. The contract must function as an epistemological tool for discovering the moral order instead of, or in addition to, a way of inventing a moral order. Assuming for the moment that there is an order to be discovered, humans would come together as a moral community not to invent a framework but to attempt as best they can—through collective reasoning, perceiving, or the receiving of revelation—to discover the moral structure that will provide the basis for their community.

As with the ideal observer problem, there is reason for dispute about who possesses the necessary skill to reason, perceive, or receive revelation. The Israelite model suggests that special skill in perceiving is held by single individuals: the prophets from Moses on down. Current-day theology, especially among Protestants, seems more in tune with modern secular thought. According to this tradition, we have not been able to identify postbiblical humans having the unique ability to know the created order, at least not in the sphere of morality. The doctrine of the priesthood of all believers, if it means anything at all for modern man, means that no one has been accorded the privilege of being the channel through which the divine will is revealed. As applied to the sphere of morality, it means that the fundamental moral structures of society cannot be known or defined by a specific person or persons.

If this is the case, those whose ethics is rooted in these theological traditions will join with proponents of the ideal observer theory to seek some common expression for articulating fundamental moral principles and practices.

We now have several approaches to the discovery or generation of a universally applicable framework for morally structuring a society, and they are not so different from each other as they originally appeared. In the end, they all turn on some notion of reasonable people coming together, attempting to approximate the moral point of view, in order to contract to or at least agree on a framework. Some would hope to discover the content of the original covenant between God and man, others to discover what an ideal observer—if such an observer existed—would approve of. These two groups should have very little separating them methodologically in the task of generating a common framework. Their product in either case might be called the basic social contract. Still others would see themselves as reasonable people coming together collectively to use their rational processes in discovering the moral order. All of these groups are engaged in contracting; all concede that real, finite people can only approximate the moral point of view required of them and that the real moral order would be the one acknowledged by a hypothetical group of contractors who are capable of perfect knowledge and of perfectly taking the moral point of view.

The term *contract* is used guardedly, since for some it means a basic social contract only epistemologically because another earlier and more fundamental contract between God and man precedes it. For others it is a basic social contract only epistemologically because it is the best way to approximate what an ideal observer would approve or what reason would require. An ethic rooted in a social contract is, with these emendations, not at odds with the view that the moral order can be discovered. Hobbes and Locke may not have been able to reconcile natural law theory with their contract theory, but modern man certainly can.

Moreover, the model of contractors trying to discover the moral order is not very different from the one where contractors create or invent the moral framework. Both approaches require acknowledgment of man's real, finite limits and of an impartial point of view. They also include full and equal consideration of everybody's interests.

In the case of the moral-framework creators, real people come together with the task of inventing the basic principles constitutive of their society. They will be successful to the extent that they respect each person's liberty and treat everybody's interests equally. Fallible humans, they attempt to mimic a hypothetical contract that would have been drawn by those who could meet completely the conditions of the moral point of view. In the other case, real people come together because they have the task of discovering the basic principles constitutive of their society. They will be successful to the extent that they take an impartial point of view, becoming an approximation of the ideal observer or the ideal rational agent. Also fallible humans, they attempt to mimic a hypothetical contract that would be drawn by those who can completely meet the imposed conditions.

Is there any reason why real people coming together to establish or reaffirm the most fundamental principles and practices of their society should disagree if they are working from these various perspectives? There are at least two quite different reasons why people seeking the moral framework use the heuristic device of thinking of themselves as impartial contractors. For one group it is a very sophisticated technique based on enlightened self-interest. For the other, it is the best epistemological tool it has for discovering the moral order. For the former group the principles are agreed to because they reflect self-interest; for the latter it does not make much sense to ask why they are agreed to, they simply are. (Reason dictates so, or the moral sense perceives them so. To ask why people should agree to the basic moral framework makes no more sense than to ask why objects should act according to the laws of gravity or why two plus two should equal four. It is simply the way of the universe, according to the combined wisdom of our best powers of perception and/or reason.)

There is, thus, a moral community constituted symbolically by the metaphor of the contract or covenant. There is a convergence between the vision of people coming together to discover a preexisting moral order—an order that takes equally into account the welfare of all—and the vision of people coming together to invent a moral order that as well takes equally into account the welfare of all. The members of the moral community thus generated are bound together by bonds of mutual loyalty and trust. There is a fundamental equality and reciprocity in the relationship, something missing in the philanthropic condescension of professional code ethics.

Some may want to insist that the proper term for the relationship described should be covenant rather than contract. William May[25] and Roger Masters,[26] for example, challenge the term *contract* as too legalistic sounding and/or too individualistic in its implications. There is some risk that it can be misunderstood as having those implications. Nevertheless, I prefer to recognize *covenant* as a kind of contractual relationship, with special emphasis on the morally binding communal qualities of mutual loyalty and reciprocity that are essential to all contractual relationships. Our normal usage reveals a linguistic confusion of the two terms. We speak of the marriage "contract," wanting to retain the moral elements of trust and loyalty, and we speak of restrictive real-estate "covenants" in a highly legalistic way. I want to hold on to this tension, affirming that the basic social contract or covenant expresses a moral community bound together in reciprocal pledges of trust and loyalty, but at the same time recognizing that the moral relationship affirmed by the contract will sometimes have more public, more formal, more legal ramifications. This is especially true in a complex moral community, including the communities of marriage and of lay-professional relationships. If one considers contract, then, as an epistemological device, the traditional criticisms of social contract theory, such as those offered by May and Masters, seem not to be decisive. I shall thus continue to refer to that basic social relationship which underlies a moral community and articulates its principles as either a contract or a covenant.

We are working gradually toward the solution of Dr. Moore's problem. We have the source of a framework within which we can begin to determine whether society should be structured with practices and principles that induce a psychotherapist to disclose a patient's confidence under certain circumstances. Before we have an answer, however, we shall need to know what the basic content of the social contract is; that is, we need to know substantively what the basic principles and practices for the society ought to be.

This is not to say that those basic principles, if known, could tell us for certain what Dr. Moore should do; basic principles are very general. We may need to develop further rules, guidelines, or rights claims that specify how to move from the most general principles to the specific case. We may also need to know whether there are special role-specific duties that might lead to a different obligation regarding confidentiality for a health professional or a psychotherapist than for citizens not in those roles.

It seems clear that both the articulation of the moral rules and the spelling out of role-specific duties for professionals will have to be derived from the basic social contract. In part III of this volume the possible content of a basic social contract and the moral rules that follow from it will be outlined. Before that, however, we need to say a word about how a special set of role-specific duties for professionals could be derived from the basic social contract.

THE CONTRACT BETWEEN SOCIETY AND A PROFESSION

In Dr. Moore's case we are not so much interested in the general question of whether a person outside a professional relationship should disclose potentially lifesaving confidential information as in the more specific question of whether a person in the role of a health professional should disclose the confidence. For this particular medical ethical problem, we shall have to understand how health professionals might have special obligations and privileges not applicable to other members of the society.

There are, of course, other roles in society that require specific duties, but in all three of the cases we have presented thus far—that of the physician asked for information on killing, that of a professional association's right to limit advertising, and that of a psychotherapist's dilemma on disclosure of useful information—the problems concern the special duties of medical professionals. Likewise, lay people, when interacting with professionals, have special, role-specific duties that do not apply when they interact with nonprofessionals. These might include not only special duties of keeping appointments and paying bills, but others, such as disclosure of one's personal life situation or plans, that are not normally disclosed socially. The patient's special duties often relate to reporting symptoms honestly.

I have already conceded that there may be such role-specific duties, but I have argued that they cannot exist simply because a profession itself imposes them or alleges it alone possesses the ability to know what is ethical for professionals or patients. If the possibility, indeed the necessity, exists then that in certain circumstances professionals and patients will have obligations not shared by those in other roles, where can such duties come from? If they are moral duties, as we have developed that term, they must derive at least indirectly from the basic social contract.

In ancient Greece, healers were not organized into a profession in the sense that we understand the term; anyone could set out to practice the healing arts.[27] There was no system of licensure, no single kind of healer with a monopoly on the practice of medicine, and no single school of thought so dominant as to separate orthodox practitioner from heterodox or reputable healer from charlatan.[28] Practitioners took on patients at their own discretion and had no special duties to treat. As Darrel Amundsen summarizes, "Bound by no duty to a licensing authority or professional organizations, the physician exercised his art

127

at his own pleasure. He sold his services at his own discretion to those who asked and paid for treatment.[29] The lay population of that period faced substantial uncertainty about the knowledge, ability, style, and habits of the usually itinerant physician-entrepreneur. Only through knowledge of a practitioner's association with a cult or ideology, such as the Hippocratic, could a potential patient garner some sense of the physician's commitments. There was no special ethic for the practitioner as a member of a specially identified professional group. He was subject to the same norms, religious injunctions, laws, and political forces of the society applicable to all citizens. Private agreements could be made with those willing to pay for the healer's services. A quasi-contractual arrangement was made within the context of the basic social framework. To be sure, the basic social framework was not always thought of in the contractarian terms, as it was in certain religious communities. However, there was a basic social structure, one comparable to what we can understand now as having been invented or discovered in the basic social contract.

In the early Middle Ages, the pattern had not changed appreciably. It gradually became apparent, however, to practitioner and patient alike, that it would be useful to regulate in some way the practitioner's behavior and to specify what the lay person could expect. Visigothic law, promulgated in the sixth and seventh centuries, includes several provisions governing physician behavior.[30] According to one law, the contractual understanding between physician and patient had to be drawn up in writing before treatment could begin. Another law specified that if the treatment were rendered under contract and the patient died, the physician lost his fee. (That same law, in turn, protected the practitioner from suit.) If a physician debilitated a free man by phlebotomy (bloodletting), he had to pay a substantial fine. If the patient died during the process, "the physician must immediately be handed over to the relatives of the patient so that they would have the power to do with him whatever they wish."[31] If a slave was debilitated or killed by phlebotomy, the physician had to replace him with one of equal value. Thus begins the structuring of the relationship between medical professionals and lay people.

The emergence of craft guilds added structure to the professional role. In the eleventh and twelfth centuries, groups of practitioners banded together. Surgeons, apothecaries, and physicians organized into worker associations. They attempted to control standards of training and education, enforce high standards of quality, and assure conformity to a minimal level of etiquette.[32] They could privately limit membership in their guilds as well as set working laws, wages, and prices.[33] The physicians, in contrast to the surgeons and apothecaries, saw their guild structures evolve into corporate associations of students and teachers, and finally into universities.[34] The responsibility for regulation of entry into the professional group was taken on by the universities and medical faculties,[35] (hence the term *doctor*, which means teacher).[36]

During the eleventh and twelfth centuries, the guilds were still private associations without public recognition, legal privileges and responsibilities, or monopoly on the practice of the craft—all characteristics that would soon come and add appreciably to practitioners' status and fortune. It became apparent that the public had a great deal to gain by having a voice in determining the physician's terms of practice and responsibilities; they also had a lot to offer: the right of monopoly practice. By the late Middle Ages, public recognition of the guilds in exchange for a role in setting the terms of professional practice emerged. Thus, a second basic contract, one between the public as a whole (or agents for the public) and the profession as a group, could be said to have been initiated. A public bestowal of a license on the professional is a visible sign of the contractual bond between the society and the professional. Both public and profession gain greatly by the contract of licensure.[37]

In 1140, the Norman king, Roger II, initiated a state examination in Sicily for those who wanted to practice medicine. His order proclaimed the public interest in the practice of medicine:

> Who, from now on wishes to practice medicine, has to present himself before our officials and examiners, in order to pass their judgment. Should he be bold enough to disregard this, he will be punished by imprisonment and confiscation of his entire property. In this way we are taking care that our subjects are not endangered by the inexperience of the physicians.[38]

In the fourth decade of the thirteenth century, Emperor Frederick II of the Holy Roman Empire published regulations for physicians based on the old Norman codes.[39] His code gave a monopoly in the practice of medicine to those who passed exams and were licensed. The understanding between the government and the profession was that a public exam would be given and a certificate issued "not only by the professor of medicine, but also by one of our civil officials, which declares his [the physician's] trustworthiness and sufficient knowledge."[40] In exchange for the license, stiff requirements specified by the government had to be met. A detailed course of study was outlined (nine years, including the study of grammar and rhetoric, theology, and music). The physician had to take an oath of loyalty, not to the profession, but to the state, indicating that he would faithfully fulfill all the requirements of the law. He had to agree to report any apothecary selling drugs of less than normal strength (a precedent that will be important in our discussion of Dr. Moore's duty to break confidence). He also had to agree to advise the poor without asking for compensation. In addition, detailed fee schedules were included. Violations were punishable by the "confiscation of their movable goods."

In short, new privileges and duties were generated for the profession by agreement or contract in exchange for a commitment by physicians to assure adequate standards and to abide by the terms of practice spelled out. Similar legislation was adopted in Spain in 1283 and in Germany in 1347.[41] While a real monopoly in the practice of medicine probably did not emerge until the nineteenth century, we can see that the structure of an understanding between the profession and the society, with each gaining something in exchange for taking on certain obligations, had its origins much earlier.

This model of generating a special set of obligations for the members of a profession is radically different from the mere internal professional generation of a code. Although the ethical content of the licensure law under Frederick II was minimal, it is quite reasonable to see that role-specific duties for health professionals (or other professionals) could be grounded in this second level of social contract. Under this model the basic norms of a society are those that would be invented or discovered by people coming together to form a society from the moral point of view, that is, assuming that each person's welfare is taken fully into account. Within that framework, the members of society might determine that special roles such as physician or patient should carry with them special rights and responsibilities. Some of those roles— what the sociologist calls achieved roles—one can choose to enter. Those who do can enhance their status from time to time by making a contract or covenant as a group with the rest of society. In that second contract or covenant the special norms for the role can be identified and made explicit. (Whether they are invented or discovered at this point is once again contingent upon one's views on the complex theoretical questions we have already discussed.)

The second contract will be generated within the context of the more basic social contract. Therefore, it will be limited by the principles of that contract. The basic social contract will tell us what the fundamental ethical principles for the society are: those that would be agreed to if the contractors treated the interests of all as equal; if, in Rawls's term, they assumed the veil of ignorance. Since real people cannot fully assume this ideal status, the contract is hypothetical. Real contractors must attempt to approximate this moral point of view in order to invent or discover the basic principles.

In the same fashion, if members of a society (including professionals) want to determine the special duties of those in a specific role, such as nurses, pharmacists, physicians, or patients, the same tension between an ideal vantage point and man's limited reality would be apparent. The ethically appropriate special duties are those that would be agreed to by ideal, disinterested observers taking the moral point of view. In the real, finite world, the best we can do is approximate that hypothetical contractual position. The actual contract between the profession and society, therefore, to the extent it attempts to articulate a morality for the professional and lay roles, will, at best, approximate the ideal. Still, the actual contract can attempt to formulate an understanding of the role-specific duties within the framework of the basic social contract.

The relationship will be a complex one, however. For example, if it turns out that one of the principles of the basic social covenant is a principle of equity establishing what is a fair distribution of resources in, say, health planning, then any social contract between a profession and a society would have to be in accord with that principle of equity. Exactly how that requirement is met, however, is open to further discussion between the society and the profession. It might turn out that representatives of the profession and the public agree that individual practitioners, in the normal course of their day-to-day practice of medicine, should not be responsible for equitable allocation of health resources. Perhaps the profession as a whole would be given that responsibility, with society exerting its continuing influence by specifying what kinds of physicians be licensed and where those physicians may practice. The result would be a special exemption for the individual practitioner from the general duty of equity because society has determined that that duty can be met more effectively at a broader level. Both sides gain as well because the individual practitioner in the context of his patient-physician relationships is unburdened of the worry that someone else somewhere in the world may have a claim of equity on his services.

This second contract, the one between the profession and society, may provide a basis for resolving Dr. Moore's problem about whether to disclose his knowledge of Prosenjit Poddar's intent to the Tarasoff family. There are, in this situation, good reasons why society might want to have the confidences broken. It might, therefore, agree to a general duty to warn. There are also good reasons why a society might in general want to seal confidences between people, and particularly good reasons why it might want people in certain roles to keep confidence.

The lawyer, for example, might further a system of justice in the long run by keeping confidence rather than disclosing his client's guilt. Society tends to believe that, within limits, defense attorneys should have that "privilege," and it grants such an exemption in its contract with the legal profession. In fact, nondisclosure is a duty, even though society could conceivably gain in the short run from the disclosure.

Likewise, society might plausibly see that health professionals, particularly psychotherapists, could contribute most, on balance, if they were under a special obligation to keep confidences. Such an exemption, for example, might encourage a dangerous patient to remain in therapy, thus minimizing the long-term risk to others. Society might establish a special set of duties and exemptions for psychotherapists in the area of confidentiality. On the other hand, society would almost certainly want to place some limits on the principle of confidentiality. If Dr. Moore faced a patient carrying several loaded revolvers and confessing to a plan to immediately murder a large number of people, it seems likely that many members of the society would draw the line—in a case like this, they would conclude, there is a limit to that special exemption from the duty to warn. (In fact, there may be a more stringent duty in this case to make the risk known because a trained professional might be in a better position to evaluate the individual's real intentions.) Exactly where the limits of the exemption come and when the special duties begin is probably arbitrary. Society and the profession may both have views on exactly where these lines should be drawn; agreement by all that a clear line should be drawn at this point is probably more important than that it be drawn at any one precise spot.

It should now be clear why a professional group's unilateral declarations on Dr. Moore's duty of confidentiality should not be definitive in deciding what his moral (or legal) duty is. The members of society have a legitimate stake in articulating both the role-specific duties of the health care professional and the reciprocal duties of the patient. They will (or they should) incorporate those duties into the contract made with the professional at the time of licensure. That contract, in turn, should reflect as accurately as possible the one that would be agreed to by our ideal, hypothetical contractors. The health professions (or any other profession) should participate in the decision, setting out the content of this second contract, but should not unilaterally set the terms. In the end, society will outline its terms for granting the privileges of licensure. If the members of the profession (and new members coming up for licensure) are so offended morally (or any other way) by the terms, they can refuse to complete the agreement. If necessary, society will reformulate its understanding of the character of both the professional and the lay roles, taking into account the profession's own understanding of those roles until such time as there is an adequate meeting of the minds.

If the morality of a professional role is linked to this second social contract (which itself is linked to the rights and responsibilities that society grants to the professional along with licensure), then one major problem confronts us. Are the terms of the second contract spelled out once and for all at the time of licensure? If so, our understanding of the professional's moral obligation is fixed in perpetuity at the time he or she is licensed. There is then no room for rethinking the content of the unique moral obligations of the professional, no room for society to readjust its expectations of the professional, and no chance of the professional making a case for reformulation. In short, there is no chance to bring the real second contact into line with what the hypothetical ideal contractors would promise. It thus seems likely that both sides would want the right to renegotiate from time to time, to make more refined attempts at summarizing what the ideal moral relationship is.

One way to adjust our social understanding of the professional's moral obligation may be through reformulation at the time new people enter the professional role. As with the traditional Hippocratic physician, young medical students will be presented (at least figuratively) the moral framework of their anticipated new role, be socialized into that framework, and either accept or reject the moral stipulations accompanying it. This means that if society develops a new understanding of what it thinks ought to be the moral conditions, the role-specific duties, and the practice of a profession, such a shift would gradually be introduced so that over a generation a new understanding of the morality of the role would be established.

An alternative is to place limits on the length of time of licensure. Renewed negotiation could take place, every five years. At that time, if society wanted to change its understanding of the conditions under which confidences had to be disclosed, it could do so at this periodic renegotiation. The profession also would have a chance to articulate its understanding of the duty of the professional and a new bargain would be struck. Insofar as this is moral bargaining, the moral point of view would be taken. All contractors would ask what the role-specific duties should be for, say, psychotherapists; for example, they would try to imagine that they did not know whether they were to be therapists, future patients with homicidal tendencies, future lovers of mentally deranged patients with homicidal tendencies, or merely bystanders.

This approach has the added advantage of allowing reformulation of the lay person's role-specific duties in relationships with a professional. Periodically, we as a society might become convinced that we can articulate a better approximation of the ideal social contract between the profession and the society, specifying more appropriately the moral structure of both lay and professional roles.

We still have not really addressed what the content of the professional's duty should be when faced with the question of keeping confidences or any other problem. We now have a framework, however, for understanding how the question can be asked. The framework is in principle accessible to all and is perceived by all as morally legitimate.

THE CONTRACT BETWEEN PROFESSIONALS AND PATIENTS

At this point we have a framework of a basic social contract by which we can understand what it means to affirm a basic set of ethical principles. Within that basic social contract we also have a framework for generating a set of role-specific duties regarding relations between professionals and lay people via the mechanism of a second social contract. The result will be a general moral framework for the society and a more narrowly formulated moral framework for lay and professional roles.

In a liberal society, these two contracts will not fix all the dimensions of a social choice. There will be points on which the original social contractors would be indifferent; these would be left as matters of taste or preference or personal beliefs and values. Likewise, it can be assumed that lay and professional options for action will not be rigidly determined by the second contract. Professional and lay person will retain some discretion for acting according to his or her personal beliefs and values. Those decisions will have to be in accord with the two contracts, but substantial latitude will remain—for example, to practice surgery or psychiatry, to opt for high risk–high gain options or low risk–low gain ones, to treat aggressively or conservatively, to emphasize prevention or therapy, and so forth.

At the same time, patients in interactions with the professional will have a range of views about these same variables. Some of the variables may be universally recognized as matters of life-style preference or taste. Others may possibly be perceived as moral matters.

It is at first puzzling to understand how matters that are moral could stand outside the moral principles growing out of the basic social contract and the second contract. Several reasons can be offered. First, some questions may not be considered by all to be matters of morality. Card playing, contraception, and the use of narcotics for pain control are all ambiguously regarded issues. Some see them as issues of morality, others as mere matters of prudence or preference.

Second, some of the residuum may actually include matters of morality—those that would be resolved by the principles agreed upon by social contractors taking the moral point of view. But it is possible that one of the principles would itself be a principle of liberty, permitting individual discretion in interpreting the ethical principles for action and even permitting limited departures from what is moral in the name of individual choice. At the very least, the principle of liberty is likely to leave room for individual discretion in understanding how the basic principles apply to the individual case.

From these sources it is quite possible that some choices within a social contract framework, even moral ones, will remain for individual practitioners and individual lay people. Both practitioner and lay person should have the right to make such choices based on their own beliefs and values as well as their understanding of the implications of the social contract for specific medical ethical problems. If lay persons are given complete authority for specifying the framework of the lay–professional relationship (within the bounds of the first two contracts), the professional loses all sense of being an autonomous agent with the right to make moral and other value choices. If, on the other hand, the professional is given complete authority to specify the terms of the relationship, the lay person is similarly disenfranchised and dehumanized. The solution seems to be that a third contract or covenant be negotiated between the professional and the lay person. (Here and elsewhere I use these terms to refer either to individuals or to groups. The professional may be a professional team: a group practice with physicians, nurses, social workers, and other health professionals or a Health Maintenance Organization. The lay person may be a couple, a family, or even a whole community.[42])

This contract or covenant between the professional and the lay person would fill in the gaps—it would stipulate the belief system, the residuum of moral values, the specific understanding of how basic ethical principles apply to specific problems, and lifestyle preferences that will constitute the basis of the specific relationship. For example, some professional–lay relationships might be established with the agreement that certain kinds of treatment for the terminally ill are not appropriate. The more basic social contract and the secondary professional contract probably would establish certain broad rights to have or refuse treatment. They can never, however, specify in any detail what the trusting, harmonious relationship will be at the individual level. If professional and lay persons can agree ahead of time on some of the constitutive elements of that relationship, neither will be forced into the intolerable situation of having to choose between violating one's conscience and violating the conscience of the other party.

Probably the basic social contract and the contract between the professional and society also will specify some broad right for patients to have access to certain kinds of information. State laws and court cases are currently clarifying that right in law. It seems reasonable to believe, however, that all professionals and lay persons will not reach exactly the same conclusion on precisely what information should be transmitted or how it should be done. Within the limit of the first two contracts, individual professionals and lay persons should develop a clear understanding of this right of access in their particular relationship. Will it include a right to the actual documents or only the information in them? Will it include psychological information or only organic medical information? Will it cover information that physicians sincerely believe will not be in the patient's interest to know? Some of these questions will probably be answered in the first two contracts, but a range of discretion is likely to remain. That should be specified in the third contract, the contract between the professional and the lay person, within the bounds of the earlier, broader contracts.

Medical institutions have begun to articulate a moral identity—a set of beliefs and values—that can be the professional starting point for this third social contract. The clearest present-day example is the hospice, where a philosophical stance about important matters of belief and world view is articulated more or less explicitly. Lay people know (or should know) when they choose to enter a relationship in such an institution that certain attitudes prevail about aggressive intervention and so-called "extraordinary" measures.

Likewise, lay people have begun to cluster in groups around the sets of values and beliefs that they consider crucial, that they want to incorporate into their lay-professional relationships. We see this happening in feminist health collectives as well as in certain religious groups.

It would seem wise for small "sectarian" groups sharing a common ideology of health care to come together. They could include both lay people and professionals holding a common moral, philosophical, theological, or ideological framework. Christian Science, Jehovah's Witnesses, Seventh Day Adventists, holistic health centers, and Oral Roberts's medical complex in Tulsa are the ideal models of this, even if they have not chosen the right system of beliefs and values. Lay people and practitioners in such a community would share a common framework. They might share a common story, history, or world view—an option that Stanley Hauerwas recently suggested ought to be the basis for articulating opposition to abortion.[43] No one then would be foolish enough to select a health professional or accept a patient without a common understanding of beliefs and values adequate to the circumstances. A health collective could not organize around a commitment to extensive use of heroin; to active, intentional mercy killing; or to extend parents and physicians the right to work together to withhold safe, simple, and sure treatments from children even if they were convinced these were important. They could, however, organize around commitments that are within the constraints of the first two contracts.

CONCLUSION

The result, finally, is what I have called a triple-contract theory of medical ethics. The first contract specifies the basic content of an ethical system. It is what contractors taking the moral point of view (the outlook that other people's welfare is considered on the same scale as one's own) would invent or discover or have revealed to them as the basic ethical principles for society. Real humans, being finite, can only approximate this hypothetical condition, but it is the best system we have for knowing the basic content of an ethical system. It is a system usable by those who are convinced that morality is objective and absolute (whether they derive their ethical theory from a theological system, attempt to determine the ethical principles by use of reason, or believe they can use the moral sentiments to discover them). It is also usable by those who are convinced that morality is subjective. (They would see real people coming together assuming the moral point of view for more practical purposes of trying to reach an agreement on a system that would lead to joint harmonious survival.) I find it hard to discover what differences in principle would result, what differences in content of the social contract could be expected from these approaches that appear to be so different. In either case, a set of basic principles for organizing society will emerge. The inventors should have no problem with those who approach morality believing they are pursuing something that is objective. If anything, it will give their fellow contractors an added incentive to be fair in assuming the moral point of view. On the other hand, the discoverers should not be overly troubled by those among their fellows who think they are only inventing an ethic. Assuming the inventors take the moral point of view, they should be in roughly the same position as those who set out to discover a morality. From the point of view of those who believe ethical principles are there for humans to discover or have revealed to them—for those who believe they are in the created order, in nature, in reason, or in the empirical reality—it should not be surprising if the inventors come up with the set of principles that the discoverers believe actually exists. They might feel sorry for the inventors, believing they do not understand the true basis of the apparently subjective conclusions. If the inventors think they have created the basic principles, it may tell on their character; it may lead to a false sense of pride and anthropocentrism, but it should not affect the content. If those principles turn out to be there for the discovering, however, it would not be surprising if the inventors find them or at least some approximation of them. From either approach, a set of principles will be articulated that will constitute the foundation for a morality.

Once that basic social contract articulates these fundamental principles, a second contract, one between the society and a profession, can then spell out (again from the moral point of view) the special role-specific duties regarding interactions between lay people and professionals. The only limit of that second contract will be that as a whole it cannot contravene the morality of the prior, more basic, social contract.

Finally, within the context of these two contracts, individual professionls and lay persons (or the groups that function as individual units) have the opportunity to spell out further the terms, moral and otherwise, of their relationship. The result is a triple-contract theory of medical ethics, one that in principle is accessible to all and applicable to all. We are left only with the problem of what the content of these various contracts will be, and to that question we now turn.

PART III

The Principles of Medical Ethics

Chapter 6

Why Not Always Benefit the Patient: Personal and Social Consequences

---

Case 4 *Breaking Confidentiality to Try to Benefit a Patient*

Miss X, at sixteen years old, was described in the official record of her case as a highly intelligent, attractive, and mature young woman. When she reached the decision to begin using birth control, she apparently realized that her long-term family physician, Dr. Robert John Denis Browne, would not look favorably on a request for contraceptives. He was 63 years old, had practiced in Miss X's community of Birmingham, England, for thirty years, and had provided medical care for her since her birth. She went, instead, to the Birmingham Brook Advisory Centre, where an oral contraceptive was prescribed for her. To permit monitoring of possible side effects and to avoid prescribing contraindicated medication, the clinic routinely informed each patient's family physician of its service, unless specifically forbidden by the patient to do so. Miss X, perhaps without thinking about potential implications, agreed to let her physician be informed.

141

Dr. Browne, upon receiving the unsolicited medical information, was faced with a dilemma. He was worried about his young patient using the contraceptive pill without her physician's prior knowledge or consultation.

He had two concerns: first, the physical hazards of the pill, and second, the "moral and psychological hazards"—the potential sense of guilt that could harm her emotionally. He struggled with the problem, discussing it with his colleagues without revealing his patient's identity. He finally felt compelled to conclude that it was in Miss X's best interests to inform her parents. He viewed them as sympathetic and kindly and in the best position to counsel her with tact and care. He considered asking Miss X first for permission to discuss the matter with her parents, but was afraid of arousing their suspicion. He felt finally that it was his obligation to do what he judged to be in her best interests. Even if she had not given her permission, he apparently would still have felt that she would be best served by a disclosure to her parents. Happening to meet her father one day, he first asked if the girl were planning to marry. When the father responded that she had a steady boy friend, but was not contemplating marriage, Dr. Browne "thought hard" and then decided to disclose, "bearing in mind that girl's best interests, and solely for that reason."

The Birmingham Brook Advisory Centre brought a complaint of "serious professional misconduct" against Dr. Browne to the British General Medical Council, the body responsible for adjudication of such disputes. That Dr. Browne was highly regarded as a practitioner was not a matter of dispute. Nevertheless, the Centre's spokesperson charged that he had violated his professional obligation by disclosing information without permission of the patient.

In his defense, Dr. Browne turned to Dr. Walter Wolley, ex-chairman of the Central Ethical Committee of the British Medical Association. Dr. Wolley emphasized that in his view a third party, in this case the clinic, could not fetter the physician's right to use his own judgment.

The British Medical Association's Code of Ethics at the time (1971) said:

It is a practitioner's obligation to observe the rule of professional secrecy by refraining from disclosing voluntarily without the consent of the patient (save with statutory sanction) to any third party information which he has learnt in his professional relationship with the patient. The complications of modern life sometimes create difficulties for the doctor in the application of this principle, and on certain occasions it may be necessary to acquiesce in some modification. Always, however, the overriding considerations must be adoption of a line of conduct that will benefit the patient, or protect his interests.

It thus appears that Dr. Browne's behavior was in accord with the Medical Association's position. Dr. Browne's position was also supported by another practitioner, Dame Annis Gillie. In her view, professional secrecy exists for the interest of the patient. She believed that situations occur requiring disclosure in order to benefit the patient. Every case, she concluded, must be judged by the practitioner on its own merits.

Dr. Browne was viewed by all as a dedicated practitioner trying to serve the interests of his patients. He was acquitted on all counts of professional misconduct.[1]

For purposes of understanding medical ethical theory, this may be the most important case in twentieth-century medical ethics. It reveals some of the problems of reliance on a professionally generated code of ethics as a basis for resolving medical ethical disputes. Many argue that the British Medical Association's instruction on confidentiality at the time, no matter how clear, was simply wrong. In particular, many have held that in such cases the physician should try to get the consent of his patient to break the confidence but, if permission is not forthcoming, should respect the refusal. That, in fact, was the position adopted by the British Medical Association in 1971, soon after this case was resolved in Dr. Browne's favor.[2]

Why should a society by guided by the consensus of a professional group on establishing a principle of confidentiality? There are, after all, many professionally generated codes of ethics in other countries, and even within Britain at a later time, that have taken a different view. The American Medical Association, until 1980, also endorsed the breaking of confidence by a physician when it was necessary to protect the welfare of the patient. (In fact, the AMA's position also permitted the physician to break confidence if it was necessary to protect society, an exemption not found in the British version.) Still other codes, though, seem to give other answers. The Hippocratic Oath is ambiguous on the matter. It says, "Whatever, in connection with my professional practice, or not in connection with it, I see or hear, in the life of men, which ought not to be spoken abroad, I will not divulge, as reckoning that all such should be kept secret." That leaves open, of course, the decisive question of what ought to be spoken abroad. The Oath gives no direct answer but does tell us repeatedly that the physician should do what he thinks will benefit the patient, thus logically subordinating the duty of keeping confidence to the principle of patient benefit—as the British and American medical associations held. On the other hand, the World Medical Association, a confederation of national medical organizations, makes the physician pledge bluntly, "I will hold in confidence all that my patient confides in me," an apparently exceptionless requirement that would bind all practitioners in all circumstances. It would bind Dr. Moore in the Tarasoff case and others who could save countless lives by breaking confidence, as well as Dr. Browne in the contraception case.

If there is no agreement among professional codes about a principle as fundamental to medical ethics as that of confidentiality, then it is literally impossible to resolve disputes about problems like Dr. Browne's with a simplistic appeal to the codes. Even, if they did agree, however, it is not clear why Miss X, her parents, and the rest of society should be bound by the medical profession's consensus on a principle of confidentiality.

I have suggested that it is wrong in principle to rely on the majority view of a minority segment of the population as a way to resolve ethical disputes or to generate a set of principles for resolving them. Rather, reasonable people—lay people and professionals—should ask themselves what fundamental ethical principles they can discover (or invent, if necessary) to provide a basic moral structure for the society. Once those basic social principles are agreed upon, then lay people and professionals should ask themselves what they reasonably would want the principles governing the relationships between physicians and patients to be. Presumably this second set of principles would be subordinate to the first, or at least compatible with it. Thus, we should approach Dr. Browne's case not by looking to the British Medical Association's interpretation of the principle of confidentiality, but rather by asking what reasonable people would identify as the principle governing lay–professional relationships. This leads us to the decisive question: Would reasonable people agree to be governed by the Hippocratic principle, which says the physician's sole or primary duty is always to do what he or she believes to be in the interests of the patient?

From this point on, a normative theory of medical ethics will be more speculative. The structure that has been generated for creating the principles is such that there are no clear a priori ways of knowing what is ethical and there are no identifiable experts in providing the answers. No group in any profession can determine what it is that reasonable people would covenant together to establish as the principles of professional ethics. This, of course, goes for professional ethicists as well as professionals in any field. There is simply no evidence that any group (including ethicists) has expertise in estimating what reasonable people who take the moral point of view would conclude. The best we can do is try as a society to place ourselves in a position as close as possible to the ideal contractors and see what answers are forthcoming. Various individuals will offer firm positions and even back them up with reasons, but the ethically correct principles and the ethically correct answers to case problems based on those principles can be known with no more certainty than can other, nonmoral facts about the state of the world. All I shall be able to do from this point on is to offer my set of suggestions, as if I were at the table trying to take a moral point of view in negotiating a set of ethical principles for a society and a second set governing relationships between lay people and professionals. I shall try to give what I hope are persuasive reasons in support of my suggestions, but these would have to be tested by others who also are trying to develop a social contract for the two sets of principles. With that important qualifier, I believe it can be shown that establishing the Hippocratic principle as the fundamental principle for the physician-patient relationship would be irrational for people to covenant.

THE PRINCIPLE OF BENEFICENCE

If a principle of benefiting the patient according to the physician's ability and judgment is to be the product of the covenant between the profession and society, a connection must be found, at least in part, to a more fundamental notion of the duty to benefit. Reasonable people coming together to adopt a set of basic ethical principles for the structuring of their moral community might well agree to some form of what might be called the principle of beneficence. At the very least, people usually recognize that they have an interest in getting benefits for themselves, other things being equal. But we must remember that the contractors discovering or inventing the basic principles would be doing so from what we labeled "the moral point of view"; that is, one in which other people's interests are given the same weight as their own. They would be deciding under the hypothetical Rawlsian veil of ignorance, with no awareness of a social hierarchy or with the principle of reversibility applied. People might adopt this moral point of view for several reasons. They might do so out of a conviction that it was in their best interests to do so (perhaps because it is the only condition under which others will agree to bargain). They might be convinced that it is simply the nature of the human that people take the moral point of view, or feel they ought to take it, when discussing the basic moral principles. In either case, people would reasonably agree that some form of a principle of beneficience would tend to result in right action. Other things being equal, it is morally preferable to take a course of action that will produce more benefit than harm. In fact, among all courses, if other things are equal, one might be tempted to say—along with Bentham, Mill, and the utilitarians—that the society should adopt as its basic moral principle the one which states that the right course is that which will produce at least as much net benefit as alternative courses.

It turns out that there may be real problems with adopting that position or at least adopting it as the only basic normative ethical principle. It seems to require that for every choice in a human life, one is obliged to choose the one course that would maximize net aggregate total consequences. It is a principle that seems to require perfection in every moment in order for one to lead a moral life. But most people feel that they need not always conduct themselves in a way that will produce more good results on balance than other course. While producing good is often considered relevant to deciding what is morally required, there are times when doing what will produce the most good is supererogatory, that is, morally commendable but not necessarily morally required.

Employing the principle of beneficence as the sole principle for moral conduct would mean that no other characteristics of actions have any bearing on whether an action is right or wrong. Many hold, however, that there are other relevant characteristics. These may include whether promises have been kept, whether a person is being truthful, whether human lives are purposely taken, and whether the good consequences are distributed fairly.[3]

Later I shall explore the problems of an ethic that focuses exclusively on producing good consequences, and suggest why reasonable people might not opt for that principle alone. For now I shall allow the case against consequentialism and its principle of beneficience emerge as we explore the Hippocratic principle, which seems to be so closely related to it.

Even if one concludes that there are problems with the principle of beneficence as the foundation for a social system of morality, the principle of producing good results does seem relevant to moral judgment. Let us see how far it can take us in defending the Hippocratic principle as the appropriate choice of reasonable people coming together to agree on a guiding principle for the medical professional–patient relationship.

AGAINST THE DANGEROUS HIPPOCRATIC PRINCIPLE

When the Hippocratic author, together with the members of the British Medical Association and the American Medical Association, specified that physicians in a moral bind like that of Dr. Browne act to benefit their patient (even if it means violating a confidence), they must have been somewhat in tune with the principle of beneficence. They may have decided that as members of their group they had a right and a responsibility to invent a principle of conduct for their members, thus coming up with the Hippocratic formula. They may have decided that even though the principle comes from some source beyond their group, only its members have the skill or knowledge in the moral realm to articulate the principle. In any case, they opted for emphasizing only benefits and harms in establishing a basis for moral decision making in the treatment of patients. We have seen that this agreement among professionals is not a sufficient reason for the rest of society to accept a principle as the foundation of a contract between the profession and society. What if, however, someone proposed the Hippocratic principle at the time of contracting between two groups? Should the society accept it as the basic principle of medical ethics as it applies to the professional in relation to the patient?

If we are to understand why reasonable people would not accept the Hippocratic principle, we are going to have to analyze it in some detail. It will be found to have three essential characteristics: It is consequentialistic; it is paternalistic; it is individualistic.[4]

HIPPOCRATIC CONSEQUENTIALISM

First, the Hippocratic formula is consequentialistic: It focuses on outcomes. In that sense, it is related to the more general principle of beneficence in contrast to ethical positions rooted in notions of duties or rights that may exist independently of consequences. The Hippocratic Oath speaks of benefiting the sick and keeping them from harm, a formula which has a ring of utilitarianism about it. It is almost as if the Hippocratic author had been reading Bentham: To determine the right course, determine the one that on balance will produce the most util-

147

ity. To Bentham this meant producing benefit, advantage, pleasure, good, or happiness. For both Bentham and the Hippocratic author, utility alone determines what we ought to do. What could be controversial about such a platitude?

Dr. Browne's decision has been criticized first for the breadth of his vision when he calculated benefits and harm. He is blunt in admitting that he included not only the physical benefits and harms—the pharmacological dangers of the pill—but also the psychological and even moral dangers. But the Hippocratic formula does not say that the physician should do what he or she thinks is for the benefit of the physical health of his patient. Dr. Browne, like the Hippocratic author, had a more holistic perspective. In this they are contemporary to the point of being avant garde. Dr. Browne has in his frame of reference the total well-being of his patient. He conforms to the liberal interpretation of the World Health Organization when it defines *health* as a state of "complete physical, mental, and social well-being, and not merely the absence of disease or infirmity."[5] In fact, Dr. Browne goes even further by including moral well-being as well. Certainly if we are concerned about benefiting the whole person and not merely the body, then the moral and even the spiritual well-being cannot be summarily excluded. A Bentham or a Mill would have been puzzled by a moral principle affirming that benefit should be maximized while limiting consideration to only physical, or even psychological and physical, health benefits. The beauty of the utilitarian formula is that it reduces everything to one calculus. And if we want Dr. Browne to limit his attention to only physical well-being, then we must abandon the more general Hippocratic and utilitarian concern with net benefits over harm (regardless of the kind of benefit).

Limiting the principle to physical benefit would seriously compromise its power. No rational person would say that anyone—himself, lay people, or physicians—should ever act solely on the basis of physical health consequences. If physicians are to be limited to the realm of the physical (or even the physical and psychological), then almost never will they have enough information about the total benefits to a patient to make any kind of decision. We are left with a dilemma. If total benefits are the relevant consideration, then physicians seem to be in no position to assess them since they have no particular expertise in economic, spiritual, aesthetic, intellectual, or other nonmedical dimensions of benefit to the patient. Alternatively, if health benefits are the relevant concern, it is hard to see why decisions should be made on that basis alone, excluding all other dimensions of benefit and harm.

148

HIPPOCRATIC PATERNALISM

It is possible, of course, that physicians can in some cases really know what is "in the interest" of their patients, in the full sense of the term. Dr. Browne, for example, might have been correct in his assessment of the total consequences. In at least some cases, physicians are probably in a position to estimate benefits and harms correctly, perhaps even more accurately than the patient can. A young woman without the benefit of moral counsel from her parents and her physician might make a mistake. Many patients assessing what is in their interest may err. If we are willing to be consequentialistic in at least some cases, we might accept some version of the Hippocratic formula.

This raises a second problem with the formula, however. It is paternalistic. Some would respond to the possibility that the physician might really know what is in the patient's interest by saying that it is not altogether decisive. The Hippocratic ethic gives remarkable authority to the physician to use his judgment to decide what will be beneficial. The Oath says, "I will follow that system . . . which, *according to my ability and judgment, I consider* for the benefit of the sick." (Italics mine.) It is a bizarre ethic that bases correctness of moral action on what one happens to think is beneficial, without specifying rigorous criteria for testing the individual's intuitions of right and wrong, good and bad.

If one is going to focus on benefits and harms, several alternatives are available for deciding how to calculate the consequences. Consider the Hippocratic formula and five alternatives to it:

1. The physician should benefit the patient according to his ability and judgment (the Hippocratic formula).
2. The physician should benefit the patient according to the consensus of the medical profession.
3. The physician should benefit the patient according to the most objective judgment available.
4. The physician should benefit the patient according to the patient's own judgment.
5. The physician should benefit the patient according to the most objective judgment available unless the patient autonomously chooses some other course.
6. The physician should benefit the patient according to the most objective judgment available unless the patient autonomously chooses some other course, provided the physician's own conscience is not violated beyond limit.

Given these six options it seems that no rational person would choose the first. It permits physicians with bizarre and confused notions of benefit and harm to wreak havoc on unsuspecting patients. It would allow the deviant physician who really believed in the wonder-cure potential of laetrile to administer it to the cancer patient, without the patient's consent if necessary. It would permit a Dr. Jacobson to dispense amphetamines without restriction when he thinks patients need them to overcome depression or lethargy. It permits Dr. Browne to violate a confidence totally independent of an objective basis for believing that Miss X would benefit.

At the very least one would choose option two, the action based on the consensus of the medical profession. It would at least eliminate the bizarre or deviant subjective judgments physicians could make about benefits and harms. It is the "standard of the professional colleagues," which, until recently, had great support in the law. But this alternative is not all that helpful. At best it shifts the standard so that patients would be subject to the whims of a professional consensus rather than of individual practitioners. For both health and nonhealth benefits, the value constellation governing the professional group may not be the same as that of the lay population. For example, oncologists may tend to believe that cancer is an evil to be combated, making the pain and suffering of surgery, radiation, and even experimental toxic chemotherapy almost always worth the risk. Yet there must be something that led oncologists to their specialization, something that influences their judgment in specific cases. There is some evidence that they have views about cancer that differ from the rest of the population, that they think the struggle against cancer is particularly valuable. There is no rational reason why lay people should impose on themselves the particular and peculiar value constellation of a professional group, especially when others, including themselves, do not share that value constellation.

We might then turn to the third option, under which the physician views "the patient's interest" according to the most objective judgment available. That, at least, is what seems to be called for by the principle of beneficence. Exactly how that judgment would be made remains a serious problem. It would have to be further specified in the contract between the profession and society. In some cases the professional consensus may concur with what all agree is the best objective way of knowing what is in the patient's interest. If so, that becomes a test, but the principle remains more general. The quest is for the best objective test of the patient's best interest. Many people would probably conclude that best interest cannot necessarily be determined by the consensus of the profession. They will establish procedures for due process, require rules of evidence, and perhaps designate representatives of the society for the special tasks of assessing best interests. The most objective answer to the question of what is in someone's general best interest is unlikely to come from any group with a uniquely strong commitment to only one relatively small subcategory of total human benefits. It does not matter whether that category be the aesthetic, economic, spiritual, intellectual, legal, psychological, or physical.

This suggests, then, that the third option could work for rational people trying to formulate a principle for the physician–patient relationship based solely on the principle of beneficence. They might opt for the formula that tells the professional to assess patients' interests according to the best, most objective judgment available.

It is not at all clear, however, that rational persons would ultimately give such a mandate to a professional group or include such a notion in their contract. This forces us to consider one way in which people might want to move beyond a simple principle of beneficence. There may be good reason why rational members of the society would not always want professionals to do what even objectively is in the lay person's best interests. Later we shall see how even in the case of incompetents or infants parents may have limited authority to make judgments that diverge from the best ones available. For now, it is sufficient to ask whether rational people would want to consider the fourth option, the one instructing the physician to do what is in the interests of the patient according to the patient's own judgment.

It seems overwhelmingly clear that in at least some cases people want the freedom to act as they choose even if a particular action is not decisively shown to be in their best interest. Moreover, some people want the freedom to act even if there is no question that the action is against their best interest.

Society's best technique for judging what is "really" in the patient's interest often may produce an answer that is different from the patient's own answer. Many in our society believe that the principle of autonomy or self-determination should override the principle of beneficence in such a situation, at least in certain circumstances. If that is the case, the Hippocratic formula would have to be qualified further. It might read something like option four above: Benefit the patient according to the patient's own judgment.

That still is not quite satisfactory, however. Autonomous patients may sometimes prefer to act in such a way that they are not promoting their self-interest, even according to their own judgment. All altruistic actions, for example, are actions chosen on grounds other than self-interest and many are contrary to the individual's self-interest. Volunteering for research, donating a kidney, and sacrificing parental interests to provide medical care for one's children are all examples.

If we are going to incorporate the principle of autonomy as well as of beneficence into our basic social contract, then the second contract between the professions and the society might best be based on still another modification of the Hippocratic principle. Option five states: "The physician should benefit the patient according to the most objective judgment available unless the patient autonomously chooses some other course."

If, however, we discover that the principle of autonomy is an essential qualifier to the principle of beneficence, then we must recognize that the physician also has to retain autonomy. The representatives of the professional group at the contract bargaining table would certainly want to insist that the physician not be obligated to act in a way that egregiously violated his or her conscience. They might push for the sixth option, namely, option five with the added qualifier: "provided the physician's own conscience is not violated beyond limit." It may be necessary to place still other restraints on the principle, including requirements that the professional act in such a way that he or she keep promises made, tell the truth, avoid killing morally protected life, and distribute resources fairly. They may want to mandate that the requirements apply even if they do not promote the greatest benefit to the patient. These qualifiers will have to be explored when we discuss the principles of promise keeping, autonomy, honesty, avoiding killing, and justice in more detail in the chapters ahead. At this point, it is sufficient to point out that the Hippocratic formula is consequentialistic in a particular way. The first three of the six versions are all paternalistic. The first formula, the original Hippocratic ethic, betrays its paternalism by placing the physician in the central position to judge what is in the patient's best interest without requiring that it be the most reliable basis for judging benefit. The first variation moves toward correcting this, but still leaves open the question of whether the consensus of the profession is the best objective test of what will benefit the patient. The third option overcomes this problem (while begging the question of the appropriate test for "objective judgment"), but still remains paternalistic because it imposes an external judgment on the patient. It is this paternalism, as much as the breadth of Dr.

Browne's concept of benefit, that has lead to such controversy over his decision.

Some might argue that this reads too much into the Hippocratic position, that physicians really have not claimed that they should impose their own judgment on that of their patients. Yet the evidence is quite convincing that this is precisely what they have meant. The Hippocratic Oath itself has generated scholarly controversy over what is meant when the physician is asked to pledge that he will keep his patients "from harm and injustice." Ludwig Edelstein, the respected scholar of the Hippocratic tradition previously cited, deals with the question of who might cause the potential harms and injustices that the Oath's author had in mind. He named several candidates: the patient's friends, family members, the physician, and the patient himself. On the basis of careful textual and contextual analysis he concludes that the physician

> . . . promises to guard his patients against the evils which they may suffer through themselves. That men by nature are liable to inflict upon themselves injustice and mischief and that this tendency becomes apparent in all matters concerned with their regimen, this is indeed an axiom of Pythagorean dietetics.[6]

Dr. Browne then was standing in the center of a long and noble tradition. The principle of confidentiality of the British Medical Association that was then in effect did not emphasize the importance of the physician's own judgment. It simply instructed the physician to focus on the welfare of the patient. The testimony surrounding the case, however, suggests that the welfare of the patient was to be assessed in Hippocratic fashion, that is, according to the physician's judgment.

Thus we are left with a tension between the Hippocratic principle and what reason seems to dictate. I believe that reasonable people might advance at this point a revision of the principle for relations between professionals and lay people, namely the sixth option that reads: "The physician should benefit the patient according to the most objective judgment available unless the patient autonomously chooses some other course, provided the physician's own conscience is not violated beyond limit." Admittedly, this is more clumsy than the easier Hippocratic version and will require more specification: how the principle of autonomy of the patient should come into play and how the autonomy of the professional might permit his or her conscientious objection. Besides autonomy, other considerations not based on consequences may have to be taken into account and adjustments made.

153

There are other problems, however, which are suggested by the third characteristic of the Hippocratic principle: individualism.

HIPPOCRATIC INDIVIDUALISM

The Hippocratic principle deviates from what would seem to be the most straightforward implications of the principle of beneficence by giving priority to the medical professional's own subjective judgment of benefit rather than to the best and most objective estimate attainable. It also deviates in another important way. It limits the relevant consequences to the individual patient.

It is not clear that the Hippocratic corpus itself is individualistic. The Edelstein translation says that the physician's duty is to benefit "the sick," a translation made by Jones as well. Does this mean the Hippocratic physician was to benefit the sick patient with whom he was interacting or was he to benefit his sick patients as a group? Or did the physician's oath pledge him to benefit the sick in general, whether they were his patients or not? The Greek is consistently in the plural—the physician is to benefit sick people. The prescription in "The Epidemics" that the physician is to help, or at least do no harm,[7] does not restrict itself to helping one's own patient or even one's own patients. That it is in the context of a treatise on epidemics suggests that broader issues—we might call them public health questions—were at stake. The immediate context of the maxim is the "second constitution," a discussion of the problems of what is apparently a kind of malaria which was a major problem for Greece at that time.

Most striking is the fact that the tradition, even in the Hippocratic corpus, is remarkably silent on the question of whether the physician has duties to the sick of society or only to individual patients with whom the physician is engaged. The practice of medicine in classical Greece was not a profession in the sense we know it today. There was no equivalent of what we would consider to be a social contract between a professional group and the society at large. A notion of professional obligation was not to emerge until the days of the Middle Age medical guilds. There was no generalized sense of a duty to patients or to society beyond the private pledges made by individual physicians to individual patients or by physicians to one another in such forms as the Oath. There appears to have been widespread commitment beyond the individual patient, however. On the other hand, the fact that neither scholars of the classical period nor modern scholars have concerned themselves with questions of the physician's duty to the society as a whole is at least suggestive of the charge that the Hippocratic focus was quite individualistic. That characteristic may account for the sorry state of the health-care delivery system in the modern West, particularly in those countries where medical policy and practice is reserved primarily to those in the profession.

Whether or not the classical Hippocratic physician was committed only to the interests and welfare of the patient with whom he was interacting, this individualism has, at least until recently, become dominant in the mainstream of modern Hippocratic ethics. The physician has been committed with zeal to the "ideal" of excluding the interests of the state, of the patient's family (who may have competing interests), and of any other societal segment that might be perceived as diverting the physician's attention from what the physician takes to be the welfare of the patient.

Physicians in the Hippocratic tradition who have "read Bentham" seem to have carefully considered and then rejected his seventh factor in the calculation of total utility. After Bentham explains how one calculates the net benefits for each person, he then claims that a final step is necessary: "Sum up the numbers expressive of the degrees of good tendency, which the act has, with respect to each individual. . . ." That is to say, Bentham insists upon maximizing total aggregate utility. His goal is the proliferation of good no matter to whom that good accrues. The Hippocratic physician is thus a 'modified utilitarian', one who limits the relevant good to the individual immediately under consideration. This is no small deviation from classical utilitarianism and creates no mean dilemma in the moral decision-making process.

Perhaps the relation between the general principle of beneficence and the Hippocratic version is one in which there is a subtle working out of the general principle to apply to the special role of the health professional. Perhaps reasonable people at the time of contracting with the profession might consider it wise to generate a special role-specific duty for professionals that will, in the end, maximize good consequences. They might realize that if physicians are permitted to abandon their patients in order to pursue what appears to be a greater good at the moment, more total harm than good will be done in the end. Thus, rational members of the society might agree that one in the role of physician should be permitted to forget about the larger, more social consequences and act *as if* the benefit to the immediate patient were the only concern. They might believe that if those in the role of physician did that, in the end the greater good would be served. An invisible hand with genetic links to Adam Smith's would see to it that pursuing the individual patient's good ended up also serving the good of society overall.

There are problems with that defense, however. First, most physicians seem not to favor the individualism of the Hippocratic formula (or some variant of it) only because it seems a clever way of serving the general welfare. They seem to believe that they have a unique obligation to their individual patients, independent of the aggregate benefits, which moves them to make decisions to an end beyond that of producing the best aggregate consequences. In this sense, they are really not utilitarians after all. Moreover, even if physicians accepted the notion of compatibility of the Hippocratic principle with the general principle of beneficence, using this Adam Smith-like technique, there is good reason to believe that the defense does not work; that is, there are some cases, perhaps rare, in which the aggregate could be served if the physician were not limited to considering patient welfare alone.

Several simple case problems illustrate the difficulty. A physician in private practice conducting a physical examination on an apparently well patient is interrupted by someone who bursts into his office saying that an auto accident victim is lying on the street bleeding profusely. Should the physician temporarily abandon his patient in order to benefit someone else who is not his patient? The answer given by the Hippocratic principle is striking. He must do what he thinks will benefit his patient; in other words, in this instance, do not abandon the person in the office. The results are still striking if we use one of the modified forms of the principle. Either the physician should do what he thinks will benefit his patient (the original form) or he should benefit his patient according to the best objective judgment unless the autonomous patient chooses some other course and then only if the physician's own personal conscience is not violated beyond limit. Thus, the physician would be justified in going to the aid of the accident victim only if permitted to do so by the patient in his office. Yet it seems that morality requires something else. There has to be some reason why society might want a professional physician ethics that would justify or even require the physician to respond to the accident victim if it meant only briefly abandoning a healthy patient. Perhaps for other reasons we would say that the physician should try to get the approval of the patient in his office for the temporary abandonment (and maybe add that he should not go if he cannot get it), but certainly we must consider the welfare of the nonpatient to be morally relevant. Were the physician to stay with his patient, even because of the patient's insistence, we would not consider the outcome perfectly moral. It seems as if the social contract between society and the profession should include some dimension of benefit to those other than the patient.

Some medical professionals now routinely conduct research in addition to engaging in patient care. Some of that research involves the use of procedures not undertaken primarily for the benefit of the patient. Under the original Hippocratic formula, all such research is immoral. The World Medical Association, in 1949, adopted a code that follows the Hippocratic tradition in affirming that, "under no circumstances is a doctor permitted to do anything that would weaken the physical or mental resistance of a human being except from strictly therapeutic or prophylactic indications imposed in the interests of his patient." Six years later this same group accepted the moral licitness of what it called "non-beneficial research" on healthy subjects although that, by definition, violates the earlier, more traditional moral principle. The modification of the Hippocratic formula that permits doing something contrary to the patient's interest, if the autonomous patient consents, corrects some of the problem, but not all of it. If that were the only basis for justifying research on human subjects, then research could never be done on nonautonomous subjects (children, for example). Also, the physician would be unable to distinguish morally between research that would expose the consenting subject to harm in order to attempt to answer a question vitally important to society and research exposing him to equal harm but with only trivial benefits to society. Yet we know that a researcher is more justified in engaging in the first type of research than in the second. If research interventions on human beings are to be morally acceptable, the Hippocratic formula will have to be modified still further so that benefits to others in the society are taken into account.

The same problem emerges in public health. If the physician is morally bound to serve the individual isolated patient, then it is unacceptable for a physician to take actions designed to protect the health of the community as a whole, especially if those actions are not for the benefit of some specific individuals. Yet many public health decisions require certain compromises with the liberty and even the welfare of individuals in order to serve the common welfare of the public.

Finally, consider the problem of health cost containment. The public is currently pressing the medical profession to reduce the costs of medical procedures where possible. Reduction can come in two ways. First, some procedures may be doing the patient no good at all, so no rational reason exists for continuing them once their uselessness has been established. That will eliminate some costs, but probably not enough to bring them down to an acceptable level. The interesting case is the one where a patient wants a very costly medical procedure that the best objective judgment deems only marginally beneficial to the patient. An example of the kind of marginal benefit I have in mind is an expensive diagnostic test with a one-in-a-thousand chance of discovering something that would extend an elderly cancer patient's life, and then only by a matter of weeks. According to the Hippocratic principle, it would be immoral for a physician to take into account costs to third parties—insurers, Medicare, Medicaid, and so forth—in exploring the alternatives with the patient. Even under the modifications of the principle he would be obligated to provide whatever he is capable of, unless the patient, who by hypothesis might gain some slight benefit (even taking into account pain, suffering, and inconvenience), autonomously chooses another course.

Even if we bracket the conflict between the individual and society, there is another problem in the individualism of the Oath's norm. If a physician views his duty as that of benefiting his patient, he is given no guidance whatsoever in allocating his concern among his patients. What is the physician to do if he has a choice between staying in his office to see three moderately ill patients and making one house call to see another patient too sick to come to the office? The choices for allocating scarce medical resources, including time, are not particularly guided by the principle of benefiting the individual patient. Certainly choices must be made, choices that may fall to the detriment of at least some patients. Even if the physician takes a pledge to work for the benefit of his patients—in the plural—he is given no guidance on how to allocate his resources. If this plural interpretation is made, are we to conclude that it is the physician's duty to maximize total benefit among his patients taken as a group? If so, the physician once again becomes a Benthamite, but on a small scale.

It seems as though, at some level in the contract between the society and the profession, consequences to other parties must become relevant to the moral mandate of the profession. The Soviet physician's oath and the principles of ethics of the AMA since 1957 have recognized as much. The AMA principles say that "the responsibilities of the physician extend not only to the individual, but also to society, where these responsibilities deserve his interest and participation in activities which have the purpose of improving both the health and the well-being of the individual and the community." The AMA, as we have seen, also permits the physician to break a patient confidence when that becomes necessary to protect the welfare of the community. In this regard, the AMA has been "socialistic" since 1957. The newest (1980) revision retains this same social commitment. Thus, both the AMA and the Soviet physicians are not traditionally Hippocratic in the sense I have summarized the Hippocratic principle. Yet, some kinds of consequences to people other than the patient simply have to be relevant to some professional physician decisions. Perhaps they are not always relevant at the level of the individual. The cost containment decision, for example, might be taken out of the hands of the individual practitioner by having others—professionals or lay people—place some constraints on the kinds of services provided. That would free the practitioner to try to do whatever was in the interest of the patient (subject to the other preliminary qualifiers about autonomous choice and the physician's right of conscientious objection).

This might handle the cost containment problem. Other adjustments would have to be made to deal with the experimentation and public health problems. Perhaps some members of the profession could be given a moral mandate to pursue social benefits, and others be required to focus only on the welfare of individual patients. Reasonable lay people coming together with reasonable members of the profession would have to amend the Hippocratic formula still further in other ways.

In the case of the bleeding accident victim, even the strategy of a division of labor among professionals (some focusing on social benefits, others on individual benefits) would not be sufficient. If we want physicians to be morally justified in abandoning certain patients temporarily in order to save a nonpatient's life, we need some additional qualifier. Perhaps the solution is to revert to the nonindividualistic, social utilitarian form of the principle of beneficence.

VARIANTS ON THE HIPPOCRATIC PRINCIPLE

Before turning to the principle of social utility as a possible alternative to the Hippocratic principle, we should consider two important variants on the Hippocratic formula that were mentioned in chapter 1. Both of them seem to qualify still further the physician's duty to do what he thinks will benefit his patient. Physicians sometimes summarize what they take to be the core of their professional obligation with the maxim, "first of all, do no harm." Other times, they say that their first duty as physicians is to prolong life. These two formulations can be seen as variants on the Hippocratic formula.

Do No Harm   Especially in recent physician writing, the principle "first of all, do no harm" has gained great prominence. In its Latin form, *primum non nocere*, it appears literally hundreds of times in the contemporary folk ethic of physicians without a sense that the formula is either controversial or reformative.[8] If it means anything other than the Hippocratic principle, however, it is indeed controversial and reformative. Widely accepted as the summary principle in modern Hippocratic medicine, there is virtually no perception that "first of all, do no harm" is in potential conflict with the Hippocratic patient-benefiting principle.

It is sometimes hard to tell whether the maxim is meant to be a short form of what I have called the Hippocratic principle—benefit the patient and keep him from harm—or an expression of something different and even more controversial. If the former, then all of the problems of the Hippocratic principle apply and no more analysis is needed. It seems, however, that at least some users of the slogan are revising the Hippocratic principle. It is sometimes held that the duty not to harm is especially stringent, that it takes precedence over the general duty to help. The principle of nonmaleficence is separated from, and given special standing over, the principle of beneficence.[9] In this form it is significantly different from the Hippocratic notion of benefiting *and* preventing harm, in which benefits and harms are to be viewed as pluses and minuses on the same scale. The priority in the principle of not harming over helping has Western roots in Aristotle, Kant, W. D. Ross, and others. We have also seen it in the Hindu and Buddhist notion of ahimsa. Kant considered the avoidance of harm to be a perfect obligation, as opposed to producing good which he saw as merely an imperfect obligation. In twentieth-century ethics, giving special weight to avoidance of evil has been defended by Ross.[10] He demonstrates, whether he means to or not, that the emphasis on not harming can be an especially conservative doctrine leading in the extreme case to the conclusion that the physician should never take on a patient since then at least he could never be the direct cause of any harm. Thus *primum non nocere* is a principle that can be quite incompatible with the more general Hippocratic patient-benefiting principle, as well as with other more universal ethical norms. Its conservative, antiinterventionistic implications are quite opposed to those doctrines that see the human as cocreator and cosustainer of his environment, including his bodily environment.

The origins of the phrase are unclear. Some, as I have said—perhaps conflating the 'do no harm' formula with the more general Hippocratic notion—trace the principles behind it back to the Hippocratic corpus.

"The Epidemics," written by the unknown Hippocratic author, contains the maxim, "As to diseases, make a habit of two things—to help, or to do no harm." It appears in the work somewhat unexpectedly. "The Epidemics" contains descriptions of case histories from various parts of the Greek Isles. At the end of chapter eleven (in Book One), several apparently unrelated aphorisms are given without explanation or obvious reasons, including the one in focus. English scholarship has been misled somewhat by Jones's definitive translation in which, without apparent reason, the words "at least" are added, as follows: "to help, or at least do no harm."[11] This still, however, does not suggest the stronger formulation of "primarily" or "first of all."

For many years I have tried without success to find Greek, Latin, or even early English versions conveying this notion. Albert Jonsen, a professor in medical ethics at the University of California Medical Center, San Francisco, has recently published an essay on the 'do no harm' principle in which he reveals a similar abortive search for the origin of the *primum non nocere* concept.[12] I am led to suspect that the specific formulation may be quite modern, perhaps rendered into Latin by some nineteenth- or twentieth-century physician to endow it with a certain social and literary cachet.

The only other scholarly commentary on the history of the maxim is the obscure article *"Primum Non Nocere"* by one C. Sandulescu in the *Acta Antiqua Hungarica.*[13] Sandulescu also notes that modern users of the phrase must mean some kind of balancing of helping against harming, thus rendering the maxim compatible with the Hippocratic tradition. He refers to *primum non nocere* as the "concentrated Latin aphorism,"[14] implying that the full form would be that found in "The Epidemics" of balanced benefiting against harming. He travels through relevant Greek and Latin texts without finding any citation of the locution.

Jonsen suggests four possible interpretations of the phrase, the first three of which imply the familiar general formulas relating benefits to harms in a way that does not give priority to harms. The fourth interpretation, he suggests, may give special moral consideration to not harming in a manner similar to the double effect principle of Catholic moral theology. This requires that the harming be in proportion to the potential benefit, but at the same time not be a means to a good end. Even that does not endow harming with the special weight implied by the *primum non nocere* formula.

Whether or not ancient medical ethics gave this special priority to not harming, those formulating a contemporary ethic of professionals in relationship to patients need to consider whether this approach is preferable to the more general Hippocratic version of the principle of beneficence. Consider the following case.

Case 5 *High Risk—High Gain*

Donald Merriam, a young man in his early twenties, was suffering from leukemia. His disease had advanced to the point where a radical, new and potentially toxic chemotherapy regimen was being considered. He was told by his physician that the likelihood of long-term benefit was small, but that the experimental compounds possibly could work. On the other hand, the toxicity was great, causing nausea, loss of hair, and occasional severe depression and weakness—and carrying as well a one to two percent mortality risk from the drugs themselves. The physician described the situation as "high risk-high gain." The alternative was the more standard therapy—low risk-low gain. The physician estimated that the medical benefit-risk ratios were similar, with both benefit and risk much higher in the experimental treatment. To these medical determinations, of course, one would have to add the other dimensions of benefit and harm that are unique to the patient's own system of beliefs and values. Some patients would have great fear of the experimental treatment and would suffer more than others if they decided to undertake it. Others might be traumatized by the knowledge that there were treatments that could have been tried but were not. These people would be inclined to the experimental alternative. Some patients might be influenced by close relatives who had been well or poorly served by one of the approaches. Others might get special satisfaction out of participating in an experiment. All of these personal benefit-and-harm variables would have to be included in the calculus. That alone reveals that these decisions can never, in principle, be made without reference to the patient's own values.

In this particular patient's case, no decisive additional benefit or harm was anticipated from either of the alternatives so that their benefit-harm ratios remained about the same. Morally, what should be taken into account?

If the goal is to maximize net benefit over harm, then the more aggressive option might be chosen since the difference between the benefit and the harm would be greater (while the ratios remained the same). If the goal is to select the best ratio between benefit and harm, however, the choice should be viewed as a toss-up. If, however, the goal is *primum non nocere*, and this is taken literally to mean that avoiding harm takes precedence over producing benefit, then the conservative course (or no treatment at all) is the preferred one. The physician, Ray W. Gifford, accuses the FDA of being pervaded with, and unduly influenced by, the doctrine of *primum non nocere* when it bans potentially risky drugs from the market.[15] In doing so he seems to follow this last interpretation, that is, the one making avoiding harm take precedence over helping.

It is not obvious why rational people selecting among these alternative ways of combining benefits and harms would be impelled toward any one of the choices. The third one, the one that simply minimizes harm, is especially unappealing. In the extreme, no people follow that principle in their own lives or with the lives of others. If they did, no physician could ever engage in any activity. Surgery and chemotherapy would always be immoral. If failing to benefit is morally different from, and less onerous than, actually harming, one could always avoid doing harm simply by doing nothing.

Perhaps medical professionals and others have been tempted to give "not harming" a priority over "helping" because they mistake the nature of the problem. In some cases we can help one person by harming another. In medicine we could save the lives of many kidney patients if we did universal tissue typing and by compulsion took one kidney from a healthy person whenever it was needed to benefit another person in chronic kidney failure. The donor would be harmed somewhat while the recipient would be helped greatly. Yet many are repulsed by the idea, even though the scheme increases net benefit. They may explain their repulsion by saying not harming gets the highest priority, ergo *primum non nocere*.

That explanation overlooks the fact, however, that in addition to doing the unwilling kidney sources harm, we may be doing other things to them. We may be violating their rights. We may be treating them unfairly. The real test of the difference between the duty not to harm and the duty to help would come when the case is not cluttered by these other considerations, when it does not involve this particular distribution of benefits and harms (with most of the harm going to one and the benefit to another). The best test might be cases like Donald

Merriam's where the benefits and harms all accrue to the same person and, for purposes of discussion, the option is chosen by the patient himself or at least with his consent. It is clear that in these situations we sometimes decide to harm in order to produce net benefit. Perhaps people making the contract between society and the medical profession would find some reason to give a special priority to not harming over and above the concern for producing benefit, but I cannot see why. That seems to me more like the kind of choice where rational contractors would perceive no clear societal reason for emphasizing one way of relating benefit to harms over another. That is the kind of choice that could be left to individual lay people in discussion with individual practitioners at the level of the third contract. Of course, it would be unfortunate if a conservative lay person were paired up with an aggressive, interventionistic, high risk–high gain professional, but the reverse would be just as unfortunate. The Hippocratic Oath seems to relate benefits and harms equally with no priority given to not harming. It has been necessary to propose several modifications of the Hippocratic principle, but I see no reason why we would want to push for this further modification to give precedence to not harming. Other considerations are much more important: producing net objective benefit, protecting the autonomy of the patient, protecting other rights of the patient and other parties, promoting fairness, and so forth. Perhaps the formula ought to be changed to read *ultimum non nocere,* "last of all, do no harm."

Prolong Life   There is a second variant on the Hippocratic principle, which, like the "do no harm" variant, may or may not be a modification. Several important traditions in medical ethics—including the Jewish, Islamic, Buddhist, and Taoist—as well as the right-to-life movement—place special emphasis on the moral duty of prolonging or preserving life. Sometimes those speaking within the tradition of Western secular professional physician ethics also say that the physician's primary obligation is to prolong life. Sociologists Talcott Parsons, Renée C. Fox, and Victor Lidz describe what they call modern medical ethics—and what I have been calling professional physician ethics—as having as a structural core the "absolutizing of the value of preserving life."[16] This ethic which, strikingly, they describe in the past tense, "permitted, indeed required, that he [the physician] pursue the 'saving' of life at almost any cost—that is, by subordinating almost all other value considerations." "This nearly absolute commitment to preserve life," they say, "strongly insulated medical ethics from any ethical system or complex that did not place a commensurate emphasis upon the value of preserving life."[17]

Some spokespersons for the professional ethic have indeed accepted this unique commitment. Jesse Dukeminier and David Sanders, in an initial defense of their proposal for routinely salvaging cadaver organs useful in transplantation, buttress their case by claiming, "The first and most important principle of medical ethics is to save life."[18] Often it is explicitly recognized that this is a uniquely professional commitment. Private practitioner August M. Kasper says, "Medical practitioners have the wistful audacity, thank God, to blindly insist that pain is bad and life is to be preserved. This patent value judgment is the basis of medicine, and only coincidentally has it anything to do with knowledge of observable reality."[19] Physician Franklin H. Epstein, in an article (expressing the folk professional ethic) that appeared in the popular physician press, says the physician's "primary concern is to preserve human life; death is his enemy."[20] He adds that this is the "attitude of his profession," and makes no effort to ground it beyond professional consensus. Some physicians, though, have begun to abandon this ethic taught to them in their professional socialization. Physician Marjorie J. McKusick says that as a medical student, "I was firmly convinced that my role was clearly defined to preserve life."[21] She goes on to reveal that more recently she has discovered problems with the simple commitment to preserving life.

Sometimes it is hard to tell whether these people are really holding to the original version of the Hippocratic principle, which focuses on subjective benefit to the patient according to the physician's perspective. They might believe that, empirically, life is so valuable that prolonging it will always, on balance, do more good than harm, thus producing a net benefit for the patient. Then the claim that the physician's duty is always to prolong life is really a summary of the evidence based on the principle of benefiting the patient. Alternatively they may have adopted the commitment to the priority of not harming suggested by the *primum non nocere*. Like the Buddha, they may believe that no creature would want to die, that the principle of avoiding harm (ahimsa) essentially always leads to the conclusion that life should be preserved when possible. If so, the duty to prolong life is just shorthand for the principle that the patient should be protected from harm. From this point of view death is *always* a harm of major proportions such that no one justifiably could conclude (as Dr. T. and Ms. R. did) that someone would be better off dead. This interpretation makes its adherents indi-

165

vidualistic consequentialists (focusing on consequences for the patient) who happen to believe that, empirically, avoidable death is always a decisive harm.

Some physicians and others in the tradition of secular, professional medical ethics, however, seem really to believe that over and above any principle of benefiting or not harming, there is an independent duty of the physician to prolong life. It then becomes not a matter of consequences, but a simple belief that failing to prolong life when one can is an inherently wrong-making characteristic of an action. If the duty to preserve a life when possible is independent of consideration of consequences, then holders of this position have departed significantly, whether rightly or wrongly, in still another way from the Hippocratic core ethic as I have summarized it.

The Hippocratic Oath does not require a physician to use his skill to preserve life. It does require the Hippocratic physician to avoid giving "a deadly drug to anybody if asked for it," but that is certainly quite different. Some interpreters understand this to mean nothing more than a prohibition against collaboration in an ordinary scheme of homicide by poisoning. The evidence for that interpretation is weak, however. Edelstein concludes that it must refer to the physician's role in assisting in suicide, which was then a common response to intolerable pain and suffering.[22] Since suicide was not generally condemned in Greek culture, however, the question arises why the collaboration of the physician in providing poison would be prohibited. Edelstein suggests that only Pythagorean philosophical dogma is compatible with the prohibition, evidence he uses in part toward his conclusion that the Oath is Pythagorean. (See chapter 1.)

If that is the case, however, modern physicians and modern lay people have even less reason to be bound by the Oath's instruction. We would have to opt for the ethic of the Pythagoreans rather than of the Stoics, Cynics, Platonists (or those of any other school) if we wanted to be good Greeks and still accept the Oath.

Except for the prohibition on the prescribing of poisons, there is no mandate for the physician to prolong life, even in the Hippocratic literature. Puzzled by the apparent absence of ancient roots for the oft-proclaimed preservation–prolongation duty, I sought, while director of the Hastings Center's Research Group on Death and Dying, a more thorough review of the literature of ancient medicine. Darrel Amundsen, a classics professor at Western Washington University and perhaps the most able scholar working on ancient medical ethics, was asked to review the literature. His conclusions were summarized in a fascinating essay, "The Physician's Obligation to Prolong Life: A Medical Duty without Classical Roots."[23] Amundsen's findings converge with those of Gerald Gruman, whose *A History of Ideas about the Prolongation of Life* finds traces of the commitment to prolong life in folklore, Taoism, alchemy, and aspects of Renaissance hygiene, but connects the evolution of the duty into a major doctrine with the development of the idea of progress that became dominant in the eighteenth century.[24]

The philosopher Francis Bacon (1561–1626) is sometimes said to have recognized the duty to prolong life as a new principle for medical ethics. In his "De augmentis scientiarum," he divided medicine into three parts: preservation of health, the cure of diseases, and the prolongation of life. About the last he observes, ". . . the third part of medicine which I have set down is that which relates to the prolongation of life, which is new, and deficient; and the most noble of all."[25] While some might interpret this as Bacon's endorsement of the physician's duty to prolong the life of the terminally ill patient, Amundsen has shown that that is not what is meant. Bacon says that "when, all hope of recovery being gone, it serves only to make a fair and easy passage from life, . . . the same *Euthanasia* [Bacon's emphasis] which likewise was observed in the death of Antonius Pius, which was not so much like death as like falling into a deep and pleasant sleep."[26] Thus by Bacon's time there was evidently some tendency for physicians to try to prolong life. He criticizes those who "make a kind of scruple and religion to stay with the patient after he is given up, whereas in my judgment, if they would not be wanting in their office, and indeed to humanity, they ought both to acquire the skill and to bestow the attention whereby the dying may pass more easily and quietly out of life."[27]

Even if the obligation to prolong life does not have ancient roots, the real question is whether rational contractors would find it reasonable to include such a notion in a general system of ethics. When our hypothetical contractors come together, taking the moral point of view, would they add to the principle of beneficence an independent provision that life should be prolonged when possible?

Very few people believe they and their fellow citizens have a general, independent duty to prolong all human life as long as possible. Of course, prolonging life would often be beneficial to the individual and therefore could be subsumed under the general principle of beneficence, but to add to that a duty to prolong all human life would make war, capital punishment, abortion, and life-threatening acts of self-defense immoral in all circumstances (an implication that will be explored later). It also would commit society to preserving life of the terminally ill patient to the last gasp. It would even exclude high-risk occupations. No society has ever held it a general duty to prolong life in all circumstances, and there seems to be no rational reason why any should do so.

A more interesting question is whether at the time of negotiating the contract between society and the profession, rational people would want to establish a special role-specific duty *for physicians* requiring them to prolong life when possible. The late Washington physician and writer Michael Halberstam has argued, "The proper function of the physician in society is implicitly and explicitly agreed upon by physicians and those they serve, and that function is to preserve biological life."[28]

His claim is an interesting one. He says not merely that Hippocratic physicians on the Isle of Cos agreed, or that modern physicians agree, but rather, that "physicians *and those they serve*" agree to the notion that the physician's function is to preserve life, and "biological life" at that. It is possible that even though society in general cannot act on the principle that life should be prolonged in all circumstances, there might be reasons for a division of moral labor so that physicians, as society's custodians of life, could act upon it. This arrangement might serve some greater purpose in the long run.

If physicians alone took this view of their role, we would be faced with the old problem of why lay people ought to concur in this role-specific duty. The evidence, though, seems to show that physicians do not hold that they have a duty of preservation. The majority of them consistently say that in at least some cases where life could be prolonged by intervention, they should not intervene.[29]

Regardless of the views of the medical professional, lay people, it seems, would want to qualify the principle that the physician has a role-specific duty to prolong life. They would at least impose the same kinds of qualifications that were placed on the original Hippocratic principle: They would want to insist that life would be prolonged "according to the best available evidence," not merely the physician's judgment. Lay people would have to ask whether they would want to have the physician instructed to prolong life against the patient's own wishes or only with the consent of the patient. They might even have to ask whether biological life should always be preserved for a few unconscious moments at great expense, even if that were the wish the patient expressed while conscious and competent.

Perhaps the duty to prolong life has been confused with the duty to avoid killing. Many traditions have opposed as unethical actions designed to kill actively another human being. Even traditions that do not prohibit all killings may favor a role-specific duty for physicians to keep them from killing even when there seems to be good reason, as perhaps when the killing is requested by the about-to-be-deceased.

We shall examine in more detail the plausibility of the principle prohibiting killing and its implications for a medical ethic in chapter 10. At this point, however, we are focusing on the more general possible duty to prolong life. The case for that duty, even as a role-specific duty for physicians and other health professionals, seems to be a weak one, one that would have to be qualified severely. I suspect that the principle either reduces to a more general Hippocratic principle of benefiting the patient—a principle which we have seen has many problems of its own—or it is a careless expression of a more narrow and sophisticated role-specific duty, the duty to avoid knowingly and actively killing human beings. Since lay people and professional groups do not hold the position that life in general always should be prolonged, or even that medical professionals always should prolong life, this variant on the Hippocratic principle probably deserves no further attention. If we can provide in some other way for the moral concerns of those who have claimed prolongation as the physician's duty, the problem will have been eliminated.

AGAINST THE DANGEROUS UTILITARIAN PRINCIPLE

We have seen that the Hippocratic principle in its most usual form presents real problems for people who are negotiating a social covenant between a society and the profession from the moral point of view. It is so subjective that it places the physician's own judgment above the reasonable consensus even of the profession as to what constitutes benefit to the individual. It makes no commitment in principle to finding out the most objective estimate of what would be most beneficial. Even if it did, it would be paternalistic. It would leave no room for an individual patient to make medical decisions based on his or her own estimate of personal benefit (except insofar as the physician believed the patient to be the best judge of what would really be beneficial). It would leave no room for individuals to be altruistic and choose to include the welfare of others in their decisions about their medical futures. It totally excludes all consideration of benefit to others: in human experimentation, in public health medicine, and in cost containment. It leaves no room for a justified temporary minor compromise of the interests of the patient in order to perform a lifesaving rescue operation on a nonpatient. It does not provide for distribution of resources among patients.

It is clear that the Hippocratic principle presents enormous problems. In fact, given all these problems, one can conclude that the Hippocratic ethic is dead. No rational person would agree that the physician should be given the role-specific duty of always doing what, according to his ability and judgment, he considered to be for the benefit of the patient regardless of these other factors. The variants, which commit the physician to doing no harm to the patient and to prolonging the patient's life, raise all the same problems and more. If there is an alternative, it certainly deserves consideration.

THE UTILITARIAN ALTERNATIVE

The most obvious alternative is to take the general principle of beneficence from the basic social contract and see if a set of role-specific duties for the medical profession can be generated in such a way that the relevant benefits are not limited to the individual patient with whom the physician is interacting. The utilitarian principle of acting so as to produce the greatest aggregate net benefit over harm has much to be said for it. It is one of the most widely accepted ethical formulas in normative ethics. Many physicians as well as lay people have opened the door to social utilitarianism in an effort to cope with the problems of traditional Hippocratic individualism.[30] Even the AMA's "Principles of Medical Ethics" has recognized the need to expand beyond Hippocratic individualism, affirming since 1957 that "the honored ideals of the medical profession imply that the responsibilities of the physician extend not only to the individual, but to society." He or she has, according to the AMA, the well-being of both the individual and the community as an essential responsibility.

In its more sophisticated forms utilitarianism can account for all or virtually all of our ethical intuitions.[31] It would justify research on human subjects even if it was not expected to produce a net benefit to the patient. It would justify public health measures. It would justify certain cost containment efforts (though probably not the ones where individuals would be hurt dramatically). It would explain why a physician might be justified in temporarily compromising the interests of his patient slightly in order to benefit a nonpatient in desperate need of otherwise unobtainable help. As powerful as the utilitarian principle is in explaining our moral intuitions, however, it does not seem to do the job completely. Consider the case of health planning on Fictitious Island.

Case 6 *Health Planning on Fictitious Island*

The legislature of Fictitious Island was deeply embedded in a debate over whether to adopt a national health plan for the island. Heretofore, their health planning had always been a mixture of individual initiative issuing from a free market in professional services and a smattering of welfare programs. Some of the latter were designed to meet the health care needs of the seriously afflicted, chronically ill who were unable to provide for themselves; some to aid those in the island nation's pockets of poverty; and some for people with specific disease entities, such as polio, diabetes, and chronic kidney failures.

There was substantial concern over the lack of any systematic plan for meeting health care needs. The legislature wanted to have a comprehensive plan. It referred the problem to the Office of Technology Projection with a mandate to review feasible alternatives. The Office was to make use of its extensive computer capability to project the full range of consequences of various options. Its goal was to rank the options on the basis of the extent to which they would produce the greatest net benefit for the society in comparison with other alternatives.

The health planners were sophisticated users of systems analysis, adept at cost–benefit/cost–effectiveness analysis. They knew that they would have to include in their projections long-term, subtle, and indirect impacts on the citizenry, including such elements as changes in mood and effects on the labor force and the family. Their first report back to the legislature said that if they had to compare alternative uses of the island's resources they would need to examine social programs other than health care ones since some of those others might produce greater net utility.

The legislature's spokespersons were aware of this complication and said they would take responsibility for comparing health care programs with other kinds of social programs. They told the health planners to attempt only to compare alternative health care programs, taking into account all potential effects of all programs and the likelihood of those effects occurring.

After several months of intensive work, the computer runs were completed. The planners discovered to their amazement that the answer was more straightforward than expected. They reported back to the legislature that for the peculiar set of circumstances on the island (circumstances that may not exist elsewhere), one program would simultaneously reduce mortality rates, morbidity rates, infant mortality, and other indicators of health problems. Furthermore, it would not be an expensive program or one that would be difficult to administer.

The program generated would require social scientists to identify the one percent of the population that was chronically ill with incurable illness, possessing insufficient intelligence to follow a medical regimen, and receiving expensive medical care. Excluding this population, which would be banned from receiving any further health care, a universal health maintenance system would be established for the island.

The planners acknowledged that morbidity and mortality rates for the one percent would increase, but said the medical resources diverted to others would improve medical indicators enough to more than offset the problems among the one percent. In fact, with the increase in mortality among the sickly, the average morbidity rates for the island would improve. The legislature's responsibility was to decide whether to enact the program.

The case is clearly hypothetical, the only one in this volume not based on a real situation. It has to be hypothetical in order to highlight the ethical principles of the case unencumbered by controversy over nonmoral facts. Some would argue that in their society, banning the bottom one percent of population would not really improve the health indicators. This could be the case in the United States, for example. By hypothesizing the facts, we are able to see whether the principle of utilitarianism provides an adequate moral answer in a case where the outcome would produce the greatest good for the greatest number (compared to other health programs).

Many will be uncomfortable with the implications of the conclusion reached by the planners. They would oppose the enactment of legislation based on the scheme even if it did produce the greatest good for the greatest number. The legislators, of course, are not blind with regard to their position in the system. They might try to take the moral point of view, but, in fact, would not be behind a veil of ignorance or be able in any way to count other people's interests as equal to their own. The striking thing about the case, however, is that if the legislators are biased with self-interest at all, one would expect them to lean toward favoring the proposal. Presumably they would know that they are less likely to be in the one percent than the random citizen of the island. Though they are not totally blind, however, they still might resist the proposal of the health planners.

There are a number of reasons we can offer to explain the tension between the principle of utility and the scheme proposed by the planners. The principle of utility supposedly takes into account all alternative uses of available resources as well as all potential benefits and harms. We have already specified in the fictitious case, however, that the planners attempted to take into account all potential effects of the alternative health care programs; the legislators promised to compare alternative uses of resources outside the health care sphere.

The legislature might, therefore, resist the proposal merely because it concludes that investments of resources into areas outside the health care sphere would produce even more benefits than the health planners' proposed ban on the one percent. Suppose, however, that the legislators make at least a crude calculation and comparison with alternative uses of the resources and conclude that, *all benefits and harms considered*, the proposed plan is better than the alternatives. No alternative use of the resources would produce such a good outcome. After all, the costs of the scheme will be relatively small. Even when nonquantifiable costs such as fear, social tension, and suffering from the loss of loved ones is taken into account, the legislators might conclude that the plan produces the greatest net benefit. Why then might they still plausibly have doubts that they would be acting morally if they adopted the plan?

We can conceive two explanations. First, they might accept the principle of utilitarianism as correct; their resistance might come from a lifetime of what would then be erroneous belief that people ought to be treated to some degree equally even if it does not produce the greatest good for the greatest number. Alternatively, their moral intuitions about the wrongness of the proposed health scheme could be correct, in which case the principle must be wrong.

There is no definitive method for resolving the tension. All that can be done at this point is to pose once again the problem of principle for the contractors. If they were coming together to invent or discover the basic principles for the society, would they hold on to the principle of utility knowing that it would justify banning the one percent if it would hypothetically maximize net benefits? Would they hold on to the principle even if it would justify, say, slavery, in a hypothetical situation where the aggregate benefit to slaveholders would outweigh the more serious harm done to a smaller number of slaves?

One of the problems of the utilitarian ethical principle is that, at least hypothetically, it seems to justify too much. It would have justified the Nazi experiments if only the Nazis had been clever enough to devise experiments that really produced benefit on balance. Since social benefits in experimentation accrue to present and future citizens, the number benefited is large, potentially almost infinitely large, while the number hurt is fixed and relatively infinitesimal. It is possible that an experiment could be devised in which sufficient benefit could be produced to justify the loss of a few lives if the only thing at stake were benefits and harms totaled up as if the recipients of the benefits and harms were interchangeable. This has led many people to conclude that the principle of utility, at least as it is applied to specific problem solving such as the decision of that legislature, is unacceptable.

We are trapped between the ultraindividualism of the Hippocratic medical ethic and the social indiscrimination of the utilitarians. A compromise between the two does not seem possible either. As long as there is some opening of the door to social benefits in a way that permits balancing them against the claim of individuals, it is hard to see how it can be shut once again. There are so many in a society who are potential recipients of benefit that any balancing of individual and social benefits is almost certainly to be dominated by the social consequences. Yet if we hold on to a pure individualistic Hippocratism, fundamental wrongs seem to result. Before we adopt the principle of beneficence as the only principle of the social contract between the profession and the society, we should see if there is some way out of our bind. We should see whether we are prepared to admit that there are right-making characteristics of actions other than the consequences they produce.

This possibility should not be a surprise to those standing within the Hippocratic tradition. They have already accepted several nonconsequentialist right-making characteristics: the idea that subjective rather than objective benefit should take precedence, the limitation of benefit to the one with whom one is interacting, perhaps the elevation to priority of not harming over helping, and the acceptance of the duty to prolong life independent of the consequences. All of these suggest that

174

nonconsequentialist factors may be morally relevant to medical ethics. In our critique of the Hippocratic principle we had cause to appeal to an independent principle of autonomy as a possible counter to Hippocratic beneficence. Perhaps other right-making characteristics also have to be taken into account as well, characteristics that can liberate us from the horns of the individualist–utilitarian dilemma.

RULE UTILITY AS AN OPTION

Before examining those nonconsequentialist considerations, there is one potential intermediate solution that must be dealt with. Perhaps these right-making characteristics of actions are not independent principles, but merely principles summarizing a set of rules which, if followed, will produce the greatest good on balance. If using utility per se to justify banning the one percent from a health care system seems wrong, it may be because a general rule promoting equal access or equity of access or fairness in the distribution of resources will produce better consequences for the society. Such a rule might produce better consequences than any other, including the one that for each policy question, benefits and harms ought to be calculated and the policy chosen that will maximize net benefit. This scheme is what philosophers have come to call the normative position of 'rule utility.'[32]

It probably comes very close to being able to account for our moral intuitions. It can usually explain, for example, why people ought to act justly, tell the truth, keep promises, and respect freedom. Following such principles and the rules derived from them will tend to produce more benefit than following other principles and rules, even if in some individual cases more harm than good might be done.

The result is a rule-utility solution to the problem of how interests of the individual and interests of a society might be balanced. The interests of society could be allowed to surface only in the formulation of principles or rules that would produce the greatest good in the long run.

Even if rule utility gives an account of how these interests might be balanced, it raises problems of its own. First, rule utility is very un-Hippocratic. It permits the subordination of the individual case problem to a general rule of conduct. No good Hippocratic physician would accept such a subordination.

Second, if there is a subclass of actions where breaking the rule would produce more utility than following it, why not amend the rule so that the exception becomes part of the rule?[33] If that is done, then rule utility will eventually reduce to utility calculations very like those done for individual cases. For example, if banning the one percent would produce greater utility, but would violate a rule-utilitarian principle of justice, why not rewrite the rule utilitarian principle of justice to read: "each should receive according to his need except in cases where more good would come from some other distribution," specifying those conditions, if necessary. That would be a rule producing even greater utility, so it seems, than the simpler rule of equal access.

Third, if our problem can be resolved by converting utility calculations to calculations of the utility of alternative sets of rules, why are we so morally certain about our moral judgments? If the ethics of slavery, for example, were contingent upon a general calculation of whether the rule favoring slavery would produce more happiness than the rule prohibiting it, could we be as certain as we are that slavery is wrong? If we are certain that slavery is wrong or that the one percent should not be banned from health care services, it may be because the judgment is not really based on utility alone, whether it be utility of the case or of the rule.

This suggests a fourth and final problem with the rule-utilitarian resolution. Even if it does produce a morally correct solution to life's medical ethical problems, it may not provide a good account of the reasons why an action or a rule is morally acceptable. If it turns out that the one percent should not be banned and coincidentally that banning would not be in accord with the rule that would maximize utility in distribution when compared with other rules, it does not follow that banning is wrong *because* it is not in accord with the rule that would maximize utility in distribution when compared with other rules. It may be wrong because it is unfair. In fact, it may be because it is unfair that it produces bad consequences (because people are justifiably disturbed by the immorality of the unfairness).

The movement to rule utility is a sophisticated attempt to recover for utilitarianism a ground it has had to abandon because it could not adequately explain our moral intuitions in cases such as slavery and the banning of the one percent. If there is no other more plausible set of principles that will provide a foundation for a medical ethic, then we shall have to return to rule utilitarianism and see if we can work out what that would mean for the contract between the profession and the society. If there is a more straightforward way of establishing the other right-making characteristics, however, the necessity of this retreat into a problematic utilitarianism will be eliminated.

Chapter 7

The Principle of Contract Keeping

The principle of beneficence with its monomaniac infatuation with consequences leaves us suspended between two equally unacceptable alternatives: Focus exclusively on the interests of the individual patient and exclude all consideration of the welfare of others, or focus on the total aggregate welfare of the society even if the welfare of the individual is overpowered. Would rational people attempting to discover or invent a basic set of principles for the society be satisfied with either version of the principle of beneficence as the exclusive foundation for social morality? Would they, when attempting to discover or invent a set of principles governing relations between medical professionals and lay decision makers, be satisfied with either the Hippocratic or the more general utilitarian form of beneficence? Given the problems encountered thus far, it seems they would at least try to look elsewhere for some additional principles to buttress their normative theory of morality.

Several should be considered. All seem to resolve moral dilemmas and square with our moral intuitions about how medical lay people and medical professionals ought to act in difficult ethical situations. They would help provide a further ethical foundation for physicians and other health professionals such as nurses, pharmacists, social workers, and various therapists. We shall consider the principles of contract keeping or promise keeping, of autonomy, of honesty, of avoiding killing, and of justice. The result can be an ethic of freedom and responsibility based on a contract or covenant binding the moral community, one to replace the Hippocratic or utilitarian ethics of consequences.

Case 7   *The Homosexual Husband*[1]

David, the oldest of three children, was the son of a well-to-do manufacturer. David's father valued physical prowess and athletic accomplishments, areas in which David showed little interest. When David was twelve or thirteen years old, conflicts with his father resulted in almost nightly arguments. It was evident that David's father had become concerned about David's mannerisms and considered them to be effeminate.

David's schoolwork deteriorated considerably and he became withdrawn. His father decided to send him to a military school, but he remained there for only six months. By this time, David had told his parents that he was a homosexual, had engaged in, and was engaging in homosexual practices. He came home and completed his high school studies, but did not go on to college and continued to live at home.

He was treated for gonorrhea, asthma, and infectious hepatitis. At the age of twenty-one, to gain him exemption from the draft, his physician attested to the fact that David was a homosexual.

Five years later, Joan visited her family physician for a premarital serological exam. The physician was the same physician who had treated David. Joan was twenty-four years old and had been under this physician's care since the age of fourteen. A close and warm relationship had developed between the physician and Joan's family, and it was thus natural for the physician to ask about her fiancé. When he did, he learned that she was about to marry David. She had known him only briefly, but well enough, she felt, to be certain about her choice. Nothing more was said at the time.

David and Joan were married shortly thereafter and lived together for a period of six months. The marriage was annulled on the basis of nonconsummation. David by this time had told Joan that he was homosexually oriented, and she had learned as well that they shared a physician who had been aware of David's homosexuality. She subsequently suffered a depression as a result of this experience and was angry that her physician had remained silent about David. She felt that she could have been spared this horrible episode in her life—if only her physician had not shirked his duty to inform her. His failure to do so was an act of negligence resulting in deep emotional scars.

To whom did the physician owe primary allegiance? Do the interests to one patient prevail over the requirements of confidentiality surrounding another's case?

CONTRACT KEEPING IN THE BASIC SOCIAL CONTRACT

This case poses (in a somewhat different fashion than Dr. Browne's violation of confidentiality about contraception) a head-on conflict between the Hippocratic principle and the duty to keep confidences. If the physician in this case has a duty to his patients to do what he thinks will benefit them, and he thinks telling Joan about her husband's sexual preference and venereal disease history would be beneficial on balance, then he has an obligation to warn her.

The AMA's principles of medical ethics in effect at the time provided an exemption from the duty of confidentiality if it were in the interest of others to break confidence, providing in essence a social utilitarian support for breaking the confidence that converges with the Hippocratic mandate.

On the other hand, if the physician were loyal to the World Medical Association's International Code of Ethics he would have found an apparently exceptionless duty to keep confidences. He would then owe silence to David in spite of the fact that Joan, another patient, would benefit from the disclosure. There is a clear, direct conflict between the two requirements and the two codes.

At the point to which this case has developed there may well be no possible solution. However, a fuller exploration of the ethical principle of contract keeping, or promise keeping, may provide a way out of future situations like this one. If the duty to keep confidence is derived from an implied or explicit promise made to patients or contractual obligation with them, then that duty will be limited by the nature of the promise or contract.

One of the most obvious candidates for a right-making characteristic that is not totally dependent upon consequences is whether the action involves keeping or breaking a promise. Contract keeping is a special case of promise keeping so any ethic that is grounded in a contract theory has to have a special place for the principle of promise keeping. Would rational contractors taking the moral point of view agree that one of the principles that ought to govern social relations in the community should be the principle of promise keeping? If so, is that only because keeping promises will produce good consequences?

Those who view a social contract as the source of ethical principles invented by people trying to construct a society in which they want to live are faced with a serious logical problem regarding the principle of contract or promise keeping. Let us assume that agreement on what the principles ought to be also implies agreement in the form of a pledge that these principles ought to be followed. If contractors generate a principle of beneficence or a principle of just distribution in this manner, they are then bound by their pledge to follow the implications of the principle for social relationships. To do so, however, requires the prior existence of the principle that pledges or promises ought to be followed. The principle of promise keeping cannot be generated and found binding on contractors, then, by the mere fact that they have come together and promised to follow the promise-keeping rule. To do so requires that they already acknowledge for some reason that promises or pledges should be kept.

This problem has been seen as so severe that some have concluded that it is therefore impossible for a morality to be generated de novo by an actual social contract among those forming a moral community. The best that can be hoped for the inventors is that they might recognize that it is in everyone's self-interest for people always to keep promises since that is the only way the society can function. After an initial trial to test the commitment of others to follow such logic, keeping of promises eventually would become a habit.

Social contract theorists who see the contract as a way of discovering preexistent moral principles do not have such a serious problem. The principles are viewed as required by reason, in the laws of nature, or generated by a deity. The contractors simply discover the principle of promise keeping much as a child discovers that promises are made to him or her long before that child accepts the principle or has the ability to act upon it. Those standing in a theological tradition perhaps have the easiest time understanding the nature of promises. Relationships of faithfulness are constitutive for them. An initial creative act of promising generated a covenental bond both making possible and requiring fidelity. From that point, fidelity to covenants is morally fundamental. Those outside of a theological tradition have reached a similar conclusion based on reason or experience. The moral community is impossible, so the reasoning goes, without the obligation of fidelity to commitments. Kant considered the possibility of someone borrowing something (money, in his example) and promising to return it, knowing one will not be able to pay it back.[2] He then applied a version of a universalizability test, asking whether he could also will that the maxim become a 'universal law of nature', and he concludes obviously that he could not. He proposed it in the universal form of the maxim— "every one believing himself to be in need can make any promise he pleases with the intention not to keep it." The maxim, said Kant, would "make promising, and the very purpose of promising itself, impossible since no one would believe he was being promised anything, but would laugh at utterances of this kind as empty shams."[3] Reason requires, then, that promise keeping be a moral duty, prior to and independent of any contractors inventing the principle.

This does not quite answer the question, however, of whether promises should be kept only when, on balance, keeping them does more good than harm, in which case the principle might be derivative from the principle of beneficence. It must be conceded that if one is sophisticated in taking into account long-term consequences of breaking promises (including the fact that one won't be trusted in the future, that the world will be less predictable, and so forth), one is forced to conclude that often keeping promises, even promises with apparently bad consequences, turns out really to be beneficial in the long run.

The contractors inventing or discovering the principles have a clear choice at this point. They can opt for the principle of promise keeping without exception or they can opt for the principle that promises should be kept unless it is beneficial (really beneficial, including long-term consequences) to break the promise. It is not quite so obvious that logic rules out the latter option.

Since we have no definitive way of knowing what our hypothetical contractors taking the moral point of view would do, we are forced to face our, by now, standard dilemma. All we can do is try to put ourselves as closely as possible into the position of the ideal contractors and attempt to determine what we would conclude. One technique for helping us in that enterprise is to pose a problem that seems to require a forced choice between the two alternatives in as stark a manner as possible. The case problem we come up with will probably be somewhat contrived since most cases do not lend themselves to posing moral alternatives crisply.

Consider then what a physician should do if she faced the following situation. She has provided long-term care for an elderly, now terminally ill, man, and is the only one in attendance at the bedside as his dying moments approach. The patient, who has two grown children, asks the physician to promise to deliver an envelope to his lawyer. The patient tells the physician she should read the letter because he wants her to see that his wishes expressed in it are carried out. The physician agrees just as the patient passes away. She then opens the letter to find that it disinherits the patient's children, leaving the money instead for a trust fund to care for his cat. It also contains derogatory remarks about the children and comments about their turning against their father in his old age.

The physician knows this was not true. She also knows that the patient had been disturbed mentally as a result of potent drug medication he had been taking. She is convinced that the letter does not express the real wishes of the patient and that there is no doubt that a great deal of harm will be done if the letter were delivered. She realizes the will probably would be overturned in court, but with great suffering for all involved. Also, no one would know if the letter were not delivered. She considers the long-term, subtle consequences of not delivering the letter, including possible guilt feelings. Finally she concludes that if destroying the letter is really the right thing to do, there should be no problem of guilt feelings. (She also considered the possibility that she had made an error in calculating utilities and decided that much greater harm would be done if she assumed she had made an error.) Is there any reason why the physician should feel at all inclined to deliver the letter?

The question is not put in terms of whether on balance it is required that the physician deliver the letter, but rather whether there is any moral weight on the side of keeping the promise. People considering such cases differ in their responses. Many, however, conclude that there is at least some pull in the direction of keeping the promise, which seems clearly to lead to less good than breaking it. These people conclude that, at least hypothetically, even if it can be established that keeping the promise produces less net utility than breaking it, still there is some moral claim in favor of keeping it. Keeping a promise, they believe, is a right-making characteristic independent of the consequences. We are left with the question of whether rational contractors would choose the version of the promise-keeping principle that permits exceptions when greater good would be done by breaking the promise.

It is questions such as this for which, as far as I am able to discern, we have no identifiable group of experts. Certainly being an expert on law or psychology or medicine does not seem to give one expertise in deciding whether promises should be kept when that produces less net utility than breaking them. Neither can I see any evidence that those trained in ethics have expertise at this point. It is for this reason that we need to turn to the standard of the reasonable person and, to make the test objective, require the possibly contrary-to-fact condition that these persons take the moral point of view, adopt a veil of ignorance, try to be like ideal observers, or meet some other condition leading to the interests of all being considered equally.

When I apply these tests to the best of my ability, I am forced to the same conclusion as most (but not all) others: Promise keeping, or contract keeping, is a right-making characteristic independent of the consequences. If rational social contractors would agree, then this becomes a second principle of the social contract in addition to the principle of beneficence.

CONTRACT KEEPING AND THE LAY–PROFESSIONAL CONTRACT

Traditional Hippocratic physicians seem to be one group that is somewhat less inclined to accept the notion that there is a general duty to keep promises even when, on balance, more good would be done by breaking them. Hippocratic physicians, though, do seem to accept a version of an ethic of promise keeping. The Hippocratic Oath is, after all, a pledge—a promise. It is a pledge made by Apollo and all the gods and goddesses presumably to one's teacher. Thus there is a clear ethic of promise keeping within the professional group. Young medical students who, upon graduation from medical school, today take some revised version of the Oath likewise make a pledge to their teachers or to their new colleagues or to the profession.

It is sheer speculation to attempt to get at the moral theory behind the pledge. Is it rooted in the presumption that the promise will produce good consequences or rather that one should be bound by it even if it turned out not to produce the best possible net consequences? The original Oath ends with the statement, "If I fulfill this oath and do not violate it, may it be granted to me to enjoy life and art, being honored with fame among all men for all time to come; if I transgress it and swear falsely, may the opposite of all this be my lot." This suggests that the original believers in all the gods and goddesses might have believed that the deck was stacked so that breaking the Oath could never produce better consequences on balance, in which case the question of whether the promise itself (or the consequences of breaking it) was decisive in deciding whether to break it would be moot. Modern physicians, however, may not come equipped with the belief in such divine punishment as the ground for keeping promises. They do appear to believe, though, that in interaction with their professional colleagues pledges can be made that are morally binding even beyond calculations of the consequences.

It is not so clear that they take the same view with regard to pledges made outside the collegial network. The Hippocratic tradition is totally devoid of any notion of promises made to outsiders. Some codes, Percival's and the AMA's of 1847, for example, speak of obligations to the society, but there is no notion of contracting with the society or promising anything to the society. Likewise, there is no ethic of promising with regard to patients. Many physicians, to be sure, seem to believe they have a trust with the patients, that the relationship is a fiduciary one, but there is no official recognition of any notion of promise-keeping responsibility to those outside the profession. There is no notion of a contract between the profession and the society in the traditional professional ethics of the Hippocratic tradition. The responsibilities of the professional are unilateral, generated out of a pledge that the physician makes to his colleagues.

To the extent that this still reflects the position on lay-professional relations, the contemporary physician is sometimes uncomfortable. Some modern physicians, like their lay counterparts, are beginning to talk about a contract between a physician and a patient or between their profession and the lay population.[4] If an ethic for medical decision making will, in part, be determined by a contract between the profession and the society, it would appear that those people engaged in that discussion would want to have some account taken of the fact that contracts and other promises ought to be kept. That means that the role-specific duties for medical professionals and medical lay people will both be based upon, and include, an obligation to keep contracts. Some of the contractual promises will be between the profession as a whole and the society. Others will be between individual professionals and lay people.

THE PROBLEM OF MEDICAL CONFIDENTIALITY

I believe that the problem faced by the physician who suddenly discovered that he was providing care for a homosexual man and the woman that man was about to marry can only be dealt with by exploring the contractual relations and promises that should underlie a relationship between lay people and professionals. If confidentiality cannot be reduced to a single-minded calculation of benefit to the patient based on the physician's own judgment—as Dr. Browne was wont to do in the birth control case—or to a calculation of total social benefit—as some have interpreted the courts to require Dr. Moore to do in the Tarasoff case—then it will have to be understood as a set of pledges made by lay people and physicians.

It is the nature of the relationship between medical lay person and medical professional that discussion of highly personal, perhaps embarrassing, information may be important. Lay people would be hesitant to disclose information if they feared that it would be revealed to others. At the same time, professionals have interests that can only be satisfied by a pledge of fidelity from the patient. They are as interested in getting information to help them do their job adequately as in having patients keep their other pledges about appointments and fees. A general solution to the problem of confidentiality would be a pledge by lay people to disclose needed information to the professional in exchange for a pledge on the part of the professional to keep the information confidential.

Normally keeping such a set of pledges is, on balance, in the interests of each party. If the lay person does not reveal the necessary information, he or she may not benefit as much from the relationship; the lay person's interest is in disclosure. On the other hand, if the professional breaks the confidence, relatively little is gained and much could be lost. The professional's reputation could be harmed and future clients lost. Occasionally, however, one of the parties might conclude that more good might be done if his or her part of the bargain were not kept. The professional such as Dr. Browne might think that the patient would benefit from a discrete disclosure. Or he or she might feel that someone else might benefit—Tatiana Tarasoff in Dr. Moore's case, or Joan in the case of the homosexual husband. If, however, a promise has been made and mere anticipated good consequences do not justify breaking a promise, then we have an understanding of why, even in such a situation, the disclosure should not be made.

If confidentiality derives from the implied or expressed promise made by the professional and the lay person, then the right to confidentiality is derived from the ethical principle of promise keeping. This makes clear that the right resides with the patient, not the physician or anyone else. New York State's Department of Social Services has been faced with the problem of disclosing information in welfare client files to the client.[5] Guidelines have been proposed requiring that, under the Freedom of Information Act, records be disclosed upon request. Safeguards of confidentiality are proposed, however, including a requirement that information pertaining to other individuals be withheld. The proposal also includes the provision that confidentiality be maintained by extracting from the file before it is released to the client any medical or psychiatric diagnosis unless a medical professional familiar with the client's medical or psychiatric history has determined that its disclosure would not be against the best interests of the client. In effect, in the name of confidentiality—a right belonging to the client—the client may not be able to see his or her own record. The pledge of confidentiality has become confused with the paternalistic patient-benefiting principle. The right has been shifted from the patient to the physician. If such a requirement is to be placed on disclosure, it cannot be in the name of the promise of confidentiality to the patient.

The Tarasoff case suggests, however, that it might not be prudent to give a blanket promise to keep all confidences no matter what the consequences. In fact, reasonable people coming together to develop a set of moral principles for lay–professional relationships might build in certain exceptions, not exceptions to the requirement about when the promise-keeping rule should be followed, but exceptions in the negotiated promise-keeping rule itself. They might, for example, conclude that there are some special, important patient conditions about which professionals should not be permitted to promise that they would keep confidences. Gunshot wounds, venereal disease, and epilepsy (especially in motorists) are all conditions in which the public might have an overwhelming interest. The contractors might prudently say that there are certain conditions that must be reported to appropriate public health officials and that it is unacceptable for professionals to promise to keep such information confidential. This notion has been recognized in some laws that require such reporting. It is also recognized, at least to a limited degree, in the principles of both the American and the British Medical Associations, which at least permit breaking of confidence when required by law. It seems that the agreement between the society and the profession would not simply permit such infringement on confidentiality, but require it.

Should all information that would be of benefit to society be excluded from the general promise of confidentiality, as was specified in the AMA principles in effect from 1957 through 1980? If so, the professional would have to be sophisticated enough to realize that some disclosures that would otherwise be beneficial to society would have serious, indirect negative effects also. Since the exemption would tend to discourage people who are a danger to society from seeking help from professionals, it could possibly do more harm than good. That would make it prudent to require serious harm to society before a disclosure is justified. Furthermore, people generally value privacy, a notion probably rooted in the principle of autonomy, which will be discussed shortly. Rational people writing the confidentiality rule would probably not insist that any disclosure that would be beneficial to society be made (even taking into account subtle, indirect consequences). The promise should therefore be articulated in such a way that whenever possible, information will be kept confidential. Reasonable people may differ somewhat on exactly what the promise should consist of. Perhaps it should pledge confidentiality except when there is a clearly identified, direct, immediate threat to life or grave bodily harm to another. To offer confidentiality in that situation is something that society probably cannot tolerate—at least it did not in Dr. Moore's case. To require or even permit a physician to disclose whenever it would benefit society, but benefit it by some lesser degree, would really be unnecessary and would do harm in the process. It seems reasonable that physicians should keep a pledge of confidentiality unless required to break it by law or by circumstance of a direct, immediate threat to life or grave bodily harm to another. The exact wording is not as critical as the need that society and the profession come to some understanding so that all involved can know what has been promised.

Would society also permit or require physicians to promise confidentiality, but with the proviso that the physician could break confidence when he or she believed, as Dr. Browne did, that the patient would benefit? It is hard to imagine why reasonable people would agree to that proviso stated in this form. Other, more restricted exclusions from the confidentiality promise might be more acceptable. For example, to take an obvious exception, it seems reasonable that medical professionals should be permitted to break confidence when they have the permission of the patient who is the subject of the confidential information. Promises do not bind when the one making them is authorized by the one to whom they are made to break them. Thus, the 1971 revision of the British Medical Association Code that urges the physician to seek the permission of the patient to break confidence, but to keep the confidence if that permission is not forthcoming, is the kind of stipulation reasonable people might accept. The general British public did not have a chance to vote on that proviso, so it should not be considered part of a covenant between patients and physicians, but it seems like the sort of stipulation they would have accepted if asked.

Some narrower patient-benefiting exclusion to the confidentiality promise might be tolerable. Physicians in most jurisdictions may now break a confidence in order to have a patient committed to a mental institution. Would that sort of exclusion be acceptable to reasonable lay people? I cannot tell for sure. At first it seems as if reasonable people would not want to have their physicians breaking confidence to have them committed against their will. If, however, the decision is being made at some distance from the specific case, if we are adopting a general principle, then people might agree that, with stringent safeguards, their physicians should be permitted to disclose limited information in such situations, at least enough to determine if the patient is competent. This proviso, sometimes called weak paternalism, will be discussed under the principle of autonomy below.

The physician in the homosexual husband case got into a moral bind because he made two implicit promises: to benefit his patient according to his ability and judgment and to keep confidences. It turned out, however, that benefiting Joan required breaking the confidence promised to David. If he had been more discreet in his promising, or if society had been more discreet in articulating the pledge between the profession and the society, the problem could have been avoided. The benefiting promise could have been qualified by saying "except when benefiting requires violating some moral obligation imposed upon the profession (such as keeping the confidentiality promise)." The confidentiality promise could have been qualified by saying "except when disclosure avoids immediate serious threat of bodily harm to another." If the qualifications had been included, the head-on conflict of principles would have been avoided. Probably both qualifiers are reasonable. If the threat to Joan is not considered to be a threat of immediate, serious bodily harm, then the duty of the confidentiality promise would prevail and no violation of the (new) obligation to her would have taken place. Even if the harm were considered to be immediate and serious, still no conflict would occur because no confidentiality promise covering such situations would have been made.

The exact specification of how serious the harm would have to be to justify breaking confidence is probably arbitrary and not terribly critical as long as everyone knows the extent of the confidentiality promise. The specification can be left to mutual agreement between the profession and the society. The core ethical principle for getting out of the confidentiality bind in which Dr. Browne, Dr. Moore, and the physician in the homosexual husband case each found himself in, however, is the recognition of the implications of the principle of promise keeping.

Chapter 8

The Principle of Autonomy

Once promise keeping is accepted as a principle that describes a right-making characteristic of actions independent of consequences, it seems reasonable to press on to see if there are other nonconsequentialist principles. In discussing the problems of the Hippocratic principle, I concluded that reasonable people might not favor a mandate to physicians to do even what is objectively most beneficial to the patient in cases where the autonomous patient chooses otherwise. The freedom of the individual might, we hypothesized, actually overcome the production of maximum benefit. The following case illustrates the problem.

Case 8   *Consent for Research on Human Placentas*

Researchers at a major metropolitan hospital and research center planned a cell physiology study requiring human endothelial cells. They proposed to obtain placentas from clinic patients in the delivery room for normal childbirth.

The research proposal was submitted to the local institutional review board (IRB), the body responsible for review of research involving human subjects. The board first reviewed the protocol to determine, as required by federal regulation, if the risks to the subject were justified by the sum of the benefit to the subject and the importance of the knowledge to be gained; that is, the utilitarian test of maximizing net aggregate utility. They determined quickly that there was no plausible benefit to the subject of this basic science study, but they concluded that there was no plausible risk either. They were satisfied with the scientific merit of the research design and the importance of the research question and so determined that on balance the protocol passed the risk–benefit test.

Federal regulations require two additional tests, however. The rights and welfare of the subject must be adequately protected and there must be a legally effective informed consent. These requirements stand independent of the evaluation of net aggregate utility. The IRB moved to the question of whether the researchers proposed a legally effective informed consent. They searched the protocol, discovering that the researchers had proposed no consent at all. The women in labor would be at no risk. In fact, obtaining consent would be as much an inconvenience to the researchers as to the subjects. Since many of the pregnant women would have had no extensive prenatal contact with the hospital, consent would have to be obtained while they were in labor. Otherwise, subjects would be limited to the small group of patients who would have had more extensive contact with the obstetrical service. The question before the committee was what would constitute a legally effective consent in such a situation. Would the researchers' plan of omitting the consent procedure be acceptable in the light of the fact that there was no risk to the subjects?

When the IRB faced this question, unexpectedly severe disagreement erupted. One group seemed Hippocratic in its approach. Its members emphasized that no harm would be done to the patient. If they were consistently Hippocratic, of course, they would have to be skeptical of the physicians' involvement in the research at all since there was no expected benefit for the patients. They seemed to approach the decision about informed consent by concentrating on the risk to the patient-subject. They could find none. They seemed to compromise the Hippocratic principle to the point that they would support research without direct therapeutic intent. They concluded that requiring subject consent would be frivolous and unnecessary.

Other members of the committee went further, seeming to take a more social utilitarian approach. They were willing to consider benefit to others as well as to the patient. That led them to an even more rigorous opposition to requiring consent. Requiring it would not only be frivolous, but malicious. Not only would patients not be harmed. If

191

consent were required, the research enterprise would be hindered, thus producing less benefit on balance.

According to this more societal calculation of benefits and harms, the only reason for getting consent would be that the benefits of getting it would outweigh the harms. This might occur, for example, when consent was necessary to recruit subjects or when the reputation of the research institution would be jeopardized if word got out that it was conducting experiments without informing patients who were unwittingly also subjects.

A third group of reviewers on the IRB raised this concern about protecting the credibility of the institution in its argument that the subjects who would donate placentas have to be informed and given an opportunity to consent. That was not the real foundation of the group members' argument, however. They contended that subjects had a right to decide whether to participate in the project. They maintained that this right pertained also to cases where subjects participated only by supplying the necessary tissues for a study without in any way risking harm to themselves. They pointed out the possible subtle benefits—both to the individuals and to the institution—of getting consent even in a case such as this one, especially the potential benefits of allowing the general consent rule to dominate over the one requiring consent only when the researchers or the IRB thinks a question of harm to the subject is involved. The core of their argument, however, was different. It rested on the principle of autonomy. It held that morality made it necessary for individuals to be permitted, among other things, personal liberty to determine their own actions according to plans they themselves had chosen. This principle of autonomy, the group held, applied particularly to control over the individual's own body and to tissues obtained therefrom.

AUTONOMY IN THE BASIC SOCIAL CONTRACT

Would the principle of autonomy, like the principle of promise keeping, hold a special place in the social contract of a moral community, a place independent of the calculation of benefits and harms? Many have held that autonomous individuals are a logically necessary prerequisite for any system of morality. Morality implies responsibility for one's actions in some way and responsibility requires some notion of freedom or autonomy of thought and action. At the very least, personal freedom must be a psychological reality.

This position has not been universally accepted in the history of human thought. Determinisms of one type or another abound from the physical determinisms of those who apply a kind of Newtonian physics to the processes of the human body to the behavioral determinisms of a B.F. Skinner to the theological determinisms of those who believe human action is controlled by a divine plan. Yet as powerful as these theories are they eventually must be rejected, at least by those who believe that human freedom and therefore human morality is possible. Theologians from Augustine on up to Luther, Erasmus, and Jonathan Edwards have struggled with the paradox of the compatibility of divine omnipotence with human freedom of the will.[1]

The theological answer has always been that, by the grace of God, man is free, whether the freedom be the robust variant of a Pelagius or an Arminius or the more subordinated freedom of the Augustinian tradition. This theologically grounded doctrine of freedom means that at least one formulation of the idea of individual autonomy posits a preestablished moral community antedating the gift of freedom. Thus it need not be, at least for the discoverers of the principle of autonomy, that contract theory is necessarily individualistic at its roots.

Secular philosophy has also made its peace with the concept of human freedom. Kant, who in some ways provides the bridge from theological to secular notions of freedom, bases his entire moral system on an affirmation that "every rational being exists as an end in himself not merely as a means for arbitrary use by this or that will."[2] From this the will is seen as autonomous, "making the law for itself."[3] Philosophers since Kant, like their theological counterparts, have had to come to terms with some notion of human freedom.[4]

Contract theorists who see the contractors as inventing the basic principle face a problem with the principle of freedom similar to the one they faced with the principle of promise keeping. Freedom of the contractor must be acknowledged prior to the contract. It is a necessary condition for contracting and therefore sometimes referred to as a "side constraint."[5] Somehow, however, they must discover such freedom and the responsibility to respect it while contracting, even if it is only because there is no other rational alternative to the use of force. To make matters more complicated there is no logical reason why free contractors would have to come out of the bargaining with the principle of autonomy intact. They might choose to surrender their autonomy in order to promote aggregate utility, peace, harmony, or tranquility.

Those who see the principle of autonomy rooted in reason, the natural law, divine decree, or experience approach the contract in a somewhat different manner. Both kinds of contractors, however, face this question: Would rational people taking the moral point of view find it necessary to include the principle of autonomy as one of the basic principles for the society in addition to the principles of beneficence and of promise keeping? Time and time again, the answer to this question has been in the affirmative. Liberty is a fundamental principle, either an inalienable right endowed by the creator or simply a rational necessity for founding a moral system. It stands beside the principle of beneficence ("the pursuit of happiness," in the language of the American founding fathers) as an essential part of the social covenant.

The only real question worth pursuing is whether the commitment to the principle of autonomy is totally unlimited, whether autonomy is fundamental even in cases such as our placenta research example, or where the person whose liberty might be restricted stands to benefit greatly from the restriction.

Those who have reflected on this problem have concluded that individual autonomy is very basic. It is to be protected even at some loss in terms of other, nonmoral goods. John Rawls, whose approach, like the one being used here, is contractarian, suggests that a principle of liberty would be the first principle of a contractarian system. As he puts it, rational contractors from behind a veil of ignorance would agree that "each person is to have an equal right to the most extensive basic liberty compatible with a similar liberty for others."[6] The implication is that liberty is basic, but also that it must give way at least at the point where it is necessary to protect like liberty for others.

It is now often argued that for there to be real liberty it is not enough for people to be free from restraint; they must also have the knowledge and resources to act following their freely chosen course. On this basis, claims of freedom have been divided into those that merely affirm an individual's freedom from constraint and those that assure the resources to act. The former are sometimes called 'liberty rights' or 'negative rights' while the latter are called 'entitlement rights' or 'positive rights.'[7] Under the former are such medical notions as the right to refuse medical treatment, the right to control one's own body (assuming that only one's body is at stake), and the right to consent to treatment. They all involve claims of autonomy in the sense of an individual's choosing to act without interference from others.

Entitlement rights, on the other hand, require some action on the part of others in order for one to be free to act. The rights of access to medical care and of Medicare payment for that care, or even the right to courteous treatment (called for in the *Patient's Bill of Rights*), are all claims that normally imply a duty on the part of another not simply to leave the person alone, but to act in a particular way.

Clearly both kinds of rights claims are related to the fundamental principle of autonomy, but clearly they are different conceptually. Entitlement claims are more obviously distributional in their implication. Providing health care resources or professional time for one person necessarily means that resources and time will not be available to another. On the other hand, liberty rights claims are much less obviously distributional. For this reason, I shall deal only with liberty rights claims at this point, leaving entitlement claims for consideration under the principle of justice.

Even liberty in this restricted sense must be constrained when it interferes with the like liberty of others. One cannot have the liberty to shoot firearms in public without seriously jeopardizing the like liberty of others. The interesting question is whether liberty (still in this narrow, more negative sense) should be constrained in order to promote the welfare of the individual whose liberty might be so constrained.

This presses the issue of the relationship between beneficence and autonomy into its starkest form. It is often referred to as the problem of paternalism. Would rational contractors ever permit beneficence to take precedence over liberty when autonomous action does not constrain the liberty of others but can be anticipated to do serious harm to the actor?

While it seems at first that the answer would be negative, it must at least be conceded that society has the right to intervene to protect the welfare of individuals who are substantially nonautonomous, whose actions are essentially nonvoluntary. While some refer to such intervention as a kind of justified paternalism (after all, fathers are justifiably paternalistic with their infant children), others maintain that such cases are really not paternalism problems at all. In any case, they do not illustrate the conflict between the principle of autonomy and the principle of beneficence. The real problem comes when the person is substantially autonomous or when we do not know whether he or she is autonomous.

There is at least one case where rational contractors might agree to paternalism: when persons are engaged in actions potentially seriously harmful to themselves and there is prima facie, but not certain, evidence that those persons do not understand what they are doing or are not free in their actions. If we see a person, acting in an apparently deranged manner, standing on the railing of a bridge but have not determined with certainty that the person is incompetent to understand his action, should society be structured in such a way that we are permitted (if not required) to intervene long enough to determine whether the person is acting rationally? This is a situation that many people consider to justify paternalism. This is sometimes called "weak" paternalism because it is limited to intervention to determine whether the person's action is voluntary.[8] Analysts of paternalism, even those critical of it in its most ordinary forms, have concluded that limited interventions of this sort would be justified, that they would be accepted by contractors taking the moral point of view (who know that they might be on the receiving as well as the giving end of the paternalistic intervention).[9] Careful qualification would have to be placed on the intervention. It would probably be limited to the minimum infringement of freedom necessary to determine whether the person were acting autonomously. As soon as possible, due process would be required if further restriction were called for on grounds that the person were acting in a substantially nonvoluntary way. The one intervening would have to conform to standards that reasonable people would find plausible.

Would these contractors be willing to accept paternalism beyond this weak paternalism? Would they, for example, favor constraint of behavior of an individual who is neither deranged nor irrational and who concedes his behavior is harmful in the long run, but lacks the will power to act in his own best interest?[10] The smoker who would like to quit smoking is an example. The answer seems to be that the society as a whole cannot justify forced control of behavior in such situations, but is willing to accept voluntary, partial surrender of freedom on the part of the individual himself. The smoker might join a club where all members contribute $100 and divide the money among those who do not smoke for one year. The mentally ill, but still substantially voluntary individual might be permitted to surrender his autonomy temporarily to commit himself to a mental hospital for a fixed period of time.

Individual contracts that surrender partial freedom under rigidly specified conditions for fixed periods will be accepted, but not made mandatory by the contractors, or so it would seem. The principle of autonomy prohibits a compulsory paternalism as part of the basic social contract, but that same principle permits individual contractors who are substantially autonomous to agree to limited surrender of their freedom.

But society might reasonably place some limits on the surrender of freedom, even if it is surrendered voluntarily. Especially for those who discover the principle of autonomy (as opposed to those who invent it), liberty might be perceived as an inalienable right in its old, literal sense as a right that cannot be surrendered.[11] It is on this basis that many societies forbid selling oneself into slavery even if the person trying to do so is convinced that he would be better off in the long run as a slave.

John Stuart Mill, who is ordinarily viewed as a pure example of a utilitarian thinker, seems to give an independent status to the principle of liberty at this point. Through the bulk of his *On Liberty*, Mill defends liberty on utilitarian grounds,[12] but when he considers slavery he rejects it not on the grounds that it will tend to do more harm than good, but simply because "by selling himself for a slave, he abdicates his liberty; he foregoes any future use of it beyond that single act. He therefore defeats, in his own case, the very purpose which is the justification of allowing him to dispose of himself."[13] It seems that in the extreme case of selling oneself into slavery, Mill himself recognized what those in the natural rights and Kantian traditions have affirmed all along: Autonomy, independent of the good it will normally produce, is by itself a right-making characteristic of actions. Although it might be surrendered voluntarily in carefully specified situations of limited duration and limited stakes, the principle of autonomy itself remains unscathed as a right-making characteristic of action in a moral community. For those who are known to possess autonomy (and have not surrendered it), the principle takes precedence over any moral obligation to produce benefit for them. That is one reason why the Hippocratic principle, in its original, most paternalistic form, is so unacceptable to those forming a social contract.

AUTONOMY AND THE LAY–PROFESSIONAL CONTRACT

When it comes time to negotiate a covenant or contract between the lay population and the profession, the negotiators will have to work out the implications of the principle of autonomy for lay–professional relations. The starting point would have to be the affirmation of the autonomy of both lay people and professionals whether acting as individuals or as small moral communities. It is on this basis that the parties are able to come together to discuss what the moral relationships should be that bind lay people and professionals. Within the constraints of the basic social contract and the moral principles contained therein, both professionals and lay people ought to be able to retain autonomy in making significant choices in their lives.

For professionals this means that, in general, arrangements with the society ought to include a respect for the professional's conscience. We shall, in the discussion of the principle of justice and the right of access to health care in chapter 11, discover that the members of a rational society would likely want to structure arrangements to allow some kind of health care opportunity for all citizens. At the same time, however, physicians and other health care personnel (especially nurses and those working in hospital settings) should be permitted to avoid participating in health care that they find morally reprehensible. This means provision ought to be made by society to protect the consciences of objectors to abortions or to sterilizations as well as that of objectors to care for the terminally ill that is either very aggressive or limited to palliation. If autonomy of the professional is to be respected in freedom of conscience, however, society will have to assure itself that other professionals will be trained and available to provide services considered essential. Until the adjustment is made so that the profession as a profession has an adequate balance of professionals willing to provide these services, there will be an inevitable conflict between the lay person's right of access and the professional's right of conscience.

The profession as a whole may find certain tasks morally unacceptable even though society feels them essential. Participation in capital punishment or military propaganda might be examples. The contract between the society and the profession will have to come to terms with such tensions, negotiating compromises where possible, or if necessary training new cadres of professionals to perform the jobs that the medical profession as we know it would find collectively objectionable.

The contract between the profession and the society will also have to spell out the sphere of autonomy for lay people. Would it be prudent to set up a system in which lay people surrendered more (or less) of their autonomy to members of the health care professions than to other members of the society? For the most part, since the contract between the profession and the society is bound within the more basic social contract, the principle of autonomy will have to be respected. Certainly it would not be prudent to permit any random member of a helping profession to dominate the liberty of a patient simply because that professional happened to believe, in Hippocratic fashion, that the patient would be helped under such domination.

Weak paternalism, however, seems to be justified within certain constraints. Could it be that members of the helping professions would have a special role to play in weak paternalism? These professionals are often in a position to encounter people in jeopardy of hurting themselves while substantially out of control. The professionals should at least have the same mandate as other members of the society to engage in the minimal intervention necessary to obtain a review with due process to determine competence. That, by itself, is a very restricted justified paternalism. It would permit seeking a court order for a blood transfusion (on the grounds that the person does not voluntarily refuse the blood), but not the forcing of the transfusion simply because the professional believes the person to be incompetent.

Is there any reason, though, why medical professionals should be given greater authority to benefit people even though it violates their autonomy? If stronger paternalism is, in general, unacceptable, even in the hypothetical case where the individual would be benefited by having his autonomy violated, it is hard to see why professionals should merit an exclusion. Even assuming that they would be uniquely talented in determining the best interests of patients, that consideration does not hold up against the principle of autonomy. The fact that physicians historically have believed that they have a duty to benefit patients (even against patients' wills) is not a significant counter that would weigh on the contractors when establishing a set of principles to govern professional conduct.

Professionals are often given special authority to commit people for psychiatric observation for short periods of time. The commitment is an example of weak paternalism that reasonable people might accept if proper safeguards are in place to minimize the infringement. Why are health professionals, especially physicians, given this authority, however? At first it seems to be because they have the expertise in psychiatry necessary to determine competence. Competence, however, is a legal term. Even when temporary commitment is made, the final authority for adjudication of competency is the court, not the psychiatrist. Furthermore, many jurisdictions give all physicians, not just psychiatrists, the authority to commit patients for observation while psychologists are not given such authority. If that is the case, then the authority cannot reasonably be based on physician expertise. Two obstetricians can commit a male for psychiatric observation in the state of

New York. It must be because the members of the profession are trusted as an identifiable group of reasonable citizens, rather than as experts on mental illness and competence.

Society might indeed choose to give professionals this special authority unrelated to their expertise but possibly related to their general reasonableness as good citizens. There are risks, however. Paternalism, even weak paternalism, requires an assessment of the individual's overall welfare, not merely his physical and mental welfare. Selecting a professional with a particular commitment to the physical or mental well-being of people is risking a skewed evaluation. It does not explain why physicians rather than nurses or psychologists or lawyers or architects should be given that special role. On balance, it seems strange that society gives such power to people licensed to practice medicine. To the extent that they are selected as a group of reasonable citizens, such an arrangement might be part of the contract between the society and the profession. Careful safeguards would be necessary, however.

THE RIGHT TO CONSENT

We are now in a position where we can begin to understand what all the fuss is about over the notion of informed consent. Those who insisted that the women in the delivery room had a right of consent in the use of their placentas probably entered the debate from a very different moral standpoint than those who thought the consent issue was either frivolous or malicious. The pro-consent group probably began with a framework that includes the principle of autonomy. Although the patterns are by no means absolute, those who favor requiring consent in such a situation tend to be the lay people while those opposing it tend to be the medical professionals. As medical professionals they stand either in the Hippocratic tradition of clinical medicine or the utilitarian tradition of research medicine, both of which have no independent principle of autonomy. The notion of self-determination so fundamental in Anglo-American secular philosophy and law is simply alien to these alternative positions in medical ethics. From this foundation of the principle of autonomy, we can begin to build a doctrine of consent.[14]

A full theory of consent in lay–professional relationships should include consent on the part of both the professional and the lay person. The terms of the relationship, financial and moral, including any special sets of values held by the lay person or professional, should be spelled out. If either stands within an identifiable special medical ethical tradition—religious or secular—that might influence moral commitments, this should be discussed. The professional should consent to the lay person's moral framework insofar as possible, as the lay person should consent to the professional's.

From the standpoint of one committed to the principle of autonomy, consent is required independent of the calculations of consequences if a person is to be touched (as in assault and battery), if privacy is to be invaded, or if the person is to be used in research. Whether the context be research, therapy, or preventive medicine, if a person is to be treated as an end and not as a means only, then permission is needed when that person is brought into the professional medical nexus. The long battles over the difference between research and therapy seem pointless once one realizes that the principle of autonomy and the right to consent that flows from it remain, regardless of the classification of the contact between lay person and professional.

Some argue that in therapeutic situations a lower standard of consent is called for since the physician is committed unequivocally to serving the patient. We have seen, however, that such a commitment is morally questionable. Even if a physician were so committed, protecting the welfare of the patient does not override the principle of autonomy. There must be some other standard.

The placenta case was selected to illustrate the principle of autonomy and the right to consent because its problematical nature gives us a chance to examine the grounding and standards for getting consent. Some may doubt that consent is required for involvement of a patient in such research. Likewise, the necessity of consent for normal therapeutic contacts between lay person and professional (such as physical exams or routine prescription of an antibiotic for an infection) may be problematic. There must be some limit to the right to consent, for the amount of information potentially transmittable is infinite.

We can get at the proper standard for the amount of information to be transmitted by asking a test question. What would the person want to be told before agreeing to become involved in or deciding to continue the lay-professional relationship (whether it be therapeutic or research)? What information should flow for autonomous choice to be preserved? This reveals the irrationality, the danger, of the traditional standards based on the amount of information professional colleagues similarly situated would have disclosed. Those standards turn out to be irrelevant unless it can somehow be established independently that the professionals would want the same information as the patient or subject. Since professionals have different knowledge, different experiences, and different values and preferences, it seems dangerous to presume they would.

There is a serious methodological problem at this point since we can never know what people would want to be told unless we ask them, and we cannot ask them without telling them what the information is. A prudent compromise seems called for. We can never determine what an individual patient or subject would want to know without asking, but we can determine what typical reasonable people would want to know before participating in the relationship. We could then insist that the professional disclose what reasonable people would want to know, realizing that professionals, as any group of experts, are atypical and therefore not necessarily good judges of what reasonable lay people would want to know.

This, of course, is a limited compromise with the principle of autonomy. The individual engaged in the discussion may not be reasonable. He or she may want more or less information. If that person signals such a desire, the principle of autonomy requires that an individual, subjective standard be substituted for it (or that the relationship be teminated at that point). If, for example, a professional pianist communicates to the medical professional that her hands are unusually important to her and that she wants to know risks to her hands—something the normal person might not care to discuss—then the professional is warned and must conform to the more personal, subjective standard. It is the duty of the person who deviates from the norm, however, to communicate his or her uniqueness (unless the professional can be expected to perceive or know about the unusual characteristics).

It is clear that the reasonable person would not want to know everything about the potential therapy or research project being undertaken. No person, not even the professional, can know or would want to know everything. The proper standard is what the reasonable lay person would want to know (unless the individual lay person has signaled otherwise). This often can be tested simply by asking a group of lay people. For example, some of us once wanted to find out if donors at a blood bank would prefer to know whether there was a chance of some or all their blood being used for research rather than for therapy. Rather than arguing in the abstract over what we would want or what reasonable people would want, we turned to a group of two hundred donors and asked them.[15]

Even with such information it is not clear what standard should be used. At first one might be inclined to disclose all those things that the majority of a group of reasonable persons would want to know. That, however, means that up to half might not be getting facts they considered necessary or desirable in order to give an informed consent, therefore involving them in a relationship violating their autonomy. On the other hand, one cannot insist on absolute proof that no one would want the information before it is excluded from the consent process. With a finite sample of reasonable people, it is impossible to prove that no one would want to know something.

There is a price for communicating too much information. Recipients will be inconvenienced and possibly even confused, so that the quality of their understanding decreases as additional information is given. Clearly information that confuses should be excluded. If the problem is only inconvenience, however, the rights infringements of those who get too much information may not be as serious as the infringements of those who do not get enough. The overinformed person is inconvenienced; the underinformed has his or her autonomy violated. Furthermore, the overinformed have the opportunity to signal that they have had enough information so that the process can stop. On balance, therefore, the reasonable standard for exclusion of a piece of information would be set very high. I see no logically compelling, definitive solution. Elsewhere, I have proposed that information should be transmitted unless fewer than five percent of reasonable people would have desired that information.[16] That still means that the right to consent of five percent may be violated (unless they signal a desire for more information), but I see no other workable solution.

In general, there are two reasons why people would not want a piece of information. First, it might be too trivial, given their system of beliefs and values and the options open to them. In the blood-use survey, for example, if only a few cubic centimeters of blood were to be used in research, some people did not even care to know about it. If, however, all the blood were to be used, then they wanted to be consulted.

Some information might be so trivial, we can presume that virtually no reasonable people would want to have it. For example, should people be asked to consent before their old medical records are surveyed for statistical information about some noncontroversial health problem? A great many people would say that if they had no information at all about such a project, they still would have been adequately informed. It is not that no consent would be required, but rather that the reasonable person might consent without being told anything at all, that is, he might give a blanket consent for the use of such records. If the names were to be disclosed, however, or if the purpose of the research were controversial (say, for testing the hypothesis of a correlation between blood type and race or IQ and race), then people might want to be told. That in itself is sufficient reason why even apparently trivial research projects such as record searches should be reviewed by a panel made up of people as close to reasonable subjects as possible. The risk of confidentiality violation or of potentially objectionable research should be ruled out. Reasonable people would want to consent, so the argument goes, if either of these factors were present in a study. They would feel as if their autonomy were being violated if they were not asked. But for some decisions, such as the statistical use of medical records or the drawing of blood in therapeutic settings for a routine set of blood tests, perhaps the reasonable person would desire to know nothing more at all. For the blood test, the person probably already knows about the momentary pain and the risk of a minor infection.

Even for routine tests, however, persons perhaps should know something about test costs, who will pay for them, what the physician is looking for, or how likely it is that something will be found. All of these are reasons why, even for routine blood tests, active patient consent might be in order. Rational people with differing value systems or different financial means would choose differently depending upon the answers to those questions; still others might consider all of these concerns too trivial. If so, then consent can be implied with no further explicit discussion of the invasion of the patient's autonomy.

This gives us a framework for the placenta case. We should ask whether reasonable women delivering a baby in that obstetrical unit would want to be asked before the placenta they contribute is used for research. Some may find it such a trivial request that they would not even want to be asked. Rather than speculate, though, there is an obvious empirical way to answer the test question: Ask women who are delivering babies in that obstetrics unit. If more than five percent (my arbitrarily chosen cutoff point) would want to be informed, then the group as a whole should be. To do so would inconvenience the researchers and possibly the women, but it would preserve the principle of autonomy. If less than five percent would have wanted to be told, their right to self-determination would have been violated, but if such a standard were well publicized they would at least know of that risk and would have an opportunity to warn the medical staff of their unusual desire for information. If some lesser standard is used, then the principle of autonomy is violated even more.

There is a second reason why people might not want to be informed even if the issues are not considered trivial. They may trust the value system that someone else would use to make the choice and may not care to take part actively. A patient who has known his physician for many years may have come to know that his own values were almost always the same as the physician's. As a matter of efficiency, that patient may be less inclined to want to have details than he would be if he were seeing a new physician.

This second reason for not wanting information tends to be idiosyncratic to a specific lay–professional relationship. Some value questions in medical decisions, however, may generate such a consensus that as a matter of public policy we can assume a convergence of the lay person's and the professional's values. This explains why the contract between the profession and the society permits the professional to presume consent in the case of life-threatening emergency to an incompetent patient. When a safe, simple, and relatively sure technique is available for starting respiration on a patient who would otherwise die, and there is no means available to check that patient's personal values, we can presume, according to this understanding, that the person would prefer to live. That presumption is not a certainty. A patient may be a member of a religious group that opposes the intervention, but society and the profession have agreed that there is such a great likelihood of consensus on the values that, given the alternatives, it is acceptable to presume the patient's approval without futher discussion.

These two legitimate reasons for not wanting information—because it is too trivial and because the professional's values are known to be similar to the lay person's—suggest a moral problem. What should happen if someone specifically requests that information be withheld, but without having the justification of either of these reasons? For example, what should be done if a terminally ill patient requests that information about diagnosis and prognosis (which certainly would be considered essential by the reasonable-person test) be withheld because the person refuses to take responsibility for important medical decisions about his or her own life? What should happen if a candidate for an important but risky research project, wanting to be altruistic, refuses to hear of the risks of the experiment for fear that he or she will then decline to participate?

If autonomy is not only a right, but an inalienable right, then it seems that there is something dehumanizing about refusal to face important decisions affecting one's future. It is more noble, more responsible, to take an active part in making these decisions. That seems to imply that individuals have not only a right but an obligation to get this kind of critical information (information that is neither trivial nor irrelevant because it is known that other decision makers will use values that are the same as the primary decision maker). The principle of autonomy, then, if it is a right-making characteristic of actions, generates at least a prima facie duty to get information that would be material to responsible decision making.

It does not follow, however, that professionals engaged in covenantal discussions related to obtaining consent have an authorization to force information on others against their will. That same principle of autonomy that generates a right to be informed gives humans the freedom to act in a less than responsible manner. Imposing information on a person would violate the individual's autonomy just as withholding information would. At least for the therapeutic situation, then, explicit requests from lay people that information not be transmitted should be honored.

There is a danger that professionals charged with obtaining consent may take this exception as a justification for withholding information that they believe is not wanted by the patient, based on, say, their reading of indirect communication, vague value expressions, or body language. The danger of misinterpreting such indirect signals is so great that it seems reasonable to insist on direct, explicit communication from the lay person if the normal requirements of consent are to be waived.

A request by the patient not to receive information often may be justified by one of the two reasons just discussed: For a particular patient with a unique set of beliefs and values the information may be too trivial, or the decision to participate may not be material because the professional is considered to have values similar to the patient's. In other cases the request may be less responsible. It seems, nevertheless, that it still should be honored, at least in therapeutic contexts.

Research not related to efforts to benefit a specific patient poses an even more complex problem. In these cases lay people have a particularly rigorous obligation to participate in decisions concerning the lay–professional relationship. The normal appeals for exceptions from consent by the patient in the therapeutic context do not apply. The normal subject cannot argue, as the patient can, that the benefits of a procedure are so obvious that virtually any value system would lead to a decision to participate or that the trauma of the illness makes full participation difficult. On the other hand, the principle of autonomy still would seem to justify the right of an individual to waive access to what seems like a reasonable amount of information. In all but the extreme situation the autonomous surrender of free and active control over one's life is not analogous to Mill's example of selling oneself into slavery where it is argued that the autonomy principle itself prohibits such ultimate surrender of freedom. Thus, from the standpoint of the subject, waiving information in research settings seems comparable to waiving it in therapeutic settings.

From the standpoint of the researcher and the research community, however, there may be an important difference. In research on normal subjects (as opposed to therapeutic interventions with at least some intention of benefiting the patient), little would be lost by excluding those subjects who want to waive a reasonable amount of information. Normally other subjects could be taken at almost no cost. Declining subjects have no right to participate in the research. The researcher, the research community, or the researcher's institution may have an obligation not to take risks with other human beings' lives without their adequately informed consent when the subjects willing to be informed are available to participate.[17]

Autonomy, then, provides an underpinning of the right to consent for both research and more routine therapeutic settings. It also provides a standard for deciding how much information must be transmitted for consent to be considered informed. People should be told what the reasonable lay person similarly situated would want to know in order to exercise autonomous choice about their life plans. No one wants fully informed consent; reasonably informed consent by the reasonable-person standard, however, is essential, unless the lay person has signaled that some other amount of information is appropriate to his or her unique situation. In rare circumstances, especially in the research setting, special requests for more or less information than the reasonable person would want to have may make continuation of the relationship impossible for the professional. In that case, the covenant between professional and lay person comes to an end, but barring such a parting of the ways, autonomy of both parties is preserved in the covenant between them.

THE RIGHT TO REFUSE TREATMENT

With this construction of the right to consent rooted in the principle of autonomy before us, the question of the right to refuse treatment, over which much controversy has taken place recently,[18] is reduced to little more than an aside. It makes no sense to talk about getting a patient's consent to nontreatment, whether that patient be terminally ill or not. Consent is a process that establishes a covenant between patient and professional within the context of a broader series of covenants or contracts. One does not consent to nontouching. Nontouching is the initial presumption of autonomous individuals barring any consent that establishes a medical relationship.

Legally and morally, treatment without consent is assault and battery. Conversely, consenting to nontreatment is like consenting to not having assault and battery committed. The only way that the notion makes any sense at all is to presume that the prior establishment of a covenant between patient and physician carries with it the presumption of continued care. Reasonable patients and physicians, however, would never contract for an open-ended relationship that bound them to one another for care in perpetuity. The physician would reserve the right to end the relationship if certain problems arose—for example, if the physician could not in good conscience participate in a course of treatment chosen by the patient. By the same token, the reasonable patient would choose to end a relationship with a physician at the point where the physician believes that the only care he or she can offer falls outside the patient's system of beliefs and values. Refusing medical care believed necessary by the physician is nothing more than the patient's expression of what is fitting in his or her system of values. It is to be hoped that in most such cases the values expressed will be sufficiently compatible with the professional's so that the covenantal relationship can be continued, with the professional providing the care chosen by the patient or with some mutually acceptable compromise negotiated at the level of this individual contract.

In this regard the fact that the patient is terminally ill would appear to count for little. Of course, we, as a society, might adopt the position that the principle of autonomy applies less rigorously once one is terminally ill. Unless we adopt such a stance, though, the right of self-determination applies equally in these circumstances. If there is any obligation to prolong life at all (independent of considerations of benefit and harm or of a duty to avoid killing), it cannot authorize professionals to violate the autonomy of the terminally ill. The society cannot let a minority of physicians who believe that they have a duty to prolong life override the principle of autonomy in such situations. Should individuals hold that there is such an independent duty to prolong life (whether or not they are members of groups we have identified with that position), that conviction can be expressed in the covenantal bonds established with the physician by the individual or by his or her agents at the appropriate time.

FAMILY AND GUARDIAN AUTONOMY

Mention of the notion of an agent for the patient introduces a final qualification in the analysis of the principle of autonomy in lay–professional relationships. I have presumed that the principle of autonomy gives the individual lay person and professional authority to make covenants and other contracts including consenting to medical interventions. The real world, however, is not populated exclusively by autonomous individuals acting as isolated, free agents. They are also members of groups—in both voluntary associations, such as clubs, churches, and professional organizations, and in ascribed communities, such as families and ethnic communities. Sometimes these groups may function as smaller moral communities for the individual. Any full theory of medical ethics must include a theory of these moral communities.

One way into this subject is to ask what should happen in cases where the individual cannot function as his or her own moral agent. When a patient is not competent, for example, to negotiate and renegotiate his or her own covenant with the health professional, what ought to happen?

The response probably depends upon the moral history of the individual. Three different types of cases deserve separate theoretical formulations. First, consider the case of the formerly competent man who had expressed, at least in some rudimentary form, his own moral position about medical decisions. This person may have written a living will or expressed wishes about terminal care. He may have developed a sufficiently consistent philosophical stance toward the world that his beliefs on medical matters can be deduced.

Whether the position is expressed in writing or merely by a consistent life-style, there will be problems in interpreting the person's system of beliefs and values when it comes time to make a specific medical decision. Since the man is no longer competent—say because of senility, comatose condition, or legal declaration of incompetency—he will not be able to negotiate the specific terms of the individual contract for medical care. Someone else must make the decisions. In this case, it seems that the decisions should be based on the person's beliefs and values as best as can be determined. The agent for the patient should be selected on the basis of ability to reflect and interpret those beliefs and values. The obvious best candidate would be someone designated for this purpose by the person. That is why I and others have recommended that people who are concerned about the quality of their terminal care (or their care in circumstances of incompetency) designate someone using a power of attorney.[19] Autonomy is preserved by the agent acting on the framework established by the person while competent.

There will be some cases where the person has not expressed wishes or even a set of beliefs and values that would give a frame of reference for making the decision on this subjective basis. In the most extreme case, which constitutes our second type of case, the patient has given no signals at all, perhaps has never even been competent to express any views on the matter. Here the principle of autonomy contributes nothing. It seems like the only thing we can do is revert to the principle of beneficence, insisting that the choice be made according to the best available objective judgment about what will best serve the interests of the patient. This is not, of course, the Hippocratic solution, unless it is independently established that the personal judgment of the physician involved in the case is the best available objective basis for deciding. Normally, especially in cases such as this where the patient is alone and without a moral community, we would want to assure maximum protection requiring standards of due process such as would be offered by judicial review to determine what is most objectively in the patient's interest. Some qualification may have to be made to this solution when we later discuss the principle of justice, but for the present it seems that a good approximation of the method for the second type of case would be to turn to the courts or to some such method of ascertaining in the light of public scrutiny what is most objectively in the patient's interest.

The third type of case is more complex; patients here have not expressed their wishes while competent, but family members are available who are plausible candidates for the guardian role. Assume (for the moment) that in cases where individual autonomy can play no role the goal is to do what is in the patient's interest. Do we as a society want to insist that the judgment be made according to the best available, objective judgment of patient interest, or do we want to permit limited familial discretion? I think that a case can be made for what I shall call limited familial autonomy.[20]

There is likely to be some disagreement over what is really in the incompetent one's best interest. This disagreement will stem from differences in interpretation of the facts, and from disagreements, as well, about the beliefs and values at stake. Even if we assume that there is some way to determine objectively what is best for the patient, it is not clear that such a criterion is precisely what we as a society should require.

In the case of the formerly competent patient, as we have seen, the individual may have been bound to smaller moral communities that have some legitimate, if limited, role in these decisions. The most obvious case would be a religious group. One might, for example, grow to have confidence in a leader in one's church and designate such a person as one's agent. This might especially be the case if the religious group had a developed position in medical ethics that differed from the broader community's.

For the never-competent person (or the one who never expressed himself while competent), however, the small moral community plays a more ambiguous role. The family is the most significant example. Should the family be given any discretion in exercising judgment over what counts as being in the patient's interest, or should it be required to accept the best available judgment of objective interest?

It is clear that the family cannot have unlimited discretion. That would give parents the right to choose extremely dangerous, even life-threatening, alternatives—such as the refusal of an apparently needed blood transfusion. But is it possible that the family as a smaller moral group should be given limited familial autonomy?

The family is an important institution in all societies. Though its role differs substantially in different cultures, all give families a broad range of decision-making choices. The same principle of autonomy that gives the individual freedom to deviate from the social consensus of what is best may also provide some limited range of familial discretion. For example, parents are given discretion in selecting a school system for their children. They are even permitted to choose alternative systems that most people would not consider to be fully in the best interests of the ward.

If that is the case, then as a society we might begin with an initial presumption that the family (or next of kin) is the agent for the incompetent patient. That agent would attempt to decide in the best interests of the patient based, if possible, on the beliefs and values of the patient. If that is not possible, then the family agent should determine what is objectively in the patient's best interest based on the family's beliefs and values. That initial presumption is now routine in cases of parents who are asked to consent to professional medical treatment for their children.

There are limits, however. The parents cannot choose to have no schooling at all. They cannot refuse needed blood transfusions or other care when the best available judgment is that such care is clearly in the interests of the ward. The presumption can, therefore, be tested in court. Anyone—another family member, neighbor, or health care professional—has the right and even the duty to ask for judicial review to see if the presumed guardian has gone beyond the limits of reasonableness. The goal is still to do what is in the interest of the patient. If review takes place, severe limits will be placed on the guardian. The guardian will not be reduced, however, to one and only one option in all cases. In some instances, perhaps in many, there will be more than one course that, according to the best objective tests the court can muster, is a reasonable approximation of what is in the incompetent one's interests. In some cases the test of objective best interest may yield two or more options of equal value. At least in those cases (and where the patient's own value system cannot be used) the guardian, using familial autonomy, should have the right to choose among them.

In some cases one course may seem the most reasonable, but other courses may be so close that some rational persons might choose them. For example, suppose parents were faced with the choice between a leukemia chemotherapy treatment program for a child that involved three years of severely burdensome treatment with projected five percent mortality and another course involving only two years of burdensome treatment and projected six percent mortality. Suppose further that the courts, applying the most objective test they could devise of best interest for the particular child, determined that the former treatment was more in the child's interest. They might at the same time concede that the two-year regimen is also plausibly defensible as being in the child's interest, although not quite as beneficial as the five-year treatment. The courts might find that parents opting for the two-year treatment plan are acting within the limits of reason. Clearly those parents would not be permitted to choose no treatment at all; that would exceed the limits of reason. But if two choices seem close the principle of familial autonomy might permit parents to choose what they consider to be objectively the best course, even if most reasonable people would go some other route.

The same kind of problem often emerges in more mundane treatment choices. Many dentists X-ray children's teeth twice a year. Let us assume for the moment that such a schedule meets the test of objective best interest of the child. Should a parent who has an unusually uniquely high fear of radiation exposure for the child be permitted limited familial autonomy to decline X rays at that frequency, perhaps choosing instead to have them made only yearly? The problem would be the same if some other frequency is judged best for the child. We still must face the problem of whether family members in the guardian role should be permitted to use deviating family values to choose

slightly deviant courses for their child's medical care. Parents who refuse all dental care for their child might well be exceeding the bounds
of which I am speaking, but it seems that limited familial discretion is
not only permissible, but desirable. Some might argue that a child in
such a case benefits in the long run from limited parental discretion,
thereby defending limited parental choice, in the end, on grounds of
the child's best interest. That probably is true, but even if it were not, it
seems that parents and other family members acting as guardians or
agents should have some limited choice based on the value of familial
autonomy (in cases, that is, where a patient's own system of beliefs and
values cannot be used either because it has never existed or is not
accessible).

Would reasonable contractors establishing a social order extend the
concept of autonomy to familial autonomy in this way? If so, they give
the family a unique place in the social system. Someone must have the
initial presumption of agency. The family has general responsibility
for the welfare of its members and is accustomed to making decisions
based on a full and complex familial pattern of beliefs and values. We
have grown to respect these choices. I see no reason why familial
autonomy should not have this limited place in a system of medical
ethics.

Chapter 9

The Principle of
Honesty

As supplements to the principle of beneficence, in addition to promise keeping and autonomy, rational people would have to consider a third principle. At the time they were formulating the basic principles for a moral community, they would also have to consider the principle of honesty. Truthfulness or veracity seems to be, like promise keeping and autonomy, a fundamental moral claim on human interaction. In medicine this principle is both crucial for lay–professional interactions, and to a remarkable degree, ignored as an independent right-making characteristic. If we are to understand the significance of honesty in the relationships between lay people and professionals, however, we shall first have to grasp the basic moral notion itself.

HONESTY IN THE BASIC SOCIAL CONTRACT

If people were to come together to discover or invent the basic principles for a society adopting the moral point of view, they would include in their agreement, so it seems, commitment to the principles of promise keeping and autonomy. Closely related to these, perhaps implied in them, is the notion of honesty or veracity. As we have seen before, the inventors of the contractual principles would have difficulty in their initial negotiations unless there were some preexisting commitment to honesty. It seems they could not even generate the honesty principle by promising or contracting because there would be no way to assure that the initial promise was made honestly. They would have to reason together that honesty serves self-interest as well as morality and that therefore those at the bargaining table could be trusted, at least provisionally, to be honest in their bargaining. Eventually the habit of honesty in social interactions might emerge. Always, however, there would be the fear that individual "free riders" would conclude in a specific case that dishonesty would pay for them even after taking into account the harmful impact on the liar's reputation.

Discoverers of the basic principles do not have this problem. Just as they might find the principles of promise keeping and autonomy in a divine decree or in the laws of nature or reason, so they could discover a similar duty to tell the truth.

Two kinds of arguments are given in support of the principle. The first, attractive to rule utilitarians, is that reasonable people would be forced by reason to conclude that a world with the rule "always to tell the truth" would be a better world on balance than a world with any alternative rule. In order for human interaction to be valuable, it must be based on the premise that communication will be honest.

Kant's vigorous defense of truthfulness is sometimes interpreted as making this appeal to consequences regarding a policy permitting dishonesty in special cases. In his fascinating short essay, the "Supposed Right to Tell Lies from Benevolent Motives," Kant writes: "If, then, we define a lie merely as an intentionally false declaration towards another man, we need not add that it must injure another . . .; for it always injures another; if not another individual, yet mankind generally."[1] It sounds as if Kant has finally been caught calculating consequences as the basis of morality. But further reading reveals that this is not the case. By "injury to mankind generally," he means doing wrong (formally) rather than merely doing harm.[2] He concludes that "to be truthful (honest) in all declarations is therefore a sacred unconditional command of reason, and not to be limited by any expediency."[3]

It is possible that subtle, sophisticated interpretations of rule utility lead to the conclusion that it is wrong to violate the principle of honesty because the rule based on that principle produces more good than any other rule. Kant and many others have concluded, however, that that is not the decisive reason for a principle of honesty. Rather, it is because dishonesty by its very nature is a violation of what is morally required. Sometimes this is interpreted as a violation of faithfulness, of the fidelity of an implied promise that communication is truthful.[4] Sometimes it is interpreted as a violation of the respect that is owed to another as an autonomous being who is an end in himself.[5] In any case, being truthful is morally, according to these views, a right-making characteristic, independent of the consequences of dishonesty. Especially as we move into problems of truthfulness in the medical sphere, it may be helpful to articulate the principle of honesty on its own in the list of principles reasonable people would accept.

HONESTY AND THE LAY-PROFESSIONAL CONTRACT

This principle of honesty will be the context within which lay people and professionals will come together to spell out the moral freamwork for lay-professional relations. The medical sphere, it turns out, is a prime area where people have from time to time argued that dishonesty might be justified. Henry Sidgwick the great utilitarian argued, for example, that, "Where deception is designed to benefit the person deceived, Common Sense seems to concede that it may sometimes be right: for example, most persons would not hesitate to speak falsely to an invalid, if this seemed the only way of concealing facts that might produce a dangerous shock."[6] In contrast to Kant, for whom expediency was of no power as a counter to honesty, Sidgwick says, "I do not see how we can decide when and how far it [dishonesty] is admissible, except by considerations of expediency."[7]

Medical professionals had, until recently, followed Sidgwick's moral conclusion rather than Kant's. Organized medicine had been silent on any requirement to deal honestly with patients, subordinating the principle of honesty to the Hippocratic principle so that the question of whether to be truthful with a patient was determined by consideration of what the physician believed would benefit the patient on balance. None of the codes made any commitment to truthfulness. Practitioners, by large majorities, reported that they at least sometimes withheld information from patients.[8] They have done so, for example, in dealing with terminally ill patients[9] and in situations such as genetic counseling where truthfulness might produce harm to the parent being counseled or to the offspring,[10] or in cases in which deception was deemed necessary to conduct research, especially social-psychological research.[11] Professionals have, on Hippocratic or broader utilitarian grounds, supported withholding the truth, deceiving the lay person, or even outright active lying.

Recently, there have been signs of change within professional

216

groups. The newly adopted "Principles of Ethics" of the American Medical Association commit the physician member for the first time to "deal honestly with patients and colleagues and strive to expose those physicians deficient in character or competence, or who engage in fraud or deception."[12] Perhaps the members of the AMA's House of Delegates did not realize how radical a break from the Hippocratic tradition this seemingly innocent commitment was. It signals, however, a shift in moral position within the profession.

That same shift is traced in the attitudes of individual practitioners. While earlier surveys of physicians' patterns of disclosing a terminal illness revealed substantial proportions who tended not to disclose, recent surveys have found a remarkable shift in favor of disclosure.[13] Some of this shift may be accounted for by a shift in the professional judgment about the consequences of disclosure. As health care delivery within larger, less personal institutional teams becomes the norm, it probably will be harder for an individual physician to withhold a diagnosis, even if he or she thought that would be beneficial. A greater part of the shift in attitude seems to be accounted for, however, by the shift in moral principle away from the paternalistic Hippocratism of an earlier day and toward a more covenantal model in which the patient is seen as an active participating member of the health care team.

Of course, the official shift in the principles of medical ethics of the AMA and the parallel shift in physician attitude cannot be decisive in determining what reasonable people would choose if they were formulating a set of moral principles for the lay–professional relationship. If the earlier professional commitment to the Hippocratic principle was not logically decisive for lay people, then neither can the more enlightened, nonconsequentialist commitment to honesty be logically decisive.

We are left with the question of whether the medical professional's roles are so sufficiently unique that reasonable people would grant a special exemption from the honesty requirement to people in those roles. It is possible that some kinds of exemptions might be consistent with, and justified under, a broader social contract that generally prohibits certain actions. The role of policeman is normally thought to carry with it a legitimate exemption from the prohibition on the use of physical force. To take a trivial example in the area of honesty, the role of magician in Western society carries with it an exception from any prohibition against deception. Technically, only deceptions integral to the performing of magic are legitimate; deceptive contracts for the magician's services would remain just as wrong.

Magicians' deceptions are exempted from the general prohibition because all parties involved, at least those who understand magic the way the modern scientific West understands it, realize that deception is integral to the art. An audience knowingly consents to the deception and enjoys the game of each trying to outwit the other.

Could medicine be similar to magic in a way not anticipated by the anthropologists of religion who study the similarities and differences between medicine in Western culture and magic in non-Western cultures? Society, at the time of bargaining with the representatives of the medical profession, could agree that physicians and other health care professionals have a special exemption to deceive, withhold the truth, and possibly even lie when they believe it would be in the interest of patients.

That eliminates the moral tension between honesty and Hippocratic beneficence, but at a great price. In special cases, individual patients might be able to contract with individual practitioners so that a professional would be permitted to withhold certain information thought harmful to the patient. As strange as it may seem, some patients might have a meeting of the minds with their physicians, establishing a general consent for the physician to withhold or even lie at some point in the future if the physician believed it would benefit the patient. Of course, that would undermine the physician's credibility to some extent, but those who agreed to such a plan might find it tolerable. There are reports that some patients given placebos (pharmacologically inactive medication prescribed to produce an anticipated benefit in the patient who falsely believes the compound to be active) and told they are getting placebos sometimes still get positive placebo effects.[14]

One of the more intriguing problems in medical ethics is whether people have a duty rather than a mere right to be actively responsible for decision making vis-à-vis their cases. The answer will depend upon one's understanding of the nature of the human being, as well as one's theory of medical ethics. The contractarian theory being constructed here is based on certain judgments in both areas. Humans are viewed as autonomous agents, as ends in themselves (although quite possibly existing within a transcendent framework where they are said to derive their fundamental worth through the grace of a transcendent power). It is their nature to possess the capacity for rational and free choice and to make covenantal relationships both as individuals and as moral communities. If this is a reasonable understanding of the human, then there seems to be something dehumanizing about a refusal to have the knowledge necessary to be an active and equal participant in decision making. When that decision making affects primarily one's own being, then responding to one's own nature with integrity seems to require knowing information necessary to take primary responsibility for those decisions. To be true to one's own nature, then, may require active assimilation of necessary knowledge.

When I have made a similar argument in the past, it has sometimes been interpreted as implying that professionals, such as physicians, therefore have a right or a duty to impose information on a person against his or her wishes.[15] That does not follow, however. If individuals, lay people, or professionals are free, autonomous beings, they retain the right (derived from the principle of autonomy) to conduct themselves in ways that may not be the most noble. Certainly, individuals should be able to decline information they find trivial or information that, because of their system of beliefs and values, they find to be irrelevant to making decisions about their own health care. But they should be able to go even further. They should be able to decline even more essential information. Respecting their autonomy in these cases requires permitting them to be less rational and less in control than they could be.

Thus, at the level of the individual contract or covenant between lay person and professional, special agreements exempting one party from open, honest, or ordinary disclosure to the other seem acceptable. But could there be a general agreement to such an exemption at the stage of the second contract, the contract between the society and the profession? It is hard to imagine that society could offer such a sweeping exemption. Even if individual practitioners and patients are of such a temperament and have such a long-term trusting relationship that it would be prudent to work out an exemption to the honesty principle, that special set of relations does not exist typically in the society. The result of a general exemption to the honesty principle for medical professionals would be a breakdown of trust in the lay–professional relationship. No patient could believe any good news received from his or her physician. Assuming this were a general policy, the word would soon spread that physicians sometimes deceived or withheld or lied. The professional's word would soon be meaningless. The contract giving the exemption would reasonably be reciprocal so that both parties had the right to lie, withhold, or decieve when they thought it would be beneficial to the other party. In that case, professionals also would not be able to depend on lay people to deal honestly with them. All too often patients have reported withholding pain or agony or anger from their physicians because they did not want to disturb the physicians, perhaps not realizing that the integrity of the relationship was in jeopardy just as it is when professionals are dishonest with their patients. Honesty, the presumption of truth telling by both parties, is necessary for a covenantal relationship between equals. If there were a general contractual understanding between professionals and lay people that dishonesty were acceptable whenever one party believed it would be in the interests of the other party, individuals would no longer be treated with the equality and respect afforded those treated as ends in themselves, but would be treated as objects subject to manipulation in order to produce good consequences. If the arguments against the Hippocratic ethic and against paternalism hold (at the level of the lay–professional contract), then rational negotiators would not want to write in an exemption for the lay–professional relationship as a whole.

This has implications for several major areas in lay–professional relations in medicine. First, if people have a right to be dealt with honestly and to receive information they need to make decisions within the lay–professional relationship, then they should have the right to processes needed to become informed. These include a right to counseling and communication with those who can convey adequately the required information. They include a right of access to medical journals and medical books (within reasonable limits of burden on libraries and other facilities) and to medical records as well. The medical record is an important symbol, a visible collection of potentially significant information. If the lay person is to be treated by the profession as an equal in moral worth and one responsible for making medical decisions about his or her own care, then the written as well as the oral version of the critical information must be open to the patient. Arguments often given against a right of access, such as the potential harms that could come (especially regarding psychiatric records), do not count against this nonconsequentialist principle of honesty and the related principles of promise keeping and autonomy. If the patient literally cannot understand the information when explained and communicated responsibly (because of inherent lack of capacity to understand or because of the traumatic nature of the information), then the patient literally cannot consent and is incompetent for the purposes of the particular relationship. A guardian should be appointed to act on behalf of the incompetent one.

A second implication of forbidding exemptions from the honesty principle concerns use of placebos. They would become almost morally impossible. Only in that special case where one has somehow consented to being so deceived would placebos be morally acceptable. Those who have analyzed the ethics of placebos have increasingly been led to this conclusion.[16] In contract perspective, it would appear that no general authorization of the use of placebos would be possible.

Third, deception in scientific research is suspect. Research deception poses a slightly different problem, however. In the first place, efforts to defend such research—in both the medical and social sciences—rely not on the Hippocratic, patient-benefiting principle, but on a more general social utilitarian principle. The opposition to deception, therefore, is not the opposition grounded in the attack on paternalism. Rather, it is grounded in a concern for the moral dangers of justifying infringement of individuals' rights simply because it is in the interests of society to do so. Furthermore, the utilitarian defense of deception in scientific research cuts a broader swath through the fabric of life than does the use of placebos.[17] With placebos, one would realize that their use would be limited to a professional cadre in those rare circumstances where the individual himself could be benefited. By contrast, in research, virtually every corner of one's life is potentially subject to such deception. The researchers may not be those identified as one's freely chosen physician, but could be all manner of scientists, including those who pose as reporters, salesmen, accident victims,[18] court officials,[19] and even fellow religious converts.[20] Virtually all of one's social interactions with fellow human beings would become suspect.

On the other hand, consent for deception in social science research is not out of the question. For example, students could be recruited for a long series of experiments by the local university's psychology department and told that, occasionally, certain pieces of information might be withheld or even falsified. Rational persons might consent to such an arrangement if they were assured, as discussed earlier, that confidentiality would be maintained adequately, that they would not likely object to the overall purpose of the experiment, and that there would be no risks of physical or mental harm. It is even possible that research subjects of adequate quality could be obtained this way. The usual objection is that if subjects are so alerted to the possibility of deception, they would not be a valid sample of the population the researchers are attempting to study. By now, however, most humans are somewhat suspicious of scientific research, so there may be no such thing as a genuine naive subject. Whether or not this provides a way out of the dilemma posed by the principle of honesty, it would appear that deception, short of this kind of individual lay–professional contract that authorizes it, violates the principle. It is hard to see how reasonable people contracting with the research-professional would authorize wider use of deception.[21]

There is one possible way out of the dilemma short of a general contract with professionals exempting them from the principle of honesty in situations where harmless deception with purposes that are not suspect seem necessary to produce valuable information. In discussing the right to consent as it derives from the principle of autonomy, it was argued that people must be told what reasonable people would want to know if they are to consent to the invasion of their autonomy. Clinicians and investigators thus carry the burden, according to this reasonable person standard, of establishing that they have disclosed what reasonable people would want to know. Theoretically, however, reasonable people might hold that they would not want to know about a particular deception (or withholding or lying), especially if the mendacity were necessary to gain important research information (as well as meeting the other conditions mentioned above). If it could be established reliably, based on empirical evidence, that subjects would not want to be told about the deception, then an adequate consent could be obtained without disclosing the key piece of information. For example, surrogate subjects drawn from the same pool from which potential real subjects will be recruited might be told the proposed deception and asked if they would have wanted to have been told about it. Evidence that they would not have wanted the information would have to be strong. Using the figure I proposed earlier, if no more than five percent of the surrogate subjects objected to the deception and wanted to be informed (and the other conditions were met), then the deception would be justified.[22] I believe, based on an unscientific sampling, that more than this percentage of reasonable people would object in principle to any deception, in which case our theoretical opening to deception research is once again closed rapidly. The model proposed, however, is not one based on *ex post facto* consent.[23] It is based on the claim rooted in empirical evidence that reasonable people would consider the consent adequate without the missing piece of information. It is always the case that some information about a therapeutic or a research interaction will be withheld from the patient. It is justifiably withheld on the grounds that reasonable people would not want that information. If virtually no reasonable subjects would want to know about a particular deception, then it would not need to be disclosed.

LYING, DECEPTION, AND WITHHOLDING THE TRUTH

Thus far I have treated lying, deception, and withholding the truth as if they were one and the same. Some may object that there are moral differences such that the immorality of lying does not extend to all cases of deception and withholding. In fact, there are subtleties within the general scope of dishonesties that need further elucidation in a general theory of medical ethics. It may turn out that even some truthful statements are morally condemned under the principle of honesty and that silence may sometimes be more honest than at others.

There is a particularly perverse dishonesty that I call "the big lie," the dishonesty that fools even the one who is being dishonest.[24] Sometimes, for example, the truth can have the moral impact of a lie because it is meant to convey a false or misleading impression. Truthful disclosure to a patient that he has cancer, using technical jargon intended to conceal the reality, is what might be called a truthful lie.

At other times, people, especially medical professionals, may convince themselves that they have spoken the truth when they say they cannot be sure what the outcome of a medical condition will be. They may say that only to assure the patient when they themselves have some idea of the likely course of events. They have learned in their scientific training that nothing is known with absolute certainty. They could make such an observation and continue to disclose the possible outcomes and some estimate of their likelihood. They may say that there is real hope for the patient's recovery, while believing internally that it is an almost groundless hope. Or alternatively, they may paint as bleak a picture as possible, "hanging crepe," even though they suspect the patient may do well.[25] In the process they may convince themselves they have fulfilled the principle of honesty to the letter. Still another version of this potential self-deception is rooted in the truism that the patient cannot be told everything. Since no reasonable person would want to be told literally everything, this, of course, leaves open the question of which things the professional has an obligation to disclose.

If honesty is a requirement of covenantal relationships among equals, if it is rooted in an implied promise to be open in communication and to treat the individual as an autonomous partner under the contract, then the futility of these rationalizations becomes apparent. The moral obligation is to disclose those things that are called for by the covenant. Normally that will be those things that a reasonable person would want to know or find material in deciding about his or her future medical care. Technically accurate statements that convey misleading messages are no less a violation of the principle of honesty because their content happens to be technically true.

One of the most important justifications given by those who feel that it is not necessary to disclose openly in a medical context is the claim that they are not lying, but merely withholding the truth. Morally, it is argued, withholding is an omission and different from the active, knowing communication of false information, which is a commission. It is not obvious, however, whether actions and omissions are morally different simply because one is an act and the other is an inaction. Philosophers have struggled over the problem in several contexts.[26] It quickly becomes apparent that both actions and omissions can have the same intention and the same consequences, and can be done with the same foreknowledge of the consequences. Yet in the context of the debate over the difference between active killing and letting die, the general public has rightly or wrongly tended to support a moral difference between omissions and commissions. In the area of lying and withholding the truth, however, the difference is much less generally supported. A full account of the argument is not possible here.[27] I suggest that the core difference between the two cannot be reduced to consequences. It may, in part, hinge upon the different relationships that may be established in the two cases. In an action (whether it be a mercy killing or a lie), the actor invariably thrusts himself or herself into a relationship with another party. Morally and legally, the actor is in the causal nexus.[28] Once the actions follow their way through the causal chain to their impact on the other party, we can say that the actor was responsible for the outcome. Whether the outcome was intentional or not, whether it was good or bad, the causal chain is established in such a way that responsibility is attributed.

In omissions, however, the pattern is more complex. There is still a causal chain such that if the actor had done some other particular act, a different impact would have been felt by the other party.[29] If, in an act of charity, someone gives a gift to a beggar on the street and not to another one nearby, we say that the charitable person was responsible for the good fortuune of the one, but we do not conclude in the same way that he was responsible for the continued poverty of the other. It was, of course, in the donor's power to have acted differently, changing the causal chain and making the second beggar better off. The donor, though, was not in either nexus of responsibility until he chose to enter one of them.

Some omissions, however, are linked more closely to responsibility.

In some situations, persons stand in special relationships—where they have a contractual obligation, a role-specific duty, or some other specially acquired obligation to another, such that there is a duty to act. In those cases, and in those cases only, one is responsible, in this full sense, for omissions.

Withholding information from a stranger with whom there is no special duty to communicate is normally an omission for which this responsibility, in the full sense, is lacking. Withholding information while in a special contractual relationship, however, is quite different. It is the nature of lay–professional relationships that contractual bonds have been established requiring open communication. In such a situation, withholding information that it is reasonable to suspect the other person would find meaningful is a violation of that covenantal bond. Withholding of information in a lay–professional relationship is really not very different in concept from the omission of medical treatment. In both cases, there is a contractual relationship. In both cases, the contract calls for some limited obligation on the part of the professional (as well as of the lay person) to act in certain ways. Normally this means providing treatment within the limits of the contract (just as it means providing information potentially meaningful to treatment of the patient). If the patient consents to having the information withheld, then a special exception is created at the level of the individual contract. The information in this new and special circumstance need not be communicated. In fact, if the terms of the contract are so specified, it *should* not be communicated.

Likewise, medical treatment should be delivered within the limits of the lay–professional contract. Reasonable patients would probably not contract to have their physicians deliver care against the patient's wishes. Omitted care that is within the contract is the same as active harming. The professional is responsible. If death occurs, the charge is murder, at least morally. Care that is omitted because it is excluded from the covenant is radically different, however. The patient has not consented to the care. It is an omission for which the professional is not responsible. In fact, were the professional to provide such care outside the scope of the contract, he or she would be violating the autonomy of the patient and, therefore, entering the causal nexus as an interloper. Thus in both withholding information and withholding treatment, the responsibility for the consequences is determined by the conditions of the lay–professional bond.

The principle of honesty in a lay–professional relationship requires open communication and respect for the covenantal bond. Except when there is good reason to conclude that a particular communication is excluded from the bond (because the patient would not find it meaningful or because the patient has explicitly excluded the communication from the relationship), then withholding information is morally the same as active lying.

Deception is, at the same time, more ambiguous and more clear. It is ambiguous in the sense that it can take place either by active telling of a falsehood or by the toleration of misleading signals in cases where one party knows the other party is being misled and omits the disclosure of that fact. It is morally more clear, however. Deception, as the knowing misleading of one person by another, is always a violation of the bonds of the covenant (unless the parties have consented to the deception).

Chapter 10

The Principle of Avoiding Killing

Many of the most crucial problems in medical ethics, like many of the important problems in ethics more generally, involve questions of the taking of human life. The merciful killing of the terminally ill, the toleration of suicide, the compassionate response to a young, unknowing, unmarried pregnant woman who does not want to bear another child, the removal of lifesaving organs from a human in irreversible coma for transplantation into another—all touch on the question of taking a human life and whether any such action is ever morally justified.

If morality were simply doing what appears to be in the interests of another, and if professional physician ethics were merely affirming the responsibility of the physician to do what he or she thinks is for the benefit of the patient, then it seems that occasionally the taking of a life (especially with the permission of the one whose life is to be taken) ought to be acceptable, morally and legally. Many people hold, however, that independent of its consequences, the taking of a life is a wrong-making characteristic of actions. The following case illustrates the problem:

Case 9 *Active Killing with Parental Consent*

Andrea was a nine-year-old girl who had been diagnosed as having cystic fibrosis at the age of thirteen months. Since then she had been hospitalized twelve times, eight during the last year.

When admitted for the last time she was already receiving an experimental antibiotic, which was being administered in an attempt to control a resistant pneumonia superimposed on severely damaged lungs, a result of her underlying disease. She was at that time a severely ill, emaciated child with moderately labored breathing. She seemed to have no interest in her environment and refused to communicate with anyone but her mother.

Because of the severity of the child's illness and because the parents had accurately perceived that the experimental antibiotic was a "last ditch" attempt to control her pulmonary infection, the physicians discussed with the parents their perceptions of "extreme medical measure" and the significance of a "No-Code" order. The parents indicated that in the event of a cardiac or respiratory arrest, they did not want their child to be resuscitated and the appropriate "No-Code" order was written. The child was not involved in these conversations or subsequent decision making, nor had the mother previously been able to answer her daughter's questions about death and dying.

As the child's condition continued to decline, the parents asked how much longer she would live and how she would die. At one point the father said: "Watching your own child die is worse than dying yourself." This comment led to a discussion of active euthanasia utilizing intravenous potassium chloride or a similar drug. The physicians pointed out that no matter how hopeless a situation or the amount of suffering that the patient and family were enduring, the law prohibited the active taking of a patient's life. They refused to consider this option.

The following day Andrea's heart began to fail. Her condition became progressively worse, and she died approximately forty-eight hours later. During these last two days her parents were appalled by her grotesque appearance (her "eyes bulged out like a frog") and were in great despair because of her steadily deteriorating condition. They felt helpless, impotent to alleviate their daughter's distress. Medical treatment was continued to the end, and no measures were taken to hasten Andrea's death.

228

Approximately two months after her death, the mother was asked if she would still have given permission for active euthanasia if she had been offered that option. She replied, "Yes."[1]

KILLING IN THE BASIC SOCIAL CONTRACT

As with Dr. T. in chapter 1, we have every indication that Andrea's physicians believed it would have been in her interest to intervene actively to hasten her death. If they had been true Hippocratic physicians, in the sense that they were committed to acting on the principle that they should do what they thought would benefit the patient, they would have been obliged morally to inject the potassium. Something was pulling against such a decision, however. Perhaps it was only the fact that such killings are illegal in the United States. That, however, simply begs the interesting question: Are they immoral, and, if not, why should they be illegal?

Clearly those involved in the case did not take the position that they had an affirmative moral obligation (or even a legal one) to prolong Andrea's life by all means at their disposal. They rejected resuscitation after cardiac or respiratory arrest. They apparently reached the conclusion I reached earlier that there is no unassailable moral obligation to prolong life. Neither they nor the parents took this interpretation of the Hippocratic principle.

They did, however, see and rely on a fundamental difference between active hastening of death, which they considered unacceptable, and allowing the child to die, which they considered acceptable. The difference is an important one in medical ethics—or at least it is often thought to be. It is similar to the difference considered in the last chapter between lying and withholding the truth. In both cases, the question is whether there is a morally significant difference between an omission and a commission.

In the case of lying and the withholding of the truth, at least some cases of withholding can be as morally reprehensible as lying. When someone is already in a causal nexus with an existing duty to act in a certain way, then failing to act is as culpable as actively bringing about a suspect result. Omission of information or treatment in such a relationship is just like a commission. In the case of mercy killing, the failure to fulfill a duty to provide for a child, feed it, and keep it from harm lets the causal chain proceed to the death of the child. This may happen even though one could have intervened to save the child without extraordinary effort. In either case, one is responsible both morally and legally. If a parent starves his or her child to death, it is as reprehensible as murdering it.

This intuitive realization that the two kinds of behavior can be equally reprehensible morally has led some philosophers to conclude that there is no moral difference between active killing and simply letting die.[2] However, it certainly does not follow logically that because one can think up two specific cases where behaviors are equally reprehensible, the two cases necessarily involve the same moral issues, or that, in general, all examples of either type of behavior are equally bad morally. Even though one could conjure up a case where slapping someone with an open hand would be as harmful as shooting that person with a gun, it does not follow that, in general, slapping is as bad as shooting.[3]

In the case of Andrea, the physicians are involved in a patient–physician relationship, but presumably it is not one that gives the physician unlimited Hippocratic authority. Were they to inject potassium chloride, they would have made a new entry into the causal chain just as surely as would one who crept into the hospital to kill the girl in the middle of the night. Yet, if I am correct about the notion of limited familial autonomy, her parents should have the authority to consent to further treatment for Andrea, including the experimental antibiotic and cardiac resuscitation. They should also have the authority to refuse consent for those treatments. Should they refuse, the physicians are not in any relationship with the patient that requires, or even permits, these treatments. Were they to render them without parental consent, they unjustifiably would be invading the familial relationship. They would be committing an assault on the patient and the family. If they follow the parents' wishes and accept an instruction not to resuscitate, as they did in this case, they are within the proper bounds of relationship with the family. This, quite clearly, is different from entering that relationship to become part of the causal chain leading to Andrea's death. In the words of Philippa Foot, "Man's right to noninterference usually extends farther than his right to be cared for. His rights may block our interference in his life; but if we may not intervene to bring a certain result, it does not follow that we may not allow it to come about."[4]

That removes the physicians from any responsibility for the death of Andrea if she is allowed to die, but it does not clarify the position of the parents. They presumably have a duty to use their judgment reasonably to do what is in her interests. If they were to simply step aside, they would be abandoning her; they have a duty to serve the interests of their ward. The parents, however, need not necessarily interpret serving the ward's interests as requiring continued treatment or consent to having others continue it. If their judgment is that the treatment would be useless or gravely burdensome to their ward, then refusing any such treatment is simply acting on their mandate to do what they consider to be within the interests of their ward.

What if, however, they consider killing her to be in her interest? It would seem to follow from the principle of beneficence and the responsibility they bear to her that, in such a case, they ought to kill her. At least if their judgment is reasonable enough to fall within the scope of familial autonomy, then society, it would seem, must use the principle of beneficence to tolerate the parental decision to kill for mercy. According to Marvin Kohl, beneficent euthanasia in such circumstances at least would be tolerable and probably would be morally required.[5]

The taking of human life however, may, not be reducible to that principle of beneficence. Whether Andrea's parents would be justified in killing for mercy may not hinge so much on the interpretation of the principle of beneficence as on whether there is a moral principle, independent of considerations of benefit and harm, that prohibits the taking of life. It might turn out that it is simply wrong to take a life (or, at least, certain kinds of life—such as human life or viable human life or viable innocent human life). Much of medical ethics hinges upon how society, taking the moral point of view to negotiate the basic social contract, resolves this question. Would our hypothetical citizens coming together to invent or discern the moral law decide it is reasonable simply to outlaw the taking of life?

I want to put aside for a moment the extraordinarily difficult problem of exactly what kind of life we are talking about. Consider, then, postnatal conscious, possibly sapient human life and the reasons why society might prohibit taking such life, even while recognizing there is no duty that such life must be maintained as long as possible. Two basic arguments have been made for the prohibition. The first is consequentialist: Even though it seems as if killing for mercy would produce more good than harm, the argument goes, the net consequences in the long run may provide good reasons to avoid killing even in those special circumstances. There may be errors made in determining what the patient wants or would want. There may be errors made in prognosis.

These initial arguments can be countered, however, by pointing out that errors may well not be made. More harm may come from presuming errors than in not presuming them, especially in cases where we have a clear idea of the patient's wishes.

The consequentialist case for the prohibition continues, however, by appealing to the possibility of abuse. If patients can be killed for mercy, some will die who should not.[6] These will probably tend to be the most vulnerable members of the community: those who are alone, unwanted, and without resources or those with people actively trying to harm them. A policy of permitting active killing for mercy would surely lead to some early deaths of such people who simply would not die for the forseeable future if a policy of letting die were adopted. (Of course, even a policy of letting die runs some of this risk, but not nearly as great a one as a policy accepting active killing. Many people simply will not die if left alone, but would die if potassium chloride were injected.) Many reach the conclusion that, in the long run, it is better simply to prohibit all active killing, even for mercy.[7] This conclusion based on consequences can sometimes be especially appealing to rule utilitarians, that is, those who claim that morality is a matter of following the rules that will tend to produce the best net consequences rather than simply doing the acts that will produce the best outcomes.

These arguments about consequences are not always entirely satisfying. It is not obvious, for example, that the rule that prohibits all killings would produce better consequences than a rule that prohibited all killings except those where rigid due process had determined that the patient's interests would be served by killing for mercy. Even if the arguments from consequences tend to work, they are always open to doubt for particular cases (or, for rule utilitarians, particular kinds of cases).[8] Furthermore, even if one were convinced that toleration of killing in special circumstances would produce bad consequences, it is not obvious that this is the reason for us to proscribe killing.

The second argument to proscribe all taking of life is more subtle, but perhaps more powerful. It says life might be viewed as inviolable for either intrinsic or extrinsic reasons. The view is as hard to articulate as it is widespread. For those whose metaphysics is theocentric, the task is a little easier. They say since life is not the mere product of human engineering—subject to human property rights—it is not man's to dispose of. Life in this view is sacred in the sense that it commands ultimate concern and respect.[9]

This commitment to the ultimate respect for life is shared by some philosophers who argue from a less explicit theological framework.

Kant, for example, treats life as an end in itself; he considers that to be self-evident.[10] Kant, then, seems to have reached an ultimate for which there can, in principle, be no argument; as with the other fundamental principles, reasonable people would have to agree. Kant's judgment is normative and, in a way, aesthetic. It says there is something fundamentally repulsive about treating a human as a means only, something surpassing even the revulsion that comes over one when contemplating the purposeful destruction to Picasso's *Guernica* or Rome's Coliseum. It is worse, in fact, since life is more ultimate and is irreplaceable.

From that does it follow that our ideal reasonable people taking the moral point of view would agree that the prohibition on killing is one of the fundamental principles of the human community? Certainly actual human beings have not accepted it as such. War, capital punishment, homicide, and abortion, as well as recorded mercy killings, all reveal that life has not been so respected in the real world.

Either life really is not sacred (that is, it really can be violated) or life is sacred and real-world behavior does not conform to what morality requires. I find myself pressured toward the second option; that is, when I try to put myself in the position of one attempting to invent the moral rules for the community, and especially when I place myself in the position of one attempting to discern the rules, I find that the prohibition on killing is one that I must cling to. It is morally an ultimate, and, therefore, no reason can be given for the conclusion any more than one can give reasons for choosing the principles of beneficence, liberty, veracity, or contract keeping. It is the very nature of a fundamental principle that no reasons can be given to explain it. If they could be, then the principle would not be truly fundamental in this ultimate sense. If that position can be maintained regarding the principle of avoiding killing (although most people seem to think it cannot), then the prohibition on active killing for mercy is easy to understand. If all killings are prohibited simply because the taking of life is fundamentally outside of human discretion, then taking of life for mercy must be prohibited as well. According to this view, it is not a matter of the bad consequences, though those may be bad enough. The prohibition is even more basic.

Even if the full force of my own conclusion is unacceptable to most people (as I assume it is), a more limited prohibition on killing might still be agreed to as part of the basic social contract. It may be agreed to either because of its consequences or for the more fundamental reason that it is simply a right-making characteristic of actions.

The most powerful counterargument to the essentially pacifist anti-killing position is that a principle requiring the avoiding of all killing would prohibit both personal and national self-defense. It would prohibit repelling aggressors. The pacifist, of course, is willing to accept these implications either because he or she believes the power of example is a weapon against aggression or because the moral principle is seen as overriding the exigency of resisting aggressors.

At a lesser extreme, many apply the principle of avoiding killing to the issue of capital punishment. Society can never be as certain of a culpable, voluntary choice to commit a crime as it is of the results of capital punishment. Even if it were doubtful, many of its members would oppose capital punishment on essentially moral-aesthetic grounds. It is cruel, unusual, barbaric punishment.

Even if it were conceded that exceptions could be made for self-defense, repelling aggressors, and capital punishment, such exceptions would not tell decisively on the problem of mercy killing. The justification for taking an aggressor's life presents, however, a test of the stringency of the commitment to the prohibition on killing. If an exception can be made for aggressors (an exception that I am not yet willing to concede), then perhaps another exception could be made for those to whom killing would be welcome acts of mercy, beneficial on balance. That seems to follow. Either life is sacred in the sense of being ultimate and an end in itself or it can be compromised for good reason. It can be argued that in both mercy killing and the aggressor case, the individuals have waived any right to life that they might possess (or that they would waive it if they could). The actions of the aggressor remove him from the community of the social contract. The one in intractable pain can give consent for the merciful act or, if necessary and with due process, permission of the guardian might be substituted.

It seems that the two kinds of exceptions are of comparable power. Clearly the justifying reasons are different. In the case of the aggressor, innocence normally has been surrendered and the welfare of society on balance favors immobilizing the one inflicting the hostility. In some instances, however, innocence is not surrendered—as in the case of the mentally deranged aggressor, for example. Aggressors often can be immobilized by methods short of killing.

Merciful killing, on the other hand, is undertaken out of concern for the welfare of someone who is suffering, possibly with the explicit consent of the one to be killed. One is forced to the conclusion that active killing for mercy is as justifiable as any kind of killing can be. Those like myself who hold to the full power of the principle of avoiding killing will not find that sufficient. Those who are willing to compromise for exceptions probably should find the moral exception for mercy persuasive.

The way the rigorous form of the principle has been stated thus far, however, might force people into absurdities. They might, for example, be forced to avoid driving cars, even if they are driven as safely as possible, for fear of actively killing someone by accident. Surgeons would never be able to operate, internists never able to prescribe any medication with any mortality risk. Each decision involves a risk that the actor will kill actively. Each clearly involves actions, so the omission–commission distinction will not get the would-be surgeon, the driver, or the internist off the hook. Traditional Catholic moral theology provides one way out of this problem.

The principle of indirect or double effect justifies some actions that lead to evil or violate prima facie moral principles. It is a moral maneuver that can be applied to any situation where moral principles conflict, but it is used frequently to distinguish moral from immoral killings. The principle, in its classic form, is stated as requiring four conditions, all of which must be met to justify an otherwise morally unacceptable action such as an active killing. The principle of the double effect justifies actions producing evil effects as well as good effects, if the following four conditions are fulfilled:

1. The action itself is good or indifferent;
2. The good effect and not the evil effect is the one sincerely intended by the agent;
3. The good effect is not produced by means of the evil effect (if the evil effect is not at least equally immediate causally with the good effect, then it becomes a means to the good effect and intended as such); and
4. There is a proportionate reason for permitting the foreseen evil effect to occur.[11]

The legitimacy of the principle of indirect effect has been attacked from two sides because it leads to wrong discriminations, excusing killings it should not and forbidding those it should allow.[12] There are those who object that the ordering of the events set out in the third criterion really cannot be decisive. Ordering, according to this view, cannot be so significant morally as to justify an unintended event if it follows the intended one in a causal sequence and not to justify it if it precedes the intended event.[13] These critics tend to reject the distinction based on directness of causality. For example, they say that if it is ever justified to remove a cancerous uterus with an implanted fetus, knowing that the indirect effect will be death of the fetus, then it must also be justifiable to remove the fetus in order to produce a benefit of equal magnitude. In other words, a killing that does not meet condition three, but meets all the others would be a direct, but still acceptable, killing (to the extent that an otherwise similar indirect killing would be).

Others attack in the opposite direction, arguing that the mere absence of intention to kill should not justify even an indirect killing if that killing is foreseen. For example, bombing a military weapons depot of an enemy may unavoidably spread debris from the secondary explosion in such a way that it would kill innocent children in a next-door schoolyard. Even though all four conditions would be met in the case, the bombing cannot be justified, according to this criticism, by the bomber's absence of intention to kill the children if he or she knew or should have had reason to know that the indirect killing was almost certain to result.

We see then that neither directness nor intention may be the critical variable. In both criticisms, the deaths could be foreseen with virtual certainty. This may be sufficient moral reason to make these killings equally reprehensible. If so, then the critical variable is neither directness of the killing nor intention of the killer, but the foreknowledge that the actor possesses or has reason to possess. Directness may be important in assessing whether the actor should have had foreknowledge of the killing, but direct killings that reasonably could not have been foreseen are *morally* tolerable. Intention may be important in judging the moral character of the actor, in deciding whether he or she was blameworthy, but not in judging the morality of the action. Unintended but foreseen killings, even though indirect, are wrong. Knowledge of the expected outcome, not directness or intention, is critical in evaluating morality of actions. If so, society might reasonably come to agree that active, foreseen killings, at least of innocents, are morally unacceptable whether intended or not and whether direct or not. It might also agree that unforeseen killings or those that involve small statistical risk for proportionally great reasons are acceptable, whether direct or indirect. If this is the principle reasonable people would accept, and intention or motive is not decisive, then active, foreseen killings for mercy would not be tolerable, although unforeseen ones would be.

Even if, hypothetically, active, foreseen killing for mercy were morally justified, it does not follow either that such killing should be legalized or that health professionals should be permitted to participate in it. Even in a hypothetical situation where it would be ethical to kill for mercy (because a person consents or is in intractable pain—either of which has been established by ample due process), there may be pragmatic reasons for prohibiting the killing. The hypothetical may be too difficult to reproduce in reality. Consent might be too difficult to determine, due process too difficult to establish. If certain conditions were met so that a prudential policy making active killing illegal created little or no hardship, then it might be plausible to enact such a law. If pain could be controlled by adequate medication, as is reportedly the case,[14] and patients and their agents retained the right to refuse medical treatment so that an existing dying process could continue, then no practical objections to the law prohibiting active mercy killing would exist. To legalize active mercy killing under these circumstances would accomplish little; a hypothetical right would be affirmed that ought never be exercised lest it lead to real abuse of people's rights through errors in assessing the quality of consent or through the intractability of pain. If active killing for mercy appears to many reasonable people to be a violation of the general principle of avoiding killing and little good would come from permitting it in any case, then a legal prohibition would be acceptable. Those who remain convinced that killing is moral and merciful in a specific case would have to justify it as an act of civil disobedience.

KILLING AND THE LAY–PROFESSIONAL CONTRACT

Even if taking of all life is not proscribed in the general social contract, even if mercy killing can be isolated enough so that the principle justifying it will not also justify other killings, even if such killing should be considered legal as well as ethical, it is still an open question whether health professionals ought to be permitted to engage in it. Andrea's parents, considering such a merciful action to be in their daughter's interest, would first have to respond to the stringent moral and legal reasons why any such taking of life would be unacceptable. I am convinced that finding a sufficient response would be an insurmountable task. Even if merciful decisions by patients or their agents could be found to be moral or legal, it still does not follow that physicians, nurses, or other health professionals ought to be involved in such activities.

In order to determine what is morally appropriate in medical relationships between professionals and lay people, a second social contract, the one between professionals and the rest of the population, would have to address the question of whether there is a special moral responsibility for health professionals, some reason why killing might be incompatible with their role. In chapter 4 I argued that Lord Brock was wrong when he said that as a professional, he knew that certain things, such as mercy killing, are excluded by the ethics of the profession. The idea that professionals and only professionals can have special knowledge of what is required morally in their role is irrational. There is no reason why Andrea's parents or any person who is not a member of the medical profession would or should feel bound by such a professional consensus. It is entirely another matter, however, to ask whether reasonable people—including lay people—reflecting on how they want the health professional's role conceived, would see purposeful, if merciful, taking of life incompatible with the psychological or moral definition of the role.

Traditionally, that role has been conceived as emphasizing healing, promotion of health (and even of well-being), as well as the preventing of premature death. A role incorporating these qualities may be incompatible with the role of killer, even for mercy. Whether or not the two roles are logically incompatible they well may be psychologically incompatible. Reasonable people might get together and decide that mercy killing is an activity they do not want health professionals engaging in. If I were at the bargaining table, attempting to establish an understanding between lay people and professionals about the moral content of the medical role, I would hold out for a separation of the health professional role from the role of killer, no matter what the motive of the one doing the killing. That, of course, is an easy conclusion if one is inclined to see all active, foreseen killing as morally proscribed, but even those who do not share that conviction may accept the moral division of labor between healers and killers.

To get a sense of what this role-specific mandate to avoid killing might mean, consider the dilemma of the military physician stationed at a base near the front lines. What ought to be his responsibility if that base is invaded by enemy soldiers who are engaging in hand-to-hand combat with the physician's colleagues? If a gun were available to the physician, either he could join the fight or abstain on the grounds that killing even the enemy is incompatible with the primary mission of the physician. Psychologically, it might be impossible for the saver of lives to take a momentary respite from the saving to do any killing. Morally we might consider whether we would want to place the physician–soldier in such a position. The physician himself or herself might have some views about whether killing is compatible with curing, but these may not be decisive. As a society negotiating the terms of the physician's role, we would want to take into account not only the physician's feelings, but also other moral and practical requirements. We might reach the conclusion that killing is so incompatible with the role-specific duty of the physician that even a military physician should be excluded from carrying a weapon for such emergencies and from using it if one happens to come into his or her possession.

At present, international law neither prohibits nor permits the bearing of arms by medical personnel.[15] They are protected from aggressive acts of the enemy and are immune from capture as prisoners of war. Their use of arms is limited to acts of protection for the wounded and sick, and to self-defense. Any physician who engages in other forms of combat is held to be a member of the fighting forces without the special status granted by international law.

The question remains whether physicians and other health care personnel ought to be prohibited from even these limited combat functions. It is possible that a single society or the international community might find even self-defense and defense of the wounded so incompatible with the healing role that these actions too would be prohibited. Chaplains, for example, cannot legally bear arms because it is thought incompatible with their religious functions and their spiritual duties.[16] A similar case can be made for health care personnel. The question in each case is not whether the members of the special groups (chaplains or physicians) themselves consider bearing arms or combat outside their role, it is whether the society as a whole so views it. I find the argument about the incompatibility of healing and killing in one role to be compelling. Killing ought to be proscribed at least as incompatible with the role-specific duties of the health care professional. It should therefore be proscribed by the second social contract, if it will not be done by the first.

If at least this argument on the structuring of lay–professional relations is persuasive, then the principle of avoiding killing gives the physicians in Andrea's case, as well as the physicians in Ms. R.'s case, a clear moral mandate from society. They ought not to participate in active, foreseen killing of anyone. If merciful killing is justified at all, it will have to be done by someone else: by the patients themselves, or their agents or delegates. It would be understandable, however, if society should prohibit all such killings.

KILLING AND THE DEFINITION OF DEATH

Until now I have finessed the question of exactly what kind of life is intrinsically valued to such an extent that it ought to be treated as sacred, as an end in itself, inviolable by active, foreseen human intervention. The assumption has been that we were dealing with conscious, perhaps sapient, postnatal human life. It seems, however, that there must be some limits on the respect-for-life principle. There are few among us sufficiently Schweitzerian to extend the principle of utter respect for life to all the animal kingdom or even to all living things.

It is at this point in the construction of a general theory of medical ethics that space is created for discussion of such fundamental and complex issues as the concept of personhood, the definition of death, abortion, and animal rights. In the last decade, voluminous literature has been devoted to the concept of the "human" or the "person."[17] One reason it has often commanded great attention is that people believe that clarifying the concept of the person will give us answers to these intriguingly complex moral problems.

I am increasingly convinced, however, that even if this literature in linguistic analysis is helpful for some other purpose, it is no way to settle these moral questions. The literature can be reduced to two approaches. One defines personhood as referring to those in the community, usually the human community, who are the bearers of full moral standing, those who are given all the rights and responsibilities of other humans. That clearly makes personhood a moral category, but leaves all the interesting debate about who should be considered as having full moral standing to be resolved. The other approach attempts a definition of personhood independent of any moral claims about whether persons have full moral standing or any standing at all.

Michael Tooley, for example, claims something is a person "if and only if it is a continuing subject of experiences and other mental states that can envisage a future for itself and that can have desires about its own future states."[18] This may be a reasonably accurate specification of the way the term *person* is used in our language, but it seems doubtful. Regardless, it tells us nothing about whether nonpersons are the bearers of rights or have any moral claims such as the right to have their lives treated as sacred.

A more direct approach would be to tackle the question of moral standing directly by asking what limits there are, if any, to the moral principles. Is there, for example, any limit on the principle of avoiding

240

killing? Does the principle apply to all animals and even plants? Does it apply to all humans? And what is the link between the right of a living creature to be preserved from killing and other rights that may accrue to it?

It seems there must be some limit to the principle of avoiding killing. Even vegetarians accept the necessity of direct active, even purposeful, killing of some life forms. The vegetarian may claim that all life is to be respected, but not to the point of treating it as sacred—as an end in itself, which must never be killed actively.

The questions of who has moral standing and what is the basis for that standing will depend heavily on the decisions made very early in the building of a medical ethical theory. If the basic moral principles are merely the principles that would be chosen or invented by rational people convening at a bargaining table (under such constraints as agreement to respect liberty and treat the welfare of all equally), then presumably those who originally have moral standing are those who could be at such a bargaining table. They would be those capable of communicating and thinking rationally about principles for organizaing a moral community. All other life, human and otherwise, would gain its respect derivatively because those in the moral community decide to value it or otherwise give it standing. For those who view morality as invented in this way, the rights claims of other humans and of all nonhumans hang on a very thin thread. Fetuses, infants, the retarded, the senile, and even the pet dog have standing only because those in the community choose to give it. From this point of view it is easy to justify abortion, killing the retarded, and the harvesting of organs from permanently unconscious, brain-injured humans.

We realize, however, that we tend not to favor many of these behaviors, or we endorse them only after careful restriction. Two explanations seem possible. First, it might just work out that those humans in the moral community contracting with one another turn out to value fetuses, infants, the retarded, and the pet dog so that they generate prohibitions on killing those (humans and other animals) who could not sit at the bargaining table. Alternatively, the moral community may not invent the basic moral principles in the first place. We have already seen that the inventors have problems in explaining why people at the original meeting where the social contract is invented would respect freedom, keep promises, and tell the truth. There has to be some leap of faith to believe that the inventors will play by the rules they pledge themselves to, including the rules about keeping pledges.

Those who view the social contract as a metaphor for describing what it would take to go about discovering the basic structure of the moral community are in quite a different position. They are merely functioning as agents discovering a moral order that preexists the metaphorical meeting of the minds. They articulate principles, such as the prohibition on killing, which in their original scope might extend will beyond those with the mental, rational capacity to sit at the meeting table. The discoverers, in short, may find that moral standing extends beyond themselves to other creatures. That standing may be vested in a supernatural creator, in a natural moral order existing unexplained in the universe, or in some other objectively conceptualized moral force. In these cases, fetuses, infants, the retarded, and so forth are not necessarily outside the bounds of those who have moral standing.

Still there must be some limit on who can be considered to have moral claims entitling them to be treated according to principles such as the one to avoid killing. One approach to discovering what those limits may be is to ask what the meaning of death is. When a person is dead, by definition, that person loses the right not to be killed. Killing a corpse is impossible. If we know what it means *morally* to be dead, we may gain some insight into the limits of the principle prohibiting killing; we may gain insight into the kind of moral standing that accrues to those creatures who have a claim against us that they not be killed.

It is crucial to realize that the problem is essentially a moral one rather than a biological one. We want to know when it is appropriate to treat a person as dead. A range of behaviors and actions is normally triggered when we make the social statement that a human is labeled by the society as dead. Grief reactions are initiated that were not appropriate as mere anticipatory grief; certain medical interventions are stopped (such as feeding) that *may* not have been stopped appropriately before; laws, such as the uniform anatomical gift act, apply that did not apply before; inheritance laws take effect and wills can be read; rights attributed to living persons are no longer attributed or are attributed differently. Labeling someone as dead is a social, moral statement.[19]

We are left with the question of when we find it appropriate to treat someone as dead, when does the moral standing of the individual change so radically that the same rights claims attributed to living persons no longer are attributed? Several possibilities exist. The older formulations may have focused too exclusively on the human's biological capacities. The human was considered living, in the moral sense of the term, when the heart and lungs, or at least their related functions, remained intact or could be restored. When there was irreversible loss of the body's capacity for circulation and respiration, moral standing shifted to the point that the person was no longer a member of the moral commmunity. What was left was viewed as the "mortal remains."

For the living, moral obligations remained vis-à-vis that body. If pledges were made to the individual in law or direct communication, those pledges still had to be carried out. A certain sense of obligation to treat the body with respect and dispose of it properly still remained.[20] The bearer of full moral standing, however, was no longer with us. The mutilation of the corpse was, legally and morally, a crime, but not the crime it would have been if done on a living individual.

It is now widely recognized that this was far too organic a view of what gives full moral standing. Moral standing is, in essence, something far more complex than the mere presence of certain biological functions. The shift to a brain-oriented definition of death was meant to correct this problem. Here there is no biological argument that moral standing in the full sense should cease when the brain is destroyed rather than the heart and lungs. In principle, it is not the kind of question that can be resolved by biological evidence. Many reasonable people, however, were convinced, morally, that the critical function had something to do with the brain rather than the heart and lungs. It was a conclusion reached after a long debate on the issue that emerged in the 1970s.[21]

During that period, however, people began to ask what it was about the brain that was so critical to moral standing in this full sense. One answer was that the brain provided an integrating capacity. A body deserved full moral standing whenever it possessed the capacity to integrate function in any significant way. By this notion, however, whenever breathing, heart regulation, and certain other lower-brain functions and autonomic nervous system functions remained intact, a case could be made that significant integrating capacity remained and that therefore the person should be treated as having full moral standing, that is, as being alive.

The mere capacity to integrate bodily function, however, seems little more impressive than the capacity to circulate blood and respire. It is still a very biological notion of the basis of moral standing. Recently it has been argued that a more plausible basis for attributing full moral standing might be the capacity for some kind of mental or social activity.[22] If the human essence is said to include mental capacity, then either consciousness or rationality are the most likely candidates for the criterion of moral standing. If the basis is social, then perhaps the capacity for social interaction is more plausible. (Since social and mental capacities are so closely linked, there may be no practical difference even if there are important theoretical differences.) According to this view, people should be treated as alive and having full moral standing when they retain a capacity either for consciousness or social interaction or both. Clearly this should not be equated with the actual presence of either activity. That would make many people dead simply because they were asleep or make their moral standing dependent upon the good will of other citizens who may refuse to interact, say, with the retarded or with social outcasts.

Some might argue that it is not really the capacity for consciousness or social interaction that is critical, but the capacity for rational thought. This narrower criterion would exclude many who lack intellectual capacity although they may possess the capacity for consciousness. This roughly may be the position of those who hold that the moral order is invented and who give moral standing only to those who have the rational capacity to take part in the inventing. The inclusion of the criterion of sapience in the New Jersey Supreme Court's opinion in the Karen Quinlan case has mistakenly been assumed by some to imply that to be alive or have moral standing, one must have such a capacity for reasoning. At most, the court opinion suggests that treatment might be rejected by the guardian of a patient who lacks a capacity for sapience. It is not clear whether the court really meant to say that the inability to return to a cognitive, sapient state alone justified a guardian treatment refusal, but in any case, there is no implication that those lacking such a capacity are already dead.

Still, we could choose rationality rather than capacity for either consciousness or social interaction (or both) as our critical point. However, it would be a messy choice, both procedurally and morally. People move in and out of conditions where the capacity for rationality is missing. Assuming a person were to be treated as having lost moral standing when he or she irreversibly lost the capacity for rationality, we would have to be able to measure that loss. We probably cannot do that and may never be able to. We would have to be able to agree on what it means to have or lack a capacity for rationality. We shall probably never be able to do that either. Rationality is a valued part of a human person, but is it a necessary part? Those who see the essence of the person in the capacity for social interaction say "no." If moral standing is discovered rather than invented by social contractors, there is no reason why infants, the retarded, the senile, and the chronically deranged cannot still be part of the human moral community, still have moral standing. The warmth of human interaction, the love of one person for another, the emotional bonding that links people in moral communities does not require the capacity for human rationality; it does require a capacity for consciousness. That seems to me to be both the more easily applied dividing line and the more correct one. What is important in establishing moral standing is an integration of the organic bodily functions with the mental and social functions. That link between the biological and the mental, between body and soul, to use the more archaic language, is the essential, necessary condition for a person to be treated as having full moral standing. To add that a person can reason, can use his mental capacity in this particularly desirable way, may be something humans find attractive, but cannot be a necessary condition for moral standing. If this is the case, then embodied capacity for consciousness or social interaction is the minimal essential condition for moral standing.

But should we treat as dead people who irreversibly lack an embodied capacity for consciousness or social interaction as a matter of policy as well as principle? It may be that we cannot even predict accurately the irreversible loss of such a capacity. There is reason to fear that errors might be made in identifying when patients have lost irreversibly such capacity. In any case, these same patients might be allowed to die justifiably, thus removing the practical concerns as well as the indignity of confusing a spontaneously respiring corpse with the formerly living person. It might be a prudent policy to require as a determination of death the complete functional destruction of the brain and the loss of integrating capacity that accompanies such destruction, rather than the more precise philosophical concept of the irreversible loss of embodied capacity for consciousness or social interaction. In contracting our social policy, however, it will be important to realize that this is a prudential short cut, not grounded on anything more solid than the pragmatic. The result is that full moral standing as part of the moral community should end when and only when it is reasonable to deduce that there has been a breakdown of the link between bodily integrity and mental or social capacity.

KILLING AND ABORTION

If this analysis is correct, then we have considerable head start in determining who should be treated as part of the moral community in the full sense that it is being discussed here. We should be able to tell who should have the principle of avoiding killing applied to them. The integration of organic function and mental or social capacity is the decisive feature. This should tell us how to analyze both the claims of fetuses and of animals other than the human.

It is often argued, I think mistakenly, that viability is an important, if not decisive, point at which full moral standing accrues to fetuses.[23] The philosophical notion underlying that position must be that sufficient capacity to integrate bodily function is important, perhaps even decisive, in giving full moral standing. That is a position analogous to that held by those who favor a whole-brain oriented definition of death. A biological capacity—probably a neurological one—is the key factor. The ability to integrate functions sufficiently to survive outside the womb somehow mysteriously gives the fetus a claim that it did not previously have. This capacity to survive independently is contingent upon technologies and interventions that, at this moment, make the point of viability somewhere in the area of twenty to twenty-four weeks in gestation. If, however, the point of viability were reduced technologically to a much earlier period, perhaps even to the point of conception, holders of the viability position would logically have to shift with the state of the art. If viability is really so critical a factor, then holders of such a position should not object to any moral and policy shift necessitated by new technology.

It is not necessary to base full moral standing on capacity for rational thinking, however, to maintain that mid-term abortion could be acceptable independent of viability. If full moral standing is linked to capacity for consciousness or social interaction, a cutoff point for acceptable abortions is found that happens to correspond to the present U.S. Supreme Court upper limit on legal abortion (at least in cases where the health of the mother is not at stake). This view entitles the human fetus prior to this time to the respect of a human organism, one that is biologically human, but not yet one that has full moral standing. That accrues only when there is an integration of bodily form and capacity for mental process.

Any systematic medical ethic needs to show consistency between the point at which moral standing begins and when it ends. The position outlined here at least retains that consistency. It does not deprive humans outside those limits of any moral claim, as some rights-based contractarian theories would. It merely maintains that those claims are not to life itself, but to other considerations: respect and fidelity to promises made or responsibility assumed.[24]

An embryo, human or otherwise, should not be treated capriciously. A human embryo is human in biological form even if it lacks the crucial integration of the mental with the organic. It deserves respect at least because of the empathic links it has with the moral community, both in its biological form and in the potential it possesses. Such embryos should not be disposed of without good reason. By extension they are already part of the moral community. But prior to the accrual of full moral standing that comes with the linking of the mental and the physical, the moral prohibition against killing does not apply.

This suggests that the abortion of a fetus prior to the time of the development of a capacity for consciousness may be a tragedy, something that we would avoid if we could, but not necessarily something that is a definitive moral violation. Women (and couples who constitute a moral unity) would, according to this position, retain the right, morally and legally, to abort if it was necessitated by strong reasons.

Once again, however, this does not make clear the role of the health professional in such killings. It might be again argued that any killing is so outside the scope of the health professional's role that no physician, nurse, or other health professional should have anything to do with any abortion. We could train a cadre of abortionists who are not part of the general medical system, just as we train executioners and killers of other kinds. The social contract between the society and the profession might include such a provision exempting the health professional if it is thought necessary, but I am not sure that it is. It may be necessary only to grant a right of conscientious objection to any health care worker who feels that he or she cannot fulfill personal or professional obligations while participating in abortions. Such a conscience clause would make sense even in a more general medical ethical theory that may not grant unlimited liberty to health professionals. Finally, individual practitioners as well as individual patients might develop more limiting personal moral standards about when, if ever, an abortion is morally acceptable. The third contract, then, the one between the individual professional and lay person, would permit expressions of more individual variation, including objections to abortion for specific indications such as rape, incest, psychological health, fetal deformity, or personal inconvenience and hardship. It is precisely for this fine tuning that the third contract is designed.

247

KILLING OF ANIMALS

If the moral prohibition against killing applies only to creatures who possess embodied consciousness, we are able to understand those who believe that on balance, certain abortions may be justified. But what does such a position entail for physicians who are trained in the physiology lab to dissect creatures with embodied capacity for consciousness, who have grown to depend upon the products of testing involving creatures with embodied capacity for consciousness, or who dine with gastronomical delight on creatures that had been possessed of embodied capacity for consciousness?

It is not normal for works in medical ethics to include discussions of vivisection and vegetarianism, but a brief note is in order, at least to mark the position where such issues should arise in any theory of medical ethics. Ethics ranging from medical student training to most basic, preclinical medical research, to the management of the hospital cafeteria all depend on how this spot is filled.

There can be no doubt that we are dealing here with embodied creatures. There is little doubt that they possess some semblance of consciousness, at least in the higher orders of the animal kingdom down as far as the mollusks.[25] Any ethical theory that incorporates notions of pleasure, pain, and suffering must address the question of whether animal pleasure, pain, and suffering count—and if not, why not. Some, such as Peter Singer, follow the implication of the problem to its logical conclusion and say that animals, at least sentient animals, have moral claims just as humans do. Animal pleasures and pains have to be taken into the calculus just as human ones do.[26] For example, in October 1980, the National Advisory Eye Council, which must review and approve research grants of the National Eye Institute, approved a statement of policy calling on researchers to adopt "effective and uniform procedures to minimize pain to cold-blooded lower vertebrates (such as frogs and turtles) used in research." The council debated whether these lower animals feel pain and concluded that it was reasonable to assume that they did. That policymaking decision shows that animal pain is morally relevant to the way federal research money is to be used.[27]

If we justify medical research and training and normal Western dietary practices, all of which inflict suffering on and take the lives of animals, it must be that the qualitative differences between the types of consciousness or the types of embodiment are critical. Some might argue that animals possess consciousness, but not self-consciousness. It is hard to imagine how such a claim could be documented and also hard to imagine what its moral significance would be if it were. Would humans, for example, who possessed only consciousness, but not self-consciousness, be reduced to the moral status of animals? Hanging moral policies about matters as fundamental as killing upon qualitative judgments about consciousness is a risky business, perhaps one that is better avoided if possible.

The only alternative justification for our present animal treatment policies is to use the criterion of a qualitative difference in the kind of embodiment. This is also a rather thin reed on which to hang the substantial differences in our normal moral treatment of animals and humans. It may have to be the basis for such a policy, however. There is something fundamentally different in the types of embodiment, so that human sympathies and empathies seem to attach more readily to a fetus (that barely possesses any capacity for consciousness or social interaction) than to an animal that routinely interacts with humans. The nature of the embodiment must be significant, if our natural sympathies are not entirely mistaken.

This at least identifies the point where the debate can be joined. If our project is simply attempting to approximate what a group of social contractors taking the moral point of view would do to invent some moral rules, both fetuses and nonhuman animals are in real jeopardy. Their status will be contingent upon the good will, empathy, and interests of the contractors. If, however, we are approximating a similarly motivated group who meet to discover a set of moral rules and principles for those in the moral community, then both fetuses and animals might well be given substantial consideration, even if they are not given the full moral standing of those who combine human embodiment with the capacity for consciousness or social interaction (or both).

Chapter 11

The Principle of Justice

Thus far our contractors have agreed upon four general principles, in addition to the principle of beneficence, that will tend to make actions among humans in a moral community ethically right. The net effect is that sometimes the producing of good consequences—for patients, health care providers, and communities—will be held in check by previous promises or contracts, by respect for the autonomy of others, by a commitment to be truthful, or by the necessity of avoiding the active, knowing taking of life. That still leaves us with a flock of problems related to the allocation of resources and the distribution of benefits when goods can be spread around in different ways.

As long as health care allocation was limited to the principle of beneficence, we found ourselves trapped. On the one side, we had a Hippocratic ethic that extended morally relevant consequences only to an isolated, individual patient, producing a socially irresponsible hyperindividualism. On the other side was a social utilitarianism that swallowed the individual and his or her rights into a massive aggregate of benefits, drowning individual claims in a massive pool of social consequences. The rights and responsibilities derived from the other basic principles suggest limits on morally acceptable sacrifice of the individual to the polluting pool of social utility, but do not give guidance for allocating scarce resources when more than one alternative allocation is possible without violating other basic principles. Thus far we also do not have any insight into possible ways of justifiably compromising individual rights and welfare in cases where the interests of third parties seem to generate powerful, overwhelming claims. It is possible that some overwhelming claims may be generated for individuals independent of their contribution to the net aggregate of good in the society.

250

Take, for example, a physician faced with three patients in moderate need of attention who could be served by brief office visits and a fourth patient in dire need of help requiring a house call. Time constraints prohibit serving both groups. The Hippocratic ethic will not help. It would merely instruct the physician to do what he or she believes would benefit the patient according to the physician's judgment. Answers in the singular, however, are singularly unhelpful for this kind of a problem. What is needed is some guidance about whether the claims of the three moderately ill patients take precedence over the claim of the one more seriously ill.

One approach would be to assume that none of the patients has a right to the physician's attention unless and until the physician makes a commitment based on offers of payment or anything else that would move him or her. Another approach would be for the physician to try to estimate whether the total contribution to the health of the four patients would be greater by treating the three moderately needy patients or the one who was most critical. Still another approach would be to take as the goal trying to help the one least well off regardless of whether the total health improvement were greater. Finally—a strategy that in this case might amount to the same thing as trying to improve the lot of the least well off—the goal might be to try to end up in a situation where all the patients were, insofar as possible, about equally healthy.

Similar alternatives are available for a society trying to allocate its health resources or any other resources. We may conclude that most health resource allocation questions should not be forced on the individual provider, but rather should be made at a broader social policy level as health insurance policy is planned, clinical facilities are built, health care providers are trained, and work places are selected by providers. Some resource allocations inevitably will be left in the hands of isolated providers, as in the case of our physician choosing among the four patients. Regardless of whether we are talking about macroallocation decisions, such as distribution of clinics and CAT scanners, or microallocation decisions, such as distributing an afternoon of a physician's time, questions of justice or equity force us to include some principle of allocation, of distributive justice, into our general theory of medical ethics.

Case 10   *Justice and Efficiency in Care for the Mentally Retarded*

The hearing for State Bill 529 had been called to order. The bill, introduced by Representative John Sheehan, provided for the establishment of community-based homes for the care and education of the mentally retarded. There would be one home for every fifteen of the presently institutionalized mentally retarded in the state. The estimated cost to the state for this care would be $70 million a year, in comparison with the present budget allocation of $55.8 million for the four state institutions for the mentally retarded. These four institutions currently served 7,600 people.

Representative Sheehan spoke in favor of the bill. He painted a picture of hundreds of human beings, many with no clothing, huddled in the dark, drab rooms of the present institutions. Built before the turn of the century, they remained as they were decades ago, without even some of the basics of furniture. Recreation and educational equipment were nonexistent; aesthetics was ignored. The institutions were terribly understaffed, and many staff members had no professional training. Representative Sheehan, who had the support of the parents' organization, the state Department of Mental Health, the local chapter of the American Civil Liberties Union, and the religious leadership, concluded his case by pleading, "Justice requires that we extend this token contribution to this group of our citizens most burdened by incredible medical expenses, by physical and psychological suffering, and by the degradation of our society's past inhumanity to its fellow humans."

Representative Janet Hudson and Dr. Robert Simmons were the primary spokespersons in opposition. Representative Hudson emphasized that she was concerned about the care of the mentally retarded but that she was also the elected representative of all citizens of her district. She argued that the representatives had an obligation to examine possible alternative uses of the $14.2 million in increased funds called for by the bill; not to do so would be fiscally irresponsible. She had some facts to back up her point. The $70 million needed for the new program would represent 1.5 percent of the state's annual budget, a budget raised by all citizens. Yet the institutionalized population to be assisted by the program equaled only one-tenth of one percent of the state population. The proposed increase of $14.2 million could also buy hot lunches for all of the schoolchildren in the state *or provide job training for persons to become productive members of society. The fairest thing to do, she argued, would be to spread the money more evenly and to spend it on those who would be productive. "Our task as legislators," she argued, "must be to serve the greatest good of the greatest number."*

Dr. Simmons took a similar position, but as a physician he felt the money would be used more efficiently in providing health care for three groups: normal or nearly normal children, thousands of whom could be reached for every mentally retarded child in the Sheehan bill; adults potentially engaged in productive labor; and pregnant women. He emphasized that he was concerned about the plight of the mentally retarded. He showed, however, that much mental retardation could be eliminated with prenatal diagnosis. He estimated the cost of the prenatal elimination of Down's syndrome, for example, to be $200 per case, compared to an average of $60,000 for the care of every child institutionalized. Although acknowledging the fact that some of the institutionalized retarded might be gainfully employed if they were in high-quality, small-scale, community-based homes, he argued that the savings from spending the funds on detection rather than on more expensive forms of institutionalization would be enormous.

The legislative committee moved into closed session to make its decision on the bill.[1]

JUSTICE AND THE SOCIAL CONTRACT:
FOUR POSSIBLE THEORIES

Would reasonable people committed to the moral point of view, taking equal account of all persons while trying to discern or create basic social principles, include an independent principle of justice or equitable distribution of resources in addition to the other principles already agreed upon? In other words, is there a principle of justice or equity in moral theory?

Aristotle, in the *Nichomachean Ethics*,[2] warns of a linguistic problem once we start talking justice. Justice is sometimes used in a broad sense as "the whole of virtue," or as equivalent to what is lawful or morally right. Injustice is, by this usage, simply "the whole of vice." The Hippocratic ethic requires any member of a group that accepts that professional pledge to keep patients from "harm and injustice." One might try to force on the Hippocratic author a commitment to an equitable distribution pattern, but no such sophisticated normative theory was intended. Rather, those who take the Hippocratic pledge are simply saying that they will keep their patients from wrong or harm. Injustice is a loose, broad term without explicit distributional implications.

Aristotle, however, points out that justice is also used in a narrower, more provocative sense as "fairness in distribution."[3] In this sense, justice refers only to the ethically appropriate way to spread limited resources throughout the moral community. This is the dilemma of the legislature trying to decide whether to spend its funds on community-based homes for the retarded, a school lunch program, or well-baby health care. This is the choice forced on the physician who can care for the three relatively healthy patients or the one in desperate need. Whenever cost containment is introduced into the health care resource allocation debate, the problem of a fair distribution of resources is lurking close to the surface.

One of the basic principles constituting a moral community must provide a perspective for beginning to grope for an answer to these questions. If the community of reasonable people taking the moral point of view tried to articulate a principle of distributive justice, four basic choices seem plausibly worth considering. Two possibilities, the entitlement and utilitarian answers, are derived from and reduce to other principles already agreed upon: the principle of autonomy and the principle of beneficence. The other two, the maximin and egalitarian strategies, introduce totally new and independent considerations into the reflection on moral principles.

THE ENTITLEMENT THEORY

In the debate over the proposal for community-based homes for the retarded, we might simply view the retarded as unlucky losers in the lottery of life. Some have maintained that the natural lottery distributes health as well as other natural endowments such as intelligence, physical ability, and personality in an unequal, random way and that the human community bears no responsibility for adjustment of any imbalances. It is possible that one is entitled to what one gets in the lottery so that others in the community have no particular responsibility to improve the lot of the unfortunate. It is possible that those who are unusually well-endowed have no obligation to help the less fortunate.

Harvard philosopher Robert Nozick, in the volume *Anarchy, State, and Utopia*, argues that one is entitled to what one possesses, provided it has been acquired justly—by appropriation from goods not previously possessed, by gift, or by exchange.[4] His is a world where one is free to use one's natural endowments to make whatever deals one can. The state's role is limited to protection against unjust appropriation.

According to this view, no one would have a claim of justice against others to have needs met unless commitments had been made through free promising or contracting. Individuals, out of the goodness of their hearts, may act charitably toward the unfortunate, but they have no obligation to do so. There is no right to health care or any other basic good that can be claimed against members of the society.

Physician Robert Sade has written an article that serves as a crude example of how a notion of entitlement as a basis for distributing health care leads to an untenable moral position. In "Medical Care as a Right: A Refutation," writing in a manner potentially consistent with the libertarian entitlement theorists, Sade says that man has a right to his own life and that this is the basis for deciding whether there is a right to health care. For reasons that he never explains, though, he maintains that this gives the human (and the physician in particular) the right to select the values deemed necessary to sustain one's own life; the right to exercise one's own judgment of the best course of action to achieve the chosen values; and the right to dispose of those values, once gained, in any way one chooses. The proper function of government, he says, is to provide defense from individuals who would take lives or property by force. Sade's conclusion is that "the concept of medical care as the patient's right is immoral because it denies the most fundamental of all rights, that of a man to his own life and the freedom of action to support it."[5]

The entitlement theory of justice is really, then, a nontheory of justice. It justifies inequalities provided they derive from free choices made by people forced to use the resources imposed upon them by the natural lottery. The view that the needy have no claim of justice against the rest of the community can be attacked on two levels. Sade is vulnerable on both of them. First we can argue that no one today has obtained anything as a good that has not been previously possessed, and that no one can claim that the bulk of what he or she has acquired has, at all previous points, been transferred justly. At some point in the past, unfair advantage was taken by slavery, or deceptive business practices, or transactions pursued by force rather than free bargaining, and so forth. Thus, even if, in theory, entitlements could be claimed based on libertarian side constraints, they cannot be claimed in practice because the existing distribution of resources over the generations has been so complex and so unfair that no one in the present stands in full, unfettered possession of the property, skill, knowledge, and talent he or she currently possesses.

Sade somehow misses the fact that virtually all of what a physician possesses has been acquired either through class, familial, or status advantages of dubious history, or through public support—education, the monopoly practice conveyed with the license to practice medicine, and the body of knowledge generated by, and now in the possession of, the community as a whole. It is reasonable to assume that the physician acquires obligations in exchange for those acquisitions. Likewise, when hospitals acquire resources and advantages from the public through licensure, public approval, and public support (through programs like Hill-Burton funding), they acquire the obligation to serve the public, to render care to the physicianless. At least the public would be foolish not to impose such minimal obligations.

Sade and the entitlement theorists also miss at a second level. Even if individuals, including health care professionals, had not acquired most of what they possess as a public trust, even if they could appropriate a full medical education as isolated individuals in the state of nature without any unjust acquisition, this would not provide an adequate account of what is fair. The world is not ours to possess, and the entitlement theorists never justify the view that it is. The theological account, of course, makes the clearest case that the earth is the Lord's and the fullness thereof. What humans possess, they possess temporarily, as if on loan. Those adopting a more secular view, who attempt to discern a moral principle of distribution or even try to invent one based on the moral point of view, cannot ignore the needs of the unfortunate.

Nozick gets to his position by means of a contract model that is superficially like the one I have developed. To be sure, he has no use for the image of humans discovering the basic principles—whether through God's revelation, the laws of nature, the moral senses, or reason. His humans come together to agree upon a set of moral constraints that make human community possible without the constant threat of violence and unjust appropriation. The primary moral constraint, which he calls a "side constraint," is the principle of liberty, "a libertarian side constraint that prohibits aggression against another."[6] This notion of liberty as a basic principle does appear to lead to the conclusion that one is entitled to what one possesses, provided it has been acquired fairly.

One who is inventing what I have called the basic principles is limited only by a vision of what will produce an acceptable or at least a tolerable society. For some reason, defenders of the invention of the libertarian view of distribution, unencumbered by any conviction that the basic principles have a reality beyond social convention, believe that liberty alone, without a commitment to what I have called the moral point of view, will produce a tolerable moral society. This, of course, is contrary to my earlier contention that liberty alone simply would produce the chaos of despair from the less fortunate or the less well-endowed and lead them to reject this libertarian side constraint in favor of the world of force, if those were the only two choices.

It is only when the moral point of view, the taking of all equally into account, is incorporated that the inventors of the basic principles have a sustainable set of basic principles. But when that condition is added, the interests of the unfortunate are taken to count in the same way as those who have the physical or mental power that would lead to inevitable victory in a world with liberty as the only moral constraint. The result is that the inventors will be forced to include some distributional principles of justice that push them beyond a liberty-based entitlement position. They are pushed to a concern for distribution that is uniformly reflected in theories attempting to discern morality as more objectively grounded in reality.

If the hypothetical contractors are to count the needs of others equally with their own, it seems impossible that rational contractors would ignore those needs and totally subject the bearers of those needs to the natural lottery. They would want the society structured in such a way that somehow those in greatest need would, if possible, have their needs met. Anything less would be intolerable from the moral point of view. The entitlement view of distribution, no matter how coherent, fails the test that generates basic social principles. We could not base principles of distribution solely on the principle of autonomy and the exercise of the right to liberty. When any human takes the moral point of view, he or she is bound more directly to the welfare of others. Those mentally retarded citizens do not yet have a claim on the $14.2 million of the state legislature. It is absurd, however, to claim that the only way they can generate a claim morally is by using their natural abilities to make a deal with the legislature or to rely on the charity of the legislators.

THE UTILITARIAN THEORY

Representative Hudson and Dr. Simmons opposed the proposal to spend the extra $14.2 million on community-based homes for the retarded. However, they did not, as the entitlement theorists might, exclude any claims that might belong to those 7,600 retarded citizens.

Their approach was one of balancing the interests of the retarded against the interests of other citizens and attempting to determine which of several alternatives for expending the funds would do the greatest total good. Their approach, "serving the greatest good for the greatest number," is the classical utilitarian method of resolving conflicting claims over limited resources.

This is a favorite strategy of health planners and economists. They say that when we cannot buy every service everyone would like, we should calculate the benefits and costs of the alternatives and choose the plan that maximizes the benefit–cost ratio or the one that maximizes the net benefits over costs. This is the ethics, as we have seen, of the utilitarians, of Jeremy Bentham[7] and John Stuart Mill.[8] While the Hippocratic ethic is militantly individualistic in taking into account the interests of the isolated patient, the utilitarian formula takes all benefits and harms into account. In principle, then, it can provide a method of comparing the interests of the retarded with those who would benefit from Representative Hudson's hot-lunch program in the schools or her job training program to turn out productive members of society. Since both of her favored programs are likely to improve the efficient productivity of a large group while the community-based homes for the retarded will make, at best, marginal improvements in productivity for a small number of citizens, it is likely that when the $14.2 million is spent on her programs, a great deal of good will result. However, if the money is spent on Representative Sheehan's program, the benefits might reasonably be smaller.

To be sure, the benefits for the retarded will be hard to quantify. We would be remiss if we failed to take into account the greater happiness of the retarded in the new homes and the subtle improvement in the quality of their lives, but still, it is quite likely that the net aggregate benefits from Representative Hudson's plan would be greater than that of Representative Sheehan's.

Dr. Simmons's argument was structurally exactly like Representative Sheehan's. He simply focused on another set of benefits—health benefits to three groups: normal children, adults potentially engaged in productive labor, and pregnant women. His plan, like Representative Hudson's, focused on small investments in a large group of people whose productivity is subject to great increase with the small investments. Whether Dr. Simmons's or Representative Hudson's scheme would produce the most benefit for the dollar invested is debatable. In fact, this reveals an initial technical problem with utilitarian and cost-benefit strategies for solving resource allocation problems. It is probably not accidental that the physician—who places high value on health—concludes that the money can best be spent on health care services. The real question, though, is whether this approach of trying to get the most return for the dollar is the correct way of solving the resource allocation question.

At first it seems as if reasonable people, taking the moral point of view, would opt for utilitarian strategies for resource allocation. These do take into account the interests of all, and they grant legitimacy to the claims of all, including the retarded. It just so happens that with any plausible quantification of the benefits and costs, the retarded are likely to lose.

Two kinds of problems are presented to those who believe that reasonable people would opt for the utilitarian formula. First, there are the problems we have seen with the accounting. Most important benefits and harms may be subtle and nonquantifiable: pain and suffering, death of loved ones, destruction of principles held dear, the suffering of the warehoused retarded. In the health area, it is particularly difficult to compare benefits and harms. Do we consider mortality or morbidity? How do we quantify and compare physical and mental suffering? Do we consider present health or anticipated future health status?

All of these are serious problems, but they sidetrack us from the real issue. Policymakers make these estimates constantly. Any estimates of benefit in these highly subjective areas are going to be approximations, but approximations can be estimated. Quantification difficulties turn out to seem minor next to the ultimate problem of utilitarian resource allocation strategies.

This is the fundamental problem: the utilitarian strategy does not take into account the distribution of benefits and harms; it merely examines aggregate net benefits. In the words of Bentham, "... sum up the numbers expressive of the degrees of good tendency, which the act has, with respect to each individual [and] take the balance."[9] The method sums up the net benefits for each individual and, in the process, loses the information about who is benefited and who is harmed. Of course, it is usually the case that people who are in great need will benefit more from a fixed amount of resources than those who are relatively well off. Usually, marginal utility from a given amount of a resource decreases as the amount of need decreases. In aggregating benefits, those effects will be correctly taken into account. Thus, utilitarians are quick to explain why we often feel a sense of moral requiredness in distributing resources in favor of the least well off. However, this is felt, they argue, only because such a distribution will tend to produce more net utility. There is, according to Mill and his followers, no means of resolution of conflicts over distribution except the utilitarian, the one that compares aggregate impacts of alternatives.[10] It is a useful approach in that it permits a comparison of the benefits generated by highly complex social programs. It permits the comparison of the benefits to the mentally retarded with the benefits to other, more productive groups. But it justifies too much. By itself, it justifies any scheme that produces the greatest net aggregate benefit. As we have said, it would justify the Nazi experiments if only the Nazis were clever enough to design an experiment that would produce great good for the masses while harming a small number of people in such a way that the aggregate net good was enhanced. If enough people receive the benefits, it is plausible that even enormous harms to a small number will be outweighed by the aggregate benefit to the masses.

The psychology of egoism, of one who claims that people are only capable of pursuing their own happiness or good, is understandable. Utilitarians are not taking that position, however. Rather, they abandon egoism in favor of an altruism (or neutralism) that takes into account all goods equally, regardless of whether they accrue to the individual himself or to others. It is not obvious, however, why people would have an interest in maximizing aggregate good in the world without regard to how it is distributed. The position certainly lacks the psychological power of the egoistic position. In order to affirm the utilitarian answer to the question of how to distribute goods, one must accept the moral legitimacy of placing the interests of others on a par with one's own interests.

Even among utilitarians there is disagreement over exactly what combination of total benefits is morally relevant. Some press for choosing the policy that would produce the most net good if the policy were followed by all members of the society.[11] Others opt for the policy that would produce the most good if generally accepted by society (granting that there will be some deviations from the policy).[12] Still others distinguish between choosing among isolated acts on the basis of their compared net consequences and choosing among alternative general rules on the basis of the consequences of alternative rules or even systems of rules.[13]

Utilitarians face the problem of choosing among various competing ways of producing the greatest net good.[14] None of them squares with the obvious, if simplistic, psychology of egoism. Moreover, many of the utilitarianisms seem to lead to highly implausible, counterintuitive implications: that superhuman acts normally referred to as supererogatory are morally required provided they produce even slightly more good on balance than alternative actions; that even trivial choices among actions are elevated to moral obligations if they produce even slightly greater benefit (the choice among breakfast cereals, for example); that the only reason to keep promises is because keeping them produces or tends to produce the best consequences; that punishment should be meted out on the basis of the consequences rather than on the basis of who deserves the punishment; and that the distribution of the benefits and harms counts for nothing in the concept of justice except as it has an impact on total aggregate consequences.[15]

The utilitarian approach is particularly troublesome in that it does not take into account the fact that one person may benefit while another is harmed. Morally, the problem is whether it matters that the one who is harmed is not the one who is helped. Entitlement theory at least recognizes this. There is no obvious reason why reasonable contractors, having abandoned egoism for the moral point of view, would be interested in the aggregate good produced to the exclusion of how the goods are distributed.

The answer to the question of what is a just distribution, then, will depend on exactly how reasonable people would go about taking the welfare of all equally into account. If that simply means summing up the interests of each person, then the utilitarians have carried the day. The policy choice would be the one that produces the greatest total net benefit under the conditions of the various utilitarian options. But there are other ways that the welfare of all can be taken into account. The other two strategies for resource allocation pay much more attention to how the goods are distributed.

THE MAXIMIN THEORY

Some say that reasonable people considering alternative policies or principles for a society would not opt to maximize the aggregate benefits that exist in the society. Rather, they say that at least for basic social practices that determine the welfare of members of the moral community, they would opt for a strategy that attempts to assure fundamentally that the least well off person would do as well as possible. Representative Sheehan, in defending his bill, may have been working from this perspective when he said that "justice" requires increasing aid to those "most burdened by incredible medical expenses, by physical and psychological suffering, and by the degradation of our society's past inhumanity to its fellow humans." Presumably that is not the same as saying more good on balance will come from investing in the retarded citizens than alternative investments. Representative Sheehan may have believed that greater good would come from his strategy than from those proposed by Representative Hudson and Dr. Simmons. He did not mount the argument that way, however, and there is reason to believe that he would not insist that his policy be justified by the utilitarian argument.

Representative Sheehan's stated argument is one based on justice, on the burdens of a group of "most burdened" citizens. The implication is that those having the greatest burden have some claim on the society independent of whether responding to their needs is the most efficient way of producing the greatest net aggregate benefit. Holders of this view say that the commitment of a principle of justice is to maximize not net aggregate benefit, but the position of the least advantaged members of the society. If the principle of justice is a right-making characteristic of actions, a principle that reasonable people would accept as part of the basic social contract independent of the principle of beneficence, it probably incorporated some moral notion that the distribution of benefits and burdens counts as well as the aggregate amount of them. One plausible alternative is to concentrate, insofar as we are concerned about justice, on the welfare of the least well off.

This is part of those principles of justice defended by Rawls as derived from his version of social contract theory. He asks what people would choose if acting rationally to establish the basic principles for the society under the "veil of ignorance" (which essentially serves the same function as what I have called the moral point of view). Rawls claims their first concern would be the equal distribution of liberty: "Each person is to have an equal right to the most extensive total system of equal basic liberty compatible with a similar system of liberty for all." Denial of equal liberty can only be acceptable if it, in due course, enhances the equal freedom enjoyed by all. A less equal liberty must be acceptable to those with the lesser liberty. This priority of liberty is necessary, according to Rawls, because it is the basis of self-esteem, which rational people would not sacrifice for increase in material possessions (at least in a society capable of meeting the basic needs of the members).[16]

Following the principle of equal right to liberty, Rawls offers his second principle: that social and economic inequalities are to be arranged so that they are to the benefit of the least advantaged. This emphasis on the welfare of the least advantaged takes priority in an absolute way over maximizing the sum of advantages in the society or over the principle of efficiency. The fair thing to do in a society is to arrange social institutions and practices so as to improve the lot of the least well off.[17]

Since Rawls's scheme is designed to provide insights into only the basic practices and social institutions, it is very hard to discern what the implications are for specific problems of resource distribution such as the allocation of health care resources. Some have argued that no direct implications can be read from the Rawlsian principles. That seems, however, to overstate the case. At the least, basic social practices and institutional arrangements must be subject to the test of the principles of justice.

It appears, then, that this view will not justify inequalities in the basic health care institutions and practices simply because they produce the greatest net aggregate benefit. Its notion of justice, concentrating on improving the lot of the least advantaged, is much more egalitarian in this sense than the utilitarian system. It would distribute health care resources to the least well off rather than just on the aggregate amount of benefit.

There is no obvious reason why our hypothetical contractors articulating the basic principles for a society would favor a principle that maximized aggregate utility any more than one that maximized minimum utility. Our contract model, as an epistemological device for discovering the basic principles, views them, after all, as committed to the moral point of view, as evaluating equally the welfare of each individual from a veil of ignorance, to use the Rawlsian language. This perspective retains the notion of individuals as identifiable, unique personalities, as noncommensurable human beings, rather than simply as components of an aggregate mass. Faced with a forced choice, it seems plausible that one would opt for maximizing the welfare of individuals, especially the least well-off individuals, rather than maximizing the aggregate.

Nevertheless, the interpretation of justice that attempts to maximize the minimum position in the society (and is hence sometimes called the "maximin" position), still permits inequalities and even labels them as just. What, for example, of basic health care institutional arrangements that systematically single out elites with unique natural talents for developing medical skill and services and gives these individuals high salaries as incentives to serve the interests of the least well off? What if a special health care system were institutionalized to make sure these people were always in the best of health, were cared for first in catastrophes, and were inconvenienced least by the normal bureaucratic nuisances of a health care system?

It is conceivable that such an institutional arrangement would be favored by reasonable people taking the moral point of view. They could justify the special gains that would come to the elites by the improved chances thus created for the rest of the population (who would not have as great a gain as the favored ones, but would at least be better off than if the elite were not so favored). The benefits, in lesser amounts, would trickle down in this plan to the consumers of health care so that all, or at least the least advantaged, would gain. The gap between the elite of the health profession and the masses could potentially increase by such a social arrangement, but at least all would be better off in absolute terms.

So it is conceivable that reasonable people considering equally both the health professionals and the masses would favor such an arrangement, but it is not obvious. Critics of the Rawlsian principles of justice say that in some cases alternative principles of distribution would be preferred. Brian Barry, for example, argues that rational choosers would look not just at the welfare of the least advantaged, but also at the average or aggregate welfare of alternative policies.[18] On the other hand, Barry and many others suggest that in some circumstances, rational choosers might opt for the principle that would maximize equality of outcome.[19] At most, considering the institutionalization of advantages for a health care elite, they would be supported as a prudent sacrifice of the demands of justice in order to serve some other justifiable moral end.

From this perspective, favoring elites with special monetary and social incentives in order to benefit the poor might be a prudent compromise.[20] It might mediate between the demands that see justice as requiring equality of outcome (subject to numerous qualifications) and the demands of the principle of beneficence requiring maximum efficiency in producing good consequences. If that is the case, though, then there is still a fourth interpretation of the principle of justice that must be considered, one that is more radically egalitarian than the maximin strategy.

THE EGALITARIAN THEORY

Those who see the maximin strategy as a compromise between the concern for justice and the concern for efficient production of good consequences must feel that justice requires a stricter focus on equality than the maximin understanding of the principle of justice. The maximin principle is concerned about the distribution of benefits. It justifies inequalities only if they benefit the least well off. But it does justify inequalities—and it does so in the name of justice.

Rawls recognizes that there is an important difference between a right action and a just or a fair action.[21] Fairness is a principle applying to individuals along with beneficence, noninjury, mutual respect, and fidelity. The list is not far removed from the basic principles I have identified. But, given this important difference between what is right in this full, inclusive sense and what is fair, if one is convinced that incentives and advantages for medical elites are justified, why would one claim that the justification is one based on the principle of fairness? One might instead maintain that they are right on balance because they are a necessary compromise with the principle of fairness (or justice) in order to promote efficiently the welfare of a disadvantaged group. It is to be assumed, given the range of basic principles in an ethical system, that conflicts will often emerge so that one principle will be sacrificed, upon occasion, for the sake of another.

The egalitarian understanding of the principle of justice is one that sees justice as requiring (subject to certain important qualifications) equality of net welfare for individuals.[22]

Representative Sheehan may have had something slightly different in mind from the maximin theory when he argued that justice requires that the mentally retarded have a claim on the society for support of the community-based homes. Instead of taking the maximin position that they have a claim as a least advantaged group to improvement, he may have held that justice demands greater equality and that they have a right to be more equal in total welfare to others in the society. In practice it might amount to the same thing—resources under either argument would be justly committed to the retarded rather than other groups—but the interpretation of the meaning of the claim of justice is somewhat different. Everyone, according to the principle of egalitarian justice, ought to end up over a lifetime with an equal amount of net welfare (or, as we shall see shortly, a chance for that welfare). Some may have a great deal of benefit offset by large amounts of unhappiness or disutility, while others will have relatively less of both. What we would call "just" under this principle is a basic social practice or policy that contributes to the same extent to greater equality of outcome (subject to restrictions to be discussed). I am suggesting that reasonable people who are committed to a contract model for discovering, inventing, or otherwise articulating the basic principles will want to add to their list the notion that one of the right-making characteristics of a society would be the equality of welfare among the members of the moral community.

The Equality of Persons   The choice of this interpretation of the principle of justice will depend upon how the contractors understand the commitment to the moral point of view—the commitment to impartiality that takes the point of view of all equally into account. We certainly are not asserting the equality of ability or even the equality of the merit of individual claims.

Bernard Williams, in an important essay on the idea of equality,[23] suggests that what is meant must be interpreted beginning with the recognition of a common humanity, what I have referred to as a common membership in the moral community. He identifies an equality of moral worth rooted in moral capacities, independent of "natural capacities, unequally and fortuitously distributed." Each human is, in Kantian terms, an end in himself, a member of the Kingdom of Ends. Equality of respect is commanded, not "in respect to any empirical characteristics that he may possess, but solely in respect of the transcendental characteristic of being a free and rational will." Secularized, this conveys the idea of respect, with persons regarded "not merely under professional, social, or technical titles, but with consideration of their own views and purposes." Each person is "owed the effort of understanding and that in achieving it, each man is to be (as it were) abstracted from certain conspicuous structures of inequality in which we find him."

If this is what is meant by the moral point of view, taking into account equally the individuality of each member of the community, then in addition to the right-making characteristics or principles of beneficence, promise keeping, autonomy, truth telling, and avoiding killing, the principle of justice as equality of net welfare must be added to the list. The principle might be articulated as affirming that people have a claim on having the total net welfare in their lives equal insofar as possible to the welfare in the lives of others.

Of course, no reasonable person, even an egalitarian, is going to insist upon or even desire that all the features of people's lives be identical.[24] It seems obvious that the most that anyone would want is that the total net welfare for each person be comparable.

If this is the proper understanding of the principle of justice that will eventually be incorporated into a medical ethic, it is closely related in implication to, but structurally somewhat different from, the maximin interpretation of the principle. Striving to improve the lot of the least advantaged is not precisely the same as striving for equality. Often the

266

outcomes of pursuit of the two objectives will be the same. Representative Sheehan may have justified his defense of the community-homes bill on either interpretation.

However, there might be some differences in policy implications. If the strategy for the $14.2 million in extra funds was to spend most of it for highly paid administrators and professional staff, an egalitarian Representative Sheehan would be forced to pause, recognizing that equality was not necessarily being promoted even though the retarded would benefit as well as the elites. He might be forced to say that justice was being sacrificed in order to promote efficiently the welfare of the retarded through an indirect, trickle-down means. A maximin Representative Sheehan, on the other hand, would feel no such tension; the financial investment in incentives for elites would be seen as just or fair if it were the best strategy for improving the lot of the least advantaged.

If this egalitarian understanding of the principle of justice would be acceptable to reasonable people taking the moral point of view, it provides a solution to the dilemma of the tension between focusing exclusively on the patient and opening the doors to considerations of social consequences such as in classical utilitarianism. The principle of justice provides another basis for taking into account a limited set of impacts on certain other parties. If the distribution of benefits as well as the aggregate amount is morally relevant, then certain impacts on other parties may be morally more relevant than others. A benefit that accrues to a person who is or predictably will be in a least well-off group would count as a consideration of justice while a benefit of equal size that accrued to other persons not in the least well-off group would not. The hypothetical benefits of a Nazi-type experiment would not accrue to a least well-off group (while the harms of the experiment presumably would). They are thus morally different from, in fact diametrically opposed to, a redistribution scheme that produced benefits for only the least advantaged group.

Equality and Envy Critics of the egalitarian view of justice have argued that the only way to account for such a position is by attributing it to a psychology of envy.[25] Freud accounted for a sense of justice in this way.[26] They feel the only conceivable reason to strive for equality is the psychological explanation that the less well off envy the better off, and they hold that contractors take that psychological fact into account. Since they believe that envy is not an adequate justification for a commitment to equal outcome, they opt instead for an alternative theory of justice.

Nozick, for example, in an extended discussion of equality and envy, accounts for the egalitarian love of equality by claiming it derives from envy—the view that if one cannot himself have a thing, then he prefers that no one else have it either.[27] This, however, is certainly an inadequate account of the egalitarian sense of justice, the love of equality of total welfare among persons in a moral community.[28] It is clear from history that many advocates of the egalitarian sense of justice are not those have-nots who long for the possessions of others, but those who are themselves advantaged and who regret the fact that others are not similarly blessed. They, in fact, have taken the position that they would prefer that all those who have, including themselves, lose their good fortune if all others cannot be so blessed. Whatever that position involves, it is not envy.[29]

The egalitarian holds that there is something fundamentally wrong with gross inequalities, with gross differences in net welfare. The problem is encountered when people of unequal means must interact; say, when representatives of an impoverished community apply to an elite foundation for funds to support a neighborhood health program. There is no way that real communication can take place between the elites of the foundation and the members of the low-income community. It is not simply that the poor envy the foundation executives or that the executives feel resentful of the poor. Rather, as anyone who has been in such a relationship knows, the sense of community is fractured. Not only do the less well off feel that they cannot express themselves with self-respect, but the elites realize that there is no way the messages they receive can be disentangled from the status and welfare differentials. Neither can engage in any true interaction. A moral relationship is virtually impossible.

An analogous problem exists at the microlevel, in relationships between lay people and health professionals. Lay people, generally grossly unequal to providers in income, educational, and social class, are unable to communicate their system of beliefs and values to the provider standing in a radically different tradition. A moral bond between such a lay person and physician is impossible. It is not mere envy of the position of the other party; it is far more fundamental. If human beings are equal in the fundamental sense of which Bernard Williams spoke, then insofar as justice is at stake a balancing out of the differentials is required to make human interaction possible. It is a goal that is legitimately on the agenda of both groups regardless of the aggregate social consequences of the production of equality.

The Implications of the Egalitarian Formula   It turns out that incorporating health care into this system of total welfare will be extremely difficult. Let us begin, temporarily, therefore, by considering a simpler system dealing only with food, clothing, and shelter. Fairness could mean, according to the egalitarian formula, that each person had to have an equal amount of each of these. No reasonable person, however, would find that necessary or attractive. Rather, what the egalitarian has in mind with his concept of justice is that the net of welfare, summed across all three of these goods, be as similar as possible. We could arbitrarily fix the amount of resources in each category, but nothing seems wrong with permitting people to trade some food for clothing, or clothing for shelter. If one person preferred a large house and minimal food and could find someone with the opposite tastes, nothing seems wrong with permitting a trade. The assumption is that the need of people for food, clothing, and shelter is about the same in everybody and that marginal utilities in the trades will be about the same. It so, then permitting people to trade around would increase the welfare of each person without radically distorting the equality of net overall welfare. Up to this point, then, the egalitarian principle of justice says that it is just (though not necessarily right) to strive in social practices for equality of net welfare. The matter gets more complex, however, when health care is added to the system.

JUSTICE, THE BASIC SOCIAL CONTRACT, AND HEALTH CARE

Food, clothing, and shelter are obviously not the only needs of the human. Any reasonable distribution will have to include consideration of recreation and leisure, as well as education and health care. Recreation and leisure can be handled in much the same way as food, clothing, and shelter. Everyone's needs can be presumed to be about equal.[30] Trades of one kind of resource for another seem perfectly acceptable. A generalized medium like money distributed justly would make the trading much simpler and seems to present no problem of justice.

For health care and education, however, the situation is much different. Here it is reasonable to assume that human needs vary enormously. Nothing could be more foolish than to distribute health care or even the money for health care equally. The result would be unequal overall well-being for those who were unfortunate in the natural lottery for health, objectively much worse off than others.[31] If the goal of justice is to produce a chance for equal, objective net welfare, then the starting point for consideration of health care distribution should be the need for it. Education (or the resources to buy education) initially would be distributed in the same way. The amount added to the resources for food, clothing, and shelter should then be in proportion to an "unhealthiness status index" plus another amount proportional to an "educational needs index."[32]

However, that proposal raises two additional questions: Should people be permitted to use the resources set aside for health care in some other way? And who should bear the responsibility if people have an opportunity to be healthy and do not take advantage of it?

THE CASE FOR AN EQUAL RIGHT TO HEALTH CARE

Even for the egalitarian it is not obvious why society ought to strive for an equal right to health care. Certainly it ought not to be interested in obtaining the same amount of health care for everyone. To do so would require forcing those in need of great amounts of care to go without or those who have the good fortune to be healthy to consume uselessly. But it is not even obvious that we should end up with a right to health care equal in proportion to need, though that is the conclusion that many, especially egalitarians, are reaching.

Several arguments have been developed leading to that conclusion. Ronald Green, a professor of religion at Dartmouth College, has attempted to apply Rawls's maximin strategy to the health care sphere. He acknowledges that Rawls himself is silent on the implications of the general principles of justice for health care resource allocation. Green argues, however, that health care ought reasonably be seen as a primary social good and thus distributed according to Rawls's basic principles.[33] Although the basic determinants of health are, like intelligence and vigor, natural endowments distributed randomly by luck or fortune not directly subject to social control, interventions to ameliorate the impacts of the natural lottery are certainly social and thus under control of the moral community.

While this might imply that health care should be put into the pool along with other social goods for distribution according to the difference principle, Green argues that rational people would treat health care more like liberty, as having a priority over other social goods so that trades between health care and other goods is impermissible. This tactic has the effect of escalating health care into a special, privileged status. "We can expect," says Green, "the parties finally to opt for a principle of equal access to health care: each member of society, whatever his position or background, would be guaranteed an equal right to the most extensive health services the society allows."[34]

This makes Rawls a health care egalitarian in spite of himself, or so it seems. Health care is, according to this view, so important that reasonable people would not permit trades of one's fair share of health care for other social goods. The principle guarantees equal access to the health care system where health care would be distributed equally in proportion to need.

Actually, if Green is to be Rawlsian about his distribution principle, the result may not be quite equal access. As we have seen, Rawls even tolerates inequalities in the distribution of liberty. They are acceptable provided they enhance the liberty of those with lesser liberty to "strengthen the total system of liberty shared by all" in a way acceptable to those with lesser liberty.[35] By the same token it would seem that Green would accept inequalities in health care provided they were for the health benefit of the less healthy. He might then accept a scheme where an elite is temporarily given superior health care in order to keep it ready for health care emergencies.

With this qualifier, however, Green's emendation of Rawls produces a case for the kind of equality in the right of access to health care that egalitarians have in mind. But does the argument work? Is there any reason to believe that health care is any more basic than, say, food or protection from the elements? All are absolutely essential to human survival, at least up to some minimum for subsistence. All are necessary conditions for the exercise of liberty, self-respect, or any other functioning as part of the human moral community.[36] Furthermore, while the bare minimum of health care is as necessary as food and shelter, in all cases these may not really be "necessities" at the margin. If trades are to be tolerated between marginal food and clothing, is there any reason why someone placing relatively low value on health care should not be permitted to trade, say, his annual checkups for someone else's monthly allotment of steak dinners? Or, if we shall make trading easier by distributing money fairly rather than distributing rations of these specific goods, is there any reason why, based on an "unhealthiness index," we could not distribute a fair portion of funds for health care as well as for other necessities? Individuals could then buy the health care (or health care insurance) that they need, employing individual discretion about where their limit for health care is in comparison with steak dinners. Those at a high health risk would be charged high amounts for health care (or high premiums for insurance), but those costs would be exactly offset by the money supplement based on the index.

Perhaps we cannot make a case for equal access to health care on the basis that it is more fundamental than other goods. There may still be reasons, though, why reasonable people would structure the basic institutions of society to provide a right to equal health care in the sense I am using the term, that is a right equal in proportion to need.

Our response will depend somewhat upon whether we are planning a health care distribution for a just world or one with the present inequities in the distribution of net welfare. In a just world, where objective net welfare, or generalized measures of the means to obtain welfare (such as money) are distributed fairly, the case for equal access to health care is particularly difficult. Suppose that the world were structured so that each received a basic allotment, depending upon the wealth of the society. That allotment included an equal amount for everyone for food, clothing, and shelter as well as for recreation, leisure, and other needs that can be assumed to be distributed about evenly. In addition, everyone received an amount proportional to his or her need for health care and education as well as for any other needs predictably distributed unevenly.[37]

Is there any reason why one would still insist on everyone having a right to an amount of health care equal in proportion to need? At first it seems not. The only reasons to insist on equal health care access would be practical. But the practical reasons may be powerful. It would be almost impossible to determine what would be one's fair share of the resources proportional to health care needs. In order to distribute the general resources based on an "unhealthiness index," we would need an enormously complex mechanism, such as a bureaucracy, with a point system for every naturally occurring health risk factor, every adverse gene, or probability for exposure to infectious disease. Far simpler would be distributing health care services equally in proportion to need, where those health services are agreed upon by society to justify a social commitment given the general level of resources in the society and the general value preference system.

There might still be esoteric services totally outside the basic health care system that people would buy with discretionary funds. As long as funds were fairly distributed, that should present no problem.[38]

But obviously we do not live in a perfectly just world. The problem becomes more complex. How do we arrange the health care system, which all would agree is fundamental to human well-being at least at some basic level, in order to get as close as possible to equality of welfare as the outcome? Pragmatic considerations may, at this point, override the abstract, theoretical argument allowing trades of health care for other goods even at the margin.

Often defenders of free-market and partial free-market solutions to the allocation of health care resources assume that if fixed in-kind services such as health care are not distributed, money will be. Charles Fried, a law professor at Harvard University who is a defender of a partial free market solution to this question, argues that what the poor really need is not health care, but money.[39] That may well be true, but the political reality may be such that a legislature will not substitute cash grants for health care. The choice is between health care for everyone, or at least everyone with particular levels of need, and no welfare redistribution at all. Given that forced choice, an additional pragmatic reason for distributing health care equally in proportion to need is uncovered.

There is a more subtle case for an equal right to health care (in proportion to need) in an unfair world. Bargaining strengths are likely to be very unequal in a world where resources are distributed unfairly. Those with great resources, perhaps because of natural talents or naturally occurring good health or both, are in an invincible position. The needy, for example those with little earning power because of congenital health problems, may be forced to use what resources they have in order to buy immediate necessities, withholding on health care investment, particularly preventive health care and health insurance, while gambling that they will be able to survive without those services.[40]

It is not clear what our moral response should be to those forced into this position of bargainers from weakness. If the just principle of distribution were Pareto optimality (where bargains were acceptable, regardless of the weaknesses of the parties, provided all gained in the transaction), we would accept the fact that some would bargain from weakness and be forced to trade their long-term health care needs for short-term necessities. If the principle of justice that reasonable people would accept taking the moral point of view, however, is something like the maximin position or the egalitarian position, then perhaps such trades of health care should be prohibited. The answer will depend on how one should behave in planning social policies in an unjust world. The fact that resources are not distributed fairly generates pressures on the least well off (assuming they act rationally) to make choices they would not have to make in a more fair world. If unfairness in the general distribution of resources is a given, we are forced into a choice between two unattractive options: We could opt for the rule that will permit the least well off to maximize their position under the existing conditions or we could pick the rule that would arrange resources as closely as possible to the way they would be arranged in a just world. In our present, unjust society distributing health care equally is a closer approximation to the way it would be distributed in a just society than giving a general resource like money or permitting trades. The romantics, the visionaries of the world, cannot bring themselves to favor a rule of distribution that is premised on the fact of unfairness in the moral community. They insist on equal distribution, especially for something like health care—even if it does not maximize the short-term welfare of the least advantaged groups in the real, nasty, brutish, unjust world of reality. They hold to the ideal, perhaps believing that their witness in the world to that ideal will itself help bring about the greater justice they seek. In effect, holders of this position are insisting on a program of distributing resources according to a formula of equal amounts for needs distributed evenly (such as food, clothing, and shelter), for health care in proportion to the unhealthiness status index, and for education equal to the educational needs index. If in the real world they can get only the amount in proportion to the unhealthiness index (and probably another amount proportional to the educational needs index), then they should take it; perhaps the rest of the agenda will be completed in due course. They point to certain practical advantages: particularly that all (including the elites) participating in the same health care system is likely to improve that system for all, including the least advantaged groups. But their real reason is not such technical, utilitarian considerations. It is that in today's unjust world they choose to opt for the system of health care to approximate the distribution that exists in the moral world of their vision. This reflects not a paternalism—that might lead to the opposite policy—but a commitment to the ideal of justice.

Realists, of course, do not buy this dreaming. They say that if real people, especially the least advantaged group, can improve their lot by trading some of their health care for things they want even more, they should not be deprived of the right to do so. If they were in the position of contractors trying to discern the basic principles of the society, their choice might well be for the real world maximin interpretation of the principle of justice. That, however, requires acknowledgment of a policy rooted in injustice. Myself, I am more of a dreamer. I see justice not just as a way to efficiently improve the lot of the least well off by permitting them trades (even though those trades end up increasing the gap between the haves and the have-nots). That might be efficient and might preserve autonomy, but it would not be justice. If I were an original contractor I would cast my vote in favor of the egalitarian principle of justice, applying it so that there would be a right to health care equal in proportion to health care need. The principle of justice for health care could, then, be stated as follows: People have a right to needed health care to provide an opportunity for a level of health equal as far as possible to the health of other people.[41]

The principle of justice for health care is a pragmatic derivative from the general principle of justice requiring equality of objective net welfare. The result would be a uniform health care system with one class of service available for all. Practical problems would still exist, especially at the margins. The principle, for example, does not establish what percentage of total resources would go for health care. The goal would be to arrange resources so that health care needs would, in general, be met about as well as other needs. This means that a society would rather arbitrarily set some fixed amount of the total resources for health care. Every nation currently spends somewhere between five and ten percent of its gross national product (GNP) in this area, with the wealthier societies opting for the higher percentages.[42] Presumably the arbitrary choice would fall in that range.

With such a budget fixed, reasonable people will come together to decide what health care services can be covered under it. The task will not be as great as it seems. The vast majority of services will easily be sorted into or out of the health care system. Only a small percentage at the margin will be the cause of any real debate. The choice will at times be arbitrary, but the standard applied will at least be clear. People should have services necessary to give them a chance to be as close as possible to being as healthy as other people. Those choices will be made while striving to emulate the position of original contractors taking the moral point of view. The decision-making panels will not differ in task greatly from the decision makers who currently sort health care services in and out of insurance coverage lists. However, panels will be committed to a principle of justice and will take the moral point of view, whereas the self-interested insurers try to maximize profits or efficiency or a bargaining position against weak, unorganized consumers.

Applying our understanding of the implication of the principle of justice to Representative Sheehan's bill to provide homes for the mentally retarded will still require a great deal of conceptual and empirical filling. First of all, an assumption has to be made that the homes and the services taking place within the homes are really health services. That, of course, is debatable. There are good reasons to doubt the overly expansionistic subsuming of mental services under the medical model. But, especially since the homes are likely to be administered by a department of mental health, which in turn is within a state's health sphere, we might conceive of the plan as loosely a health service.

We would have to make empirical assumptions about who counts as the least well-off group among potential recipients of the state's resources. Those needing job training, school lunch programs, and well-baby clinic services might qualify, but it is likely that the retarded, especially if they have been institutionalized in inhumane conditions for many years, will win the designation as one of the least advantaged groups of the state. Then, if the principle of justice requires giving the least advantaged group an opportunity to benefit or to be equal insofar as possible to other people, then providing homes to the retarded is justified. The homes will help them more than any other expenditure of comparable funds; justice requires they get the resources.

THE PROBLEM OF VOLUNTARY HEALTH RISKS

Up to this point I have argued that, with regard to justice, people have a right to get enough health care that would allow, as far as possible, an opportunity for a level of health equal to that of other people. I have conceded that this is a pragmatic derivation from a more general principle of justice, which requires an equal distribution of net welfare among individuals in the moral community. There may be reasons based on the principle of beneficence or efficiency in producing good consequences to tilt in favor of some other distribution, such as one that gives special health status favors to elites with natural endowments so they can develop skills to promote and preserve the health of others. That is not a question of justice, however. There may be reasons based on the principle of autonomy to tilt in favor of permitting lay people to buy extra or special quality health services or of permitting health professionals to exercise freedom of choice in selecting how and where they will practice even though their choices do not promote justice. These are, however, questions of autonomy, as we said, and not of justice.

One link between the principle of autonomy and the principle of justice, though, deserves special attention. I have said that people have a right to enough health care to provide an opportunity to be healthy. But especially if we include freedom as one of the basic medical ethical principles, it is certain that some people will not take advantage of all their opportunities to be healthy. They will smoke knowing the enormous health risks involved. They will fail to exercise, although they believe with good reason they would be healthier if they did. They will consume vast quantities of alcohol, use other health-risky drugs, ski down dangerous precipices, drive automobiles recklessly, play professional football, climb dangerous mountains for the fun of it, exercise their right to autonomy by refusing life-prolonging medical treatment—in short, engage in all manner of health-risky behaviors. Does society bear a burden of justice to provide for all who voluntarily take risks with their health knowing that a right to health care is now defended by many?[43]

There may be reasons why society would want to take some limited responsibility in these cases, but it cannot be defended on the grounds that justice requires it. It may be a sense of charity that impels people to care for the maimed who show up at the hospital door after skiing accidents. A sense of the bystander's own empathetic agony on seeing the skier suffer from a broken leg may lead society to favor a social policy that provides needed medical care to those who suffer through voluntary choices of their own. These arguments too, though, are not rooted in the principle of justice. They are based on charity and beneficence, including the welfare of other parties. Would reasonable people taking the moral point of view in trying to articulate a principle of justice say that people are, by our concern generated by a sense of justice, entitled to equal net welfare outcomes or only an *opportunity* for equal net welfare outcomes?

The principle of justice is concerned with distribution of social resources on the basis of need. But need has traditionally been thought of as being derived from natural endowments and forces—genes, biochemistry, the random movement of microorganisms, and other factors beyond human control. In fact the classical formulation of the sick role includes the notion that one is not responsible for one's sickness.[44]

But it is becoming increasingly clear that one's health is, to a large extent, subject to voluntary control through conscious decisions. Not all the decisions may be made personally by the one who will suffer the illness. Parents make choices affecting genetic and nutritional components of the infant's health. Governments make choices affecting sanitation, exposure to pollutants, and public immunization levels. Industries make choices exposing their employees and others to environmental toxins. But it is increasingly clear that personal voluntary choices account for much of the variation in health among individuals. Health status increasingly is seen as correlative to life-style choices.[45]

277

Thus, we may require an amendment or a footnote to the principle of justice. It surely must not have been these personal voluntary choices affecting health status that we had in mind when we defended the principle of right to health care equal in proportion to need. That is why I added the qualifier *opportunity* to the principle of justice. Surely all that justice requires is that people have an opportunity to be as healthy as other people insofar as possible. Surely all that is necessary is that people have an opportunity to net welfare equal insofar as possible to that of other people.

Some might argue that this is really no problem at all for our account of justice. If people have an opportunity to be healthy (say by being informed of the health risks associated with skiing) and do not take the opportunity (by skiing anyway), it must be because they consider their welfare enhanced more with the skiing even taking into account the risk of the broken leg. They argue that if health care were then provided as a matter of justice on top of the joys of the exhilarating downhill plunge, justice would miscarry because the skier would have the welfare of the thrill of the hill without the burden of the risk of the health care cost. They conclude that to differentiate health care resulting from voluntary choices from health care resulting from causes beyond one's control is reasonable within the criterion of egalitarian justice.

The argument is interesting, but it may not work. There is little, if any, evidence that people make such calculations and end up balancing the benefits of the risky behavior with the potential costs of extra health care. Moreover, even if there is such a balance, it would involve the trading of health care benefits for other benefits such as the joy of skiing or the relaxation of the cigarette. I have argued, however, that there are at least pragmatic reasons why such trade-offs should not be permitted between health care and other social goods.

The more basic reason why an adjustment must be made for voluntary health risks in the principle of justice as it applies to health care is that surely it is reasonable to consider justice as requiring only an opportunity for net equality of welfare rather than actual equality in cases where people choose not to take advantage of the offered opportunity. Likewise, in the health care sphere, people are reasonably only entitled as a matter of justice to an opportunity to be as healthy as others. Should they choose not to take advantage of that opportunity, they would not be justified in turning on the society and demanding additional resources in order to restore their health. A compassionate society is likely to arrange things so that people will not be barred at the hospital door. But this is not a matter of justice; it is one of compassion and of sparing the society the burden of seeing even the voluntarily needy suffer.

For this reason many of us are searching for ways of transferring the cost of extra care to those engaging in risky behavior (and are likely to need medical care) rather than simply excluding them from coverage.[46] For example, if smoking is actuarially determined to increase the cost of providing health care to those who smoke, especially if the relationship is a linear one, then the marginal health care cost of a package of cigarettes can be calculated and added to the price of the cigarettes as a health fee.[47]

The principle of justice is focused on the fair distribution of burdens from paying for health care, not on the goal of decreasing health-risky behavior. That might be the object of a program rooted in the principle of beneficence, but such paternalistic goals would surely conflict with the principle of autonomy.[48] A program rooted in the principle of justice, on the other hand, simply concentrates on the fair distribution of the costs of the behavior. Health fees could be added to a general national health insurance or to a health-service funding pool. This would then compensate the society for the marginal costs to the extent that those costs could be calculated. Of course, if a behavior is suspected to have a health cost, but that cost has never been measured, it would be unfair and unnecessary to charge a health fee for the behavior.

Admittedly this is a dangerous suggestion. If it were applied by mistake to risks that really should not be conceptualized as voluntary, grave injustice would be done. If, for example, lung cancer involved some complex interaction including genetic predisposition and psychological causes that were perhaps related to smoking behavior, then to the extent that the risk is not one voluntarily assumed, it would be unfair to exclude health care for the lung cancer from the claims of justice.

Some conditions sometimes thought of as related to voluntary choices may really be organically determined.[49] Alcoholism, for example, may have a genetic component. Other behaviors resulting in predictable health care needs may involve life-style choices that are significantly determined by psychological factors beyond the control of the individual. Turning again to smoking, we might detect its origin in early psychological development or at least in the psychological pressures of teenage life when the individual may not have the rational capacity to exercise free choice. Other health care conditions that seem a result of individual choice also may be more socially determined than is first apparent. A very high proportion of medical conditions, perhaps all of them, have incidence rates which correlate with social class. (Those in lower socio-economic classes have higher rates.)[50] If complex social structural factors are responsible for medical need and individuals are merely the victims of their social position, then attributing personal responsibility to the individual for the medical need would be little more than blaming the victim.[51]

Furthermore, it seems clear that some risks that people take with their health in a clearly voluntary pattern are taken for the public good. The firefighter who enters the burning building may do so voluntarily, but should not be made to pay for the act. Rather he deserves public subsidy for any needed health care. This means that before the principles of justice could be used to place fees on voluntary health-risky behavior in order to distribute the costs of medical care equitably, society would have to make the judgment of whether any particular type of behavior is so socially noble than it is worth subsidizing. If, like firefighting, it is seen as a public service, then society should bear the extra cost because of its interest in promoting the voluntary behavior. It seems clear, though, that many health-risky behaviors, such as smoking, are not so ennobling, are real risks to health, are sufficiently self-willed that they fit the voluntary model, and generate enormous costs to the health care system. If and when behaviors are found to meet those conditions, justice seems to require that to be fair to others, health fees should be placed on the behaviors in order to distribute the burden of health care costs fairly. All that justice requires is an opportunity to be as healthy, insofar as possible, as other people.

Thus our recognition that some health care may be needed, at least hypothetically, as a result of voluntarily chosen individual choices that are not worthy of public subsidy, adds a minor correction to the principle of justice as applied to health care. It is only a minor correction, however, only a footnote on the otherwise egalitarian demands of justice. The consideration of voluntary health risks, for example, would seem to have no bearing at all on the debate over Representative Sheehan's proposal for community homes for the retarded. Other health care needs may be argued to be the result of individual voluntary behavior, but no one is going to consider the needs of the retarded in any way related to personal choices. At most the relative merit of the counterclaims by Representative Hudson and Dr. Simmons for the resources on behalf of some of the other potential beneficiaries might be tainted by this consideration. Conceivably, at least for the potential adult beneficiaries of the alternative proposals, their voluntary choices have led them to the needs they have. That seems quite unlikely, however. What is more likely is that even if the voluntary health risks theme is relevant to considering what justice requires for certain other policies, such as fees on tobacco, it would be irrelevant to the basic demands of justice in this case.

JUSTICE AND THE LAY-PROFESSIONAL CONTRACT

The proposal to fund community-based homes for the mentally retarded can be analyzed and probably largely resolved by considering the principle of justice as part of the basic social contract. Several tasks are essential: agreeing on which competing candidate for a theory of justice would be chosen by rational contractors taking the moral point of view; determining whether concerns rooted in the other basic principles pose insurmountable problems for the principle of justice; and making empirical judgments to determine who are the least advantaged, what would serve their interests, and whether they were to any extent voluntarily responsible for their condition. Once this is done the case is fairly well resolved. No appeal is necessary to any professional code, to any consensus of health care professionals about how health resources ought to be expended, or to any description of role-specific duties for professionals. It goes to show that we can move far in analyzing medical ethical problems without turning to problems of professional ethics.

We are left with one outstanding problem, though: What should the role of the clinical professional be in allocation decisions? The hypothetical case posed previously in this chapter presses the same problem upon us. We considered the choice a physician would have to make between one group of three patients who were well enough to be treated in the office and a fourth patient whose desperate straits required a house call that would prohibit the physician from caring for the other three. We saw, to our dismay, that the Hippocratic ethic would advise the physician to benefit "the patient" (note the singular), providing no moral clarity at all. On the other hand, if the physician routinely took it upon himself or herself to solve the problems of health resource allocation, that physician might be immobilized and might so abandon the patient perspective that patient care would suffer seriously. We are thus left with the question of whether a health professional should have a role-specific duty to push beyond the patient's perspective and deal with health resource allocation and questions of justice.

In the case involving funds of homes for the mentally retarded, we saw Dr. Simmons pushing beyond his traditional patient-centered medical role to involve himself in community affairs and health resource allocation. He advocated preventative health care services for relatively normal children, adults potentially engaged in productive labor, and pregnant women.

We are faced with the question: Did Dr. Simmons have any business getting involved in these health resource allocation issues or should he have been back in his office caring for his patient (in the singular)? He is faced with an unattractive pair of options. If he conforms to the individualistic model of duty to the isolated patient, he abandons any responsibility for broader social questions in medical ethics. That is not palatable to many—including the AMA, which has long held that the physician's duty extends beyond the individual patient. Its 1971 version of the "Principles of Medical Ethics" stated: "The honored ideals of the medical profession imply that the responsibilities of the physician extend not only to the individual, but also to society where these responsibilities deserve his interest and participation in activities which have the purpose of improving both the health and the well-being of the individual and the community."[52] The latest, 1980 version contains the same idea: "A physician shall recognize a responsibility to participate in activities contributing to an improved community."[53] Both are socially oriented. Both are very vague, not limiting the physician's commitment to medical or health concerns. The focus is on well-being and an improved community.

A principle of justice is very helpful here. It would provide a check on the shift from an individualistic ethical perspective to a more social perspective without letting social ethics collapse into sheer concern for aggregate social consequences. It is possible to take up the agenda of more social concerns, including the welfare of parties other than the individual patient, without opening the floodgates to the entire ocean of social concerns. The principle of justice would limit the morally relevant concerns to those of the least advantaged group in order to improve their lot (the maximin criterion) or to make them more equal to others (the egalitarian criterion).

However, if the physician were to follow the AMA's lead and abandon the traditional Hippocratic individualism, he would jeopardize the individual patient and any rights and responsibilities of that relationship. Neither the AMA nor the traditional alternative seem very attractive.

The matter, of course, is not one to be resolved by the AMA or any other professional group. The issues at stake are far more fundamental. Society as a whole has a vital interest in the question of whether physicians and other health care professionals should abandon their traditional commitment to the individual patient and adopt some form of a more social perspective in medical ethics. It may turn out that even though society as a moral community must take the social perspective (and can do so without fear of the dangers of pure utilitarian consequentialism because of the principle of justice), it would want to reserve for certain of its citizens an exemption from the general duty to promote justice.

Certain classes of individuals in society have special role-specific duties that may require them to be placed in this exempt category. Lawyers have a duty of confidentiality to their clients, not because they as a group want it that way or perceive that such a duty is important, but rather because society as a whole sees it that way. It perceives the importance of certain role-specific duties for lawyers, including keeping confidences. Even though a disclosure of the truth known to the lawyer might hasten retributive justice, society determines that client loyalty overrides the general duty to promote justice. Society believes basic rights are protected in the long run by giving the lawyer a special partial exemption from the duties of the ordinary citizen. The lawyer is not only permitted to avoid disclosing, he is required to do so.

Perhaps the individual physician should be given a special, partial dispensation from the general principles of justice. In this view, society as a whole would retain the duty of promoting equality of net welfare by distributing opportunities for health equal in proportion to need. It could reach an understanding with the health professions at the second contract-level that establishes the importance of opportunities for equal access to health care. This could lead to controls over entry into the profession and its various subspecialties as well as over locations of practices. It would mean that the society and the profession as a whole would come to an understanding of how the profession should be structured so as to provide equality of access.

Individual physicians, however, might be exempt from the general duty so that they can fulfill what society takes to be another important function: meeting the rights and responsibilities of the convenantal relationship with the patient. At the level of the second contract, the contract between the lay and professional communities, it seems reasonable to include such a special, limited exemption so that the physician and other health care professionals can fulfill the obligations of the lay–professional relationship.

The implications of the special, limited exemption will depend on several additional subtle issues. For example, the exemption should not be taken as a license to retreat into the individualism of Hippocratic consequentialism. The exemption permits the professional to give priority attention to the covenantal relationship between lay person and professional, but not to focus solely on the benefit to the patient, especially as judged subjectively by the physician. That, I have already argued, would not be permitted as part of the second contract between the profession and the society. Rather the priority is to the rights and responsibilities of the relationship, not the benefits to the patient. This means that the full range of rights and responsibilities for both lay person and professional dominate the rights and responsibilities related to the principles of promise keeping, autonomy, truth telling, avoiding killing, and so forth. The physician's task is to do what is right regarding the patient, not necessarily to benefit the patient.

Second, the limited exemption may or may not cover only those portions of the professional's life where he or she is in direct covenantal relationship with a patient. Many of the duties physicians and other health care professionals normally take on in today's complex world involve decision-making responsibilities that necessarily force them beyond the isolated, individual lay–professional relationship. Physicians conduct medical research; they serve on institutional review boards for the protection of human subjects; they act as public health officers, and as executives in corporations; they serve on Professional Standards Review Organizations and Health Systems Agencies where the very nature of their task is responsible health resource allocation.

It is clear that if physicians are to be exempt from any moral responsibility for allocation of goods within the community, they cannot take on any of these tasks. Two more unattractive options are thus available. Either physicians could abandon all of these roles as incompatible with their traditional patient-centered duties or they could bifurcate their moral lives, remaining fully committed to the individual in the physician–patient relationship under the limited exemption of the second contract but resuming the normal social perspective with its demands of justice when they leave their professional offices to serve in any other social capacity.

I doubt seriously that any human being has the ability to shift moral loyalties so abruptly, to eschew justice in favor of patient rights and responsibilities one moment and then wander down the hall to an institutional review board meeting where the patient's interests morally can be compromised for certain justified social benefits and the demands of equity are essential for decision making. If I am right, then physicians at the time of licensure, of the negotiating of the second contract, should opt for either a patient-centered role or a community-centered one. If they take on the community-centered role, they still will not simplistically strive to promote aggregate community net benefit. They will still work within the moral framework of the basic social contract including the principles of justice and the rights derived from the other basic principles. But they will not be limited to the individual patient–physician relationship. On the other hand, if they opt for patient care, then they should be disqualified from resource allocation and other socially oriented tasks.

Possibly physicians can bifurcate their moral lives so that they can shift from one moral framework to the other. If they can, they will have to exclude the social perspective in those moments when their role-specific duty is to fulfill the rights and responsibilities of the patient–physician relationship. For example, they should not consider cost containment for the benefit of society, insurance companies, Medicare, or Medicaid. That should be on someone else's agenda. Someone else should so structure the health care delivery setting so that it is impossible for the physician to order the sixth stool guaiac.[54] But it should not be the physician's responsibility to eliminate it on cost grounds if that physician believes on balance that the procedure is even infinitesimally beneficial to the patient. Any campaign to make the clinician more cost-conscious *in order to benefit someone other than the patient* is a campaign to get the physician to abandon his unequivocal commitment to the patient. If the second contract exempts the physician from normal resource allocation responsibilities, then benefiting other parties by saving money should not be on the physician's agenda.

In spite of this, the physician's limited exemption from the general duties derived from the principle of justice cannot totally eliminate allocational decisions from the horizon of the clinician. Normally, social welfare interests in a just allocation of resources will be someone else's worry, but there are special cases where they will necessarily belong to the medical professional. The best example is the dilemma faced by the physician with the three relatively well-off patients and the one seriously ill one. Even if he excludes all non-patient-centered concerns from his agenda, he still has a problem. It is a problem of resource allocation among the patients. It is in principle impossible for him to sidestep the issue.

I suggest that in this limited case the principle of justice appears once again on the moral agenda of the role-specific duties of the health professional (as they would be determined by reasonable lay people and professionals coming together to articulate the second contract). In this limited case, the principle would be relevant to helping the physician allocate his or her time. If the second social contract, the lay–professional agreement, is written to my interpretation of the principle of justice, it will specify that our physician has the role-specific duty to benefit the least advantaged or to make that person more equal insofar as possible to the others. Of course, other moral considerations such as efficiency in producing good and freedom of choice may counter this implication. Insofar as justice is concerned, though, the second contract will give the physician a role-specific duty of helping the sickest. Outside of this special case, a policy for promoting justice in the allocation of health resources should be almost completely off the professional's agenda.

I say "almost completely" because I doubt that the negotiators of the second contract can draw the lines quite as sharply as we have drawn them thus far. Recall the problem first considered in chapter 6. Someone rushes into a physician's private office from the street to say that a person, not the physician's patient, is bleeding to death from an auto accident and no one else is able to save the person. The physician at the time has been giving a routine physical to a patient who is not in any particular rush. Common sense says that the physician should abandon the patient temporarily to help the man in the street.

The most reasonable way of bringing this about would be for the physician to ask the patient for permission to temporarily end the physical so as to help the accident victim. That, of course, is not strictly Hippocratic since patient consent is not considered by the tradition as a justification for temporary abandonment of the patient when his interests could be served by continued care. Still the principle of autonomy combined with the principles of beneficence and justice seems to dictate our scenario.

But what if the patient, contrary to what is morally required, refuses the permission? It seems that the physician might still have a duty to help the man in the street. The only way to account for this must be that in extreme cases the principle of justice overrides considerations of the existing contractual promise between physician and lay patient. I believe society should permit—indeed perhaps require—this temporary abandonment. If so, then it must be that the second contract between the profession and the society includes within it a very limited provision allowing or requiring patient abandonment in extreme situations where justice overwhelmingly requires it (because the nonpatient's need is so much greater than the patient's).

If that is the case then the professional, in his or her professional role, is largely exempt from the requirements of the principle of justice. The principle of justice does generate a duty, though, as part of the second contract for the health professional, primarily as a way of helping him or her sort out priorities among present patients in need. It also will apply in the extreme and rare circumstance when the need of a nonpatient is so overwhelming that it overpowers the basic, normal exemption from the general requirements of justice.

The significance of the addition of a principle of justice to a set of basic principles for medical ethics is stunning. It provides a way out of the dilemma posed by the tension between the hyperindividualism of Hippocratic ethics and the societal perspective of the principle of beneficence that focuses on all benefits in aggregate. Incorporating the principle of justice into our moral framework lets us move beyond the individual without falling victim to the indiscriminate social benefits perspective. Striving to provide opportunities for health care to bring people insofar as possible to the health level of others allows certain social concerns into medicine without opening the door so wide that the entire societal wants list swamps the rights and welfare of the individual.

PART IV

Relating Cases and
Principles

Chapter 12

When Medical Ethical Principles Conflict

We now have in front of us a contractual or covenantal model that gives us an understanding of what it would mean for someone, lay person or health professional, to claim that he or she has a medical ethical right or obligation. It is merely a metaphor, but it conveys the idea that a medical ethical claim must be grounded in a reality that is universal, that extends beyond the mere consensus of a group whether professional, religious, or ethnic. It also suggests a real-life strategy for attempting to approximate the moral discourse that our hypothetical contractors would have. Real-life, fallible people—lay persons and professionals—would come together and attempt to become knowledgeable about the relevant facts, sensitive to the feelings of others, and impartial with regard to the welfare of affected parties.

These lay people and professionals, if they were to generate a medical ethic, would first come to an understanding on the basic principles for constituting the society, the moral community. They would then move on to what I have called the second contract, or covenant, in which they would try reasonably to establish a lay–professional relationship of trust and to articulate the role-specific duties for that trusting relationship.

Even after all this is done, however, the job would not be over. Even if we, as the contractors, had the moral principles completely clear, we would still need at least two more things. First we would have to have adequate data about the nonmoral facts. Some disputes in medical decision making that at first appear to be ethical disputes turn out, upon examination, simply to be disagreements over the nonmoral facts. Two physicians, for example, who disagree over whether to tell a dying woman of her cancer may think they have a moral dispute on their hands. After all, telling the truth to dying patients is quintessentially an issue of medical ethics. But it may turn out that the physicians agree on the ethics. For example, they might both see the morally relevant goal as being Hippocratic and thus doing what they think will benefit the patient—but they might disagree on the physical or psychological benefits of alternative courses. Or they may both agree that the morally relevant goal is to keep their promise to the patient, but disagree over what was promised.

We would have to agree in many more nonmoral areas: in our understanding of the law, in the definition of the group commanding our loyalty, and in the basic system of beliefs and values, including our basic cosmology. Jehovah's Witnesses only think they have a moral dispute with those who are not members of that sect. In fact, their disagreement is more theological or cosmological. If there were agreement over whether transfused blood costs the recipient eternal salvation, I suspect the moral issues surrounding the refusal of "life-saving" blood transfusions would disappear.

We should not expect all disputes that have the aura of medical ethics about them to be resolved simply because we get straight on our medical ethical theory. Much ground for fertile debate would remain, but it simply would not be medical *ethical* debate.

Even if we had all the nonmoral issues settled and had complete agreement on the moral principles, our job would still not be over. There is yet another important dimension to the development of a medical ethical theory. It is, by now, apparent that the principles so articulated are likely to come head on into conflict upon occasion. The Hippocratic principle as initially revised would charge the physician with doing what was objectively in the interests of his patient (rather than what he thought, subjectively, was in that patient's interest). Even if that objective interest could be discovered, however, that mandate to the physician can come into direct conflict with the principle of autonomy. We have, after all, a societal commitment to preserve the liberty of autonomous individuals even when that liberty may lead to something less than the greatest good for the individual.

In considering the principle of justice, I claimed that it would be reasonable for a society to affirm that one of its right-making characteristics of actions or policies or rules was that they tend to produce equal net welfare among individuals (corrected with appropriate discounts for different timing of benefits, for voluntary risks, and so forth). Such a principle, however, may conflict directly with autonomy, which might lead to toleration of inequalities growing out of free choice. It may conflict with the principle of beneficence, which identifies as a right-making characteristic of actions or policies or rules that they efficiently maximize welfare.

Everyone but Kant, it seems, has discovered that if two or more basic moral principles have bearing in a moral community, there is a good chance they will on occasion come into conflict. If a theory of medical ethics is to be complete, it will have to include some understanding of the way we move from the general principles articulated using the contract methodology and problems to specific medical ethical dilemmas. We shall need to know what to do when ethical principles conflict and whether there are any intermediate levels of moral discourse to aid in moving from these highly abstract principles to the specific case problems. The proposal that follows illustrates the problem.

Case 11 *The Physician as Executioner*

On May 11, 1977, Governor David Boren of Oklahoma signs a bill into law mandating the use of medical means to execute prisoners facing death sentences. The law calls for capital punishment by "continuous intravenous administration of a lethal quantity of an ultra-short-acting barbiturate in combination with a chemical paralytic agent until death is pronounced by a licensed physician."[1]

Three other states—Texas, New Mexico, and Idaho—have also passed laws mandating medical execution.[2] Anthony J. Chapman, Oklahoma's chief medical examiner and a drafter of the state's new execution law, faces a difficult problem with the law. Should he support the use of the medical craft for this purpose, and, if so, what role should he support, if any, for the members of his profession, one traditionally committed to benefiting the patient or even to prolonging life?

The arguments for shifting to medical injection as a way of carrying out capital punishment are powerful. There has been widespread concern about the inhumaneness of capital punishment techniques currently in use. New York introduced the electric chair in 1890 and Nevada, the gas *chamber in 1924. Both were supposed to make executions more humane, but the mental and physical suffering produced by these techniques has still been found by many to be too great.[3] University of Nebraska law professor Martin Gardner, in a detailed review of existing methods of execution, concluded that hanging, shooting, and electrocution are all clearly unconstitutional and that gas chamber likely is.[4] He maintained that lethal injection would clearly be the least cruel alternative. That method is also supported, however, as a way of restoring the death penalty—to encourage more juries to vote the death penalty and to overcome constitutional objections that it is cruel and unusual punishment. In Oklahoma's case, though, cost was an additional factor. Needed repairs on the state's electric chair would have cost $62,000, and building a gas chamber would have cost between $200,000 and $300,000.[5]*

Dr. Chapman is confronted with a number of ways the basic medical ethical principles could be brought to bear on the problem. His own judgment is Hippocratic. He reasons that he can find nothing in the Hippocratic Oath that would forbid a physician from overseeing, or even performing, an execution.[6]

On the other hand, many of his medical colleagues seem to be reaching different conclusions. Dr. Richard Hodes, a Florida physician who is president of the state's medical association and a representative in the state's legislature, argues that he feels "very uncomfortable with a technique that is used routinely for healing purposes also used to destroy human life."[7] He worries that it downgrades his professional tools. Many of Dr. Hodes's colleagues express similar concerns. Working from what is apparently the same professional Hippocratic tradition as Dr. Chapman, two other physicians, J. Christopher Perry and Carleton B. Chapman, write in a letter to the New England Journal of Medicine, *"It can never be in the patient's interest to be killed on order from the state or any other third party.[8] The clear working assumption is that the physician's duty is to serve the interest of the patient regardless of the interest of the state and that, contrary to the Oklahoma medical examiner's instincts, lethal injection for capital punishment is not in the prisoner's interest. A well-known physician, Dr. Louis Jolyon West of UCLA, has called for "a national declaration that it would be considered professionally unethical for a physician to lend his presence to an execution, even as an official examiner to certify the fact and time of death."[9]*

There has been no such national declaration in the United States, but the Idaho Medical Association's House of Delegates went on record in July 1980 opposing any physician involvement in capital punishment through lethal injections[10] and the British Medical Association has opposed any method of execution requiring the services of medical practitioners.[11]

But what should Dr. Chapman as a state official allow to influence him: his personal interpretation of the Hippocratic Oath, the growing consensus of his medical colleagues, or some more public interpretation of what the basic ethical principles require of one in the role of physician? Several options are open to him corresponding to the several roles a physician might play in executions. The Oklahoma law requires that a physician (the medical director of the Department of Corrections) "shall order a sufficient quantity of the toxic substance," conforming to laws giving physicians control over dispensing prescription drugs. Physicians might also be called upon to pronounce death as they do currently in other types of execution. They might also be asked to give preexecution physical exams to determine if the prisoner has any unusual characteristic (such as "invisible" veins) making lethal injection difficult or impossible. They might be called upon to give the injection itself or, more likely, to train a prison employee in the medical art of catheterizing a vein for injection.

Confronted with the wide range of alternatives, Chapman might be tempted to throw up his hands, agreeing with Dr. John D. King in another **New England Journal** *letter that "the matter ought to be left to individuals, not to organizations."*[12]

THE PROBLEM OF CONFLICTING PRINCIPLES

The resolution of Dr. Chapman's problem will depend, in the first instance, on how the basic ethical principles are brought to bear on the specific problem he faces. The most obvious basic principle, of course, is the principle of avoiding active, intentional killing of morally protected life.[13] If that basic principle were to dominate, the matter would be settled; in fact, the entire question of capital punishment would be settled.

Some might reject that basic principle, however, or at least reject the conclusion that it applies to criminals (who might be said to have failed to keep their obligations to the moral community as articulated by the basic social contract). Even those who are willing in general to accept killing of human beings as a necessary part of human interaction may, as we have seen, reach the conclusion that the killing is wrong for physicians. This would derive from the second contract between society and the profession, in which a physician's role-specific duty may have been articulated to avoid the intentional taking of life, even for good reason.

All of these positions short-circuit the debate about the role of the physician in medical execution. Dr. Chapman, however, seems to have reached a different conclusion. It is not clear what influenced his moral reasoning. Perhaps he has taken into account the general principle of beneficence and been led to the conclusion that more good can result on balance if prisoners are executed. Then, if execution must take place, the same principle of beneficence requires that it be carried out without any unnecessary suffering. Perhaps rather than opting for the general principle of beneficence Dr. Chapman bases his judgment on an interpretation of the role-specific duties of the physician—the kind we might generate at the level of the second contract. Dr. Chapman apparently, in spite of the arguments we have mounted to the contrary, is convinced that physicians should be Hippocratic, that they should do what they think will benefit their patients. He, as opposed to Drs. Perry and Carleton Chapman, has concluded that the prisoner will benefit, given the alternatives, from the policy of medical execution.

The AMA Judicial Council, according to an *American Medical News* article, retreated to the old variant on the Hippocratic principle, *primum non nocere*, to prohibit physician participation in capital punishment. Following the instincts of the Buddha, the article said: "It is harmful to take a life when biological death is not imminent."[14]

In addition to the principles of avoiding killing and of beneficence, some of the other commentators seemed to be basing their nonparticipation conclusions on a broader understanding of the relationship between the health professional and society, one that might bring into play the values of trust, contract keeping, honesty, and consistency of the professional role. With all of these principles and interpretations of principles at stake, a full medical ethic will have to have some method for resolving potential conflict among them.

A limited number of solutions exist to the problem of conflicting principles. None of them is terribly attractive. Still, some resolution is essential if a medical ethic is going to be anything more than a general abstract, platitudinous statement. The alternatives are worth exploring.

THE SINGLE OVERARCHING PRINCIPLES

The first and initially the most appealing solution is to attempt to identify a single, overarching principle that will provide a moral framework for the resolution of all ethical dilemmas. Although the principle of avoiding killing is the first coming to mind in Dr. Chapman's case, it seems unlikely that it could dominate in every conceivable conflict with any other principle. The principle that has come closest to being a plausible, single, overarching principle is the utilitarian principle, or the principle of beneficence. There is something initially appealing about the notion of trying to produce as much good as possible. It is similarly attractive to try to minimize the evil in the world. To combine the two along a single scale and take as our goal the maximization of the net amount of good has the potential of absorbing the entire range of our moral concern. Maybe Dr. Chapman's task is simply to maximize net good. Keeping contracts, promoting autonomy, telling the truth, avoiding killing, and distributing goods evenly all seem to tend toward promoting good outcomes. It might simply be that we have traditionally identified these as moral principles because they produce good consequences.

In this volume we have pushed that possibility about as hard as we can. It does appear that often our moral intuitions can be explained by some version of the calculation of consequences—especially if we were to adopt the version of this consequentialism known as rule utility. We might use it to explain a large portion of our moral judgments.

But we have also seen that the principle of utility by itself gets the morally reflective person into real difficulties. The problems have been analyzed earlier in the volume, especially in chapters 6 and 11. Possibly some super sophisticated version of rule utilitarianism or extended rule utilitarianism[15] could produce a rational account of an ethical system consistent with all our moral judgments. It might be consistent with a rule against physician participation in executions, for example. It does not follow, though, that such sophisticated versions of the consequentialist mode of thinking explain the *reason* we reach the moral judgments we do.

In the end, the utilitarian normative ethical principle is simply not plausible. Physicians and other health professionals insist on modifying it by considering subjective welfare as judged by the individual clinician, by limiting consequences to the individual patient, perhaps by giving priority to the negative (harms) over the positive (benefits), and perhaps also by superimposing the nonconsequentialist duty to preserve life. Most of the religiously based medical ethical systems we explored in the first part of this volume reject it or modify it by adding other moral considerations. The secular tradition of the modern West replaces it with an emphasis on moral rights and the principle of autonomy. Socialist medical ethical systems modify it with a principle of distributive justice based on need. In short, almost all find the utilitarian principle wanting, at least as a single, overarching principle. It is simply implausible.

Likewise, it is implausible that any one of the other principles, promise keeping, for example, could become the single, overarching principle that explains our moral judgments and accounts for our apparent affirmation of the other principles. The quest for the single principle of a medical ethical system, whether it be the Hippocratic principle, the utilitarian one, or any other, is likely to prove fruitless.

Even if it could be found, it is not clear how helpful it would be. It would simply shift the difficult moral calculations to the next lower level. The decision about what to tell the woman with terminal cancer becomes one of calculating the psychological and physical benefits of disclosure and then comparing them to the benefits and harms of withholding the truth, thus breaking any implied lay–professional contract as well as violating the patient's autonomy, and so forth. We are still left with an extremely complex job of balancing subtle, nonquantifiable variables. The variables would be incommensurable goods and harms rather than rights and wrongs—but they are about as incommensurable in either form. Even if we were to adopt a form of the single principle that used the principle to evaluate rules (such as rule utility), we would still be left with the problem of inevitable conflict between two rules containing apparently contradictory moral instruction.

In short, a single, overarching principle as a solution to the dilemma of conflicting principles seems most implausible and probably would not be much help even if it could be found. If we are to help Dr. Chapman out of his dilemma, we shall need another strategy.

LEXICAL ORDERING

Another alternative for moving from conflicting principles to resolution or specific case problems in medical ethics might be that among several principles certain of them always take precedence. The by now discredited maxim *primum non nocere* (if the *primum* is taken seriously) would have this quality to it. The more standard form of the Hippocratic principle, that the physician should benefit the patient according to his judgment, might be ranked so that it always took precedence in case of conflict. It would appear, however, that this would have little more going for it than the *primum non nocere* version. Giving primacy to either would suppress moral considerations other than benefits and harms and thus be unacceptable to most people.

It is possible, however, that certain principles always have priority over others. Rawls makes such a claim for the ordering of his two principles of justice.[16] With such a solution one principle would have to be fully satisfied before the next principle was brought into play. With Rawls, the equal distribution of liberty must be satisfied before any consideration is given to social and economic inequalities. It is not acceptable to sacrifice some equality of liberty in order to gain greater social or economic equality. He calls this solution to the priority problem 'serial' or 'lexical' ordering (based on the lexicographical ordering of a dictionary).

Unfortunately, while Rawls spends a great deal of time explaining the justification for giving priority to the two principles of justice, he does not move on to the larger question of how principles other than those of justice might be ranked. He does point out that the lexical ordering of principles has not had a very favorable history. Lexical ranking has generally been found implausible. He also points out that for a principle to have lexical priority it would have to generate a moral demand with quite limited application so that it is capable of being satisfied. If it could not be satisfied, no succeeding principle would have any significance. For example, Rawls cites the principle of utility as one which, if it were ranked first, "would render otiose all subsequent criteria."[17] The principle of utility (or our principle of beneficence) generates an insatiable moral demand such that, if it were given lexical priority, no other moral consideration could come into play.

That is what, in effect, happens when either the Hippocratic principle or the maxim *primum non nocere* is given priority in a medical ethics. Perhaps, though, traditional professional physician ethics have the priority just reversed—perhaps the nonconsequentialist principles should be given first priority.

Certainly this would change the character of medical ethical decisions made by lay people and professionals, but the decisions could be made. The nonconsequentialist principles could, in the normal case, be satisfied and still give leeway to pursuit of decisions under the principle of beneficence, or benefiting the patient.

In fact, if the nonconsequentialist principles are to have any power in a medical ethical system, it may be that they together have to be given a lexical priority over the principle of beneficence. Otherwise consideration of consequences can always swamp the other moral considerations. As we saw in considering the ethics of human experimentation—especially with the Nazi experiments—if enough benefit is put into the calculus other moral considerations will always be overpowered. That is why it makes sense to insist that the other principles (autonomy, with its requirement of consent, keeping of contracts, avoiding killing, telling the truth, and promoting justice) must be satisfied as prior necessary conditions before consequences of the research can be put on the agenda. No amount of good consequences can overpower the inherent moral requirements of the nonconsequentialist principles.

Some even have argued that beneficence, producing good consequences, is not a *moral* requirement at all. Kant, for instance, sees morality as related to actions based on duty, not in the consequences or the purpose of the action.[18] Including the principle of beneficence at all as an ethical principle leads, as we have seen, to strange, counterintuitive implications. Deeds normally thought of as supererogatory become morally required, and trivial choices, such as picking among breakfast cereals, become morally required choices because they will produce more good than alternative actions.

Still, at least if there are other principles in one's ethical armamentarium, there may be ways out of these implications. The benefits of not doing the work normally conceived of as supererogatory can be taken into account; and if autonomy is an opposing principle it might account for our sense that avoiding supererogatory as well as trivial ways of producing benefits is a morally acceptable action.

On the other hand, there does seem to be a duty to do good when it does not conflict with other principles. Physicians, like other persons, should strive to do good when other moral constraints do not impinge on the patient-physician relationship. It is obvious that a world with equal distribution of net welfare (including health care) at a high level is preferable to a world with equal distribution of net welfare at a low level. It probably even makes sense to say that morality requires the former if that option is available without infringing upon other moral requirements.

If egalitarian justice is the only moral principle at stake, however, we could not account for this conclusion. At least in the case of choosing among two egalitarian worlds, the principle of beneficence seems morally relevant. It may be lexically subordinated to the principle of justice, but it does at least surface when the nonconsequentialist principle is satisfied. It is at least a tie breaker when the nonconsequentialist principles do not resolve the question. The priority of the nonconsequentialist principles over beneficence helps explain the compromises in health care planning that may take place with the egalitarian demands of the principle of justice. I have consistently maintained that insofar as justice is concerned, equal objective net outcome among individuals of the moral community is what would be required by reasonable people taking the moral point of view—as a practical matter this would lead to a policy of a right to health care necessary to provide an opportunity to be as healthy as other people. I have also suggested, however, that other right-making considerations derived from the principles of autonomy and beneficence might lead to certain adjustments in the egalitarian distribution of health care. For example, the principle of autonomy might lead us to support a certain freedom of choice for health care professionals in the selection of their specialties, the location of their practices, or the setting of their fees even though such choices might conflict with the requirements of the principle of justice. Should, however, inequalities of outcome be tolerated in order to make the system more efficient (by, for example, rewarding talented producers)? We considered in the previous chapter whether it would be just for talented elites to be given special, high-quality health service in order that they might serve the less well off in the event of a medical emergency. A general institutionalization of such a practice might be justified by the Rawlsian interpretation of justice as permitting inequalities provided they benefit the least advantaged. On the other hand, I (and others including Brian Barry) have suggested that the toleration of the inequality suggested by the Rawlsian difference principle is really a compromise between justice and efficiency. I have maintained that justice would require equality while efficient production of good consequences might lead to the policy of unequal health care services for the elite.

In order to get a sense of which interpretation is more appropriate, we might ask whether it makes a difference who is making the argument for special treatment of the elite—the least well-off group or the elite themselves? It would appear that if the Rawlsian interpretation of the demands of justice is the appropriate one, it should make no difference whether it is the least well off or the elite generating the case for the inequality. Justice permits, indeed requires, inequalities provided they accrue to the benefit of the least well off (as well as the elite).

My interpretation is quite different. I think intuitively it makes a great deal of difference whether it is the least well off or the elite who argue that the elite should get special advantages and the resulting unequal enhancement of their welfare.[19] The reason, it seems to me, is that the nonconsequentalist principles take precedence. The duty of justice is a higher lexical priority than the duty to produce good. That, at first, implies that a compromise between egalitarian justice and efficient beneficence is unacceptable. This, however, is not necessarily the case.

Oftentimes the basic ethical principles generate moral obligations with correlative rights. The one to whom a promise is made has a right to have the promise kept; the one receiving information (in the context of normal human discourse) has a right to the truth; the least advantaged have a right to equality of outcomes in the distribution of welfare, including (based on pragmatic considerations) health care services. When basic principles generate rights claims, however, in at least some of these cases the bearers of the rights have the authority to waive their claims.[20] Thus, for example, if someone promises me that he will give me a book within two days, I have a right to the book in that period, but I can waive my claim to the book, thereby canceling the duty generated by the promise.

It is my contention that the least well off stand in a similar position regarding the rights they bear to equality of net welfare and, derivatively, health care services. They have a right to equal treatment based on the principle of justice. They may, however, surrender that right for good reason. A good reason sometimes (but not always) might be that such a surrender of the claim of egalitarian justice makes it possible to take into account the greater aggregate utility of inequalities. In certain cases the least advantaged would reasonably surrender their claims of justice simply to serve the goal of maximizing aggregate utility. That, however, would be a charitable act, not required by morality. It probably would not happen often. More often, this least advantaged group might surrender their claim of equality in order to encourage efficient production of benefits that, at least in part, make them better off than they otherwise would be under the regime of equality.

If this is a reasonable account of the compromise between egalitarian justice and the interests in efficient production of good consequences, it should be clear why it seems morally relevant whether it is the elite or the least advantaged group that is making the case for a maximin distribution; that is, one that deviates from the requirements of egalitarian justice in order to efficiently produce benefits to the least advantaged.

What results is an account of the relationship between a basic nonconsequentialist principle of the social contract and the consequentialist principle of beneficence. The nonconsequentialist principle is lexically ranked above the principle of beneficence; promise keeping, autonomy, honesty, the principle of avoiding killing, or justice cannot be violated simply because it would produce good consequences to do so. Should, however, one of the rights derivative from one of the principles be a type that a bearer may waive, then the nonconsequentialist principle can be suspended at the bearer's discretion in order to promote greater good consequences.

This notion of the coequal ranking of the nonconsequentialist principles and their lexical ranking over the duty to produce good consequences sets the stage for the next step. We must consider how the demands of the principle of justice might be related to those of a nonconsequentialist principle, such as the principle of autonomy.

THE BALANCING OF PRINCIPLES OF EQUAL STATUS

All of this suggests that beneficence, by itself, does not generate a counter moral imperative to the principle of justice when it comes to distributing health care (unless the least well off surrender any right they have to equal treatment). Beneficence is a lower-order principle, lexically ranked after the nonconsequentialist principles. What of the potential conflict between two nonconsequentialist principles, however? What of the conflict between the demands of justice for an equal distribution of health care services among different regions and the demands of the principle of autonomy that give providers some discretion in selecting their place of work?

This seems to raise a problem that is somewhat different from that of a conflict between the demands of justice and efficient production of good consequences. Here many would be reluctant to exclude totally from moral consideration the autonomy of providers, though they might exclude the welfare of the elites from consideration in the earlier case. If this is so, I suggest it is because the principle of justice cannot be lexically ranked over the principle of autonomy. Rather the resolution of the conflict between the two nonconsequentialist principles requires a different strategy. Both of the principles—in fact all the nonconsequentialist principles—seem to be on a par morally. One cannot be subordinated totally to the other.

The strategy that is called for is one that could be referred to as a balancing strategy. We would ask, first of all, which nonconsequentialist principles are involved and, then, to what extent the alternative courses of action violate the principles. We should opt for the course that produces the lesser violation of the nonconsequentialist principles on balance. In cases where the scales seem evenly suspended, we might then move on in the lexical ordering to consider consequences just as we would if no nonconsequentialist principles were at stake.

In the case of a proposal to promote greater justice in the distribution of physicians—by compelling them to relocate from, say, the Upper East Side of New York City to Appalachia—we would discover that relocation might be called for by the demands of justice but would be seriously violative of the demands for provider autonomy. The goal would be the mix that minimizes the moral violation by the principles on balance.

It is clear that neither alternative is going to be completely satisfactory morally. Each would involve a serious violation. Furthermore, it is clear that neither of these options would be acceptable morally if there were a third or fourth alternative that involved, on balance, less moral violation of the relevant principles (without introducing new principle violations). We might, for example, discover that rather than coercing Park Avenue psychiatrists to pick up and move to West Virginia to practice as GPs, we could attach a condition to the funding of new medical students' education so that they serve for a time in the underserved area. That might greatly alleviate the injustice without a serious infringement on the autonomy of providers.

The technique being proposed for resolution of conflict among the basic nonconsequentialist principles is probably not a very satisfying one. It does not provide a precise measuring technique permitting the balancing of counterclaims. As Bishop Butler said, however: "Everything is what it is, and not another thing." If the nonconsequentialist principles are independent and coequal in their moral priority, then it will do no good to try to force them into a lexical priority or to grope for a single principle that integrates them.

The model for conflict resolution can be devised from the earlier discussion of the contract or convenant model. If the society wants to know whether to institute a general practice of infringing upon provider freedom in order to promote greater equality of access to health care, it should, of course, first do its empirical homework and eliminate options that involve more than a necessary amount of infringement on the basic principles. Then, assuming the covenanting posture, it can ask itself how reasonable lay people and professionals coming together would balance the principles of autonomy and justice in order to resolve the moral conflict.

Real people—lay people and professionals—then would meet together attempting to assume as closely as possible the moral point of view of the hypothetical contractors.

They are likely to discover that among the options available one mix would minimize the infringement of the nonconsequentialist principles at stake. In this particular case I am convinced that some constraints on freedom of choice of providers are justified in order to promote greater equality of access to health care. This especially seems to be the case if the constraints were merely in the form of the enforcement of contracts (or promises) made during the funding of a physician's education or during licensing process. At this point, an additional basic principle, the principle of contract keeping, comes into play to support the infringement on the liberty of the providers.

This gets us part way toward a resolution of Dr. Chapman's problem about physician participation in medical execution. The most obvious case that can be made for physician participation in medical execution is one based on good consequences. Benefits might hypothetically accrue to society from the enhanced general deterrent effect of the death penalty, protected now from the onslaught of constitutional lawyers and soft-hearted juries. Benefits might hypothetically accrue to the "patient," especially if the physician believes he can consider only the options that realistically are open to those sentenced to death. Neither kind of consequentialist argument is very convincing—especially given the lack of evidence of a deterrent effect of the death penalty—but each is conceivable.

Over against these consequentialist considerations is the principle of avoiding killing. Even if reasonable people when negotiating the basic social contract reject a principle proscribing active, intentional killing, they might want to exclude execution in principle from the professional role in considering the contract between the profession and the society. The result could be a contractual or convenantal obligation for the health professional to refrain from participating in the juridical killings.

We are left with the problem of whether any moral rules will help us do the balancing when the principles come into conflict, or whether every case is so unique that individual moral judgment is called for. It appears that Dr. Chapman might still be in a position to take the advice of the physician who eschewed any institutional involvement so that each individual could simply make up his or her own ethical mind—it appears, that is, that any use of moral rules is simply impossible.

Chapter 13

Is Every Case in Medical Ethics Unique: The Use of Moral Rules

The combination of the lexical ranking of the nonconsequentialist principles over the principle of beneficence and the balancing of the nonconsequentialist principles when they come into conflict among themselves provides another step in the creation of a systematic theory of medical ethics. The clinician standing at the bedside, however, probably still will not be satisfied nor will the patient contemplating moral options for treatment decisions. Since there is no way that reasonable lay people and professionals can meet every time two principles come into conflict, it would be helpful if there were some further bridge between the general principles and the specific case problems of medical ethics.

What comes to mind is some sort of intermediate moral formulations, the kind that have shown up in many of the prototheories of medical ethics examined in the first part of this volume. It would be nice to have statements like: "Never abort a fetus except in order to save the life of the mother"; "Cadavers can never be dissected except to directly benefit a specific, identifiable living person"; "The free and competent patient always has the right to refuse medical treatment offered for that patient's own good"; or "Physicians should never participate in executions."

They have a finality about them that suggests clear, crisp moral answers not easily gleaned from principles like autonomy and justice. If reasonable people—lay people and professionals—could come together once in a while to interpret and balance the principles down to this next level of specificity, medical ethical decision making for individual lay people and professionals would be much easier. The result might be a set of moral rules applicable to specific case problems.

Many working on ethical theory have identified a level of moral discourse more specific than the abstract level of principles that have been the focus of much of this volume, but more general than a specific, ad hoc hospital-room decision by a patient or practitioner. What we are looking for has been given various names. In addition to the term *moral rules* that we have used,[1] theorists have talked of 'middle axioms'[2] or simply 'the moral level'[3] (which is contrasted with the more abstract level of ethical principle). Rights claims are also often articulated at this level—for example, the right of the woman to control her own body, the right of a research subject to give informed consent, the right of a prisoner to avoid cruel and unusual punishment. Rights claims are moral claims that are correlative to moral obligations. While sometimes they are at such a level of generality that they seem simply restatements of general principles—such as the right to autonomy—often they have a level of specificity that make them functionally the equivalent of more specific moral rules. In the latter case they are, in comparison to the basic ethical principles, more specific statements of the more or less constant moral judgments made by reasonable people when bringing the mix of ethical principles to bear on a particular type of moral problem. The rule telling health professionals to break medical confidences without the patient's permission when and only when it is necessary to protect the life of others would be an example. It mixes the impact of the principles of contract keeping (or promise keeping), autonomy, beneficence, and justice. If such a rule were accepted by reasonable people, it would be because they see it as providing a more or less uniform balancing of these principles when applied to the complex problem of confidentiality. It is possible we can develop a rule, for example, on physician participation in execution. The real issue for such moral rules (or correlative rights claims) is whether their application is *more* or *less* constant.

Clinicians and lay people soon become frustrated with philosophers' continual appeals to ethical principles—the principles of truth telling, patient self-determination, and even the physicians' own maxim 'do no harm.' If there is one characteristic that dominates what I call professional physician ethics, it is the conviction that cases are unique—that every patient presents his or her own unique set of problems that cannot be resolved by rigid application of some legalistically formulated rule that supposedly provides quick answers. The clinicians when confronted with rules by philosophers, lawyers, and others who are not clinically based, repeat in exasperation what their experience and the professional ethical tradition has taught them: No two patients are alike; no two diseases progress in the same way. The really important teaching of medical ethics goes on in informal communications on hospital rounds and in casual conversations taking place in the physicians' lounge. "Each patient should be handled individually, depending upon his temperament."[4] "The management of each case has to be decided individually."[5] These are actual quotations from physicians sensitive to patients' individuality.

Surveys of clinicians asking them their usual policy about telling patients about cancer reveal an enormous range of substantive opinions. Early surveys revealed 82 percent tending not to disclose.[6] The responses have shifted over the last decade in the direction of more willingness to disclose,[7] but one pattern is overwhelming and consistent. Virtually every clinician sees the question as one demanding flexibility. One of the earlier surveys[8] asked how often exceptions were made to the physician's usual practice. Ninety-one percent said they had to adjust their general practice tailoring their approach to the cases before them. The rule again is clear: In the clinical ethics of physicians every case is unique; no general rules can dominate clinical judgment. In fact, I would identify this as one of the dominant themes of the well developed but poorly defined tradition I am calling professional physician ethics. Any position so filled with common sense and professional consensus cannot be all wrong. On the other hand, I am perverse enough to believe that anything generating such agreement cannot be all right either, especially since humanists, some groups of patients, some public policymakers, and many philosophers and theologians examining the role of rules seem to reach a different answer. The problem of the relationship between cases and rules for moral behavior deserves fuller exploration. It will be a necessary part of a theory of medical ethical decision making. Professional physician ethics, I believe, will be found to treat the relationship differently from other ethical traditions—those of religious ethics, of Western political philosophy, and of contemporary philosophical ethics.

The debate over the relationship of cases and rules in medical ethics parallels a more general debate throughout the past decade in both theological and philosophical ethics. Many are skeptical when they hear talk of a "new morality" from some critics of traditional ethical norms. The "new morality" emphasizes the importance of sincerity and careful individual judgment, and it is skeptical of traditional moral patterns.[9] Thus, we have the examples of the young impassioned couple in the back seat of the car who decide that true love is what really matters; the blue-jeaned, long-haired user of street drugs who is sure his moral intuitions can override the moral and legal traditions of the society; the radicals who know that political kidnaping and assassination is justified because it feels like the right thing to do at the moment.

At the same time many of the same people who are skeptical of these ways of deciding realize the importance of case judgment and may occasionally feel compelled to use a very similar kind of reasoning as the new moralists. They agonize over the tension between the cases and the rules.

If I am a clinician standing at the bedside, I often face two kinds of ethical problems. First, I must ask substantively what ought I to do in this particular case? Should I stop Karen Quinlan's respirator? Should I prescribe the Laetrile I know to be useless? Should I inject the lethal drug in the prisoner? Should I abort the young woman whose parents do not know of her problem?

Second, in many cases I must also ask how seriously I should take the moral and legal rules that appear relevant to the case. I may be convinced that a treatment should continue, but be told by the hospital lawyer that the patient has the legal right to refuse any medical treatment. I may disapprove of the patient's use of the medication, but be convinced morally that the patient has the right of self-determination. I may think it is crucial for a girl's parents to know that she is pregnant, but feel bound by law and morality to protect the girl's right of confidentiality. I, like Dr. Chapman, may be convinced it is acceptable to participate in medical execution, but be told by the medical society or the state that it is unacceptable. In each of these cases my ad hoc judgment brings me to a conclusion that seems to differ from what the rule of law or the rule of morality requires of me.

Two answers to the question "How seriously should I take the rules?" are out of the question. Radical legalism is the position that rules are always to be treated as exceptionless. By legalism in this instance, I do not mean the position that ethics can be reduced to or derived from civil or criminal laws. Some of the current discussion of legalism arises as an attack on the position that the model of the law can be used as a model for the formulation, analysis, and solution of ethical issues.[10] Defending rules as a method of deciding what is right or wrong in a particular case is hard enough without reducing moral rules to legal rules. If by legalism we mean governing behavior exclusively by laws as codified in the civil law, no one finds that plausible. Everyone recognizes that the mere fact that a behavior is legal does not make it right in a moral sense. In fact most concede that behaviors required by law may actually be immoral and forbidden in an ethical sense. Legalism, then, as I use the term, is more the position developed by Judith Shklar—"the ethical attitude that holds moral conduct to be a matter of rule following, and moral relationships to consist of duties and rights determined by rules."[11] If by rules we mean moral rules as well as, or instead of, legal rules, the position gains in plausibility.

Even so, radical legalism is just not a contender in contemporary ethical theory. At least it is not if by 'radical legalism' we mean that in every case only rules rigidly applied determine the right behavior. This leaves no room for judgments by lay people or professionals to decide in particular cases that there is an exception or that one rule does not apply because it is not really meant to cover the particular situation. Anyone who recognizes that two rules can occasionally come into conflict, anyone who has moved beyond some primitive natural law ethics (with its laws-of-nature understanding of morality or its Kantian speculations about what man could will to be a law of nature) must recognize that some case-by-case judgment of what is ethically required is necessary.

Equally implausible is the position that rules of conduct are totally useless. Clinicians standing at the bedside may believe that they and they alone must make judgments focusing on particular cases, but they should at least concede that traditionally formulated rules of morality may be of some help. They may at least act as rules-of-thumb for handling easy cases. They may at least summarize ethical reasoning that has gone before by others who have found themselves in somewhat similar situations. They may at least serve as guidelines for formulating thinking about the problem at hand. People need not despise rules so passionately that they cannot grant at least these functions to rules governing clinical decisions.

The real problem is whether the rules should be given any more authority than as guidelines, whether they should even take precedence over individual judgment in a particular case. Is there any reason why individuals ought to compromise their personal judgment and yield to certain rules of behavior? Can rules of such force be established without falling into the trap of radical legalism?

310

The AMA labeled its "Principles of Medical Ethics" that were in effect during the 1970s as principles that were "not laws but standards by which a physician may determine the propriety of his conduct. . . ."[12] The new "Principles" of the AMA, adopted in 1980, made important substantive changes—including the first acknowledgment of the rights of patients—but the attitude of organized medicine in the United States about rules has remained unchanged. The principles, the new text states, "are not laws, but standards of conduct which define the essentials of honorable behavior for the physician."[13]

Yet certainly other groups are not content with viewing the rules governing the practice of medicine as mere standards or guidelines for the individual physician. They are rules to be adhered to, laws in either the moral or legal sense. What, then, is the argument about? Why the disagreement over how seriously we ought to take the rules?

It seems to me that physicians are making three kinds of claims that are in dispute. The first is the claim that determining what will benefit and harm a particular patient in a unique circumstance necessarily requires very individualized judgment. The second is that the rules are so complicated that individual judgment is necessary to determine which norms apply. The third is the claim that even if we know what benefits and harms are at stake in a particular case and even if we know what norms apply, the practice of medicine is so complicated that rules can never take into account enough of the specificities to lead to the most right actions in a particular case. This claim argues that rules must be supplemented with individualized judgments.

THE UNIQUENESS OF BENEFIT–HARM JUDGMENTS IN INDIVIDUAL CASES

I have already argued that considerations of benefit and harm are overrated in professional physician ethics. In general the principle of beneficence should be subordinated in a lexical ordering below the nonconsequentialist principles. The Hippocratic principle, which is a modification of the general principle of beneficence, is likewise subordinated. This means that any argument for the uniqueness of cases based on difficulties of calculating benefits and harms may be short-circuited. If consideration of consequences is much less significant in medical ethical decision making than traditional professional physician ethics has led us to believe, then an argument for case-by-case ethical decision making based on the uniqueness of consequences in individual cases may be less relevant.

Still, I have conceded that consequences are relevant in medical ethics. They at least come into play when other moral demands have been satisfied. When the patient has adequate information to act autonomously and when justice is reflected in the distribution of health care, then the individual making decisions about his or her own care surely should take into account consequences. The professional in relationship with a lay person, too, surely should consider what is likely to benefit the patient as well as what is right for the patient based on the prior nonconsequentialist considerations. If so, then we shall have to take into account the claim that general rules cannot be taken rigidly because of the uniqueness of benefit–harm judgments in individual cases.

First, then, let us examine the claim that judgments of benefit and harm vary tremendously from case to case so that moral rules cannot be applied rigidly. Hippocratic physicians discussing what to tell a woman with cervical cancer might appeal to the overarching ethical principle that governs traditional professional physician ethics—the physician's duty to do what he thinks is for the benefit of his patient. In another, more nonconsequentialist ethical system such as the one I have defended, the patient, out of the principle of autonomy, might yield to her physician the authority to use his judgment about what information should be disclosed. Viewed in either of these perspectives the physician, and he alone, has the job of assessing benefits and harms from possible courses of action open to him. The psychological harms the woman would suffer from the bad news, the possible anxiety and depression, are the right data for the clinician if this is the right principle. Since patients respond very differently to bad news, the only plausible course, so the argument of the clinician goes, is to evaluate on a case-by-case basis and do what will cause the most benefit or the least harm. For some patients, clear understanding of the situation may be necessary to encourage participation in therapy; for others it may be a stimulus to help make appropriate life plans; and for still others, the bad news properly presented may be less traumatic than the anxiety of uncertainty. For these patients, the wise clinician will decide to transmit the diagnosis. He will, of course, transmit it in a humane way, but he will transmit it. The goal is to provide benefit and avoid harm.

These patients are not the only ones encountered, however. Hippocratic physicians claim they see patients who would be benefited even more if certain pieces of information were withheld or judiciously doled out as the cases warrant.

Bernard Meyer, offering a clinician's perspective on what patients should be told, summarizes the idea well: "What is imparted to a patient about his illness should be planned with the same care and executed with the same skill that are demanded by any potentially therapeutic measure. Like the transfusion of blood, the dispensing of certain information must be distinctly indicated, the amount given consonant with the needs of the recipient, and the type chosen with the view of avoiding untoward reactions."[14]

As wise, compassionate, sensitive, and case oriented as that is, I think it is a mistake—a potentially dangerous mistake.

Meyer's appeal was made in classical Hippocratic fashion. The goal was to avoid "untoward reactions." The information was viewed "therapeutically," with all the risks of the term. If Meyer thinks, as the Hippocratic author did, that the physician ought to do what he thinks will benefit his patient, at first glance it is hard to challenge his advice to dole out the medicine of information just as he would the medicines of the pharmacy. It seems that no blunt rule could possibly better fulfill the Hippocratic commandment to do what one thinks will benefit the patient.

But even conceding for a moment that the clinician's goal ought to be to do what he thinks will benefit the patient (a position we have already had good reason to doubt), it is really not so obvious that using one's own judgment about benefits and harms in the isolated, individual case will always work. The human is a fallible animal. The risk of error in assessing benefits and harms can, at times, be great. Medical practitioners will disagree over what the most beneficial course would be. When they do, at least one position must be wrong. We might suggest that the less experienced practitioner should give way to those who are wiser because they are more experienced. But even experienced practitioners will disagree among themselves over precisely the same kinds of cases. If equally experienced clinicians see the same patient and disagree, we end up in a very confusing situation. The first says it is wrong to disclose, the second says it is right. But it seems one course or the other must be right.[15] Clinicians who have to decide whether bad news will be upsetting based on the Hippocratic ethic are likely to apply a morally dangerous principle called the Golden Rule. They will ask whether bad news would be upsetting to them if they were in the patient's situation. But if different people have different emotional reactions to bad news, then what we are likely to get is a judgment of how traumatic the disclosure would be for the physician rather than how traumatic it might be for the patient. That means physicians (or anyone else) may make systematic errors in deciding consequences of their actions. This danger is particularly great when the consequences will be complex and the data are inaccessible. Projections of future psychological impacts on patients who have never before been placed in the situation envisioned are certainly complex and inaccessible.

Even the substitution of the consensus of clinicians about risks and benefits does not avoid the problem. Clinicians may select certain kinds of data. Differing data would lead to different assessments of risks. Even the consensus of clinicians may be deficient. It may not include social, familial, economic, or life-style impacts. It may not include information from the patient or other family members in assessing benefits. When it comes down to it, even with such additional information, projecting the real impacts of the bad news is going to be very hard.

It might, in fact, sometimes be more reliable to follow general rules rather than relying on difficult, individualized spur-of-the-moment judgments. That is, after all, the way we approach traffic lights. It would produce far better consequences if, when we came to traffic lights, we used our own judgments about whether it was more beneficial to wait or go. It would produce far better consequences, that is, if everyone judged accurately and no time were consumed in having to guess at what others were guessing. The problems are obvious, however, and we find it produces far better consequences to simply follow the rules instead of using our judgments in each individual case.

Fortunately we have some insight into the kinds of situations where there is such a high risk of error that following the rules taught by the tradition tends to produce better consequences. These situations include cases where decision making must be hurried, action is required, and emotional stress is great; and where different actors are likely to have different assessments of the harms, where data about benefits and harms are particularly hard to come by, and where different personal involvements give rise to different sets of interests. Remarkably, every one of these arise in many clinical situations.

At the level of law we seem to have reached the societal judgment that in some situations following the rules is more likely to maximize outcomes than will using our own judgments. In Christian theology this is the direct implication of the doctrine of sin, of the predicament of man's fallibility. We do not let drivers speed over fifty-five miles an hour even if they decide it will have better consequences. We do not let citizens exempt themselves from social security even if they decide it would have better consequences for them if they did. We do not let parents keep their children out of school even if they decide it would be in a child's interest.

The last example is revealing. It is, in many ways, like the problem of the clinician trying to decide what to do in a particular case. The similarities between the parent and the physician are striking. Both are normally benevolent; both may have much relevant information (more than the one affected by the action), and both have a traditional, on-going, if limited, responsibility to provide for the welfare of the one affected.

One of the reasons for getting reasonably informed consent from patients is the belief that, on balance, they will tend to be better off if they know what they are involved in and actively participate in decisions about their care. This goal of benefiting patients may not be the only reason or the best reason for getting consent, but it is one we all understand. Of course, in rare cases getting information in order to provide a reasonably informed consent may not turn out to be beneficial for the patient on balance. Traditionally the Hippocratic physician, in a case like this, who is interested in doing what he thinks will be for the benefit of the patient would apply the doctrine of 'therapeutic privilege.' He would say consent should not be obtained—for the patient's own good.

Society has responded differently. It treats the problem of consent by simply requiring consent based on information the reasonable patient would find material for making decisions about his treatment. Society rejects the Hippocratic alternative. It rejects the policy that physicians should get consent before surgery only in those cases where they judge such consent to be better for the patient. Society recognizes that such a policy of encouraging case-by-case judgment would be self-defeating—in addition to violating autonomy. It would probably not provide as much benefit as the more rigidly applied rule that consent should be obtained before surgery.

VARYING RULES IN INDIVIDUAL CASES

Following a rule, then, just may turn out to be best even if the clinician thinks his or her medical ethics can be reduced to a single, consequentialist principle such as the Hippocratic one. But a second claim is made by the struggling practitioner standing at the bedside trying to hold off the lawyers, philosophers, clergy, and assorted bureaucrats demanding more rule following. The clinician might turn to the bystanders and loudly complain that their rules are so complicated and often in such conflict that individual, clinical judgment is necessary just to determine which rule applies. This is the response that Dr. Chapman might have given when confronted with the conflict between rules that require the physician to be a good citizen by serving the judicial system, that require him to serve the patient by treating him in a way that will protect him from suffering, and that require physicians to preserve the integrity of their special role in society by avoiding any use of medical skills to participate in capital punishment. Chapman might be forced, once again, to respond that the individual must choose what to do on a case-by-case basis, this time by picking among the various rules. This frustration with potentially conflicting rules is illustrated in another case study.

Case 12 *Choosing among the Rules*

Recently Raymond Vande Wiele of Columbia University's College of Physicians and Surgeons lost a suit because he thought he had to use his judgment.[16] As chairman of the Obstetrics and Gynecology Department he is responsible for clinical services and medical research at Columbia Presbyterian Hospital. A very clear rule at that hospital is that no research involving human subjects should take place without proper review by the Institutional Review Board and without other precautions to make sure that the rights and interests of subjects are protected.

A patient, a Mrs. Doris Del Zio, had tried unsuccessfully for many years to have a baby. One physician in New York City was willing to attempt an in vitro fertilization, a test tube conception, of her surgically removed egg. The procedure was attempted in 1973. The possibly fertilized egg was incubated in the laboratories that were under Dr. Vande Wiele's control. No review was undertaken; no approvals obtained. Dr. Vande Wiele found himself trapped between the moral rule specifying his moral obligation to prohibit human-subject research that does not have adequate review and the one specifying his moral obligation to avoid tampering with the possibly newly conceived human being. Some would argue that, based on the principle of avoiding killing, he had a moral duty to follow the rule to avoid destroying an innocent embryonic human life. Even those sympathetic to early abortion would concede he had a moral duty to avoid destroying another's property. Clinicians normally hold to the rule that one does not enter another physician's case without some sort of prior discussion with the physician in charge.

Vande Wiele had the test tube removed from the incubator and exposed to enough trauma so that little possibility remained of any living, unconta- minated cells being in the tube. He felt compelled to use his own judgment in the particular case. That universe where rules directly govern behavior must have seemed like yet another, unreal world of the philosopher's dialogues. What else could he do but plead that the rules were in such conflict that they could not be applied directly to this particular case?

But notice what is happening. Notice what would take place if the physician trying to decide what to tell the woman with cancer pleads that the moral rules are in conflict. To offer such an argument is to concede that the rules are relevant, that they would apply if only it could be determined which ones took precedence.

The problem for Dr. Vande Wiele standing there, test tube in hand, for the physician with the terrifying and private knowledge that a patient's life course is about to be altered radically, or for any clinician who is trapped in the vice of conflicting rules, is one of determining which rule is really applicable. Dr. Vande Wiele chose to struggle with his conscience and ferret out for himself in the privacy of his office the resolution of the apparent conflict in moral requirements playing on this enormously complicated case. For him the case was the reality. The rules he had absorbed from his many years of clinical training were guides informing his intuitions.

His clinical judgment seems to have been guided by that familiar classical ethical principle of Hippocratic medicine. He wanted to bene- fit his patient—or, technically, that is, the patient of his colleague. He wanted to produce benefit by avoiding the risk of producing a serious- ly deformed fetus.

But that certainly is not the only way to resolve the problem of con- flict among the rules. If the clinician is forced to choose the ethical rule that for him dominates in the particular case, the room for moral error is once again enormous. The problem now is greater than possible errors in fact or in assessment of risks to the patient, the lab, and the medical enterprise as a whole. Morally the issue is much more complex. The clinician must also choose the rules of conduct, that, for him, must dominate. Dr. Vande Wiele chose to emphasize his obligation to protect against unregulated research in his lab and his obligation to do what he thought would be most beneficial for his patient. But that was not his only option. Others similarly situated would surely have emphasized other dominating rules. Why, then, should his case judgment be "the rule of the day"?

The problem is systematic. Different people and different groups tend to give precedence to different moral commitments. We are familiar with common stereotypes of Catholic views on abortion or government economists' views on the value of cost accounting efficiency, but the differences in moral commitment are sometimes more subtle.

In the litigation over the care of Karen Quinlan—the young woman who passed into a chronic vegetative state and whose parents wanted to disconnect her respirator—the moral commitments involved her Catholic parents, her randomly assigned physician, the state welfare department paying for her care, administrators of the hospital where she lay, and lawyers for all parties. There were greatly diverging views about what rules ought to apply. Her parents supported by their local priest appealed to the rules of their tradition about the expendability of so-called extraordinary means of medical treatment. The welfare department had to be governed by its more bureaucratic rules. The lawyers tended to be concerned about the rules of law. Dr. Morse, the physician treating Karen, felt bound by the rule that he had a duty to do what he thought would benefit his patient.[17]

It might be seen as strange that he would see the life-extending treatment as really benefiting her. It should seem even more strange that he, among all the possible pickers of rules, should have the authority to pick that particular set of rules that dominated his judgment. The problem is not only that he made a bizarre choice about what would be a benefit. The more serious problem is that many would assume that his choice of possible rules was the one that should bind. We have a serious problem if the clinician standing by the bedside with a finger on the respirator switch can decide not only what is most beneficial, but also that the rule he picks should take precedence over others—such as the rule giving parents the first line of authority over the care of their offspring. Even if the outcome turns out to be the most *beneficial* course for the patient, it is still very much an open question whether it is the *right* course for the patient.

Many rules are established on the belief that there are other morally relevant concerns than producing good outcomes for patients—concerns, for example, derived from the nonconsequentialist principles that I have claimed take lexical priority over outcomes. Patients may have a right to refuse a medical treatment even if the outcome of such a decision is harmful. The rules promoting autonomy within certain constraints take precedence over the rules promoting good consequences. Rules to protect the welfare of others occasionally take precedence over those designed to protect patients' interests.

Sometimes the rules contain within them priority principles. The old AMA principles in effect from 1957 through 1980 said that normally protected confidentiality in the physician–patient relationship might be broken when in the interests of society or required by law.[18] That any interest of society could overcome the rules of confidentiality seems strange. It is not in accord with the principles I have claimed reasonable people would articulate. Most would not choose the rule that the AMA chose. But the conviction that confidentiality may be broken when required by law is a way of both recognizing that the rule of confidentiality may occasionally give way and providing a rule for when it may occur. In some cases it gives way because society has decided that gunshot wounds or venereal disease must be reported.

We could let the clinician in the situation decide the exceptions. We could as a society say to physicians that they should keep confidentiality unless in a certain situation they decide not to. Fortunately we have some more definite instruction for the doctor. It would be unfair to the beleaguered physician if we required him or her to use personal judgment without any guidance and then held him or her accountable for the results. Instead we incorporate priority rules within our rules of behavior. "Keep confidence unless forbidden by specific statutory law" is a rule that removes the agony and uncertainty of discretion in the particular case. A more complete rule might be, "Keep confidence unless forbidden by specific statutory law or unless it will predictably lead to serious, immediate threat of grave bodily harm to another." This rule might turn out to produce more good for patients in the long run. It might turn out to protect rights cherished by society even if it does not protect patients' interests. Members of society are worried that case-by-case clinical decisions might be based on rules or values that others would not have used. They fear that Dr. Morse may decide to do what he thinks will benefit Karen Quinlan rather than giving the parents the opportunity to act on the moral rules of their tradition.

Case-by-case clinical judgment, as sensitive as it is to specifics of the patient's situation, cannot avoid the enormous risk of having clinicians use their judgment to choose the wrong rules. If we are worried about these outcomes, it makes sense to choose to be governed by law rather than by ad hoc decisions.

Aristotle struggled with the question of whether it is better to be governed by law or by the judgments of good individuals. His answer is that "a feast to which all the guests contribute is better than a banquet furnished by a single man"[19] (even if he be the best of cooks). The rule of men is too dangerous—so says Aristotle. It is bad for any man, subject as he is to human commitments and fallibility, to have the supreme power. If nothing more, being excluded from the power of decision making is dishonoring. In our language it is an assault on our dignity as human beings.

Aristotle fears that human passion will corrupt the ad hoc decisions of men. Many fear that if physicians are given authority at the bedside to make case-by-case judgments, their lack of good will or of empathy or of dedication will lead to great harm for patients. Physicians, it is clear, are human like the rest of us. Some do fall short, but I think the number who lack good will and commitment to their patients is small. I do not see having to fear clinicians because they are misanthropes. Quite to the contrary, the big fear for me is that they will pursue with zeal what they think is for the benefit of the patient and, because they are human, be wrong in their well-intentioned, dedicated judgments. The misanthrope will have to be rooted out in any profession or occupation. The real problem in clinical medicine that is devoted to case-by-case decision making is the well-intentioned but erroneous judgment about what benefits or what rules ought to apply. It is for these reasons that Aristotle was right when he chose a government of law rather than of well-intentioned individuals.

This means that the moral rules will have to be taken seriously. They will be generated by reasonable people coming together taking the moral point of view, and they will be derived from the basic principles. It is likely that there will be no single definitive set of rules; real-life contractors thus will have some limited discretion in how to combine the basic principles of the first contract and the role-specific duties of the lay–professional relationship in the second contract. But the rules that flow from this covenantal process (binding lay people and professionals in a pact of mutual responsibility) will have to be given greater authority than mere rules of thumb or guidelines. They will have to become rules defining practices within the moral community.

320

A SOCIETY GOVERNED BY LAW AND INDIVIDUAL CASES

So far I have considered the problem of the clinician standing at the bedside trying to determine what will really benefit the patient. I am convinced that often we are more likely to benefit by following some rule such as, "Get informed consent before surgery" rather than forcing the clinician to use his own judgment in each case. The burdens of such complex ad hoc decisions are more than we can ask of the clinician, and some are simply beyond human capacity. I have also considered the problem faced by the clinician as he stands at the bedside of trying to discern what rules and principles he ought to use. He must not only decide what will benefit the patient, but also whether patient benefit is the decisive consideration; it could conflict with benefits to others or promotion of justice or the keeping of the promises of the physician–patient contract. In some cases it is simply unreasonable to expect that the clinician can choose the rules based on the right combination. He may not choose the ones the patient wants, the family wants, or the society wants. He may not choose the most reasonable ones. For both these reasons a case can be made for tempering individual judgment and yielding to the wisdom of the practices established by the society—for following some rules that define morally acceptable practices.

Realistically, however, such defenses of rule following will always be open to doubt. Sometimes the sensitive, long-experienced practitioner may really know what is better for the patient. Sometimes he may know that the rules he chooses are the right ones or at least the same ones the patient chooses. At least in those cases, the defender of individual judgment might argue, we should encourage the clinician to use his judgment to ferret out an exception. He might claim that the rules alone can never account for enough specificities to lead to the most right actions in a particular case; some intervening individualized judgments, he would say, are needed.

The moral risks will be great no matter which way we turn. If we encourage individual judgments to make exceptions to established practices, bad judgments about consequences will occur and sometimes the wrong rules will be chosen. If we insist blindly on the rules, however, we shall have morally wrong outcomes in particular cases.

Is this necessarily decisive, however? During the last decade there has been considerable doubt cast on evaluating cases on a situation-by-situation basis.[20] The recent development of medical execution illustrates the problem.

Regardless of which side one comes down on in this current controversy, it is interesting to look at how one might argue for a position. A defender of the possibility of physician participation in Oklahoma's executions, such as Dr. Chapman is, could say that every case is unique. The correct approach would be to examine the possible consequences of participation in each individual execution. The physician would decide, on a case-by-case basis, what rules must dominate his decision.

There is something wrong, however, with this approach. Most would say that it is the wrong way to go about deciding whether to participate. In the first place, the physician may not be asked to participate by measuring out the lethal dose and thrusting the needle into the vein. He may be asked to train an executioner in the art of intravenous injection and to advise the Department of Corrections on how to establish the practice of medical execution. If that is the case, then the physician cannot evaluate on a case-by-case basis. He must evaluate the practice as a whole and the morality of his cooperation in the practice.

More fundamentally, many would claim that the morality of the practice as a whole is really what deserves moral evaluation in the first place. Some would say it is not only impossibly difficult to evaluate the consequences of participation in each particular execution, it is also the wrong way to go about making the decisions. Many would feel obliged to say that the practice of medical execution—of using the physician's art for the purpose of producing punishment by death—is simply incompatible with the practice of the healer's art, with the role-specific duty of the physician. What is being evaluated is not the moral implications of a particular medical execution, but the practice of medical execution in general and the involvement of medically committed people in it.

It is extremely hard to show that every possible incident of slavery in every possible society, past, present, and future, produces bad consequences on balance or even violates the nonconsequentialist principles on balance. If the ethics of slavery were dependent upon our case-by-case evaluation, we should be perplexed with uncertainty. In some peculiar situation, it is conceivable, good consequences or some balancing of competing principles or rules would make some particular enslavement acceptable. However, we simply are not that uncertain about slavery. We can say, with great moral confidence, that the practice of slavery is wrong without agonizing over the details of each conceivable enslavement.

Other practices seem morally important as well, perhaps so important that abiding by the rules that define them may actually be more important than working out the consequences or the morality of the individual action.[21]

It may be that morality requires judgments about practices in general as well as judgments about individual cases. Individual judgments may also be required in a field as complex as medical ethics. But individual judgments running loose in the heat of a moment of crisis can cause bad burns, or so it seems from my much cooler vantage point.

I think of the case of the physician deciding what to tell his cancer-stricken patient. I think of the decisions that have to be made by a Dr. Vande Wiele as he stands holding the test tube that may contain embryonic human life. I think of the moment when some physician is asked to find the vein of the one who has so offended society that his life should be taken. These are some of the most difficult and complex questions of contemporary medical ethics. Those who have to make decisions will have to have substantive answers to these questions. But if we are going to be serious in our pursuit of a theory of medical ethics, we shall need more than answers to tough questions. We shall need more, even, than rules as guidelines to help us through the crises. We shall need a theory of how case-by-case decision making relates to more general rules and principles.

I have heard the claim of the clinicians that determining benefit and harm for a particular patient requires individualized judgment, but I already know of the enormous difficulty in making such judgments and also know many times when following the established rule increases the chance of good being done. I have heard the claim that the rules are so complicated that individual judgment is necessary to know which rule applies, but I also know of the enormous variation in the rules that different people would choose if left to their own judgment. I have heard the claim that the rules can never take into account enough of the details to lead to right action in particular cases, but I know of the importance of practices in a society. The struggle in trying to determine the role of rules in clinical decision making continues. Strange as it may appear at first, there are good arguments for letting the rules prevail when individual judgment seems to lead in some other direction.

Chapter 14

A Draft Medical Ethical Covenant

We have come a long way from the initial worry over whether a terminally ill woman should make the medical ethical judgment that she ought to kill her handicapped daughter in order to spare her the agony of living as an orphan. We have come a long way from the concern of the physician she approached who had to decide whether to collaborate in her act by providing information about how to murder humanely. I hope it is now obvious why it was necessary to make this long journey.

Traditional professional physician ethics at most would have provided guidance only for the physician. It has been silent regarding the vast majority of medical ethical problems, those faced by lay people such as that woman. Moreover, professional physician ethics can tell us only what particular, historically bound groups of professionals believe is their duty as professionals. Once we realize that health professionals as well as lay people stand in a variety of traditions—religious, ethnic, philosophical—we realize that a medical ethic must be grounded in something more universal and more fundamental than mere professional consensus—something all-encompassing. It is not enough that a group of professionals believes that it has a certain set of duties. It is not enough even that they believe that they have special knowledge of what is morally required for professionals. Medical ethics must be a special derivative of something far more global, something that is or ought to be perceived by all as providing a universal basis for ethical judgment.

324

I have suggested that there is a remarkable convergence among several alternative visions of what that more universal source may be. One group sees morality rooted in something that is prior to and more basic than the human community—in a deity, the laws of nature, the requirements of reason, or the empirical moral reality. They believe that the basic ethical structures can be understood as those principles that reasonable people would discover and agree to if they possessed the relevant knowledge, were sensitive to the feelings of others in the moral community, and took the moral point of view—that is, one in which all are taken equally into account. Another group sees morality rooted only in the consensus of the moral community. For its members the basic ethical structures can be understood as those principles that reasonable people would invent and agree to if they took the very same moral point of view. There is every reason to believe that people taking these two closely related points of view would agree to a set of principles, would contract or covenant together to acknowledge the basic relationships of the moral community. The result would be a set of basic ethical principles discovered by or generated by a moral community bound together in loyalty and fidelity. The resulting principles would express notions of freedom and responsibility that are the fundamental basis of morality in the community.

Once people have articulated this basic social covenant, there is also reason to believe that they would continue in the covenant mode drawing up a second covenant—one to spell out the duties of lay people and professionals when they interact in those roles with each other. The second covenant would bind lay people and professionals in trust and understanding, in equality of human dignity and respect, so that the special responsibilities of those relationships could be fulfilled and the special needs of those relationships could be met.

In the covenantal or contractual model of medical ethics, the second covenant is embedded within the first, which is the more basic prior constitutive act of the moral community. As such, no promises made at the second level will in toto contravene the commitments made at the first. Special arrangements may be necessary, however, in order to fulfill the special goals of the lay–professional relationship. Individual professionals, for example, may be exempt from some of the concerns of justice so that they may better fulfill the responsibilities of the lay–professional relationship. The profession as a whole, however, bears responsibility for working out with the rest of society ways of fulfilling the requirements of the basic principle of justice.

These two covenants or contracts, in turn, set certain limits on moral decision making in the medical sphere. Since autonomy is one of the basic principles, however, it is to be expected that many choices will not be determined decisively by the two covenants. Individual lay people and individual professionals will have the right—indeed the responsibility—to choose within a range of options remaining within the framework of the first two contracts.

The actual content of the contracts—what philosophers are wont to call normative ethics—is, by the very nature of the covenantal model, left open. The professional medical ethicist can no more than the professional physician articulate the definitive content of the covenants that reasonable people would make taking the moral point of view. Still it seems that some choices are sufficiently obvious so that an individual could at least discuss what kinds of choices reasonable people might make and for what reasons.

Thus I have criticized the principle of traditional Hippocratic ethics, which tells the physician to always do what he (or she) considers to be for the benefit of his (or her) patient. This formulation excluded all the responsibilities to the patient based on nonconsequentialist considerations and any actions (research, public health, or overwhelming medical need of nonpatients) motivated out of a concern for the welfare of others. It is silent on the question of the medical ethical duties of nonphysicians.

We shifted then to the more traditional, utilitarian form of the principle of beneficence, which includes all benefits and harms. This corrected for the individualism of the Hippocratic principle, but it also opened the gates to permit the total subordination of the individual and the loss of individual rights to the interests of the society. The solution, it was suggested, comes from the articulation of other nonconsequentialist principles that will necessarily have a bearing on medical ethical decisions: contract keeping, autonomy, honesty, avoiding killing, and justice. If these nonconsequentialist principles are collectively given priority over the production of good consequences (of either the Hippocratic or utilitarian kind), we discover a solution to the inevitable unacceptable tension between Hippocratic individualism and the utilitarian drive toward aggregate net benefit. Certain interests of others, those encompassed in the nonconsequentialist principles such as justice, are legitimately on the moral agenda, but not others.

The principles are combined by a balancing among the competing claims of the nonconsequentialist principles, which are together given lexical priority over the principle of beneficence. This principle of beneficence is nevertheless important, generating moral obligation in cases when the other moral requirements can be satisfied adequately. This combination of ranking and balancing unfortunately requires some hard, concrete judgments, some of which will be rather arbitrary. When society needs clarity in what is morally expected of lay people and professionals, even though the choices are arbitrary, it will, in many instances, be reasonable to articulate some rules—rules of practice—specifying an acceptable working out of the basic principles and the requirements of the role-specific duties for identifiable types of problems.

While the drawing up of a covenant between the profession and the rest of society, one containing these principles and rules, necessarily requires full participation by all who can approximate the role of reasonable people capable of taking the moral point of view, it might be fun to close this volume with one person's initial effort to set out what such a covenant might look like. It differs in content, in spirit, and especially in procedure from the traditional codes of professional physician ethics—those from Hippocrates to the AMA's 1980 "Principles." In that spirit then, I present a draft of the covenant I would bring to the bargaining table, if I were part of the group of citizens of the moral community trying to articulate a medical ethical covenant.

A DRAFT MEDICAL ETHICAL COVENANT

We lay people and health professionals realizing the importance of health as an important part of human welfare articulate and affirm the following basic understanding of our mutual responsibility one to another:

The common starting point of our medical ethical commitment is our recognition that we are members of a common moral community of responsible people endowed with reason, dignity, and equality of moral worth. Thus together we recognize the fundamental ethical principles.

—We acknowledge the moral necessity of keeping promises and commitments to one another, including the commitment of this covenant.

—We acknowledge the moral necessity of treating one another as autonomous members of the moral community free to make choices that do not violate other basic ethical requirements.

—We acknowledge the moral necessity of dealing honestly with one another.

—We acknowledge the moral necesssity of avoiding actively and knowingly the taking of morally protected life.

—We acknowledge the moral necessity of striving for equality in individual welfare and equality in the right of access to health care necessary to produce an opportunity for health equal insofar as possible to the health of others.

—We acknowledge the moral importance of producing good for one another and treating one another with respect, dignity, and compassion insofar as this is compatible with the other basic principles to which we are bound.

Within this basic moral commitment we grant to certain members of our community the privilege of certification by the society and its agents as health professionals who in turn acknowledge certain responsibilities different from normal moral requirements of the community and certain exemptions from those normal moral requirements. In exchange, the rest of our community acknowledges certain responsibilities for our own health and for responsible treatment of those so certified.

It is our understanding that many important choices to be made by lay people about their own health care and by professionals setting limits on the nature of their practice will be left unspecified by this covenant and that those choices should be spelled out by lay people and professionals in covenants establishing and maintaining individual lay–professional relationships.

The starting point of such relationships shall be a promise made by lay persons and professionals, as members of the moral community, to fulfill the responsibilities of the relationship including those spelled out in this covenant and any other not incompatible with this covenant agreed to by individuals. The professional member of that relationship agrees to maintain competence in his or her certified area of professional service and to serve the health of the patient insofar as that is agreed to by the patient and insofar as that is compatible with the other rights and responsibilities promised in this covenant. The lay person agrees to fulfill his or her responsibilities in the relationship as spelled out in this covenant and in individual mutual understanding with the professional.

Acknowledging the principle of promise keeping, professionals promise to keep in confidence all confided to them by lay people unless breaking that confidence is required by law or becomes necessary to protect another individual from serious, immediate threat to life or grave bodily harm.

Acknowledging the principle of promise keeping, lay people promise to keep in confidence information they should learn about other patients or about the nonprofessional lives of health care providers except when disclosures are necessary to protect another individual from serious, immediate threat to life or grave bodily harm.

Lay people and professionals promise to keep appointment times, monetary arrangements, and other normal commitments of the lay–professional relationship unless emergencies require reformulating these commitments, in which case the other party will be informed expeditiously and compassionately.

328

Acknowledging the principle of autonomy, the professional will seek the full, active participation of the lay person in his or her own health care and decisions made about that care including reasonably informed consent for all procedures, experimental or otherwise. Unless the individual covenant between the lay person and the professional spells out any other mutually acceptable arrangement based on the fact that the lay person wants more or less information, the lay person will be told what the reasonable lay person would want to know before deciding to participate in a procedure. This consent shall not be excluded because a procedure is routine or because the information may be disturbing, but only on the grounds that reasonable people would not want information before deciding to participate in the procedure. Likewise, the professional shall consent to any special, unusual agendas and goals of the lay person in the relationship, and the lay person shall inform the professional of such agendas or goals. Both lay person and professional may exercise their autonomy at any time to terminate the relationship unless suitable help would not be available for the lay person if the relationship were terminated.

Unless the individual covenant specifies otherwise, the lay person shall have a right of access to his or her medical records as a way of maintaining openness and trust in the lay–professional relationship and autonomy for the lay person in medical decision making.

Lay persons acknowledge that the free pursuit of knowledge is of unique importance to professionals and that they shall be free in such pursuit unless it conflicts with other basic ethical requirements.

Among the things lay people have a right to know are: reasonably complete current information concerning diagnosis, treatment, and prognosis including reasonable alternatives available; the financial, educational, and other ties of his or her providers and their institutions; the identity of the spokesperson for the professionals involved in the relationship; the role various professionals and students will play in the relationship (especially in surgery and other cases where the lay person may not be in a position to observe the relationship directly); the procedures, if any, that are considered experimental.

Subject to the moral requirements of this covenant, lay people shall be free to choose the professionals participating in their medical care from among those professionals willing to enter into such a covenantal relation. Subject to the moral requirements of this covenant, professionals shall be free to choose to enter lay–professional relationships with lay people willing to enter such a covenantal relation.

Both lay people and professionals shall be free to communicate information about medical services in media and other channels of communication, including types of services offered, fees, and the ethical and other values underlying the services. Any such advertising or other communication should be accurate, without any attempt to mislead, and in keeping with the dignity and significance of the lay–professional relationship.

Acknowledging the principle of honesty, both lay person and professional pledge to deal honestly with one another, the professional informing the lay person of all he or she would reasonably want to know and the lay person informing the professional of all he or she would reasonably want to know unless specific understandings are reached to the contrary.

Acknowledging the principles of avoiding killing, professionals pledge to be especially diligent in avoiding the active, knowing taking of morally protected life even for reasons of mercy. They are to be exempt from participation in executions. Lay people pledge to refrain from asking for any such participation.

Acknowledging the principle of justice, lay people and professionals as groups pledge to arrange the health care system so that all have access to the health care necessary to have health equal insofar as possible to the health of others. Professionals, as members of the moral community, accept the moral limit on their compensation in the name of justice. They accept the necessity, in emergencies, for relocating those with needed skills in order to serve human need. They accept the necessity of using incentives in the structuring and financing of medical education to encourage a fair geographical, ethnic, racial, sexual, and disciplinary distribution within the profession. Lay people, in turn, recognize the importance of giving professionals the maximum freedom of choice compatible with the requirements of justice for them to select areas of subspecialization and geographical location as well as type of practice.

Individual practitioners shall be exempt from the general moral requirements of the principles of justice, including their impact on health care planning and cost containment, insofar as they are committed to patients in ongoing lay–professional relationships. However, the needs of one's own patients shall be taken into account in deciding how to allocate one's professional time among patients in need, and the extreme needs of nonpatients shall be taken into account in deciding whether to sacrifice temporarily the marginal welfare of one's patient in order to meet the desperate need of a nonpatient. In cases where this must happen, the professional should, if possible, obtain the permission of the patient before turning to the needs of another.

Lay people and professionals acknowledge the importance of this covenant and pledge to uphold it by exposing illegal or unethical conduct of those deficient in competence or acting in ways not in accord with this covenant.

In this spirit of mutual responsibility we pledge together to establish this covenant as the basis of our medical ethical responsibility.

Notes

Introduction

1. John Locke, *The Second Treatise of Government*, ed. Thomas P. Peardon (1690; reprint ed., New York: The Liberal Arts Press, 1952); Thomas Hobbes, *Leviathan* (New York: E.P. Dutton, 1953); Jean Jacques Rousseau, *The Social Contract* (1762; reprint ed., London: Everyman's Library, 1947); Henry Sumner Maine, *Ancient Law* (1861; reprint ed., Gloucester, Mass.: Peter Smith, 1970); Ernest Barker, "Introduction," in *Social Contract* (1947; reprint ed., New York: Oxford University Press, 1962); J.W. Gough, *The Social Contract: A Critical Study of Its Development* (Oxford: Clarendon Press, 1957).

2. Robert M. Veatch, *"Value-Freedom in Science and Technology"* (Ph.D. Diss., Harvard University, Cambridge, Mass., April, 1971); idem, "Models for Ethical Medicine in a Revolutionary Age," *Hastings Center Report* 2 (June 1972):5-7.

3. Edmund D. Pellegrino, "Toward an Expanded Medical Ethics: The Hippocratic Ethic Revisited," in *Hippocrates Revisited: A Search for Meaning*, ed. Roger J. Bulger (New York: Medcom Press, 1973), pp. 133-47; Richard M. Magraw, "Social and Medical Contracts: Explicit and Implicit" in *Hippocrates Revisited: A Search for Meaning*, ed. Roger J. Bulger (New York: Medcom Press, 1973), pp. 148-57; Howard Brody, "The Physician-Patient Contract: Legal and Ethical Aspects," *The Journal of Legal Medicine* 4 (July/Aug. 1976):25-29.

4. William F. May, "Code, Covenant, Contract or Philanthropy," *Hastings Center Report* 5 (Dec. 1975):29-38; Richard A. Epstein, "Medical Malpractice: The Case for Contract," *American Bar Foundation Research Journal* 1 (1976):87-149.

5. Thus, I am using the term somewhat more loosely and giving greater emphasis to medicine in the modern West than does Wesley D. Smith in his volume *The Hippocratic Tradition* (Ithaca, N.Y.: Cornell University Press, 1979), which focuses on Hippocratic followers in the medicine of ancient Greece, Rome, and Egypt.

Chapter 1

1. Kurt Baier, *The Moral Point of View: A Rational Basis of Ethics* (New York: Random House, 1965); Richard B. Brandt, *Ethical Theory* (Englewood Cliffs, N.J.: Prentice-Hall, 1959); A. C. Ewing, *Ethics* (New York: The Free Press, 1965); William K. Frankena, *Ethics*, (Englewood Cliffs, N.J.: Prentice-Hall, 1973); Bernard Gert, *The Moral Rules* (New York: Harper and Row, 1970); Alasdair MacIntyre, *A Short History of Ethics* (New York: Macmillan, 1966); W. S. Sellars and John Hospers, eds., *Readings in Ethical Theory*, 2nd. ed. (New York: Appleton-Century-Crofts, 1970); Paul W. Taylor, *Principles of Ethics: An Introduction* (Encino, Cal.: Dickenson Publishing Co., 1975).

2. *Hippocrates*, 4 vols. (London: William Heinemann, 1923-31), vol. 1, trans. W. H. S. Jones (1923).

3. Pearl Kibre, "Hippocratic Writings in the Middle Ages," *Bulletin of the History of Medicine* 18 (1945): 371- 412.

4. See Ludwig Edelstein, "The Genuine Works of Hippocrates," in *Ancient Medicine: Selected Papers of Ludwig Edelstein* (Baltimore: Johns Hopkins University Press, 1967), pp. 133-44.

5. *Hippocrates*, 1:xliii.

6. Edelstein, "Ancient Medicine," p. 55.

7. Fridolf Kudlien, "Medical Ethics and Popular Ethics in Greece and Rome," *Clio Medica* 5 (1970): 93.

8. Edelstein, "Ancient Medicine," p. 6.

9. Ibid., p. 43.

10. Ibid., p. 20.

11. Ibid., p. 38–9.

12. Ibid., p. 6. The term for injustice is a general term sometimes translated as simply 'harm' or 'wrongdoing'.

13. "The Epidemics," bk. 1, chap. 11, in *Hippocrates*, p. 165.

14. Darrel W. Amundsen, "The Physician's Obligation to Prolong Life: A Medical Duty without Classical Roots," *Hastings Center Report* 8 (August 1978): 23–30.

15. *Hippocrates*, pp. xl–xlii.

16. Ibid., p. 291.

17. See Donald Konold, "Medical Ethics: History of," s.v. "Codes" in *Encyclopedia of Bioethics*, 4 vols., ed. Warren T. Reich (New York: The Free Press, 1978), 1:64; Loren C. MacKinney, "Medical Ethics and Etiquette in the Early Middle Ages: the Persistence of Hippocratic Ideals," *Legacies in Ethics and Medicine*, ed. C. R. Burns (New York: Science History Publications, 1977), p. 174.

18. Kibre, "Hippocratic Writings," p. 372.

19. W. H. S. Jones, *The Doctor's Oath: An Essay in the History of Medicine* (Cambridge: At the University Press, 1924), p. 23.

20. See Edelstein, Ancient Medicine, pp. 174–75; Mary Welborn, "The Long Tradition: A Study in Fourteenth-Century Medical Deontology," in *Legacies in Ethics and Medicine*, ed. Chester Burns (New York: Science History Publications, 1977), p. 206.

21. Kibre, "Hippocratic Writings," pp. 399, 402.

22. Ibid., p. 374.

23. Sanford V. Larkey, "The Hippocratic Oath in Elizabethan England," in *Legacies in Ethics and Medicine*, ed. Chester Burns (New York: Science History Publications, 1977), pp. 218–36.

24. Thomas Percival, *Percival's Medical Ethics*, ed. Chauncey D. Leake (Baltimore, Md.: Williams & Wilkins, 1927), pp. 29–32; Ivan Waddington, "The Development of Medical Ethics—A Sociological Analysis," *Medical History* 19 (January 1975): 36–51.

25. Waddington, "Development of Medical Ethics," p. 31.

26. Ibid.

27. American Medical Association, *Code of Medical Ethics* (New York: H. Ludwig and Co., 1848).

Chapter 2

1. Cited in Seymour Siegel, "Medical Ethics, History of" s.v. "Contemporary Israel," in *Encyclopedia of Bioethics*, 4 vols., ed. Warren T. Reich (New York: The Free Press, 1978), 2:896. For a fuller account, see Fred Rosner, "Autopsy in Jewish Law and the Israeli Autopsy Controversy," *Jewish Bioethics*, ed. F. Rosner and J. David Bleich (New York: Sanhedrin Press, 1979), pp. 338–45; and Fred Rosner, *Modern Medicine and Jewish Law*, Studies in Torah Judaism, no. 13. (New York: Yeshiva University Department of Special Publications, 1972).

2. Rosner and Bleich, *Jewish Bioethics*, see note 1.

3. See Immanuel Jakobovits, *Jewish Medical Ethics* (New York: Bloch Publishing Co., 1959); idem, "Judaism," in *Encyclopedia of Bioethics*, 2:791–802.

4. Moses Tendler, *Medical Ethics*, 5th ed. (New York: Committee on Religious Affairs, Federation of Jewish Philanthropies of New York, Inc., 1975).

5. David Feldman, *Marital Relations, Birth Control, and Abortion* (New York: Schocken Books, 1974).

6. Siegel, "Medical Ethics," pp. 895–96.

7. Rosner, *Modern Medicine*.

8. Jakobovits, "Judaism," p. 791.

9. Ibid., p. 799.

10. "The Physician's Oath," in Tendler, *Medical Ethics*, pp. 7–9.

11. Jakobovits, "Judaism," p. 792.

12. Fred Rosner, "The Jewish Attitude toward Euthanasia," in *Jewish Bioethics*, p. 263.

13. J. David Bleich, "The Obligation to Heal in the Judaic Tradition: A Computative Analysis," in *Jewish Bioethics*, p. 17. In some editions of the Talmud, the text reads "a single soul," not "a single soul of Israel."

14. Jakobovits, *Jewish Medical Ethics*, p. 50.

15. *Orah Hayim*, 2:338, cited in Jakobovits, *Jewish Medical Ethics*, p. 50.

16. Jakobovits, *Jewish Medical Ethics*, p. 46.

17. J. David Bleich, "The Quinlan Case: A Jewish Perspective," in *Jewish Bioethics*, p. 272.

18. Bleich, "The Obligation to Heal," p. 33; also Rosner, "The Jewish Attitude," pp. 263–64; Jakobovits, *Jewish Medical Ethics*, p. 119.

19. Rosner ("The Jewish Attitude," p. 264) seems to doubt that medical therapies are included; Bleich ("The Obligation to Heal" pp. 34–5) seems more open to their inclusion.

20. Jakobovits, *Jewish Medical Ethics*, p. 21.

21. Bleich, "The Obligation to Heal," p. 24.

22. Exodus 21:18–19.

23. Bleich, "The Obligation to Heal," p. 21.

24. Jakobovits, "Judaism," p. 798; Rosner, "Autopsy in Jewish Law," pp. 331–48; Jakobovits, *Jewish Medical Ethics*, pp. 126–52.

25. Loren C. MacKinney, "Medical Ethics and Etiquette in the Early Middle Ages: The Persistence of Hippocratic Ideals," *Legacies in Ethics and Medicine*, ed. C. R. Burns (New York: Science History Publications, 1977), pp. 175–76.

26. Darrel Amundsen, "Medical Ethics, History of" s.v. "Medieval Europe: Fourth to Sixteenth Century," in *Encyclopedia of Bioethics*, 4 vols., ed. Warren T. Reich, 3:945.

27. David F. Kelly, *The Emergence of Roman Catholic Medical Ethics in North America*, Texts and Studies in Religion, no. 3 (New York: The Edwin Mellen Press, 1979), p. 50.

28. Ibid., p. 24.

29. Ibid., pp. 25–26.

30. Even Loren MacKinney makes this clear when he observes that monastic compilers cited Christian rather than classical authorities ("Medical Ethics and Etiquette," p. 195). MacKinney's work is difficult to interpret because he is determined to show that early medieval monastic medicine "had medical ideals that are worthy of a place in the historical record alongside the Hippocratic and Salernatan 'codes.'" His objective seems to be to show that early Christian medicine was as sound and sophisticated as what he calls classical medicine. He often tries to do this by arguing that the moral premises of monastic medicine had Hippocratic analogs. The result is a certain tendency to look for similarities. Had he entertained the possibility that in some respects, early Christian medicine was morally preferable to the earlier Hippocratic and other classical tradtions, he might not have struggled so hard to find the similarities.

31. Amundsen, "Medical Ethics," p. 945.

32. Kelly, *Roman Catholic Medical Ethics*, pp. 7–12.

33. Thomas Aquinas, *Summa Theologica* I–II, Q.91. Art. 2., trans. The Dominican Fathers of the English Province, and ed. Thomas Gilbey (Cambridge: Blackfriars, 1966), vol. 28, pp. 21–24.

34. *Ibid.*, Q. 94, Art. 2. There recently have been efforts by theologians who purport to work within an orthodox framework to provide moral theologies not so closely tied to natural-law thinking. At times they modify the formulations of the principles, and the conclusions reached on specific issues of medical ethics may vary accordingly. What is presented here is meant to be the core of the traditional formulation.

35. See Charles E. Curran, "Roman Catholicism," in *Encyclopedia of Bioethics*, 4 vols., ed. Warren T. Reich (New York: The Free Press, 1978), 4: 1526–30; Patrick Finney and Patrick O'Brien, *Moral Problems in Hospital Practice: A Practical Handbook* (St. Louis: B. Herder Book Co., 1956), pp. 1–46; Frederick L. Good and Otis F. Kelly, *Marriage, Morals and Medical Ethics* (New York: P. J. Kenedy & Sons, 1951), pp. 22–28; Edwin F. Healy, *Medical Ethics* (Chicago: Loyola University Press, 1956), pp. 1–12; Gerald Kelly, *Medico-Moral Problems* (St. Louis: The Catholic Hospital Association of the U.S. and Canada, 1958), pp. 1–16; John P. Kenny, *Principles of Medical Ethics* (Westminster, Maryland: The

Newman Press, 1962), pp. 1–16; Charles J. McFadden, *Medical Ethics*, 6th ed. (Philadelphia: F. A. Davis Co., 1967), pp. 11–38; idem, *The Dignity of Life: Moral Values in a Changing Society* (Huntington, Indiana: Our Sunday Visitor, 1976), pp. 108–9, 146–52; Thomas J. O'Donnell, *Medicine and Christian Morality* (New York: Alba House, 1976), pp. 3–49; idem, *Morals in Medicine* (Westminster, Maryland: The Newman Press, 1956), pp. 3–40; Thomas A. Shannon, "The Tradition of a Tradition: An Evaluation of Roman Catholic Medical Ethics," in *Bioethics: Basic Writings on Key Ethical Questions*, ed. Thomas A. Shannon (New York: Paulist Press, 1976), pp. 2–10; and Warren T. Reich, "Medical Ethics in a Catholic Perspective: Some Present-Day Trends," in *Pastoral Care of the Sick: A Practical Guide for the Catholic Chaplain*, ed. National Association of Catholic Chaplains (Washington: United States Catholic Conference, 1974), pp. 171–84.

For works in a somewhat different style, but which reflect this tradition throughout, see Bernard Häring, *Medical Ethics*, ed. Gabrielle L. Jean (Notre Dame, Indiana: Fides Publishers, Inc., 1973); idem, "Religious Directives in Medical Ethics: Roman Catholic Directive," in *Encyclopedia of Bioethics*, 4 vols., ed. Warren T. Reich (New York: The Free Press, 1978), pp. 1431–34; and Richard A. McCormick, *How Brave a New World: Dilemmas in Bioethics* (Garden City, N.Y.: Doubleday and Company, 1981).

36. G. Kelly, *Medico-Moral Problems*, p. 5; Curran, "Roman Catholicism," p. 1528; Kenny, *Principles of Medical Ethics*, pp. 116–23; O'Donnell, *Medicine and Christian Morality*, pp. 42–43.

37. Kenny, *Principles of Medical Ethics*, pp. 113–16; O'Donnell, *Morals in Medicine*, pp. 51–68; idem, *Medicine and Christian Morality*, pp. 41–58; McFadden, *Medical Ethics*, pp. 239–40.

38. Joel Feinberg, "Voluntary Euthanasia and the Inalienable Right to Life," *Philosophy and Public Affairs* 7 (Winter 1978): 93–123; cf. Curran, "Roman Catholicism," p. 1528.

39. Healy, *Medical Ethics*, p. 10.

40. Curran, "Roman Catholicism," p. 1528.

41. Ibid.

42. G. Kelly, *Medico-Moral Problems*, pp. 8–11; Curran, "Roman Catholicism," pp. 1528–29; O'Donnell, *Medicine and Christian Morality*, pp. 65–67; idem, *Morals in Medicine*, pp. 70–72; Kenny, *Principles of Medical Ethics*, 151–54; D. Kelly, *Roman Catholic Medical Ethics*, pp. 262–64, 267–70, 333–40, 347–49; McFadden, *Dignity of Life*, pp. 183–86; idem, *Medical Ethics*, pp. 271–74.

43. McFadden, *Medical Ethics*, pp. 46–47; Frederick L. Good and Otis F. Kelly, *Marriage, Morals and Medical Ethics*, pp. 6–7; G. Kelly, *Medico-Moral Problems*, pp. 5–6; cf. Curran, "Roman Catholicism," p. 1529.

44. G. Kelly, *Medico-Moral Problems*, p. 6.

45. Ibid.

46. Curran, "Roman Catholicism," p. 1529; G. Kelly, *Medico-Moral Problems*, pp. 12–16; Finney and O'Brien, *Moral Problems in Hospital Practice*, p. 18; D. Kelly, *Roman Catholic Medical Ethics*, pp. 244–74; Kenny, *Principles of Medical Ethics*, pp. 153–54, 203–4; O'Donnell, *Morals in Medicine*, pp. 39–44; idem, *Medicine and Christian Morality*, pp. 27–31.

For a sophisticated debate covering recent critical variations on the principles, see Paul Menzel's chapter, "Cash or In-Kind Aid?," in his manuscript, "Costworthy Health Care" (unpublished). Recently secular philosophical scholarship has addressed the principle in works such as: Glen C. Graber, "Some Questions About Double Effect," *Ethics in Science and Medicine* 6, no. 1 (1979): 65–84; Jonathan Bennett, "Whatever the Consequences," *Analysis* 26 (1966): 83–102; G. E. M. Anscombe, "Modern Moral Philosophy," *Philosophy* 33 (1958): 1–19; and Philippa Foot, "The Problem of Abortion and the Doctrine of the Double Effect," in *Moral Problems in Medicine*, ed. Samuel Gorovitz, et al. (Englewood Cliffs, N.J.: Prentice-Hall, 1976), pp. 267–76.

47. G. Kelly, *Medico-Moral Problems*, p. 13. Current scholarly debate within Catholicism struggles over possible modification of these criteria. These will be discussed below.

48. O'Donnell, *Morals in Medicine*, pp. 44–49; idem, *Medicine and Christian Morality*, pp. 31–38; McFadden, *Medical Ethics*, pp. 359–67; Good and O. Kelly, *Marriage, Morals and Medical Ethics*, pp. 25–28; Finney and O'Brien, *Moral Problems in Hospital Practice*, pp. 30–33; Curran, "Roman Catholicism," pp. 1529–30; Healy, *Medical Ethics*, pp. 101–19.

49. Karl Barth, *Church Dogmatics*, trans. A. T. Mackey, T. H. Thomson, and Harold Knight, 4 vols. (Edinburgh: T. and T. Clark, 1961), 3:pt. 4.

50. Helmut Thielicke, *Theological Ethics*, trans. William H. Lazareth (Philadelphia: Fortress Press, 1966).

51. Kenneth Vaux, ed., *Who Shall Live?* (Philadelphia: Fortress Press, 1970); Harmon L. Smith, *Ethics and the New Medicine* (New York: Abingdon Press, 1970); Paul Ramsey, *The Patient as Person* (New Haven: Yale University Press, 1970); idem, *Ethics at the Edges of Life* (New Haven: Yale University Press, 1978); idem, *Fabricated Man* (New Haven: Yale University Press, 1970); idem, *The Ethics of Fetal Research* (New Haven: Yale University Press, 1975); James B. Nelson, *Human Medicine* (Minneapolis: Augsburg Publishing House, 1973); James M. Gustafson, *The Contribution of Theology to Medical Ethics* (The 1975 Pere Marquette Theology Lecture, Marquette University, 1975); Joseph Fletcher, *Morals and Medicine* (Boston: Beacon Press, 1954); Willard L. Sperry, *The Ethical Basis of Medical Practice* (New York: Paul B. Haeber, Inc., 1950).

52. Ramsey, *Patient as Person*.

53. Ibid., p. xii.

54. This is especially the case in his newer formulation of a "medical indications" policy in *Ethics at the Edges of Life* (New Haven: Yale University Press, 1978), pp. 160–71.

55. William F. May, "Code, Covenant, Contract, or Philanthropy," *Hastings Center Report* 5 (December 1975):29–38.

56. Ramsey, *Patient as Person*, p. xiii; cf. Ramsey, *Basic Christian Ethics* (New York: Charles Scribner's Sons, 1950), where the agapeic love ethics is developed much more fully.

57. Joseph Fletcher, *Situation Ethics: The New Morality* (Philadelphia: The Westminster Press, 1966), pp. 57–86; idem, *Moral Responsibility: Situation Ethics at Work* (Philadelphia: The Westminster Press, 1967), pp. 29–41.

58. Joseph Fletcher, *The Ethics of Genetic Control: Ending Reproductive Roulette* (Garden City, N.Y.: Anchor Press/Doubleday, 1974), pp. 121–231.

59. Ramsey, *Basic Christian Ethics*, p. 76.

60. Fletcher, *Situation Ethics*, p. 21.

61. James T. Johnson, "Protestantism: History of Protestant Medical Ethics," in *Encyclopedia of Bioethics*, 4 vols., ed. Warren T. Reich (New York: The Free Press, 1978), 4:1364–73.

62. Barry D. Sibermann, "The Right of a Patient to Refuse Blood Transfusions: A Dilemma of Conscience and Law for Patient, Physician, and Hospital," *San Fernando Valley Law Review* 3(1974):91–104. See also In re Estate of Brooks, 32 Ill. 2d 361–62, 205 N.E. 2d 435, 436–37 (1965); and "Authorization of Involuntary Blood Transfusion for Adult Jehovah's Witness Held Unconstitutional—In re Brooks Estate," *Michigan Law Review* 64 (January 1966): 554–61.

63. Leo XIII, "Libertas Praestantissimum," in *The Church Speaks to the Modern World: The Social Teachings of Leo XIII*, ed. Etienne Gilson (Garden City, N.Y.: Doubleday, 1954), pp. 75–78.

64. Natanson v. Kline 393, 350 P.2d 1093 (1960), pp. 57–82.

65. The Belmont Report—*Ethical Principles and Guidelines for the Protection of Human Subjects and Research*, ed. National Commission for the Protection of Human Subjects of Biomedical and Behavioral Research (Washington, D.C.: U.S. Government Printing Office, DHEW Publication no. [OS] 78–0012, 1978), pp. 4–10.

66. Laurence B. McCullough, "The Right to Health Care," *Ethics in Science and Medicine* 6 (1):1–9

67. American Hospital Association, *A Patient's Bill of Rights*, (Chicago: American Hospital Association, 1972).

68. Willard Gaylin, "The Patient's Bill of Rights," *Saturday Review [of the Sciences]* (24 February 1973) 1:22.

69. Parliamentary Assembly of the Council of Europe, "On rights of the sick and dying," Recommendation 779 (1976), 27th ordinary session. Also see Clarence Blomquist, "A New Era in European Medical Ethics," *Hastings Center Report* 6 (April 1976): 7–8.

70. Joel Feinberg, *Social Philosophy* (Englewood Cliffs, N.J.: Prentice-Hall, 1973), pp. 33–35, 71–73; idem, "Limits to the Free Expression of Opinion," in *Philosophy of Law*, ed. Joel Feinberg and Hyman Gross (Encino, Cal.: Dickenson Publishing Co., 1975), pp. 135–51.

Chapter 3

Note: Citations in this chapter to *Encyclopedia of Bioethics* refer to *Encyclopedia of Bioethics*, 4 vols., ed. Warren T. Reich (New York: The Free Press, 1978).

1. N. G. Karlsen and I. I. Kosarev, "O prepodavanii deontologii v meditsinskom vuze" [Instruction in deontology in a medical school], *Sovetskoe zdravookhranenie* 30, no. 4 (1971):46–49; L. M. Gol'dshtein, "Rol deontologii v meditsinskom obrazovanii" [The role of deontology in medical education], *Sovetskoe zdravookhranenie* 30, no. 4 (1971):49–50; F. M. Priduvalov, R. P. Chernega, and V. A. Abrosimov, "Deontologiia v sisteme meditsinskogo obrazovaniia" [Deontology in the medical education system], *Sovetskoe zdravookhranenie* 31, no. 9 (1972):66–67; D. K. Sokolov, "Opyt prepodavaniia deontologii v meditsinskom institute" [Experience in the teaching of deontology in a medical institute], *Sovetskoe zdravookhranenie* 31, no. 9 (1972):64–65.

2. The Revolutionary Committee, Hua Shan Hospital, Shanghai First Medical College, Shanghai, "Hospital-run Medical Colleges are Fine," *Chinese Medical Journal* n.s. 1 (1975):315–24.

3. Z. Ander, "Aspects from the History of Medical Ethics in Romania," *International Symposium on Society, Medicine and Law*, ed. H. Karplus (New York: Elsevier Scientific Publishing Co., 1973), p. 153.

4. "The Oath of Soviet Physicians," *Journal of the American Medical Association* 217 (1971):834, where a translation of the full text appears.

5. The JAMA translation substitutes the word *morale* for *morality*, the term used in some other translations, which seems to fit better here. (See Michael Ryan, "Aspects of Ethics," *British Medical Journal* 2 [8 September 1979]:586. Ryan's translation also refers to the "Soviet State" rather than the "Soviet government.")

6. American Medical Association Judicial Council, *Opinions and Reports: Including the Principles of Medical Ethics and Rules of the Judicial Council* (Chicago: American Medical Association, 1977), p. 5.

7. See Benjamin B. Page, "Eastern Europe in the Twentieth Century," in *Encyclopedia of Bioethics*, 3:978; and Michael Ryan, "Aspects of Ethics," p. 586.

8. Janey Milcinski, "Abortion and Infanticide in Yugoslavia," in *International Symposium on Society, Medicine and Law*, ed. H. Karplus (New York: Elsevier Scientific Publishing Co., 1973), p. 163.

9. Page, "Eastern Europe," p. 977; Milton I. Roemer and Ruth Roemer, *Health Manpower in the Socialist Health Care System of Poland* (Washington, D. C.: U. S. Department of Health, Education, and Welfare, 1977), p. 4. Cf. William T. Blackstone, "On Health Care as a Legal Right: Philosophical Justifications, Political Activity, and Adequate Health Care," *Georgia Law Review* 10 (Winter 1976):391–418; Edward V. Sparer, "The Legal Right to Health Care; Public Policy and Equal Access," *Hastings Center Report* 6 (October 1976):39–47; Robert M. Sade, "Medical Care as a Right: A Refutation," *New England Journal of Medicine* 285 (2 December 1971):1288–92.

10. Vincente Navarro, "Health, Health Services, and Health Planning in Cuba," *International Journal of Health Services*, 2 (1972):397–432; "Health Care as a Human Right: A Cuban Perspective," *Science* 200 (June 16, 1978):1246–50; Ross Danielson, "The Cuban Health Area and Polyclinic: Organizational Focus in an Emerging System," *Inquiry*, supplement to vol. 12 (June 1975):86–102.

11. Ryan, "Aspects of Ethics," p. 586; Page, "Eastern Europe," p. 978.

12. Ander, "Aspects from History of Medical Ethics," p. 152.

13. Revolutionary Committee, "Hospital-run Medical Colleges," p. 319.

14. Zhores Medvedev and Roy Medvedev, *A Question of Madness* (New York: Alfred A. Knopf, 1971); cf. Jonas Robitscher, *The Powers of Psychiatry* (Boston: Houghton Mifflin Co., 1980), pp. 319–46.

15. Medvedev and Medvedev, *A Question of Madness*, pp. 126–27.

16. Ibid., p. 136.

17. Milcinski, "Abortion and Infanticide," p. 168.

18. Darrel W. Amundsen, "Medical Ethics, History of," s.v. "Ancient Near East," in *Encyclopedia of Bioethics*, 2:882.

19. Ibid., p. 881.

20. Rahmatollah Eshraghi, "Medical Ethics, History of," s.v. "Persia," in *Encyclopedia of Bioethics*, 2:885.

21. Manfred Ullman, *Islamic Medicine* (Edinburgh: Edinburgh University Press, 1978), pp. 20–22; Donald Campbell, "The Historiography of Islam, with Special Reference to the Development of Arabic Medicine and Philosophical Literature," in *Arabian Medicine and Its Influence on the Middle Ages*, Trubner Oriental Series, 2 vols. (London: Kegan Paul, Trench, Trubner and Co., 1926), 1:2; J. C. Bürgel, "Islam," in *Encyclopedia of Bioethics*, 2:785–90; and Samuel P. Asper and Sami Haddad Fuad, "Medical Ethics, History of" s.v. "Contemporary Arab World," in *Encyclopedia of Bioethics*, 2:888–91.

22. Martin Levey, "Medical Deontology in Ninth-Century Islam," *Legacies in Ethics and Medicine*, ed. Chester R. Burns (New York: Science History Publications, 1977) pp. 129–45.

23. Ibid., p. 132.

24. W. H. S. Jones, *The Doctor's Oath:, An Essay in the History of Medicine* (Cambridge: At the University Press, 1924), pp. 29–32.

25. See H. A. R. Gibb, *Mohammedanism: An Historical Survey* (New York: Oxford University Press, 1962); Huston Smith, *The Religions of Man* (New York: Harper & Row, 1958), pp. 193–224; Wilfred Cantwell Smith, *The Meaning and End of Religion* (New York: Mentor Books, 1962), pp. 75–108; idem *The Faith of Other Men* (New York: Mentor Books, 1962), pp. 50–62, for general accounts of the core of Islamic thought. Smith's *The Faith of Other Men* includes an especially interesting account of how "the word" symbolizes the core of the Muslim faith.

26. Muhammad Abdul-Rauf, "Medical Ethics, History of," s.v. "Contemporary Muslim Perspective," in *Encyclopedia of Bioethics*, 2:892.

27. Abdul-Rauf, "Contemporary Muslim Perspective," p. 894.

28. See Richard M. Fagley, "Doctrines and Attitudes of Major Religions in Regard to Fertility," in *Proceedings of the World Population Conference, Belgrade, 30 August–10 September 1965. [Vol. 2: "Selected Papers and Summaries: Fertility, Family Planning, Morality"]* (New York: United Nations, Dept. of Economic and Social Affairs, 1967); cf. Basim Musallam, "Population Ethics," s.v. "Religious Traditions: Islamic," in *Encyclopedia of Bioethics* 3:1264–69. By a fascinating twist of fate, this fatalism has also been used to justify contraception. Muhammad is quoted as saying, regarding coitus interruptus, "Do as you please, whatever God has willed will happen [anyway], and not all semen result in children."

29. Mohammed Marmaduke Pickthall, *The Meaning of the Glorious Koran: An Explanatory Translation* (New York: Mentor Books, 1953), chap. 5, v. 32.

30. K. R. Srikanta Murthy, "Professional Ethics in Ancient Indian Medicine," *Indian Journal of the History of Medicine* 18 (1973):46; Henry R. Zimmer, *Hindu Medicine* (Baltimore: Johns Hopkins University Press, 1948), p. 60; Henry E. Sigerist, *A History of Medicine*, 2 vols. (New York: Oxford University Press, 1961), 2 *[Early Greek, Hindu and Persian Medicine]*: 182; Rastom Jal Vakil, *Our Glorious Heritage* (Bombay: The Times of India Press, 1966), p. 58.

31. I. A. Menon and H. F. Habman, "The Medical Students' Oath of Ancient India," *Medical History* 14 (1970): 295–96; Zimmer, *Hindu Medicine*, pp. 80–81; S. L. Bhutia, *A History of Medicine with Special Reference to the Orient* (New Delhi: Office of Medical Council of India, 1977), pp. 36–41; Murthy, "Professional Ethics," p. 46.

32. M. B. Etziony, *The Physician's Creed: An Anthology of Medical Prayers, Oaths and Codes of Ethics Written and Recited by Medical Practitioners Through the Ages* (Springfield, Ill.: Charles C Thomas, 1973), p. 15.

33. Zimmer, *Hindu Medicine*, p. 81.

34. Franklin Edgerton, trans., *The Bhagavad Gita* (New York: Harper and Row, 1944), pp. 157–63.

35. Zimmer, *Hindu Medicine*, p. 81.

36. O. P. Jaggi, "India," in *Encyclopedia of Bioethics*, 3:906–10.

37. Paul U. Unschuld, "Medical Ethics, History of," s.v. "South and East Asia—General Historical Survey," in *Encyclopedia of Bioethics*, 3:902; Jaggi, "India," p. 910; S. Cromwell Crawford, *The Evolution of Hindu Ethical Ideals* (Calcutta, India: Firma K. L. Mukhopadhyay, 1974), p. 123.

38. Edgerton, *The Bhagavad Gita*, I. 45, II. 8.

39. Crawford, *Evolution of Hindu Ethical Ideals*, p. 153.

40. John McKenzie, *Hindu Ethics: A Historical and Critical Essay* (New Delhi: Oriental Books Reprint Corporation, 1971), p. 62.

41. R. C. Zaehner, *Hinduism* (London: Oxford University Press, 1962), p. 159; A. L. Basham, "Hinduism," in *Encyclopedia of Bioethics*, 2:664.

42. Marc Lappé, "The Genetic Counselor: Responsible to Whom?" *Hastings Center Report* 1 (September 1971):9.

43. Paul U. Unschuld, "Medical Ethics, History of," s.v. "Prerepublican China," in *Encyclopedia of Bioethics*, 3:911; and Norman J. Girardot, "Taoism," in *Encyclopedia of Bioethics*, 4:1631.

44. Paul U. Unschuld, *Medical Ethics in Imperial China* (Berkeley: University of California Press, 1979).

45. Ibid., p. 5.

46. Ibid., p. 36.

47. Unschuld, "Prerepublican China," p. 913.

48. Ho Ch'i-pin, epilogue to Hsü Yen-tso's *I-ts' ui ching-yen*, translated in Unschuld, *Medical Ethics*, p. 109.

49. See Unschuld, *Medical Ethics*, pp. 70–73, 85, 86, 93, 95; and Girardot, "Taoism," p. 1624. This contrasts dramatically with the attitudes of some contemporary Western physicians and some Talmudic sources where the fee is seen as adding impact to the treatment. The Talmud, for example, says, "Look to your pay, oh physician; for that for which nothing is paid, the same never cures" [cited in J. H. Baas, *Outlines of the History of Medicine and the Medical Profession*, trans. H. E. Henderson (New York: W. R. Jenkins, 1910), p. 38].

50. Unschuld, *Medical Ethics*, pp. 24–34; idem, "Prerepublican China," pp. 914–15.

51. Sun Szu-miao, Ch'ien-chin fang, translated in Unschuld, *Medical Ethics*, pp. 29–33.

52. Unschuld, *Medical Ethics*, p. 28.

53. Ibid., pp. 63, 67.

54. Ibid., pp. 75, 78, 86, 93.

55. Ibid., pp. 68, 75, 76.

56. Arnold D. Hunt and Robert B. Crotty, *Ethics of World Religions* (Minneapolis: Greenhaven Press, Inc., 1978), pp. 135–40; Paul U. Unschuld, "Confucianism," in *Encyclopedia of Bioethics*, 1:200.

57. Thomas Percival, *Percival's Medical Ethics*, Chauncey D. Leake, ed. (Baltimore, Md.: Williams and Wilkins, 1927) p. xv.

58. T'ao Lee, "Medical Ethics in Ancient China," *Bulletin of the History of Medicine* 13 (1943):268. The text, from Sun Szu-miao, is translated somewhat differently in Unschuld, p. 30.

59. Chu Hui-ming, Tou-chen ch'uan hsin lu, ch. 16, translated in Unschuld, *Medical Ethics*, p. 63.

60. Kung T'ing-hsien, *Wan-ping hui-ch'un*, ch. 8, translated in Unschuld, *Medical Ethics*, p. 74. Countless other references of a similar nature can be found. Kung Hsin (ca. 1600) said, "prescribe drugs according to a formula which is valid for everyone" [translated in Unschuld, *Medical Ethics*, p. 69]; Ch'en Shih-kung (A.D. 1605) begins his five admonitions to physicians: "Firstly. When called to a patient, the physician is to go there immediately, regardless of whether it is a question of high-ranking or low-ranking people, poor ones or rich ones" [translated in Unschuld, *Medical Ethics*, pp. 76–77].

61. Hsü Yen-tso, *I-ts' ui ching-yen*, ch. 2, translated in Unschuld, *Medical Ethics*, p. 112.

62. John J. Kao and Frederick F. Kao, "Medical Ethics, History of" s.v. "Contemporary China," in *Encyclopedia of Bioethics*, 3:917.

63. Chu Hui-ming, *Tou-chen* in Unschuld, *Medical Ethics*, p. 65.

64. Frank Reynolds, "Natural Death: A History of Religious Perspective," in *Life Span: Values and Life-Extending Technologies*, ed. Robert M. Veatch (New York: Harper and Row, 1979), pp. 148–49; idem, "Death," s.v. "Eastern Thought," in *Encyclopedia of Bioethics*, 1:230; Girardot, "Taoism," 4:1635.

65. Girardot, "Taoism," 4:1636.

66. Unschuld, *Medical Ethics*, pp. 30, 110.

67. Ibid., p. 86.

68. Huai Yüan, *Ku-chin i-ch'e*, translated in Unschuld, *Medical Ethics*, p. 105.

69. Sun Szu-miao, *Ch'en-chin i-fang*, ch. 29. translated in Unschuld, *Medical Ethics*, p. 33.

70. Unschuld, "Confucianism," 200.

71. Bernard Hung-Kay Luk, "Abortion in Chinese Law," *American Journal of Comparative Law* 25 (Spring 1977): 373.

72. Girardot, "Taoism," 4:1636.

73. Luk, "Abortion," p. 386.

74. Edward Alexander Westermarck, "The Killing of Parents, Sick Persons, Children—Feticide," in *The Origin and Development of Moral Ideas*, 2 vols. (London: Macmillan & Co., 1906–08), 1: 393–413.

75. Joseph M. Kitagawa, "Medical Ethics, History of" s.v. "Japan through the Nineteenth Century," in *Encyclopedia of Bioethics*, 3: 922.

76. Smith, *The Meaning and End*, p. 67.

77. Kitagawa, "Japan," 3: 922.

78. Ibid.

79. Rikuo Ninomiya, "Medical Ethics, History of" s.v. "Contemporary Japan: Medical Ethics and Legal Practice," in *Encyclopedia of Bioethics*, 3: 926.

80. John Z. Bowers, *Western Medical Pioneers in Feudal Japan* (Baltimore: The Johns Hopkins Press, 1970), p. 6.

81. Ibid., p. 8.

82. Cited in Taro Takemi, "Medical Ethics, History of" s.v. "Traditional Professional Ethics in Japanese Medicine," in *Encyclopedia of Bioethics*, 3:925.

83. Ibid.

84. Cited in Bowers, *Western Medical Pioneers*, p. 9.

85. Ninomiya, "Contemporary Japan," p. 927.

86. For a fuller account of the four noble truths and the eightfold path, see Smith, *Religions of Man*, pp. 97–109.

87. Ninomiya, "Contemporary Japan," 3:928.

88. H. Saddhatissa, *Buddhist Ethics* (New York: George Braziller, 1970), p. 87.

89. Takemi, "Traditional Professional Ethics," 3: 925.

90. Dhammapada 130; Udānavarga v. 19; Ācārānga Sūtra 1. 2. 3. 92, 93; Suyagada 1. 11. 9, 10; cited in Saddhatissa, *Buddhist Ethics*, pp. 87–88.

91. Kitagawa, "Japan through the Nineteenth Century," 3: 922.

92. See W. R. La Fleur, "Japan," in *Death and Eastern Thought*, ed. Frederick H. Holck (Nashville and New York: Abingdon Press, 1974), pp. 248–53; Winston L. King, "A Japanese Buddhist Perspective: Practicing Dying: The Samurai-Zen Death Techniques of Suzuki Shosan," in *Religious Encounters with Death*, ed. Frank E. Reynolds and Earle H. Waugh (University Park, Pa.: The Pennsylvania State University Press, 1977), pp. 143–50; George A. DeVos, "Deviancy and Social Change: A Psychocultural Evaluation of Trends in Japanese Delinquency and Suicide," in *Japanese Culture: Its Development and Characteristics*, ed. Robert J. Smith and Richard K. Beardsley (New York: Wenner-Gren Foundation for Anthropological Research, Inc., 1962), pp. 161–64.

93. Hajime Nakamura, "Buddhism," in *Encyclopedia of Bioethics*, 1: 137.

94. Saddhatissa, *Buddhist Ethics*, p. 89.

95. Bowers, *Western Medical Pioneers*, p. 9.

96. Japanese National Commission for UNESCO, *Japan: Its Land, People and Culture* (Tokyo: Ministry of Education, 1958), p. 901.

97. Ibid

98. DeVos, "Deviancy," p. 162.

99. See Moses Burg, "A Psychocultural Analysis and Theoretical Integration of the Dynamics of Japanese Parent-Child Suicide," in *Tōyō Daigaku Shakai Kiyō* [Bulletin, Department of Sociology, Tōyō university], 2:127–54, 1961, cited in DeVos, "Deviancy;" but see also Masaaki Kato, "Self-Destruction in Japan: A Cross-Cultural Epidemiological Analysis of Suicide," in *Japanese Culture and Behavior*, ed. Takie Sugiyama Lebra and William P. Lebra (Honolulu: University Press of Hawaii, 1974), p. 368, who consider infanticide and maternal suicide different and not genuinely Japanese.

100. John Whitney Hall and Richard K. Beardsley, *Twelve Doors to Japan* (New York: McGraw-Hill, 1965), pp. 145–49.

101. Japanese National Commission for UNESCO, *Japan: Its Land*, p. 901.

102. See Kato, "Self-Destruction," p. 369, for examples.
103. Westermarck, "The Killing of Parents," p. 394.
104. Saddhatissa, *Buddhist Ethics*, p. 88.
105. DeVos, "Deviancy," p. 162.
106. Chie Nakane, *Japanese Society* (Berkeley and Los Angeles: University of California Press, 1970), pp. x, 21.
107. Ibid., pp. 96, 127–78.
108. Takeo L. Doi, "Amae: A Key Concept for Understanding Japanese Personality Structure," in *Japanese Culture: Its Development and Characteristics*, eds. Robert J. Smith and Richard K. Beardsley (New York: Wenner-Gren Foundation for Anthropological Research, Inc., 1962); idem, *The Anatomy of Dependence*, trans. John Bester (Tokyo: Kodansha International, Ltd., 1973).
109. John Bester, "Foreword," in Doi, *Anatomy of Dependence*, p. 7.
110. DeVos, "Deviancy," p. 163.
111. Nakane, *Japanese Society*, p. 137.
112. Doi, *Anatomy*, p. 8.

Chapter 4

1. In the Matter of the American Medical Association, a corporation, the Connecticut State Medical Society, a corporation, the New Haven County Medical Association, Inc. United States of America Before the Federal Trade Commission. Docket No. 9064, October 12, 1979.
2. American Medical Association, "United States of America Before the Federal Trade Commission" (Trial Brief), Docket No. 9064 (1977).
3. Ibid., p. 65.
4. Robert N. Smith, "FTC Charges Illegality in Curb on Doctors' Ads," *New York Times*, December 23, 1975.
5. Russell B. Roth, "Medicine's Ethical Responsibilities," *Journal of the American Medical Association* 215 (March 22, 1971):1957.
6. *Code of Medical Ethics. Adopted by the American Medical Association at Philadelphia, May 1847, and by the New York Academy of Medicine in October 1847.* (New York: H. Ludwig and Co., 1848), p. 17.
7. American Medical Association, *Judicial Council Opinions and Reports* (Chicago: American Medical Association, 1971), p. 23.
8. Bates v. State of Arizona, 433 U.S. 350, 45 U.S.L.W. 4895 (1977).
9. The British Medical Association, *The Handbook of Medical Ethics* (London: British Medical Association, 1980).
10. See Émile Durkheim, *Professional Ethics and Civil Morals* (Glenview, Illinois: The Free Press, 1958); Talcott Parsons, *The Social System* (Glenview, Illinois: The Free Press, 1951); Bernard Barber, "Some Problems in the Sociology of the Professions," *Daedalus* 92 (1963): 669–88; Everett C. Hughes, "Professions," *Daedalus* 92 (1963): 655–68.
11. For a fascinating compilation of their codes see Jane Clapp, *Professional Ethics and Insignia* (Metuchen, N.J.: The Scarecrow Press, Inc., 1974).
12. John Calvin, *Institutes of the Christian Religion*, 2 vols. (Philadelphia: Westminster Press, 1960) 1:724; F.H. Bradley, *Ethical Studies*, 2d ed. rev. (Oxford: Clarendon Press, 1927), pp. 160–206.
13. Joel Feinberg, *Doing and Deserving: Essays in the Theory of Responsibility* (Princeton, N.J.: Princeton University Press, 1970), pp. 5–6; Benjamin Freedman, "A Meta-Ethics for Professional Morality," *Ethics* 89 (October 1978): 5.
14. H. Thomas Ballantine, "Annual Discourse—The Crisis in Ethics, Anno Domini 1979," *New England Journal of Medicine* 301 (1979): 634–38.
15. See Kenneth Kipnis, "Professional Ethics," *Business and Professional Ethics* 2 (Fall 1978): 2, where an earlier version of this argument is misinterpreted. Kipnis assumes that I have contended there can be no role-specific duties at all. Clearly, I do not mean that. Rather, I am arguing that to avoid charges of metaethical relativism the role-specific duty must be based on claims in principle accessible to all. Likewise, Larry Churchill in his

Notes

essay, "Tacit Components of Medical Ethics: Making Decisions in the Clinic" (*Journal of Medical Ethics* 3 [1977]: 129–32), misunderstands the argument made by those of us stressing the necessity of a universal basis for medical ethics. No one denies that there is a special moral context in medicine that generates special role-specific duties for health professionals. But those health professionals cannot abandon their identity as members of the society when they seek a grounding for their special professional ethical obligation. Moral reasoning really must, contrary to Churchill, "appeal to men *as* men" (see p. 129) although all men (and women as well) will surely perceive that there are special duties for physicians and other health care professionals.

16. W.H.S. Jones, *The Doctor's Oath: An Essay in the History of Medicine* (Cambridge: At the University Press, 1924), p. 45.

17. The reason given was that it was part of the association's members' handbook. The fact remains that the basic ethical rules of conduct for the British physician were not known and not accessible to nonmembers until recently. That situation has changed with the 1980 publication of a separate volume that is circulated more generally.

18. William May, "Code, Covenant, Contract, or Philanthropy," *Hastings Center Report* 5 (December 1975):29–38.

19. Ibid., p. 31.

20. Thomas Percival, *Percival's Medical Ethics*, ed. Chauncey D. Leake (Baltimore: Williams and Wilkins, 1927), p. 71.

21. AMA, *Code of Medical Ethics*, Chap. I, Art. I, Paragraph 1, p. 13.

22. Roth, "Medicine's Ethical Responsibilities," p. 1957.

23. American Medical Association, *Judicial Council, Opinions and Reports* [Including the Principles of Medical Ethics and Rules of the Judicial Council] (Chicago: American Medical Association, 1977), p. 9.

24. Percival, *Percival's Medical Ethics*, p. 63.

25. Ludwig Edelstein, *Ancient Medicine: Selected Papers of Ludwig Edelstein* (Baltimore: Johns Hopkins University Press, 1967), pp. 26–32. Also see Donald Konold, "Medical Ethics: History of," s.v. "Codes" in *Encyclopedia of Bioethics*, 4 vols., ed. Warren T. Reich (New York: The Free Press, 1978), 1:163.

26. AMA, *Code of Medical Ethics*, Chap. II, Art. I, Paragraph 2, p. 17.

27. Ibid., Paragraph 3, p. 17.

28. For a fuller account of metaethical relativism see Richard B. Brandt, *Ethical Theory* (Englewood Cliffs, N.J.: Prentice-Hall, 1959), pp. 271–94; Paul W. Taylor, *Principles of Ethics: An Introduction* (Encino, Cal.: Dickenson Publishing Co., 1975), pp. 13–30; John Ladd, *Ethical Relativism* (Belmont, Cal.: Wadsworth Publishing Co., 1973): William K. Frankena, *Ethics* (Englewood Cliffs, N.J.: Prentice-Hall, 1973), pp. 109–110; and Arthur Dyck, *On Human Care: An Introduction to Ethics* (Nashville, Tenn.: Abingdon Press, 1977), pp. 127–31.

29. For good examples of this position see William Graham Sumner, *Folkways* (Boston: Ginn and Company, 1906), and Ruth Benedict, "Anthropology and the Abnormal," *Journal of General Psychology* 10 (1934):49–80.

30. Edward Westernarck, *Ethical Relativity* (Paterson, N.J.: Littlefield Adams & Co., 1960; Brandt, *Ethical Theory*, pp. 283–84.

31. G. E. Moore, *Principia Ethica* (Cambridge: At the University Press, 1966), p. 12; Brandt, *Ethical Theory*, 1959, pp. 164–66; Taylor, *Principles of Ethics*, pp. 182–84.

32. William K. Frankena, "The Naturalistic Fallacy," in *Readings in Ethical Theory*, ed. Wilfrid Sellars and John Hospers (New York: Appleton-Century-Crofts, 1952), pp. 54–62.

33. Quoted in *AMA Newsletter: A Weekly Report from the Executive Vice President's Office* 12 (October 13, 1980):2.

34. Lord Brock, "Euthanasia," *Proceedings of the Royal Society of Medicine* 63 (1970):662.

35. Robert M. Veatch, *Case Studies in Medical Ethics* (Cambridge, Mass.: Harvard University Press, 1977), pp. 61–64.

36. Levy v. Parker, Brief of Petitioner, U.S. Dist. Court for the Middle District of Pennsylvania, p. 165.

37. "So You Think You Know What's Ethical," *Medical Economics* (July 23, 1973), pp. 90–95.

38. British Medical Association, *Medical Ethics* (London: British Medical Association, 1970), p. 8.

39. General Medical Council, *Professional Discipline* (London: General Medical Council, 1971), p. 2.

40. Ibid.

41. Joseph J. Berman, "Legal Mechanisms for Dealing with the Disabled Physician in Maryland: Partnership Between the Medical Society and the State Commission on Medical Discipline," *Maryland State Medical Journal* 25 (February 1976):42.

42. Article 43, Section 130, *Annotated Code of Maryland* (Discipline of Physicians). As reprinted in *Laws Regulating the Practice of Medicine in Maryland* (Charlottesville, Va.: The Mitchie Company, 1979), p. 15.

43. Ibid., p. 44.

44. Stanley E. Gitlow, "Opening Remarks: Medical Discipline: Dealings with Physicians Who Are Unscrupulous, Disabled, and/or Incompetent: A Symposium," *New York State Journal of Medicine* (June 1979):1019.

45. California Medical Association and the Board of Medical Quality Assurance, State of California, "Physician Responsibility . . . A Joint Statement," January 1980.

46. Boyce Rensburger, "Amphetamines Used by a Physician to Lift Moods of Famous Patients," *New York Times,* December 4, 1972, p. 34.

47. Jane Brody, "Medical Unit to Weigh Filing of Charges Against Dr. Jacobson," *New York Times,* December 6, 1972, p. 34.

48. Robert M. Veatch, "Medical Ethics: Professional or Universal," *Harvard Theological Review* 65 (1972):531–59.

49. Jones, *The Doctor's Oath,* p. 42.

Chapter 5

1. Based on Tarasoff v. Regents of University of California. Supreme Court of Calif. Sup., 131 Cal. Rptr. 14 (July 1, 1976); see also Dennis W. Daley, "Tarasoff and the Psychotherapist's Duty to Warn," *San Diego Law Review* 12 (1975):932–51; Joseph Al Latham, "Torts—Duty to Act for Protection of Another—Liability of Psychotherapist for Failure to Warn of Homicide Threatened by Patient," *Vanderbilt Law Review* 28 (1975):631–40; and Howard Gurevita, "Tarasoff: Protective Privilege Versus Public Peril," *American Journal of Psychiatry* 134 (March 1977):289–92.

2. See my earlier discussion of this notion in Robert M. Veatch, *Value-Freedom in Science and Technology* (Missoula, Montana: Scholars Press, 1976), pp. 56–67.

3. Ibid., pp. 249–60.

4. Roderick Firth, "Ethical Absolutism and the Ideal Observer Theory," *Philosophy and Phenomenological Research* 12 (March 1952):318–19.

5. Thomas Aquinas, *Summa Theologica,* I-II, Q. 91, Art. 2.

6. Emil Brunner, *The Divine Imperative* (Philadelphia: The Westminster Press, 1947), p. 269.

7. Paul Tillich, *Systematic Theology,* 3 vols. (Chicago: University of Chicago Press, 1951), 1:186.

8. Ernst Troeltsch, "The Ideas of Natural Law and Humanity in World Politics," in *Natural Law and the Theory of Society: 1500 to 1800,* ed. Otto Gierke (Boston: Beacon Press, 1960, trans. Ernest Barker); idem, "Das stoische-christliche Naturrecht und die moderne profane Naturrecht," in *Gesammelte Schriften* IV (Tübingen: Verlag von J.C.B. Mohr, 1925).

9. Otto Gierke, *Natural Law and the Theory of Society 1500 to 1800* (Boston: Beacon Press, 1960).

10. Firth, "Ethical Absolutism," p. 333.

11. Robert Nozick, *Anarchy, State, and Utopia* (New York: Basic Books, 1974), pp. 33–35.

12. Kurt Baier, *The Moral Point of View: A Rational Basis of Ethics* (New York: Random House, 1965).

13. Ibid., p. 108.

14. John Rawls, *A Theory of Justice* (Cambridge, Mass.: Harvard University Press, 1971).

15. Ibid., p. 18.

16. Ibid., p. 12; cf. pp. 136–42.

17. See Robert M. Veatch, "Generalization of Expertise: Scientific Expertise and Value Judgments," *Hastings Center Studies* 1, no. 2 (1973):29–40, for a fuller development of this thesis.

18. Gen. 9:1–17.

19. Gen. 17.

20 See, for example, George E. Mendenhall, "Law and Covenant in Israel and the Ancient East," *Biblical Archaeologist* 17 (May 1954):26–46 and (Sept. 1954):49–76; and Bernhard W. Anderson, *Understanding the Old Testament* (Englewood Cliffs, N.J.: Prentice-Hall, 1957), pp. 388–90.

21. Mendenhall, "Law and Covenant," p. 5 (in a repaginated edition reprinted by the Presbyterian Board of Colportage of Western Pennsylvania).

22. Ibid.

23. Ibid.

24. See John Locke, *The Second Treatise of Government*, ed. with an introduction by Thomas P. Peardon (New York: The Liberal Arts Press, 1952); and Thomas Hobbes, *Leviathan* (New York: E. P. Dutton, 1953). For the most helpful discussions of their contractarian views, see Ernest Barker, "Introduction," in *Social Contract* (New York: Oxford University Press, 1962; J. W. Gaugh, *The Social Contract: A Critical Study of its Development* (Oxford: The Clarendon Press, 1957), and Henry Sumner Maine, *Ancient Law* (Gloucester, Mass.: Peter Smith, 1970). Even some who have generally been interpreted as hostile to contractarian thinking, such as David Hume, have recently been reinterpreted in a more contractarian perspective. See David Gauthier, "David Hume: Contractarian," *Philosophical Review* 88 (January 1979):3–38.

25. William F. May, "Code, Covenant, Contract, or Philanthropy," *Hastings Center Report* 5 (December 1975):29–38.

26. Roger D. Masters, "Is Contract an Adequate Basis for Medical Care?" *Hastings Center Report* 5 (December 1975):24–28.

27. Darrel W. Amundsen, "The Physician's Obligation to Prolong Life: A Medical Duty Without Classical Roots," *Hastings Center Report* 8 (August 1978):23.

28. Eliot Friedson, *Profession of Medicine: A Study of the Sociology of Applied Knowledge* (New York: Dodd, Mead and Company, 1971), p. 19.

29. Amundsen, "Physician's Obligation," p. 24.

30. Amundsen, "Medical Ethics, History of," s.v. "Medieval Europe: Fourth to Sixteenth Century," in *Encyclopedia of Bioethics*, 4 vols., ed. Warren T. Reich (New York: The Free Press, 1978):3:945.

31. Ibid.

32. Henry E. Sigerist, *On the History of Medicine*, ed. Felix Marti-Ibañez (New York: MD Publications, 1960), p. 29; idem, "The History of Medical Licensure," in *On the Sociology of Medicine*, ed. Milton I. Roemer (New York: MD Publications, 1960), p. 311; and Friedson, *Profession of Medicine*, p. 19.

33. Sigerist, "History of Medical," p. 311.

34. Vern Bullough and Bonnie Bullough, "A Brief History of Medical Practice," in *Medical Men and their Work: A Sociological Reader*, ed. Eliot Friedson and Judith Lorber (Chicago: Aldine-Atherton, Inc., 1972), p. 91; Erwin H. Ackerknecht, *A Short History of Medicine* (New York: The Ronald Press, 1968), p. 92.

35. Sigerist, *On the History*, p. 29.

36. Vern Bullough, "The Term 'Doctor,'" *Journal of the History of Medicine and Allied Sciences* XVIII(1963):285.

37. Eliot Friedson, *Professional Dominance: The Social Structure of Medical Care* (New York: Atherton Press, Inc., 1970), p. 83.

38. Cited in Sigerist, "History of Medical," p. 312; cf. John P. Dolan and William N. Adams-Smith, *Health and Society: A Documentary History of Medicine* (New York: The Seabury Press, 1978), p. 72.

39. Frederick II, "Medieval Law for the Regulation of the Practice of Medicine," in *Ethics in Medicine: Historical Perspectives and Contemporary Concerns*, ed. Stanley Joel Reiser, Arthur J. Dyck, and William J. Curran (Cambridge, Mass.: MIT Press, 1977), pp. 10–12.

40. Ibid., p. 11.

41. Ackerknecht, *A Short History*, p. 92.

42. See Robert M. Veatch, *Value-Freedom in Science and Technology* (Missoula, Montana: Scholars Press, 1976), pp. 52–54, for a fuller account of the claim that lay and professional actors are often more appropriately thought of as groups rather than individuals.

43. Stanley Hauerwas, "Abortion: Why the Arguments Fail," *Hospital Progress* 61 (January 1980):38–47.

Chapter 6

1. For more detailed accounts of this case see Robert M. Veatch, *Case Studies in Medical Ethics* (Cambridge, Mass.: Harvard University Press, 1977), pp. 131–35; and the original report in "General Medical Council: Disciplinary Committee," *British Medical Journal Supplement* no. 3542, (March 20, 1971), pp. 79–80.

2. The official *Handbook of Medical Ethics*, the revision of the British Medical Association's ethical positions that was published in 1980, seems to have reversed this requirement once again. Patient consent is not required, according to this version "when it is undesirable on medical grounds to seek a patient's consent." Arguably, medical problems (that is, psychological problems) could have occurred in Dr. Browne's case if Miss X's consent were sought. See British Medical Association, *The Handbook of Medical Ethics* (London: British Medical Association, 1980), p. 12.

3. The arguments against having a normative theory of ethics based exclusively on the principle of choosing the action that produces the best aggregate of consequences on balance have a long and rich history. For several of the more important examples see Immanuel Kant, *Groundwork of the Metaphysics of Morals*, trans. and analyzed by H.J. Paton (New York: Harper and Row, 1964); W.D. Ross, *The Right and the Good* (Oxford: Oxford University Press, 1930); John Rawls, *A Theory of Justice* (Cambridge, Mass.: Harvard University Press, 1971; and J.J.C. Smart and Bernard Williams, *Utilitarianism: For and Against* (Cambridge: At the University Press, 1973). Among the better secondary sources summarizing the controversy are Richard B. Brandt, *Ethical Theory* (Englewood Cliffs, N.J.: Prentice-Hall, 1959), pp. 380–406; and Paul W. Taylor, *Principles of Ethics: An Introduction* (Encino, Calif.: Dickenson Publishing Co., 1975), pp. 55–113. The discussion in this volume presumes knowledge of this important history of normative ethical theory.

4. I first developed this analysis in Robert M. Veatch, "The Hippocratic Ethic: Consequentialism, Individualism, and Paternalism," in *No Rush to Judgment: Essays on Medical Ethics*, ed. David H. Smith and Linda M. Bernstein (Bloomington, Ind.: The Poynter Center, 1978), pp. 238–64.

5. See Daniel Callahan, "The WHO Definition of Health," *Hastings Center Studies* 1, no. 3 (1973): 59–88 for a critique of the WHO's definition of health that expresses a concern similar to the one developed here.

6. Ludwig Edelstein, *Ancient Medicine: Selected Papers of Ludwig Edelstein* (Baltimore: Johns Hopkins University Press, 1967), p. 23.

7. E. Capps, T.E. Page, and W.H.D. Rouse, eds., *Hippocrates*, 4 vols. (London: William Heinemann, 1923–31), vol. 1, trans. W.H.S. Jones, p. 165.

8. Ray W. Gifford, "Primum Non Nocere," *Journal of the American Medical Association* 238 (August 15, 1977): 589–90; Thomas Szasz, "The Moral Physician," *The Center Magazine* (March–April 1975): 2–9; Walter F. Tauber, "Whither *Nil Nocere*," *Journal of the American Medical Association* 227 (January 14, 1974): 202; Richard J. Duma, "First of All Do No Harm," *New England Journal of Medicine* 285 (November 25, 1971): 1258–59; Charles A. Schwartz, "*Primum Non Nocere* and Disability Certification," *New England Journal of Medicine* 294 (April 15, 1976): 907–8; and Steven R. Kaplan, Richard A. Greenwald, and Arvey I. Rogers, "Neglected Aspects of Informed Consent," *New England Journal of Medicine* 296 (May 12, 1977):1127 are all typical examples. The latter two are examples of a subclass. They are both letters to the editor that end with the Latin *primum non nocere* standing alone, implying that their argument is clinched by this appeal.

9. See Tom L. Beauchamp and James F. Childress, *Principles of Biomedical Ethics* (New York: Oxford University Press, 1979), pp. 97–167.

10. Ross, *Right and the Good*, p. 22; and W. David Ross, *Foundations of Ethics* (Oxford University Press, 1939), p. 75.

11. *Hippocrates*, 1:165. The same change occurs in the definitive French translation by E. Littre, to which Jones had access when producing the English version.

12. Albert R. Jonsen, "Do No Harm: Axiom of Medical Ethics," in *Philosophical Medical Ethics: Its Nature and Significance*, ed. Stuart F. Spicker and H. Tristram Engelhardt, Jr. (Boston: D. Reidel Publishing Co., 1977), p. 27; see also Albert R. Jonsen, "Do No Harm," *Annals of Internal Medicine* 88 (1978): 827–32.

13. C. Sandulescu, "*Primum non nocere*: Philological Commentaries on a Medical Aphorism," *Acta-Antiqua Hungarica* 13(1965):359–88.

14. Ibid., p. 360.

15. Gifford, "*Primum Non Nocere*," p. 590.

16. Talcott Parsons, Renée C. Fox, and Victor M. Lidz, "The 'Gift of Life' and its Reciprocation," *Social Research* 39 (1972): 395.

17. Ibid.

18. Jesse Dukeminier and David Sanders, "Organ Transplantation: A Proposal for Routine Salvaging of Cadaver Organs," *New England Journal of Medicine* 279 (August 22, 1968): 419.

19. Quoted in Herman Feifel, ed., *The Meaning of Death* (New York: McGraw-Hill Book Company, 1959), p. 262.

20. Franklin H. Epstein, "No, It's Our Duty to Keep Patients Alive," *Medical Economics* (April 2, 1973):114.

21. Marjorie J. McKusick, *Delaware Medical Journal* 45 (February 1973):31 (editorial).

22. Edelstein, *Ancient Medicine*, pp. 9–10, especially the references discussed in footnote 28.

23. Darrel W. Amundsen, "The Physician's Obligation to Prolong Life: A Medical Duty without Classical Roots," *Hastings Center Report* 8 (August 1978):23–30.

24. Gerald Gruman, *A History of Ideas About the Prolongation of Life* (Philadelphia: Transactions of the American Philosophical Society, 1966).

25. Francis Bacon, "De augmentis scientiarum," in *The Philosophical Works of Francis Bacon*, ed. J. M. Robertson (Freeport, N.Y.: Books for Libraries Press, 1970), pp. 485, 489.

26. Ibid., p. 487.

27. Ibid.

28. Michael Halberstam, "A Startling Proposal," *Redbook*, April 1970 (as quoted in Herbert Ratner, "Humanity of the Fetus: Commonwealth v. Brunelle II. Commentary," *Child and Family* 9, no. 2 [1970]: 159–83).

29. See Norman K. Brown, Roger J. Bulger, Harold Laws, and Donovan J. Thompson, "The Preservation of Life," *Journal of the American Medical Association* 211 (January 5, 1970):76–81; Russell Noyes and Terry A. Travis, "The Care of Terminally Ill Patients," *Archives of Internal Medicine* 132 (October 1973); 607–11; Diana Crane, "Decisions to Treat Critically Ill Patients: A Comparison of Social versus Medical Considerations," *Milbank Memorial Quarterly* (Winter 1975): 1–33; Anthony Shaw, Judson G. Randolph, and Barbara Manard, "Ethical Issues in Pediatric Surgery: A National Survey of Pediatricians and Pediatric Surgeons," *Pediatrics* 60 (October 2, 1977): 588–99; Carolyn Winget, Frederic T. Knapp, and Rosalie C. Yeaworth, "Attitudes Towards Euthanasia," *Journal of Medical Ethics* 3 (March 1977): 18–25.

30. See Howard Hiatt, "Protecting the Medical Commons: Who Is Responsible," *New England Journal of Medicine* 293 (July 31, 1975): 235–41; Theodore Cooper, "In the Public Interest," *New England Journal of Medicine* 300 (May 24, 1979): 1185–88.

31. Jeremy Bentham, *An Introduction to the Principles of Morals and Legislation* (New York: Hafner Publishing Co., 1948); John Stuart Mill, *Utilitarianism*, ed., Oskar Priest (New York: Bobbs-Merrill, 1957); Henry Sidgwick, *The Methods of Ethics* (New York: Dover Publications, 1966); G. E. Moore, *Principia Ethica* (Cambridge: At the University Press, 1966); David Lyons, *Forms and Limits of Utilitariansim* (Oxford: Clarendon Press, 1965); Michael D. Bayles, ed., *Contemporary Utilitarianism* (Garden City, N.Y.: Anchor Books, 1968).

32. See Fred Feldman, *Introductory Ethics* (Englewood Cliffs, N.J.: Prentice-Hall, 1978), chap. 5, pp. 61–79; John Rawls, "Two Concepts of Rules," *The Philosophical Review*, vol. LXIV (1955): 3–32; William K. Frankena, *Ethics* (Englewood Cliffs, N.J.: Prentice-Hall, 1973), see pp. 39–43; Lyons, *Forms and Limits*, pp. 119–60; Richard B. Brandt, *A Theory of the Good and the Right* (Oxford: Clarendon Press, 1979).

33. My treatment here is a very simplified version of the argument given by David Lyons in *Forms and Limits,* pp. 119–60.

Chapter 7

1. This case originally appeared in the case study series of the *Hastings Center Report* as Harvey Kuschner, Daniel Callahan, Eric J. Cassell, and Robert M. Veatch, "The Homosexual Husband and Physician Confidentiality," *Hastings Center Report* 7 (April 1977): 15–17.
2. Immanuel Kant, *Groundwork of the Metaphysic of Morals,* trans. and analysed by H.J. Paton (New York: Harper and Row, 1964).
3. Ibid., p. 90.
4. Richard M. Magraw, "Social and Medical Contracts: Explicit and Implicit," in *Hippocrates Revisited,* ed. Roger J. Bulger (New York: Medcom Press, 1973), pp. 148–157; Edmund D. Pellegrino, "Toward an Expanded Medical Ethic: The Hippocratic Ethic Revisited," in *Hippocrates Revisited,* pp. 133–47; Howard Brody, "The Physician-Patient Contract: Legal and Ethical Aspects," *Journal of Legal Medicine* (July–August 1976): 25–29.
5. See Westchester County (N.Y.), Department of Social Services, Administrative Memorandum No. 332, July 7, 1980. In spite of the fact that the state guidelines are only proposed, the memorandum carries the notation it is effective upon receipt.

Chapter 8

1. Aurelius Augustine, *The Free Choice of the Will,* in *Saint Augustine: The Teacher, The Free Choice of the Will, and Grace and Free Will,* trans. Robert T. Russell, Fathers of the Church Series, vol. 59 (Washington, D.C.: Catholic University of America Press, 1968), pp. 65–141; and *The Enchiridion* (Chicago: Henry Regnery Co., 1961); Erasmus-Luther, *Discourse on Free Will,* ed. and trans. Ernest F. Winter (New York: Frederick Ungar Publishing Co., 1961); Jonathan Edwards, *Freedom of the Will,* ed. Paul Ramsey (New Haven: Yale University Press, 1957).
2. Immanuel Kant, *Groundwork of the Metaphysic of Morals,* trans. and analysed by H.J. Paton (New York: Harper and Row, 1964), p. 95.
3. Ibid., pp. 98–99.
4. Patrick H. Nowell-Smith, "Free Will and Moral Responsibility," *Mind* 57 (1948):45–61; cf. C.A. Campbell, "Is 'Freewill' a Pseudoproblem?" *Mind* 60 (1951):441–65.
5. Robert Nozick, *Anarchy, State, and Utopia* (New York: Basic Books, 1974), pp. 30–35.
6. John Rawls, *A Theory of Justice* (Cambridge, Mass.: Harvard University Press, 1971), p. 60; cf. pp. 195–257.
7. Joel Feinberg, *Social Philosophy* (Englewood Cliffs, N.J.: Prentice-Hall, 1973), pp. 59–61, 94–96; Michael D. Bayles, *Principles of Legislation* (Detroit: Wayne State University Press, 1978), pp. 92–93, 189–91.
8. Joel Feinberg, *Social Philosophy* (Englewood Cliffs, N.J.: Prentice-Hall, 1973), p. 33.
9. See Gerald Dworkin, "Paternalism," *Monist* 56 (January 1972): 64–84; idem, "Paternalism," in *Morality and the Law,* ed. Richard Wasserstrom (Belmont, Calif.: Wadsworth Publishing Co., 1971), pp. 107–26; Bernard Gert and Charles M. Culver, "Paternalistic Behavior," *Philosophy and Public Affairs* 6 (Fall 1976): 45–57; idem, "The Justification of Paternalism" *Ethics* 89 (January 1979): 199–210; and idem, "The Justification of Paternalism," in *Medical Responsibility: Paternalism, Informed Consent, and Euthanasia,* ed. Wade L. Robinson and Michael S. Pritchard (Clifton, N.J.: The Humana Press, 1979), pp. 1–14.
10. Dworkin, "Paternalism," in *Morality,* pp. 119–20.
11. Joel Feinberg, "Voluntary Euthanasia and the Inalienable Right to Life," *Philosophy and Public Affairs* 7 (Winter 1978):93–123; William K. Frankena, "Natural and Inalienable Rights," *Philosophical Review* 64 (1955): 212–32.
12. John Stuart Mill, *On Liberty* (New York: The Liberal Arts Press, 1956), p. 13.
13. Ibid., p. 125.

14. For earlier accounts of the doctrine of consent that follows see Robert M. Veatch, "Ethical Principles in Medical Experimentation," in *Ethical and Legal Issues of Social Experimentation*, ed. Alice M. Rivlin and P. Michael Timpane (Washington, D.C.: The Brookings Institution, 1975), pp. 21–59; idem, "Why Get Consent," *Hospital Physician* (December 1975): 30–31; and idem, "Three Theories of Informed Consent: Philosophical Foundations and Policy Implications," in *The Belmont Report—Ethical Principles and Guidelines for the Protection of Human Subjects of Research*, ed. National Commission for the Protection of Human Subjects of Biomedical and Behavioral Research (Washington, D.C.: U.S. Government Printing Office, DHEW Publication no. [OS] 78–0014), pp. 26-1 through 26-66.

15. Norman C. Fost, "A Surrogate System for Informed Consent," *Journal of the American Medical Association* 233 (August 18, 1975):800–803; Richard Winer, Robert M. Veatch, Victor W. Sidel, and Morton Spivack, "Informed Consent: The Use of Lay Surrogates to Determine How Much Information Should be Transmitted" (unpublished manuscript).

16. See Richard Winer et al., "Informed Consent," p. 16; see also Robert M. Veatch, "Three Theories of Informed Consent," pp. 26–51.

17. This, I hope, is a clearer statement of the reason why researchers might exclude from research those who want less information than is necessary for responsible decisionmaking. It is not that subjects should not be free to decline information; of course they should be. Rather, it is an obligation of the researcher to minimize risks and avoid dealing with uninformed subjects when possible, breaking the research-subject relationship if necessary. See Tom L. Beauchamp and James F. Childress, *Principles of Biomedical Ethics* (New York: Oxford University Press, 1979), p. 78.

18. For a review of the debate and the court cases, see Robert M. Veatch, *Death, Dying, and the Biological Revolution* (New Haven: Yale University Press, 1976).

19. Ibid., pp. 84–86; Sissela Bok, "Personal Directions for Care at the End of Life," *New England Journal of Medicine* 295 (August 12, 1976):368.

20. Robert M. Veatch, "Courts, Committees, and Caring," *American Medical News* (May 23, 1980):1, 2, 11–13 (Impact Section); and idem, "Guardian Refusal of Life-Saving Medical Procedures: The Standard of Reasonableness" (unpublished manuscript).

Chapter 9

1. Immanuel Kant, "On The Supposed Right To Tell Lies from Benevolent Motives," trans. T.K. Abbott, in Kant's *Critique of Practical Reason and Other Works on the Theory of Ethics* (London: Longmans, 1909), pp. 361–365.

2. Ibid., p. 365.

3. Ibid., p. 363.

4. W. D. Ross, *The Right and the Good* (Oxford: Oxford University Press, 1930), p. 21.

5. Charles Fried, *Right and Wrong* (Cambridge, Mass.: Harvard University Press, 1978), p. 67.

6. Henry Sidgwick, *The Methods of Ethics* (New York: Down Publications, 1966), p. 316.

7. Ibid.

8. For a review of the literature and the arguments used by the medical professionals, see my earlier discussion in Robert M. Veatch, *Death, Dying, and the Biological Revolution* (New Haven: Yale University Press, 1976), chap. 6, pp. 204–48.

9. Robert M. Veatch, *Case Studies in Medical Ethics* (Cambridge, Mass.: Harvard University Press, 1977), pp. 141–47.

10. Robert M. Veatch, "The Unexpected Chromosome . . . A Counselor's Dilemma," *The Hastings Center Report* 2 (February 1972): 8–9.

11. Robert M. Veatch, *Case Studies in Medical Ethics*, pp. 280–82; cf. Stanley Milgram, *Obedience to Authority* (New York: Harper and Row, 1974).

12. American Medical Association, "Text of the American Medical Association's New Principles of Medical Ethics," *American Medical News* (August 1–8, 1980): 9.

13. See Robert M. Veatch and Ernest Tai, "Talking About Death: Patterns of Lay and Professional Change," *Annals of the American Academy of Political and Social Science* 447 (January 1980): 29–45, for a summary of the recent shift in professional attitudes.

14. L.C. Park and L. Covi, "Nonblind Placebo Trial: An Exploration of Neurotic Outpatients' Responses to Placebo When Its Inert Content is Disclosed," *Archives of General Psychiatry* 12 (1965):336; see also Robert M. Veatch, "Three Theories of Informed Consent: Philosophical Foundations and Policy Implications," in *The Belmont Report*, Appendix, vol. 2, pp. 26-48 through 26-49.

15. Tom L. Beauchamp and James F. Childress, *Principles of Biomedical Ethics* (New York: Oxford University Press, 1979), pp. 207-8.

16. Sissela Bok, "The Ethics of Giving Placebos," *Scientific American* 231 (November 1974): 17-23; Howard Brody, "Persons and Placebos: Philosophical Dimensions of the Placebo Effect" (Ph.D. diss., Michigan State University, 1977); Park and Covi, "Nonblind Placebo Trial"; Beth Simmons, "Problems in Deceptive Medical Procedures: An Ethical and Legal Analysis of the Administration of Placebos," *Journal of Medical Ethics* 4 (December 1978): 172-181.

17. See Leonard Berkowitz, "Some Complexities and Uncertainties Regarding the Ethicality of Deception in Research With Human Subjects," *The Belmont Report*, Appendix, Vol. II, pp. 24-1 through 24-34.

18. Israel Shenker, "Test of Samaritan Parable: Who Helps the Helpless?" *New York Times*, April 10, 1971, p. L-25; Bibb Latane and John M. Darley, *The Unresponsive Bystander: Why Doesn't He Help?* (New York: Appleton-Century-Crofts, 1970).

19. Ted R. Vaughan, "Governmental Intervention in Social Research: Political and Ethical Dimensions in Wichita Jury Recordings," in *Ethics, Politics, and Social Research*, ed. Gideon Sjoberg (Cambridge, Mass.: Schenkman Pub. Co., 1971), pp. 50-77.

20. Leon Festinger, H.W. Riecken, and Stanley Schachter, *When Prophecy Fails* (New York: Harper and Row, 1956).

21. Diana Baumrind, "Nature and Definition of Informed Consent in Research Involving Deception," *The Belmont Report* Appendix, Vol. II, pp. 23-1 through 23-71.

22. Robert M. Veatch, "Three Theories of Informed Consent," pp. 26-48 through 26-52.

23. Alan Soble, "Deception in Social Science Research: Is Informed Consent Possible?" *Hastings Center Report* 8 (October 1978): 40-46.

24. Robert M. Veatch, *Death, Dying*, pp. 222-29.

25. Mark Siegler, "Pascal's Wager and the Hanging of Crepe," *New England Journal of Medicine* 293 (October 23, 1975): 853-57.

26. See Jonathan Bennett, "Whatever The Consequences," *Analysis* 26 (1966): 83-102; James Rachels, "Active and Passive Euthanasia," *New England Journal of Medicine* 292 (January 9, 1975):78-80; idem, "Killing and Starving to Death," *Philosophy* 54 (April 1979):159-71; Daniel Dinello, "On Killing and Letting Die," *Analysis* 31 (January 1971):83-86.

27. See Bennett, "Whatever the Consequences"; Judith J. Thomson, "Killing, Letting Die and the Trolley Problem," *The Monist* 59 (April 1976): 204-17; Tom L. Beauchamp, "A Reply to Rachels on Active and Passive Euthanasia," in *Social Ethics: Morality and Social Policy*, ed. T.A. Mappes and J.S. Zembaty (New York: McGraw-Hill, 1977), pp. 67-75; Philippa Foot, "Euthanasia," *Philosophy and Public Affairs* 6 (Winter 1977): 85-112; Tom L. Beauchamp and Arnold L. Davidson, "The Definition of Euthanasia," *Journal of Medicine and Philosophy* 4 (September 1979): 294-312.

28. George P. Fletcher, "Prolonging Life," *Washington Law Review* 42 (1967): 999-1016; idem, "Legal Aspects of the Decision Not to Prolong Life," *Journal of the American Medical Association* 203 (January 1, 1968): 65-68.

29. In an omission, normally almost all other actions the actor could have committed would lead to the same consequences for the other party, while one or a very few other actions would have led to a different outcome for the party. When I omit to start a life-saving respirator (and spend the time caring for another patient), virtually everything else I could have done would have led to the same outcome for the patient. If I inject potassium chloride, virtually everything else I could have done would have led to a different outcome for the patient. The same is true in the case of lying and withholding the truth. If I lie, almost anything else I could have done would have led to a different impression on the one lied to; if, however, I simply withhold the truth, spending my time doing something else such that a patient is misled, virtually anything else I could have done with that time would have led to the same confused perception on the part of

the patient. This is the analysis that has led Jonathan Bennett to distinguish between omissions and commissions. He concludes that there is no morally significant difference between the case where many alternatives would have led to the same result and where only a few would have led to that result, and that therefore the distinction between commission and omission is not morally significant (see Bennett, "Whatever the Consequences"). Daniel Dinello has shown, however, that though there are some cases in which virtually any move made would lead to death (what Bennett considers an omission), all would agree the move that actually is made is a killing. Dinello claims, correctly, I believe, that this bare difference in the number of alternative moves is not the morally relevant difference (see Dinello, "On Killing and Letting Die").

Chapter 10

1. This case originally appeared in the series, "Case Studies in Medical Ethics," as Hunter D. Leake, III, "Active Euthanasia with Parental Consent," *Hastings Center Report* 9 (October 1979):19.
2. James Rachels, "Active and Passive Euthanasia," *New England Journal of Medicine* 292 (January 9, 1975):78–80; Jonathan Bennett, "Whatever the Consequences," *Analysis* 26 (1966):83–102; James Rachels, "Killing and Starving to Death," *Philosophy* 54 (April 1979):159–71.
3. The argument is a variant on that used by Judith Thomson in "Killing, Letting Die and the Trolley Problem," *The Monist* 59 (April 1976):204–17.
4. Philippa Foot, "Active Euthanasia with Parental Consent," *Hastings Center Report* 9 (October 1979):20–21.
5. Marvin Kohl, "Voluntary Beneficent Euthanasia," in *Beneficent Euthanasia*, ed. Marvin Kohl (Buffalo, N.Y.: Prometheus Books, 1975), pp. 130–44.
6. R.B. Zachary, "Life With Spina Bifida," *British Medical Journal* (December 3, 1977):1460–62.
7. Tom L. Beauchamp, "A Reply to Rachels on Active and Passive Euthanasia," in *Medical Responsibility: Paternalism, Informed Consent, and Euthanasia*, ed. Wade L. Robison and Michael S. Pritchard (Clifton, N.J.: The Humana Press, 1979):181–94.
8. See Paul J. Menzel, "Are Killing and Letting Die Morally Different in Medical Contexts?" *Journal of Medicine and Philosophy* 4 (September 1979):269–93.
9. William K. Frankena, "The Ethics of Respect for Life," in *Respect for Life: in Medicine, Philosophy, and the Law*, ed. Owsei Temkin, William K. Frankena, and Sanford H. Kadish (Baltimore: Johns Hopkins University Press, 1977), pp. 24–62.
10. Immanuel Kant, *Groundwork of the Metaphysic of Morals*, trans. and analysed by H. J. Paton (New York: Harper and Row, 1964).
11. Charles E. Curran, "Abortion: Contemporary Debate in Philosophical and Religious Ethics," *Encyclopedia of Bioethics*, 4 vols., ed. Warren T. Reich (New York: The Free Press, 1978), 1:23; see also Richard A. McCormick, "Ambiguity in Moral Choice," in *Doing Evil to Achieve Good: Moral Choice in Conflict Situations*, ed. Richard McCormick and Paul Ramsey (Chicago: Loyola University Press, 1978), p. 7; Patrick Finney and Patrick O'Brien, *Moral Problems in Hospital Practice: A Practical Handbook* (St. Louis: B. Herder Book Co., 1956), p. 18; David F. Kelly, *The Emergence of Roman Catholic Medical Ethics in North America*, Texts and Studies in Religion, no. 3 (New York: The Edwin Mellen Press, 1979), pp. 244–74; John P. Kenny, *Principles of Medical Ethics* (Westminster, Md.: The Newman Press, 1962), pp. 201–4, 153–54; Thomas J. O'Donnell, *Morals in Medicine* (Westminster, Md.: The Newman Press, 1956), pp. 39–44; idem, *Medicine and Christian Morality* (New York: Alba House, 1976), pp. 27–31; Philippa Foot, "The Problem of Abortion and the Doctrine of the Double Effect," *Oxford Review* 5 (1967):5–15.
12. For a good summary of the criticism, see William K. Frankena, "McCormick and the Traditional Distinction," in *Doing Evil to Achieve Good: Moral Choice in Conflict Situations*, ed. Richard McCormick and Paul Ramsey (Chicago: Loyola University Press, 1978), pp. 145–64.
13. Glenn C. Graber, "Some Questions About Double Effect," *Ethics in Science and Medicine* 6 (1979):65–84. A similar argument is being mounted by those within Catholic moral theology who are offering critical reformulations of the traditional double effect

principle. Much of this literature, however, fails to maintain a sharp distinction between directness and intentionality. It seems that the clear meaning implies that the two terms are analytically separate. Directness has to do with the position in the causal chain. A direct effect, according to this formulation, comes intermediately in the causal chain between the action and the intended effect so that the bad effect is not *directly* between the act and the intended effect. Intentionality, on the other hand, would appear to be independent of position in the causal chain, focusing instead on the motive or state of mind of the actor.

Much of the literature in Catholic moral theology, however, assumes that if something is a means to an end (and therefore directly in the causal chain) it is necessarily intended. Thus the third of the four criteria defining an indirect effect says, "If the evil effect is not at least equally immediate causally with the good effect, then it becomes a means to the good effect and intended as such." This equation of means directly in the line of causation with intention is what is worth questioning. (See McCormick, "Ambiguity in Moral Choice," p. 7.)

It seems clear, however, that the mere fact that an effect is directly in the line of causation (a means) does not necessarily make it intended. There must be such a thing as an unintended direct effect. For example, we often give drugs for an intended beneficial effect not knowing precisely the mechanism of action. In effect, the causal chain passes through a black box. If one of the intermediate steps "inside the black box" turned out to be an evil effect unknown at the time to anyone involved, it would certainly be a direct effect (a means to the intended end) and yet not itself intended.

It seems that what is called for is a disentangling of directness and intentionality so that the relevance of each to whether an act is right or wrong can be assessed. Instead, many who are currently modifying the principle of double effect, especially in Catholic moral theology, have taken another course. They have challenged the legitimacy of subdividing miscroscopically a complex chain of events into discrete elements in which the earlier events are viewed as the means to the later events. Some complex causal chains are indivisible. In such cases some thinkers are now arguing that the entire indivisible event should be viewed as of equal psychological immediateness. (See Cornelius Van der Poel, "The Principle of Double Effect," in *Absolutes in Moral Theology*, ed. by Charles Curran (Washington, D.C.: Corpus Books, 1968), pp. 186–210; and Germain Grisez, *Abortion: The Myths, the Realities, and the Arguments* (Washington, D.C.: Corpus Books, 1970), p. 340.

Roughly the position seems to be that anything that is direct is intended, but in certain cases (those that are indivisible chains of events) some that are somewhat earlier in the direct causal line will not be viewed as direct effects. That permits them potentially to be unintended. That means, however, that criterion three collapses into criterion two, that of intentionality. It seems what they really want to say is that even though the bad effect is direct, it is unintended. As we shall see, however, intentionality may not be decisive in evaluating the morality of actions.

14. J.M. Hunt, et al., "Patients with Protracted Pain: A Survey Conducted at the London Hospital," *Journal of Medical Ethics* (June 1977): 3:72; Cecily M. Saunders, "A Death in the Family: A Professional View," *British Medical Journal* (January 6, 1973): 30–31; idem, "The Treatment of Intractable Pain in Terminal Cancer," *Proceedings of the Royal Society of Medicine* 56 (1963):195; D.S. Shimm, et al., "Medical Management of Chronic Cancer Pain," *Journal of the American Medical Association* 241 (June 1979): 2408; R.G. Twycross, "Diseases of the Central Nervous System: Relief of Terminal Pain," *British Medical Journal* 4 (October 25, 1975): 212.

15. Liselotte B. Watson, "Status of Medical and Religious Personnel in International Law," *JAG Journal* XX, no. 2 (September–October–November 1965): 46.

16. Ibid, p. 54.

17. H. Tristram Engelhardt, Jr., "The Beginnings of Personhood: Philosophical Considerations," *Perkins Journal* 27 (1973): 20–27; idem, "Ethical Issues in Aiding the Death of Young Children," *Beneficent Euthanasia*, ed. Marvin Kohl (Buffalo: Prometheus Books, 1975), pp. 180–92; idem, "Ontology and Ontogeny," *Monist* 60 (Jan. 1977): 16–28; Joseph F. Fletcher, "Four Indicators of Humanhood: The Enquiry Matures," *Hastings Center Report* 4, no. 6 (1974): 1–4; idem, "Indicators of Humanhood: A Tentative Profile," *Hastings Center Report* 2, no. 5 (1972): 1–4; idem, "Medicine and the Nature of Man," in *The*

Teaching of Medical Ethics, ed. R.M. Veatch, W.W. Gaylin, and Councilman Morgan (Hastings-on-Hudson, N.Y.: Institute of Society, Ethics and the Life Sciences, 1973), pp. 47–58; Richard A. McCormick, "To Save or Let Die: The Dilemma of Modern Medicine," *Journal of the American Medical Association* 229 (July 8, 1974): 172–76; Michael Tooley, "Abortion and Infanticide," *Philosophy and Public Affairs* 2 (Fall 1972):37–65; idem, "Decisions to Terminate Life and the Concept of Person," in *Ethical Issues Relating to Life and Death*, ed. John Ladd (New York: Oxford University Press, 1979), pp. 62–93; Lawrence C. Becker, "Human Being: The Boundaries of the Concept," *Philosophy and Public Affairs* 4 (1975): 334–59.

18. Michael Tooley, "Decisions to Terminate Life and the Concept of Person," p. 91.

19. Robert M. Veatch, "The Whole–Brain-Oriented Concept of Death: An Outmoded Philosophical Formulation," *Journal of Thanatology* 3 (1975):13–30; idem, "The Definition of Death: Problems for Public Policy," a paper prepared for the President's Commission for the Study of Ethical Problems in Medicine and Biomedical Research (June 1980); idem, *Death, Dying, and the Biological Revolution* (New Haven: Yale University Press, 1976).

20 William May, "Attitudes Toward the Newly Dead," *Hastings Center Studies*, 1, no. 1 (1973):3–13.

21. Alexander M. Capron and Leon R. Kass, "A Statutory Definition of the Standards for Determining Human Death: An Appraisal and a Proposal," *University of Pennsylvania Law Review* 121 (1972): 87–118; Joseph Fletcher, "Our Shameful Waste of Human Tissue," in *Updating Life and Death*, ed. Donald R. Cutler (Boston: Beacon Press, 1969); pp. 1–27; Bernard Häring, *Medical Ethics* (Notre Dame, Indiana: Fides Publishers, 1973), pp. 131–36; Dallas M. High, "Death: Its Conceptual Elusiveness," *Soundings* (Winter 1972): 438–58: Paul Ramsey, *The Patient as Person* (New Haven, Conn.: Yale University Press, 1970), pp. 59–164.

22. Sheff D. Alinger, "Medical Death," *Baylor Law Review* 27 (Winter 1975): 22–26; William H. Smett, "Brain Death," *New England Journal of Medicine* 299 (1978): 410–11; Häring, *Medical Ethics*; Veatch, "The Whole–Brain-Oriented Concept."

23. Roe v. Wade, 410 U.S. 113 (1973), pp. 163–65; Sissela Bok, "Ethical Problems of Abortion," *Hastings Center Studies* 2 (January 1974):44–45.

24. Judith Jarvis Thomson, "A Defense of Abortion," *Philosophy and Public Affairs* 1 (1971):57, 64.

25. Peter Singer, *Animal Liberation: A New Ethics for Our Treatment of Animals* (New York: A New York Review Book, Random House, 1975), pp. 185–89.

26. Singer, *Animal Liberation*, pp. 1–26; Tom Regan and Peter Singer, eds., *Animal Rights and Human Obligations* (Englewood Cliffs, New Jersey: Prentice-Hall, 1976), pp. 148–62.

27. Luther J. Carter, "NEI Votes to Protect Cold-Blooded Animals," *Science* 206 (December 21, 1979):1383.

Chapter 11

1. Robert M. Veatch, *Case Studies in Medical Ethics* (Cambridge, Mass.: Harvard University Press, 1977), pp. 200–201.

2. Aristotle, *Nicomachean Ethics*, tr. Martin Ostwald (Indianapolis: Bobbs-Merrill, 1962), 5:1–2, pp. 112–17.

3. Ibid., p. 118.

4. Robert Nozick, *Anarchy, State, and Utopia* (New York: Basic Books, 1974), pp. 150–53.

5. Robert M. Sade, "Medical Care as a Right: A Refutation," *New England Journal of Medicine* 285 (December 2, 1971):1288–92; see also his "Concept of Rights: Philosophy and Application to Health Care," *Linacre Quarterly* (November 1979):330–44.

6. Nozick, *Anarchy*, pp. 26, 30, 33.

7. Jeremy Bentham, *An Introduction to the Principles of Morals and Legislation* (New York: Hafner Publishing Co., 1948).

8. John Stuart Mill, *Utilitarianism*, ed. Oskar Priest (New York: Bobbs-Merrill, 1957). For twentieth-century examples of this normative commitment, see G.E. Moore, *Principia*

Ethica (Cambridge: At the University Press, 1966); Henry Sidgwick, *The Methods of Ethics* (New York: Dover Publications, 1966); A.C. Ewing, *Ethics* (New York: The Free Press, 1952); and J.J.C. Smart and Bernard Williams, *Utilitarianism: For and Against* (Cambridge: At the University Press, 1973). For good critical discussions of the position, see Richard B. Brandt, *Ethical Theory* (Englewood Cliffs, N.J.: Prentice-Hall, 1959), pp. 380–405, esp. pp. 396–400; Fred Feldman, *Introductory Ethics* (Englewood Cliffs, N.J.: Prentice-Hall, 1978), pp. 21–24, 30–47; Paul W. Taylor, *Principles of Ethics: An Introduction* (Encino, Cal.: Dickenson Publishing Co., 1975), pp. 55–81; David Lyons, *Forms and Limits of Utilitarianism* (Oxford: Clarendon Press, 1965); and Michael D. Bayles, *Contemporary Utilitarianism* (Garden City, New York: Anchor Books, 1968).

9. Bentham, *An Introduction to the Principles*, p. 386.

10. Mill, *Utilitarianism*, p. 71.

11. Known as "conformance utility," this is the amount of utility that would be produced by everyone's conforming to a rule or policy when in a situation governed by that rule or policy. This is not the kind of utility produced by everyone's *belief* in the rule or policy and not a measure of the utility produced by *all* acts performed by people if they were to conform to the rule. Conformance utility is only the utilities of acts that are done in accordance with certain rules; for example, the acts of promise keeping done in conformance to the rule of promise keeping. For a detailed discussion of this idea, see Feldman, *Introductory Ethics*, pp. 63–67.

12. This is the notion of "currency utility" or the measure of the amount of utility that would be produced by a moral code's wide acceptance in a society. According to Richard Brandt, a major supporter of this view, a moral code is a complete and consistent set of moral rules subscribed to by members of the society. If each rule in the moral code is subscribed to by at least ninety percent of the adult members of society, *and* a large proportion of the adults in society respond correctly to the rule regardless of whether other members subscribe to the rule, then the moral code of the society is said to be current. Thus the currency utility of a moral code is the amount of good per person produced within the society by the currency of the moral code. See Richard B. Brandt, "Toward a Credible Form of Utilitarianism," in *Contemporary Utilitarianism*, ed. Michael Bayles (Garden City, N.Y.: Anchor Books, 1968), pp. 143–86; idem, "Some Merits of One Form of Rule Utilitarianism," in *Utilitarianism: John Stuart Mill with Critical Essays*, ed. Samuel Gorovitz (Indianapolis: Bobbs-Merrill, 1971), pp. 324–44; and Feldman's analysis of Brandt's theory in *Introductory Ethics*, pp. 67–71.

13. John Rawls, "Two Concepts of Rules," in *Contemporary Utilitarianism*, ed. Michael Bayles; Bayles, ed. *Contemporary Utilitarianism*; and Lyons, *Forms and Limits*.

14. David Braybrooke, "The Choice Between Utilitarianisms," *American Philosophical Quarterly* 4 (1967):180–87.

15. This standard list of the counterintuitive implications of the utilitarianisms is taken from Feldman, *Introductory Ethics*, pp. 48–60.

16. Rawls, *A Theory of Justice* (Cambridge, Mass.: Harvard University Press, 1971), pp. 302, 542.

17. Ibid., pp. 79–80, 302. The full statement includes other important conditions: that the inequalities are to the *greatest* benefit of the least well off, that the arrangement is consistent with the just savings principle, and that "the inequalities are attached to offices and positions open to all under conditions of fair equality of opportunity."

18. Brian Barry, *The Liberal Theory of Justice: A Critical Examination of the Principle Doctrines in "A Theory of Justice" by John Rawls* (Oxford: Clarendon Press, 1973), p. 109; see also Robert L. Cunningham, "Justice: Efficiency or Fairness?" *Personalist* 52 (Spring 1971):253–81.

19. Barry, *The Liberal Theory*; idem, "Reflections on 'Justice as Fairness,' " in *Justice and Equality*, ed. H. Bedau (Englewood Cliffs, N.J.: Prentice-Hall, 1971), pp. 103–115; Bernard Williams, "The Idea of Equality," reprinted in Bedau, *Justice and Equality*, pp. 116–37; Christopher Ake, "Justice as Equality," *Philosophy and Public Affairs* 5 (Fall 1975):69–89; Robert M. Veatch, "What is 'Just' Health Care Delivery?" in *Ethics and Health Policy*, ed. R.M. Veatch and R. Branson (Cambridge, Mass.: Ballinger, 1976), pp. 127–53.

20. Barry, "Reflections," p. 113.

21. Rawls, *A Theory of Justice*, pp. 108–11.

22. See Ake, "Justice as Equality," for a careful development of the notion.

23. Bernard Williams, "Idea of Equality," pp. 121, 122, 124, 125.
24. Hugo A. Bedau, "Radical Egalitarianism," in *Justice and Equality*, ed. H.A. Bedau, p. 168.
25. Rawls, *Theory of Justice*, p. 538, note 9.
26. Sigmund Freud, *Group Psychology and the Analysis of the Ego*, rev. ed., trans. James Strachey (London: Hogarth Press, 1959), pp. 51f. (as cited in Rawls, *A Theory of Justice*, p. 439).
27. Nozick, *Anarchy*, p. 239.
28. Rawls, *Theory of Justice*, pp. 534-41.
29. Nozick's extensive footnote on page 239 of *Anarchy, State, and Utopia* reflects a conception of the love of equality rooted in envy that totally overlooks the possibility that the advantaged, as well as the disadvantaged, are among the lovers of equality. He defines several relevant psychological adjectives, including "envious" and "jealous" as well as "begrudging" and "spiteful," with reference to the relation between oneself and another regarding differences in possession. He works with the following table:

HE	YOU
1. Has it	have it
2. Has it	don't have it
3. Doesn't have it	have it
4. Doesn't have it	don't have it

He says you are envious when you prefer 4 to 2 while also preferring 3 to 4. You are jealous, he says, if you prefer 1 to 2 while being indifferent between 3 and 4. The egalitarian, the lover of equality of net welfare, however, will, insofar as justice is concerned, prefer 4 to 3 but be indifferent between 2 and 3. By Nozick's own definition, this person is not envious or jealous. The holder of such a position might be confused, but I suggest that he correctly perceives a fundamental relationship in the moral community, the inherent value of equality of welfare.

30. See Norman Daniels, "Rights to Health Care and Distributive Justice: Programmatic Worries," *Journal of Medicine and Philosophy* 4 (June, 1979): 180, for development of the notion that health care differs from other basic needs in this regard.
31. Barry, *Liberal Theory*, p. 55.
32. This is approximately "strategy one" as proposed by Daniels, in "Rights to Health Care." Daniels summarizes two arguments against this way of incorporating health care into the principle for distribution of social resources by indexing for unhealthiness status. First, he argues that such a strategy would "drain excessive resources into satisfaction of the special needs of some persons, perhaps to a point at which the rest of society is reduced to poverty" (p. 182). Here he follows Kenneth Arrow in the essay, "Some Ordinalist-Utilitarian Notes on Rawls's Theory of Justice," *Journal of Philosophy* 70, no. 9 (1973): 245-63. The model I shall suggest, however, allocates on the basis of reasonable social judgment a fixed portion of total social resources to the health care sphere (somewhere between 5 and 10 percent of GNP) and then allocates that fixed amount in proportion to the unhealthiness index. Under such an approach, it would be impossible to drain the system. A fair portion of social resources would be reserved for other basic needs.

Daniels cites a second objection: that adding health care into the construction of the index, and allowing its tradeoff against income and wealth, would force defenders of the strategy into the interpersonal comparisons of want satisfaction—which all involved in the debate agree we should avoid. I see no reason why that is the case, however. An objective health needs factor is added to the index. There is no reason why one would have to or should take into account interpersonal comparisons of want satisfaction. In any case, I am going to propose, largely for pragmatic reasons, that health care resource tradeoffs against income and wealth should be excluded.

Daniels correctly points out that adding an "unhealthiness factor" to the general index of net welfare introduces an element of indeterminacy (pp. 182-3). We will not know until we examine the particular features and preferences of a particular society exactly what portion of total social resources ought to go to health care. We do know, however, that a portion ought to be so expended and, given the historical consistency in the proportion of overall resources going to health care, we can even have a pretty good idea what the approximate proportion will be. This simply means that some of the specifics in determining what a fair proportion of total resources devoted to health care would be will have to be reserved to judgments made by real-life people.

33.   Ronald Green, "Health Care and Justice in Contract Theory Perspective," in *Ethics and Health Policy*, ed. R. M Veatch and R. Branson (Cambridge, Mass.: Ballinger, 1976), p. 112.

34.   Ibid., p. 117.

35.   Rawls, *A Theory of Justice*, p. 302; cf. p. 542.

36.   Daniels, "Rights to Health Care," p. 185.

37.   Of course, this is a distributional formula only insofar as the principle of justice is concerned. Considerations based on other basic principles may call for other adjustments in the distributional formula. For example, the principle of autonomy suggests that people ought to be free to expend extra effort in their leisure time in order to reap some marginal extra benefit. People should not be prohibited, for example, from spending their weekends tending their rose gardens even though they will then get a joy that others not similarly inclined will not get. It might be argued that this arrangement is still compatible wih the egalitarian principle of justice since it can be assumed, at least as a rough approximation, that the effort expended by the pro–rose-garden faction just about equals the benefit they gain. The principle of autonomy suggests, however, that extra welfare to those who tend their garden would be morally acceptable even if the result were a difference in net welfare. The implications for health care resource allocation of this autonomy-based correction in the principle of justice, which might produce small adjustments in real distributions of resources, will be discussed in the next section of this chapter.

38.   Likewise, small adjustments in the distribution principle might have to be made based on the principle of beneficence, in order to maximize efficient production and distribution. Small incentives creating inequalities in objective net welfare might be tolerated based on the principle of efficient production of benefits. I cannot imagine, however, that the variation would reasonably have to be larger than a range of one-half to double the median income.

39.   Fried, *Right and Wrong*, p. 127; idem, "Health Care; Cost Containment, Liberty," in *Ethics and Health Cost Containment*, ed. Robert M. Veatch and Ronald Bayer, forthcoming.

Fried proposes a guarantee of health services up to a "decent minimum" with discretionary buying beyond that minimum ("Equality and Rights in Medical Care," *Hastings Center Report* 6 [February 1976]: 32). He, however, makes this sound like a mere modification of the free-market system by implying that the floor of services guaranteed as the decent minimum would be quite low. Later he abandons this formulation entirely, favoring instead a scheme where all could use their fair share of general resources (money) to buy insurance up to the point where their preference for eliminating the burden of concern over the risk of encountering health care costs is exceeded by their preference for some other good (*Right and Wrong* [Cambridge, Mass.: Harvard University Press, 1978], pp. 126–7).

Even in the ideal world where income is distributed fairly, this poses serious problems. Aside from the burdens on the psyches of others who might have to suffer from witnessing the uncared-for medical crises of those who choose not to insure, Fried must face the fact that many people are in no position to exercise free choice to buy insurance. Children, for example, are not substantially autonomous, rational agents who could decide for or against long-term insurance purchases and they should not be subject to the whims of their parents' decisions about their insurance. Presumably, at least they would be entitled to societal protection with some right to health care services. Fried concedes they should get a minimum accrual of health care coverage. The parents of the congenitally afflicted are another group who might not be able to buy insurance even if they wanted to; or at the least they would have to pay a premium price. Justice would demand that they get supplemental aid to help pay for this extra cost. When children reach the age of majority one would expect that Fried would then give them the option to buy health insurance in greater or lesser amounts. But by that time, individuals are already in well-recognized risk groups either because of specific medical problems or because of their membership in social groups with known statistical risks. Would Fried also provide a supplement to subsidize the insurance purchases in order to compensate for those predictable differences in insurance cost? It may turn out that there is no such thing as the typical rational agent setting out to exercise his autonomy to buy or reject fairly priced insurance on the open market.

40. For an excellent summary of these arguments for in-kind aid and a powerful critique of them, see Paul Menzel, "Cash or In-Kind Aid?" in Menzel, *Costworthy Health Care* (unpublished).

41. This formula is first developed in Veatch, "What is 'Just' Health Care Delivery?"

42. John Fry and W.A.J. Farndale, *International Medical Care* (Wallingford. Pa.: Washington Square East, 1972), pp. 215–16; Milton I. Roemer, *Comparative National Policies on Health Care* (New York: Marcel Dekker, Inc., 1977), pp. 25–48; David Mechanic, "Growth of Medical Technology and Bureaucracy: Implications for Medical Care," *Milbank Memorial Fund Quarterly* 55 (Winter 1977):162; Victor Fuchs, "Economics, Health and Post-Industrial Society," *Milbank Memorial Fund Quarterly* 57 (Spring 1979):162.

43. I first raised the question in Peter Steinfels and Robert M. Veatch, "Who Should Pay for Smokers' Medical Care?" *Hastings Center Report* 4 (1974):8–10, and developed the analysis more fully in Veatch, "Voluntary Risks to Health: The Ethical Issues," *Journal of the American Medical Association* 243(January 4, 1980):50–55. Others pressing the question are Robert S. Morison, "Rights and Responsibilities: Redressing the Uneasy Balance," *Hastings Center Report* 4 (1974):1–4; Anne R. Somers and Mary C. Hayden, "Rights and Responsibilities in Prevention," *Health Education* 9 (1978):37–39; Daniel I. Wikler, "Persuasion and Coercion for Health: Ethical Issues in Government Efforts to Change Life-Styles," *Milbank Memorial Fund Quarterly* 56 (1978):303–38; and Tom Beauchamp, "The Regulation of Hazards and Hazardous Behaviors," *Health Education Monographs* 6 (1978):242–57.

44. Talcott Parsons, *The Social System* (New York: The Free Press, 1951), p. 437.

45. Nedra B. Belloc and Lester Breslow, "Relationship of Physical Status Health and Health Practices," *Preventive Medicine* 1 (1972):409–21; Nedra B. Belloc, "Relationship of Health Practices and Mortality," *Preventive Medicine* 2 (1973):67–81; Lester Breslow, "Prospects for Improving Health through Reducing Risk Factors," *Preventive Medicine* 7 (1978):449–58; and idem, "Cigarette Smoking and Health," *Public Health Reports* 95 (September–October 1980):451–55.

46. Beauchamp, "The Regulation of Hazards," p. 252.

47. "The Health Tax on Cigarettes," *Lancet* (December 17, 1977):1293–94; Marcia Kramer, "Self-Inflicted Disease: Who Should Pay for Care," *Journal of Health Politics, Policy, and Law* 4 (Summer 1979):140.

48. Beauchamp, "The Regulation of Hazards," p. 245.

49. Dan E. Beauchamp, "Alcoholism as Blaming the Alcoholic," *International Journal of Addiction* 11 (1976):41–52.

50. Leonard Syme and Ira Berkman, "Social Class, Susceptibility, and Sickness," *American Journal of Epidemiology* 104 (1976):1–8; P.W. Conover, "Social Class and Chronic Illness," *International Journal of Health Services* 3 (1973):357–68.

51. William Ryan, *Blaming the Victim* (New York: Vintage Books, 1971); Robert Crawford, "Sickness as Sin," *Health Policy Advisory Center Bulletin* 80 (1978):10–16; idem, "You Are Dangerous to Your Health," *Social Policy* 8 (1978):11–20; Dan E. Beauchamp, "Public Health as Social Justice," *Inquiry* 13 (1976):3–14.

52. American Medical Association, *Judicial Council Opinions and Reports* (Chicago: American Medical Association, 1971), p. vii.

53. Judy Alsofrom, "New Ethical Principles for Nation's Physicians Voted by AMA House," *American Medical News* (August 1–8, 1980):9.

54. Duncan Neuhauser and Ann M. Lewicki, "What Do We Gain from the Sixth Stool Guaiac?" *New England Journal of Medicine* 293 (July 31, 1975):226–28.

Chapter 12

1. Oklahoma Stat. Ann., title 22, n. 1014.

2. See William J. Curran and Ward Casscells, "The Ethics of Medical Participation in Capital Punishment by Intravenous Drug Injection," *New England Journal of Medicine* 302

(January 24, 1980):226–230, and George J. Annas, "Doctors and the Death Penalty" (editorial), *Medicolegal News* 8 (April 1980):17.

3.   Patrick Malone, "Death Row and the Medical Model," *Hastings Center Report* 9 (October 1979):5–6.

4.   Martin R. Gardner, "Executions and Indignities: An 8th Amendment's Assessment of Methods of Afflicting Capital Punishment," *Ohio State Law Journal* 39(1978):1–96–130.

5.   Malone, "Death Row," p. 5; Curran and Casscells, "The Ethics of Medical Participation," p. 227.

6.   Anastasia Toufixis, "Injection-Death Laws Pose Ethical Problems," *Medical Tribune* (January 18, 1978): 1.

7.   Malone, "Death Row," p. 5.

8.   Christopher J. Perry and Carleton B. Chapman, "Medical Participation in Capital Punishment," *New England Journal of Medicine* 302 (April 24, 1980):971.

9.   Lawrence Altman, "Pharmacy, Science and Society: The Ethics of Execution by Drugs," *U.S. Pharmacist* (August 1980), p. 72.

10.   "Idaho MDs Oppose Lethal Injection Role," *American Medical News* 23 (August 15, 1980): 18.

11.   Simon Berlyn, "Execution by the Needle," *New Scientist* 75 (September 15, 1977):676–77.

12.   John D. King, "Medical Participation in Capital Punishment," *New England Journal of Medicine* 302 (April 24, 1980):971.

13.   Civil libertarians have criticized medical execution by lethal injection on the grounds that all capital punishment is unacceptable. See Annas, "Doctors and the Death Penalty," and Henry Schwarzschild, "Lethal Injection and the Death Penalty," (letter). *Hastings Center Report* 10 (February 1980):4.

14.   "Death Injection Laws Cause Problems," *American Medical News* 23 (July 11, 1980):13.

15.   Richard B. Brandt, *Ethical Theory* (Englewood Cliffs, N.J.: Prentice-Hall, 1959), p. 404.

16.   John Rawls, *A Theory of Justice* (Cambridge, Mass.: Harvard University Press, 1971), pp. 42–45, 541–48.

17.   Ibid., p. 44.

18.   Immanuel Kant, *Groundwork of the Metaphysic of Morals*, trans. H.J. Paton (New York: Harper and Row, 1964), p. 67.

19.   Rawls himself makes a distinction between least advantaged and more advantaged groups advocating the inequalities permitted in his principles of justice, but only when he is discussing inequalities in the distribution of liberty. In order for such an inequality to be acceptable, it would, among other things, have to be "acceptable to those with the lesser liberty" (*A Theory of Justice*, p. 302). I am suggesting that the same point can be made regarding the difference principle, an opinion which can be explained only by viewing the difference principle as a compromise between the demands of justice and the demands of efficiency—a compromise that, because of the lexical priority of justice, only the least advantaged have the moral authority to authorize.

20.   This does not hold for rights that are inalienable (or nonsurrenderable, the sense in which I used the term in the discussion of the right to life). Thus, for example, if the right to life is inalienable in the sense of nonsurrenderable, one cannot authorize the killing of oneself by giving permission and surrendering the right to life.

Chapter 13

1.   Used also, for example, by Bernard Gert, *The Moral Rules: A New Rational Foundation for Morality* (New York: Harper and Row, 1973); and Henry David Aiken, *Reason and Conduct: New Bearings in Moral Philosophy* (Westport, Conn.: Greenwood Press, 1962). pp. 69–75.

2.   J. H. Oldham, "The Function of the Church in Society," in *The Church and its Function in Society*, eds. W.A. Visser't Hooft and J.H. Oldham (London: George Allen and

Unwin, 1937), p. 210; John C. Bennett, "Principles and the Context," in *Storm Over Ethics,* ed. J.C. Bennett et al. (Philadelphia: United Church Press, 1967), pp. 16–17.

3. James M. Gustafson, "Context versus Principles: A Misplaced Debate in Christian Ethics," *New Theology 3,* ed. Martin Marty and Dean G. Peerman (New York: Macmillan, 1966), p. 71.

4. L. M. Piatt, "Physician and the Cancer Patient," *Ohio State Medical Journal* 42 (1946): 371–72, cited in W.D. Kelly and S.R. Friesen, "Do Cancer Patients Want to be Told?" *Surgery* 27:6 (June 1950): 822.

5. John Lister, "By the London Post: Clinical and Legal Death," *New England Journal of Medicine* 298:17 (April 27, 1978): 956.

6. Donald Oken, "What to Tell Cancer Patients: A Study of Medical Attitudes," *The Journal of the American Medical Association* 175:13 (April 1, 1961): 1120.

7. Russell Noyes, Jr., Peter R. Jochimsen, Terry A. Travis, "The Changing Attitudes of Physicians Toward Prolonging Life," *Journal of the American Geriatrics Society* 25:10 (1977): 470–74; Dennis H. Novack et al., "Changes in Physicians' Attitudes Toward Telling the Cancer Patient," *Journal of the American Medical Association* 241 (March 2, 1979): 897–900.

8. Oken, "What to Tell," p. 1122.

9. For this argument, see Joseph Fletcher, *Situation Ethics* (Philadelphia: The Westminster Press, 1966). A critique is found in Paul Ramsey, *Deeds and Rules in Christian Ethics,* especially in chap. 8, "A Letter to John of Patmos from a Proponent of the 'New Morality'" (New York: Charles Scribners, 1967), pp. 226–40.

10. See John Ladd, "Legalism and Medical Ethics," in *Biomedical Ethics,* ed. John W. Davis et al. (New York: Humana Press, 1978), pp. 1–35; also his shorter version under the same title in *Journal of Medicine and Philosophy* 4 (March 1979): 70–80.

11. Judith Shklar, *Legalism* (Cambridge, Mass.: Harvard University Press, 1964), p. 1.

12. American Medical Association, Judicial Council, *Opinions and Reports* [including the Principles of Medical Ethics and Rules of the Judicial Council] (Chicago: American Medical Association, 1977), p. 5.

13. Judy Alsofrom, "New Ethical Principles for Nation's Physicians Voted by AMA House," *American Medical News* (August 1–8, 1980): 9.

14. Bernard Meyer, "Truth and the Physician," in *Ethical Issues in Medicine,* ed. E. Fuller Torrey (Boston: Little Brown, 1968), p. 172.

15. Of course, both judgments may be true. The clinician's ability to disclose may be the decisive factor, but that is a crude basis for deciding to transmit information. It could mean that both physicians should assess whether deferral to the other regarding their skills in disclosure (or lack thereof) would produce more benefit for the patient.

16. Tabitha M. Powledge, "A Report from the Del Zio Trial," *Hastings Center Report* 8 (October 1978): 15–17.

17. See *In the Matter of Karen Quinlan: The Complete Briefs, Oral Arguments, and Opinions in the New Jersey Supreme Court* (Arlington, Va.: University Publications of America, Inc., 1976).

18. American Medical Association, "Opinions and Reports."

19. Aristotle, "Politics," Book III, Chapter 15, Sec. 1286a in *The Basic Works of Aristotle,* ed. Richard McKeon (New York: Random House, 1941), p. 1200.

20. See P. Ramsey, *Deeds and Rules.* Also Gene H. Outka and Paul Ramsey, *Norm and Context in Christian Ethics* (New York: Charles Scribner's Sons, 1968); and Harvey Cox, ed., *The Situation Ethics Debate* (Philadelphia: Westminster Press, 1968).

21. John Rawls, "Two Concepts of Rules," in Michael D. Bayles, ed., *Contemporary Utilitarianism* (Garden City, N.Y.: Anchor Books, 1968), pp. 59–98.

Bibliography

Abdul-Rauf, Muhammad. "Medical Ethics, History Of: Contemporary Muslim Perspective." In *Encyclopedia of Bioethics*, vol. 2, edited by Warren T. Reich, pp. 892–95. New York: The Free Press, 1978.

Ackerknecht, Erwin H. *A Short History of Medicine*. New York: Ronald Press, 1968.

Aiken, Henry D. *Reason and Conduct: New Bearings in Moral Philosphy*. Westport, Conn.: Greenwood Press, 1962.

Ake, Christopher. "Justice as Equality." *Philosophy and Public Affairs* 5 (1975):69–89.

Al-Karmy, Ghada. "Medical Education in Islam." *Journal of the Kuwait Medical Association* 12 (1978):241–47.

Alsofrom, Judy. "New Ethical Principles for Nation's Physicians voted by AMA House." *American Medical News* (August 1–8, 1980):1, 9.

Altman, Lawrence, "Pharmacy, Science and Society: The Ethics of Execution by Drugs." *U.S. Pharmacist* (August 1980): 71–72.

American Medical Association. *Judicial Council Opinions and Reports*. Chicago: American Medical Association, 1971.

————. *Judicial Council Opinions and Reports: Including the Principles of Medical Ethics and Rules of the Judicial Council*. Chicago: American Medical Association, 1977.

————. *Code of Medical Ethics: Adopted by the American Medical Association at Philadelphia, May, 1847, and by the New York Academy of Medicine in October, 1847*. New York: H. Ludwig and Company, 1848.

————. Trial Brief, "United States of America Before the Federal Trade Commission." Docket Number 9064, 1977.

Amundsen, Darrel W. "Medical Ethics, History of: Ancient Near East." In *Encyclopedia of Bioethics*, vol. 2, edited by Warren T. Reich, pp. 880–83. New York: The Free Press, 1978.

————. "Medical Ethics, History of: Medieval Europe, Fourth to Sixteenth Century." In *Encyclopedia of Bioethics*, vol. 2, edited by Warren T. Reich, pp. 938–51. New York: The Free Press, 1978.

————. "The Physician's Obligation to Prolong Life: A Medical Duty Without Classical Roots." *Hastings Center Report* 8 (August 1978): 23–30.

Ander, Z. "Aspects from the History of Medical Ethics in Romania." In *International Symposium on Society, Medicine and Law*, edited by Heinrich Karplus, pp. 149–55. Amsterdam: Elsevier, 1973.

Anderson, Bernhard W. *Understanding the Old Testament*. Englewood Cliffs, N.J.: Prentice-Hall, 1957.

Annas, George J. "Doctors and the Death Penalty." Editorial in *Medico-legal News* 8 (April 1980): 17.

Annoted Code of Maryland. Article 43, Section 130, "Discipline of Physicians." Reprinted in *Laws Regulating the Practice of Medicine in Maryland*. Charlottesville, Va.: Mitchie, 1979.

Anscombe, G. E. M. "Modern Moral Philosophy." *Philosophy* 33 (1958):1–19.

Aquinas, Saint Thomas. *Introduction to St. Thomas Aquinas*. Edited by Anton C. Pegis. New York: Random House, the Modern Library, 1948.

Aristotle. *The Basic Works of Aristotle*. Edited by Richard McKeon. New York: Random House, 1941.

————. *Nicomachean Ethics*. Translated by Martin Ostwald. Indianapolis: Bobbs-Merrill, 1962.

Ashley, Benedict M., and O'Rourke, Kevin D. *Health Care Ethics: A Theological Analysis*. St. Louis: The Catholic Hospital Association, 1978.

Asper, Samuel P., and Fuad, Sami Haddad. "Medical Ethics, History of: Contemporary

Arab World." In *Encyclopedia of Bioethics*, vol. 2, edited by Warren T. Reich, pp. 888–91. New York: The Free Press, 1978.

Augustine, Saint Aurelius. *The Enchiridion*. Chicago: Henry Regnery, 1961.

—————. "The Free Choice of the Will." In *Saint Augustine: The Teacher, The Free Choice of the Will and Grace and Free Will*, translated by Robert T. Russell, pp. 65–241. Fathers of the Church Series, vol. 59. Washington, D.C.: Catholic University of America Press, 1968.

"Authorization of Involuntary Blood Transfusion for Adult Jehovah's Witness Held Unconstitutional—In re Brooks Estate." *Michigan Law Review* 64 (1966): 554–61.

Bacon, Francis. "De augmentis scientiarum." In *The Philosophical Works of Francis Bacon*, edited by J. M. Robertson. 1905. Reprint, Freeport, N.Y.: Books for Libraries Press, 1970.

Baier, Kurt. *The Moral Point of View: A Rational Basis of Ethics*. New York: Random House, 1965.

Ballantine, Thomas H. "Annual Discourse—The Crisis in Ethics, Anno Domini 1979." *New England Journal of Medicine* 301(1979):634–38.

Barber, Bernard. "Some Problems in the Sociology of the Professions." *Daedalus* 92 (1963):669–88.

Barker, Ernest. "Introduction." In *Social Contract*. 1947. Reprint, New York: Oxford University Press, 1962.

Barry, Brian. *The Liberal Theory of Justice: A Critical Examination of the Principle Doctrines in "A Theory of Justice" by John Rawls*. Oxford: Clarendon Press, 1973.

—————. "Reflections on 'Justice as Fairness.' " In *Justice and Equality*, edited by Hugo A. Bedau, pp. 103–15. Englewood Cliffs, N.J.: Prentice-Hall, 1971.

Basham, A. L. "Hinduism." In *Encyclopedia of Bioethics*, vol. 2, edited by Warren T. Reich, pp. 661–66. New York: The Free Press, 1978.

Bates v. State Bar of Arizona. 433 U.S. 350, 45 U.S. L.W. 4895. 1977.

Baumrind, Diana. "Nature and Definition of Informed Consent in Research Involving Deception." In *The Belmont Report: Ethical Principles and Guidelines for the Protection of Human Subjects of Research*, Appendix, vol. 2. Washington, D.C.: 23–1 through 23–71. DHEW Publication No. (OS) 78–0014.

Bayles, Michael D. *Contemporary Utilitarianism*. Garden City, N.Y.: Anchor Books, 1968.

—————. "Criminal Paternalism." In *The Limits of Law: Nomos XV*, edited by J. Roland Pennock and John W. Chapman, pp. 174–89. New York: Lieber-Atherton, 1974.

—————. *Principles of Legislation*. Detroit: Wayne State University Press, 1978.

Beauchamp, Dan. "Alcoholism as Blaming the Alcoholic." *International Journal of Addiction* 11 (1976):41–52.

Beauchamp, Tom L. "A Reply to Rachels on Active and Passive Euthanasia." In *Medical Responsibility: Paternalism, Informed Consent, and Euthanasia*, edited by Wade L. Robison and Michael S. Pritchard, pp. 181–94. Clifton, N.J.: The Humana Press, 1979.

—————. "A Reply to Rachels on Active and Passive Euthanasia." In *Social Ethics: Morality and Social Policy*, edited by Tom A. Mappes and J. S. Zembaty, pp. 67–75. New York: McGraw-Hill, 1977.

—————. "The Regulation of Hazards and Hazardous Behaviors." *Health Education Monographs* 6(1978):242–57.

Beauchamp, Tom L., and Childress, James F. *Principles of Biomedical Ethics*. New York: Oxford University Press, 1979.

Beauchamp, Tom L., and Davidson, Arnold L. "The Definition of Euthanasia." *Journal of Medicine and Philosophy* 4(1979):294–312.

Becker, Lawrence C. "Human Being: the Boundaries of the Concept." *Philosophy and Public Affairs* 4(1975):334–59.

Bedau, Hugo Adam. *The Courts, the Constitution, and Capital Punishment*. Lexington, Mass.: D.C. Heath and Company, 1977.

—————. "Radical Egalitarianism." In *Justice and Equality*, pp. 168–80. Englewood Cliffs, N.J.: Prentice-Hall, 1971.

Belloc, Nedra B. "Relationship of Health Practices and Mortality." *Preventive Medicine* 2(1973):67–81.

Belloc, Nedra B., and Breslow, Lester. "Relationship of Physical Status, Health and Health Practices." *Preventive Medicine* 1(1972):409–21.

Benn, Stanley I. "Abortion, Infanticide, and Respect for Persons." In *The Problem of Abortion*, edited by Joel Feinberg, pp. 92–104. Belmont, Calif.: Wadsworth, 1973.

Bennett, John C. "Principles and the Context." In *Storm Over Ethics*, edited by John C. Bennett, et al., pp. 1–25. Philadelphia: United Church Press, 1967.

Bennett, Jonathan. "Whatever the Consequences." *Analysis* 26(1966):83–102.

Bentham, Jeremy. *An Introduction to the Principles of Morals and Legislation.* 1789. Reprint, New York: Hafner, 1948.

Berkowitz, Leonard. "Some Complexities and Uncertainties Regarding the Ethicality of Deception in Research with Human Subjects." In *The Belmont Report*, Appendix, vol. 2. Washington, D.C.: 24–1 through 24–34. DHEW Publication No. (OS) 78–0014.

Berlyn, Simon. "Execution by the Needle." *New Scientist* 75(1977):676–77.

Berman, Joseph I. "Legal Mechanism for Dealing with the Disabled Physician in Maryland: Partnership Between the Medical Society and the State Commission on Medical Discipline." *Maryland State Medical Journal* 25 (1976):41–45.

Bhagavad Gita, The. Translated by Edgerton Franklin. New York: Harper and Row, 1944.

Bhutia, Maj. Gen. S. L. *A History of Medicine with Special Reference to the Orient.* New Delhi: Office of Medical Council of India, 1977.

Blackstone, William T. "On Health Care as a Legal Right: Philosophical Justifications, Political Activity, and Adequate Health Care." *Georgia Law Review* 10(1976):391–418.

Bleich, J. David. "The *A Priori* Component of Bioethics." In *Jewish Bioethics*, edited by Fred Rosner and J. David Bleich. New York: Sanhedrin Press, 1979, pp. 11–19.

————. "The Obligation to Heal in the Judaic Tradition: A Comparative Analysis." In *Jewish Bioethics*, edited by Fred Rosner and J. David Bleich. New York: Sanhedrin Press, 1979, pp. 1–44.

————. "The Quinlan Case: A Jewish Perspective." In *Jewish Bioethics*, edited by Fred Rosner and J. David Bleich. New York: Sanhedrin Press, 1979, pp. 266–76.

Blomquist, Clarence. "A New Era In European Medical Ethics." *Hastings Center Report* 6 (April 1976):7–8.

Boffey, Philip M. "Health Care as a Human Right: A Cuban Perspective." *Science* (June 16, 1978):1246–50.

Bok, Sissela. "Ethical Problems of Abortion." *Hastings Center Studies* 2 (January 1974):33–52.

————. "The Ethics of Giving Placebos." *Scientific American* 231(November 1974):17–23.

————. "Personal Directions for Care at the End of Life." *New England Journal of Medicine* 295(1976):367–69.

Bowers, John Z. *Western Medical Pioneers in Feudal Japan.* Baltimore: Johns Hopkins University Press, 1970.

Bradley, F. H. *Ethical Studies.* 1876. Reprint, 2d rev. ed. Oxford: Clarendon Press, 1927.

Brandt, Richard B. *Ethical Theory.* Englewood Cliffs, N.J.: Prentice-Hall, 1959.

————. "Some Merits of One Form of Rule Utilitarianism." In *Utilitarianism: John Stuart Mill with Critical Essays*, pp. 324–44. Indianapolis: Bobbs-Merrill, 1971.

————. *A Theory of the Good and the Right.* Oxford: Clarendon Press, 1979.

————. "Toward a Credible Form of Utilitarianism." In *Contemporary Utilitarianism*, edited by Michael Bayles, pp. 143–86. Garden City, N.Y.: Anchor Books, 1968.

Braybrooke, David. "The Choice Between Utilitarianisms." *American Philosophical Quarterly* 4(1967):180–87.

Breslow, Lester. "Prospects for Improving Health through Reducing Risk Factors." *Preventive Medicine* 7(1978):449–58.

British Medical Association. *The Handbook of Medical Ethics.* London: The British Medical Association, 1980.

————. *Medical Ethics.* London: British Medical Association, 1970.

Brock, Lord. "Euthanasia." *Proceedings of the Royal Society of Medicine* 63 (1970):662.

Brody, Howard. "Persons and Placebos: Philosophical Dimensions of the Placebo Effect." Ph.D dissertation, Michigan State University, 1977.

————. *Placebos and the Philosophy of Medicine: Clinical, Conceptual and Ethical Issues.* Chicago: University of Chicago Press, 1980.

————. "The Physician-Patient Contract: Legal and Ethical Aspects." *The Journal of Legal Medicine* 4(July-August 1976):25–29.

360

Bibliography

Brody, Jane. "Medical Unit to Weigh Filing of Charges against Dr. Jacobson." *New York Times*, December 6, 1972:34.

Brown, Norman K.; Bulger, Roger, et al. "The Preservation of Life." *Journal of the American Medical Association* 211(1970):76–81.

Brunner, Emil. *The Divine Imperative*. Philadelphia: Westminster Press, 1947.

Bullough, Vern L. "The Term 'Doctor.'" *Journal of the History of Medicine and Allied Sciences* 18(1963):284–87.

Bullough, Vern L., and Bullough, Bonnie. "A Brief History of Medical Practice." In *Medical Men and their Work: A Sociological Reader*, edited by Eliot Friedson and Judith Lorber, pp. 86–102. Chicago: Aldine-Atherton, 1972.

Burg, Moses. "A Psychocultural Analysis and Theoretical Integration of the Dynamics of Japanese Parent-Child Suicide." *Tōyō Daigaku Shakaigakubu Kiyo* [Bulletin, Department of Sociology, Tōyō University] 2(1961):127–54.

Burgel, J. C. "Islam." In *Encyclopedia of Bioethics*, vol. 2, edited by Warren T. Reich, pp. 785–90. New York: The Free Press, 1978.

Callahan, Daniel. "The WHO Definition of 'Health.'" *Hastings Center Studies* 1 (No. 3, 1973):59–88.

Calvin, John. *Institutes of the Christian Religion*. Philadelphia: Westminster Press, 1960.

Campbell, Charles A. "Is 'Freewill' a Pseudo-Problem?" *Mind* 60(1951):441–65.

Campbell, Donald. "The Historiography of Islam, with Special Reference to the Development of Arabic Medical and Philosophical Literature." In *Arabian Medicine and Its Influence on the Middle Ages*, pp. 32–59. Trubner Oriental Series, vol. 1. London: Kegan Paul, Trench, Trubner, 1926.

Capron, Alexander M., and Kass, Leon R. "A Statutory Definition of the Standards for Determining Human Death: An Appraisal and a Proposal." *University of Pennsylvania Law Review* 121(1972):87–118.

Carone, Pasquale A., et al. "Medical Discipline: Dealings with Physicians Who Are Unscrupulous, Disabled, and/or Incompetent." *New York State Journal of Medicine* (June 1979):1018–35.

Carter, Luther J. "NEI Votes to Protect Cold-Blooded Animals." *Science* 206(1979):1383.

Childress, James F. "A Right to Health Care?" *Journal of Philosophy and Medicine* 4(1979):132–47.

Childress, James F., and Harned, David B. *Secularization and the Protestant Prospect*. Philadelphia: Westminster Press, 1970.

Churchill, Larry R. "Tacit Components of Medical Ethics: Making Decisions in the Clinic." *Journal of Medical Ethics* 3(1977):129–32.

Clapp, Jane. *Professional Ethics and Insignia*. Metuchen, N.J.: The Scarecrow Press, 1974.

Conover, Patrick W. "Social Class and Chronic Illness." *International Journal of Health Services* 3(1973):357–68.

Cooper, Theodore. "In the Public Interest." *New England Journal of Medicine* 300(1979):1185–88.

Coriden, James A. "Church Law and Abortion." *Jurist* 33(1973):184–98.

Cox, Harvey. *The Situation Ethics Debate*. Philadelphia: Westminster Press, 1968.

Crane, Diana. "Decisions to Treat Critically Ill Patients: A Comparison of Social Versus Medical Considerations." *Milbank Memorial Fund Quarterly* (Winter 1975):1–33.

Crawford, Robert. "You are Dangerous to Your Health." *Social Policy* 8(1978):11–20.

Crawford, S. Cromwell. *The Evolution of Hindu Ethical Ideals*. Calcutta, India: Firma K. L. Mukhopadhyay, 1974.

Cunningham, Robert L. "Justice: Efficiency or Fairness?" *Personalist* 52(1971):423–81.

Curran, Charles E. "Abortion: Contemporary Debate in Philosophical and Religious Ethics." In *Encyclopedia of Bioethics*, vol. 1, edited by Warren T. Reich, pp. 17–25. New York: The Free Press, 1978.

_____. "Roman Catholicism." In *Encyclopedia of Bioethics*, vol. 4, edited by Warren T. Reich, pp. 1522–33. New York: The Free Press, 1978.

Curran, William J., and Casscells, Ward. "The Ethics of Medical Participation in Capital Punishment by Intravenous Drug Injection." *New England Journal of Medicine* 302(1980):226–30.

Daley, Dennis W. "*Tarasoff* and the Psychotherapist's Duty to Warn." *San Diego Law Review* 12(1975):932–51.

Daniels, Norman. "Rights to Health Care and Distributive Justice: Programmatic Worries." *Journal of Medicine and Philosophy* 4(1979):174–89.

Danielson, Ross. "The Cuban Health Area and Polyclinic: Organizational Focus in an Emerging System." *Inquiry*, supplement to vol. 12 (June 1975):86–102.

"Death Injection Laws Cause Problems." *American Medical News* 23(July 11, 1980):13.

DeVos, George A. "Deviancy and Social Change: A Psycho-cultural Evaluation of Trends in Japanese Delinquency and Suicide." In *Japanese Culture: Its Development and Characteristics*, edited by Robert J. Smith and Richard K. Beardsley, pp. 162–64. New York: Wenner-Gren Foundation for Anthropological Research, Inc., 1962.

Dinello, Daniel. "On Killing and Letting Die." *Analysis* 31(1971):83–86.

Doi, Takeo. *The Anatomy of Dependence*. Translated by John Bester. Tokyo: Kodansha International, 1973. (Originally published as *Amae no kōzō*. Tokyo: Kōbundō Publishers, 1971.)

———. "Amae: A Key Concept for Understanding Japanese Personality Structure." In *Japanese Culture: Its Development and Characteristics*, edited by Robert J. Smith and Richard K. Beardsley, pp. 132–36. New York: Wenner-Gren Foundation for Anthropological Research, Inc., 1962.

Dolan, John P., and Adams-Smith, William N. *Health and Society: A Documentary History of Medicine*. New York: The Seabury Press, 1978.

Dukeminier, Jesse, and Sanders, David. "Organ Transplantation: A Proposal for Routine Salvaging of Cadaver Organs." *New England Journal of Medicine* 279(1968):413–19.

Durkheim, Emile. *Professional Ethics and Civil Morals*. Glenview, Ill.: The Free Press, 1958.

Dworkin, Gerald. "Paternalism." In *Morality and the Law*, edited by Richard Wasserstrom, pp. 107–26. Belmont, Calif.: Wadsworth, 1971.

———. "Paternalism." *Monist* 56(1972):64–84.

Dyck, Arthur. *On Human Care: An Introduction to Ethics*. Nashville, Tenn.: Abingdon Press, 1977.

Edelstein, Ludwig. *Ancient Medicine: Selected Papers of Ludwig Edelstein*. Baltimore, Md.: Johns Hopkins University Press, 1967.

Edwards, Jonathan. *Freedom of the Will*. 1754. Edited by Paul Ramsey. New Haven: Yale University Press, 1957.

Engelhardt, H. Tristram. "The Beginnings of Personhood: Philosophical Considerations." *Perkins Journal* 27(1973):20–27.

———. "Bioethics and the Process of Embodiment." *Perspectives in Biology and Medicine* 18(1975):486–500.

———. "Ethical Issues in Aiding the Death of Young Children." In *Beneficent Euthanasia*, edited by Marvin Kohl, pp. 180–92. Buffalo, N.Y.: Prometheus Books, 1975.

———. "Ontology and Ontogeny." *Monist* 60(1977):16–28.

Epstein, Franklin H. "No, It's Our Duty to Keep Patients Alive." *Medical Economics* 50(April 2, 1973):97–114.

Epstein, Richard A. "Medical Malpractice: The Case for Contract." *American Bar Foundation Research Journal* 1(1976):87–149.

Eshraghi, Rahmatollah. "Medical Ethics, History of: Persia." In *Encyclopedia of Bioethics*, vol. 2, edited by Warren T. Reich, pp. 884–87. New York: The Free Press, 1978.

Etziony, M. B. *The Physician's Creed: An Anthology of Medical Prayers, Oaths, and Codes of Ethics Written and Recited by Medical Practitioners Through the Ages*. Springfield, Ill.: Charles C Thomas, 1973.

Ewing, A. C. *Ethics*. New York: The Free Press, 1953.

Fagley, Richard M. "Doctrines and Attitudes of Major Religions in Regard to Fertility." In *Proceedings of the World Population Conference: Belgrade, 30 August through 10 September, 1965*, vol. 2. New York: United Nations, Department of Economic and Social Affairs, 1967.

Feifel, Herman, ed. *The Meaning of Death*. New York: McGraw-Hill, 1959.

Feinberg, Joel. *Doing and Deserving: Essays in the Theory of Responsibility*. Princeton: Princeton University Press, 1970.

———. "Limits to the Free Expression of Opinion." In *Philosophy of Law*, edited by Joel Feinberg and Hyman Gross, pp. 135–51. Encino, Calif.: Dickenson Publishing, 1975.

———. *Social Philosophy*. Englewood Cliffs, N.J.: Prentice-Hall, 1973.

_____. "Voluntary Euthanasia and the Inalienable Right to Life." *Philosophy and Public Affairs* 7(1978):93–123.

Feldman, Fred. *Introductory Ethics*. Englewood Cliffs, N.J.: Prentice-Hall, 1978.

Festinger, Leon; Riecken, H. W.; and Schachter, Stanley. *When Prophecy Fails*. New York: Harper and Row, 1956.

Finney, Patrick, and O'Brien, Patrick. *Moral Problems in Hospital Practice: A Practical Handbook*. St. Louis: B. Herder, 1956.

Firth, Roderick. "Ethical Absolutism and the Ideal Observer Theory." *Philosophy and Phenomenological Research* 12(1952):317–45.

Fletcher, George P. "Legal Aspects of the Decision Not to Prolong Life." *Journal of the American Medical Association* 203(1968):65–68.

_____. "Prolonging Life." *Washington Law Review* 42 (1967):999–1016.

Fletcher, Joseph. *The Ethics of Genetic Control: Ending Reproductive Roulette*. Garden City, N.Y.: Doubleday, Anchor Press, 1974.

_____. "Four Indicators of Humanhood: The Enquiry Matures." *Hastings Center Report* 4(December 1974):4–7.

_____. "Indicators of Humanhood: A Tentative Profile." *Hastings Center Report* 2(November 1972):1–4.

_____. "Medicine and the Nature of Man." In *The Teaching of Medical Ethics*, edited by Robert M. Veatch, Willard W. Gaylin, and Councilman Morgan, pp. 47–58. Hastings-on-Hudson, N.Y.: Institute of Society, Ethics and the Life Sciences, 1973.

_____. *Moral Responsibility: Situation Ethics at Work*. Philadelphia: Westminister Press, 1967.

_____. *Morals and Medicine*. Boston: Beacon Press, 1954.

_____. "Our Shameful Waste of Human Tissue." In *Updating Life and Death*, edited by Donald R. Cutler, pp. 1–27. Boston: Beacon Press, 1969.

_____. *Situation Ethics: The New Morality*. Philadelphia: Westminster Press, 1966.

Foot, Philippa. "Active Euthanasia with Parental Consent" *Hastings Center Report* 9(October 1979):20–21.

_____. "Euthanasia." *Philosophy and Public Affairs* 6(1977):85–112.

_____. "The Problem of Abortion and the Doctrine of the Double Effect." *Oxford Review* 5(1967)5–15.

Fost, Norman C. "A Surrogate System for Informed Consent." *Journal of The American Medical Association* 233(1975):800–03.

Frankena, William K. *Ethics*. Englewood Cliffs, N.J.: Prentice-Hall, 1963.

_____. "The Ethics of Respect for Life." In *Respect for Life in Medicine, Philosophy, and the Law*, edited by Owsei Temkin, William K. Frankena, and Sanford H. Kadish, pp. 24–62. Baltimore: Johns Hopkins University Press, 1977.

_____. "McCormick and the Traditional Distinction." In *Doing Evil to Achieve Good*, edited by Richard McCormick and Paul Ramsey, pp. 145–64. Chicago: Loyola University Press, 1978.

_____. "Natural and Inalienable Rights." *Philosophical Review* 64(1955):212–32.

_____. "The Naturalistic Fallacy." *Mind* 48(1939):103–14.

Frederick II. "Medieval Law for the Regulation of the Practice of Medicine." In *Ethics in Medicine: Historical Perspectives and Contemporary Concerns*, edited by Stanley J. Reiser, Arthur Dyck, and William Curran, pp. 10–12. Cambridge, Mass.: MIT Press, 1977.

Freedman, Benjamin. "A Meta-Ethics for Professional Morality." *Ethics* 89(February 1976):1–19.

Fried, Charles. "Equality and Rights in Medical Care." *Hastings Center Report* 6(1976):29–34.

_____. "Health Care, Cost Containment, Liberty." In *Ethics and Health Cost Containment*, ed. Robert M. Veatch and Ronald Bayer, forthcoming.

_____. "Rights and Health Care: Beyond Equity and Efficiency." *New England Journal of Medicine* 293(1975):241–45.

_____. *Right and Wrong*. Cambridge, Mass.: Harvard University Press, 1978.

Friedson, Eliot. *Professional Dominance: The Social Structure of Medical Care*. New York: Atherton Press, 1970.

_____. *Profession of Medicine: A Study of the Sociology of Applied Knowledge*. New York: Dodd, Mead, 1971.

Fuchs, Victor R. "Economics, Health and Post-Industrial Society." *Milbank Memorial Fund Quarterly: Health and Society* 57(1979):153–82.

Gardner, Martin R. "Executions and Indignities: An 8th Amendment's Assessment of Methods of Afflicting Capital Punishment." *Ohio State Law Review* 39(1978):96–130.

Gauthier, David. "David Hume: Contractarian." *Philosophical Review* 88(January 1979):3–38.

Gaylin, Willard. "The Patient's Bill of Rights." *Saturday Review (of the Sciences)* 1(February 24, 1973):22.

General Medical Council. *Professional Discipline.* London: General Medical Council, 1971.

Gert, Bernard. *The Moral Rules: A New Rational Foundation for Morality.* New York: Harper and Row, 1970.

Gert, Bernard, and Culver, Charles M. "The Justification of Paternalism." *Ethics* 89(1979):199–210.

————. "The Justification of Paternalism." In *Medical Responsibility: Paternalism, Informed Consent, and Euthanasia,* edited by Wade L. Robison and Michael S. Pritchard, pp. 1–14. Clifton, N.J.: Humana Press, 1979.

————. "Paternalistic Behavior." *Philosophy and Public Affairs* 6(1976):45–57.

Gibb, H.A.R. *Mohammedanism: An Historical Survey.* 1949. Reprint. New York: Oxford University Press, 1962.

Gierke, Otto. *Natural Law and the Theory of Society 1500 to 1800.* 1913. Reprint. Boston: Beacon Press, 1960.

Girardot, Norman J. "Taoism." In *Encyclopedia of Bioethics,* vol. 4, edited by Warren T. Reich, pp. 1631–37. New York: The Free Press, 1978.

Good, Frederick L., and Kelly, Otis F. *Marriage, Morals and Medical Ethics.* New York: P. J. Kenedy and Sons, 1951.

Gough, J. W. *The Social Contract: A Critical Study of Its Development.* Oxford: Clarendon Press, 1957.

Graber, Glenn C. "Some Questions about Double Effect." *Ethics in Science and Medicine* 6(1979)65–84.

Green, Ronald. "Health Care and Justice in Contract Theory Perspective." In *Ethics and Health Policy,* edited by Robert M. Veatch and Roy Branson, pp. 111–26. Cambridge, Mass.: Ballinger, 1976.

Gruman, Gerald J. *A History of Ideas About the Prolongation of Life.* Transactions of the American Philosophical Society. Philadelphia, 1966.

Gurevitz, Howard. "Tarasoff: Protective Privilege Versus Public Peril." *American Journal of Psychiatry* 134(1977):289–92.

Gustafson, James M. "Context Versus Principles: A Misplaced Debate in Christian Ethics." In *New Theology* No. 3, edited by Martin E. Marty and Dean G. Peerman, pp. 69–102. New York: Macmillan, 1966.

————. "The Contributions of Theology to Medical Ethics." The 1975 Pere Marquette Theology Lecture. Milwaukee: Marquette University, 1975.

Hall, John Whitney, and Beardsley, Richard K. *Twelve Doors to Japan.* New York: McGraw-Hill, 1965.

Häring, Bernard. *Medical Ethics,* edited by Gabrielle L. Jean. Notre Dame, Ind.: Fides Publishers, 1973.

————. "Religious Directions in Medical Ethics: Roman Catholic Directions." In *Encyclopedia of Bioethics,* vol. 4, edited by Warren T. Reich, pp. 1431–34. New York: The Free Press, 1978.

Health of the Disadvantaged: Chart Book. Hyattsville, Maryland: U.S. DHEW publication No. (HRA) 77–628. Public Health Service, 1977.

Healy, Edwin F. *Medical Ethics.* Chicago: Loyola University Press, 1956.

Hiatt, Howard. "Protecting the Medical Commons: Who is Responsible?" *New England Journal of Medicine* 293(1975):235–41.

High, Dallas M. "Death: Its Conceptual Elusiveness." *Soundings* 55(Winter 1972):438–58.

Hill, Denis. "The General Medical Council: Frame of Reference or Arbiter of Morals?" *Journal of Medical Ethics* 3(1977):110–14.

Hindery, Roderick. *Comparative Ethics in Hindu and Buddhist Tradition.* Delhi: Motilal Banarsidars, 1978.

Hobbes, Thomas. *Leviathan.* 1651. Reprint. New York: E. P. Dutton, 1953.

Hollis, Harry N. *A Matter of Life and Death: Christian Perspectives.* Nashville: Broadman Press, 1977.

Hourani, George F. *Islamic Rationalism: The Ethics of 'Abd al-Jabbār.* Oxford: Clarendon Press, 1971.

Hughes, Everett C. "Professions." *Daedalus* 92(1963):655–68.

Hunt, Arnold D., and Crotty, Robert B. *Ethics of World Religions.* Minneapolis: Greenhaven Press, 1978.

Hunt, Jennifer M., et al. "Patients with Protracted Pain: A Survey Conducted at the London Hospital." *Journal of Medical Ethics* 3(1977):61–73.

"Idaho MDs Oppose Lethal Injection Role." *American Medical News* 23(August 15, 1980):18.

In the Matter of the American Medical Association, a Corporation, the Connecticut State Medical Society, a Corporation, the New Haven County Medical Association, Inc. United States of America Before the Federal Trade Commission. Docket No. 9064, October 12, 1979.

In re Estate of Brooks, 32 Ill.2d 361, 362, 205. N.E.2d 435, 436–37(1965).

In the Matter of Karen Quinlan: The Complete Briefs, Oral Arguments and Opinions in the New Jersey Supreme Court. Arlington, Va.: University Publications of America, 1976.

Jaggi, O. P. "Medical Ethics: History of, Indian." In *Encyclopedia of Bioethics,* vol. 3, edited by Warren T. Reich, pp. 906–10. New York: The Free Press, 1978.

Jakobovits, Immanuel. *Jewish Medical Ethics.* New York: Block, 1959.

————. "Judaism." In *Encyclopedia of Bioethics,* vol. 2, edited by Warren T. Reich, pp. 791–802. New York: The Free Press, 1978.

Japanese National Commission for UNESCO. *Japan, Its Land, People, and Culture.* Tokyo: Printing Bureau, Ministry of Finance, 1958.

Johnson, James T. "Protestantism: History of Protestant Medical Ethics." In *Encyclopedia of Bioethics,* vol. 4, edited by Warren T. Reich, pp. 1364–73. New York: The Free Press, 1978.

Jones, W. H. S. *The Doctor's Oath: An Essay in the History of Medicine.* Cambridge: At the University Press, 1924.

Jonsen, Albert R. "Do No Harm: Axiom of Medical Ethics." In *Philosophical Medical Ethics: Its Nature and Significance,* edited by Stuart F. Spicker and H. Tristram Engelhardt, Jr., pp. 27–41. Boston: D. Reidel, 1977.

————. "Do No Harm." *Annals of Internal Medicine* 88(1978):827–32.

Kant, Immanuel. *Groundwork of the Metaphysic of Morals.* 1785. Translated and analysed by H. J. Paton. New York: Harper and Row, 1964.

————. "On the Supposed Right to Tell Lies from Benevolent Motives." 1797. In Kant's *Critique of Practical Reason and Other Works on the Theory of Ethics,* translated by Thomas Kingsmill Abbott, pp. 361–65. London: Longmans, 1909.

Kao, John J., and Kao, Frederick F. "Medical Ethics, History of: Contemporary China." In *Encyclopedia of Bioethics,* vol, 3., edited by Warren T. Reich, pp. 917–21. New York: The Free Press, 1978.

Karplus, Heinrich. "Medical Ethics in Paolo Zacchia's *Questiones Medico-Legales.*" In *International Symposium on Society, Medicine, and Law,* edited by Heinrich Karplus, pp. 125–33. Amsterdam: Elsevier, 1973.

Kato, Masaaki. "Self-Destruction in Japan: A Cross-Cultural Epidemiological Analysis of Suicide." In *Japanese Culture and Behavior,* edited by Takie Sugiyama Lebra and William P. Lebra, pp. 359–82. Honolulu: The University Press of Hawaii, 1974.

Kelly, David F. *The Emergence of Roman Catholic Medical Ethics in North America.* Texts and Studies in Religion, No. 3. New York: The Edwin Mellen Press, 1979.

Kelly, Gerald. *Medico-Moral Problems.* St. Louis: The Catholic Hospital Association of the U.S. and Canada, 1958.

Kenny, John P. *Principles of Medical Ethics.* Westminster, Md.: The Newman Press, 1962.

Kibre, Pearl. "Hippocratic Writings in the Middle Ages." *Bulletin on the History of Medicine* 18(1945):371–412.

King, John R. "Medical Participation in Capital Punishment." *New England Journal of Medicine* 302(1980):971.

King, Winston L. "A Japanese Buddhist Perspective: Practicing Dying: The Samurai-Zen Death Techniques of Suzuki Shōsan." In *Religious Encounters with Death,* edited by Frank

E. Reynolds and Earle H. Waugh, pp. 143–58. University Park, Pa.: The Pennsylvania State University Press, 1977.

Kipnis, Kenneth. "Professional Ethics." *Business and Professional Ethics.* 2(1978):2–3.

Kitagawa, Joseph M. "Medical Ethics, History of: Japan through the Nineteenth Century." In *Encyclopedia of Bioethics*, vol. 3, edited by Warren T. Reich, pp. 922–24. New York: The Free Press, 1978.

Kohl, Marvin. "Voluntary Beneficent Euthanasia." In *Beneficent Euthanasia*, edited by Marvin Kohl, pp. 130–144. Buffalo, N.Y.: Prometheus Books, 1975.

Konald, Donald. "Codes of Medical Ethics: History." In *Encyclopedia of Bioethics*, vol. 1, edited by Warren T. Reich, pp. 162–71. New York: The Free Press, 1978.

Kudlien, Fridolf. "Medical Ethics and Popular Ethics in Greece and Rome." *Clio Medica* 5(1970):91–121.

Kuschner, Harvey, et al. "The Homosexual Husband and Physician Confidentiality." *The Hastings Center Report* 7(April 1977):15–17.

Ladd, John. *Ethical Relativism.* Belmont, Calif.: Wadsworth, 1973.

————. "Legalism and Medical Ethics." In *Biomedical Ethics*, edited by John W. Davis, et al, pp. 70–80. New York: Humana Press, 1978.

La Fleur, W. R. "Japan." In *Death and Eastern Thought*, edited by Frederick H. Holck, pp. 226–56. Nashville, Tenn.: Abingdon Press, 1974.

Lappé, Marc. "The Genetic Counselor: Responsible to Whom?" *Hastings Center Report* 1(September 1971):6–8.

Larkey, Sanford V. "The Hippocratic Oath in Elizabethan England." *The Bulletin of the History of Medicine* 4(1936):201–19.

Latane, Bibb, and Darley, John M. *The Unresponsive Bystander: Why Doesn't He Help?* New York: Appleton-Century Crofts, 1970.

Latham, Joseph Al. "Torts—Duty to Act for Protection of Another—Liability of Psychotherapist for Failure to Warn of Homicide Threatened by Patient." *Vanderbilt Law Review* 28(1975):631–40.

Lee, T'ao. "Medical Ethics in Ancient China." *Bulletin of the History of Medicine* 13(1943): 268–77.

Levey, Martin. "Medical Deontology in Ninth-Century Islam." In *Legacies in Ethics and Medicine*, edited by Chester R. Burns, pp. 129–45. New York: Science History Publications, 1977.

Lister, John. "By the London Post: Clinical and Legal Death." *New England Journal of Medicine* 298(1978):956.

Little, David, and Twiss, Sumner B. *Comparative Religious Ethics.* New York: Harper and Row, 1978.

Locke, John. *The Second Treatise of Government.* 1690. Edited with an introduction by Thomas P. Peardon. New York: The Liberal Arts Press, 1952.

Luk, Bernard Hung-Kay. "Abortion in Chinese Law." *American Journal of Comparative Law* 25(1977):372–92.

Luther, Martin. *The Bondage of the Will.* 1526. Translated by Philip S. Watson in collaboration with Benjamin Drewery. In *Luther's Works*, edited by Philip S. Watson, vol. 33. Philadelphia: Fortress Press, 1972.

Lyons, David. *Forms and Limits of Utilitarianism.* Oxford: Clarendon Press, 1965.

McCarthy, Donald G., ed. *Responsible Stewardship of Human Life: Inquiries into Medical Ethics, II.* St. Louis: The Catholic Hospital Association, 1976.

McCormick, Richard A. "Ambiguity in Moral Choice." In *Doing Evil to Achieve Good: Moral Choice in Conflict Situations*, edited by Richard A. McCormick and Paul Ramsey, pp. 7–53. Chicago: Loyola University Press, 1978.

————. *How Brave a New World: Dilemmas in Bioethics.* Garden City, N.Y.: Doubleday, 1981.

————. "To Save or Let Die: The Dilemma of Modern Medicine." *Journal of the American Medical Association* 229(1974):172–76.

McCormick, Richard A., and Paul Ramsey, eds. *Doing Evil to Achieve Good: Moral Choice in Conflict Situations.* Chicago: Loyola University Press, 1978.

McCullough, Laurence B. "Medical Ethics, History of: Introduction to the Contemporary Period in Europe and the Americas." In *Encyclopedia of Bioethics*, vol. 3, edited by Warren T. Reich, pp. 975–76. New York: The Free Press, 1978.

Bibliography

————. "The Right to Health Care." *Ethics in Science and Medicine* 6(1979):1–9.

McFadden, Charles J. *The Dignity of Life: Moral Values in a Changing Society.* Huntington, Ind.: American Sunday Visitor, 1976.

————. *Medical Ethics.* 6th ed. Philadelphia: F. A. Davis, 1967.

McKenzie, John. *Hindu Ethics: A Historical and Critical Essay.* New Delhi: Oriental Books Reprint Corporation, 1971.

MacKinney, Loren C. "Medical Ethics and Etiquette in the Early Middle Ages: The Persistence of Hippocratic Ideals." In *Legacies in Ethics and Medicine,* edited by Chester R. Burns, pp. 173–203. New York: Science History Publications, 1977.

Magraw, Richard M. "Social and Medical Contracts: Explicit and Implicit." In *Hippocrates Revisited: A Search for Meaning,* edited by Roger J. Bulger, pp. 148–57. New York: Medcom Press, 1973.

Maine, Henry Sumner. *Ancient Law.* 1861. Reprint, Gloucester, Mass.: Peter Smith, 1970.

Malone, Patrick. "Death Row and the Medical Model." *Hastings Center Report* 9(October 1979):5–6.

Masters, Roger D. "Is Contract an Adequate Basis for Medical Cure?" *Hastings Center Report* 5(December 1975):24–28.

May, William F. "Attitudes Toward the Newly Dead." *Hastings Center Studies* 1(1) (1973):3–13.

————. "Code, Covenant, Contract, or Philanthropy." *Hastings Center Report* 5(December 1975):29–38.

Mechanic, David. "Growth of Medical Technology and Bureaucracy: Implications for Medical Care." *Milbank Memorial Fund Quarterly* 55(1977):61–78.

Medvedev, Zhores, and Medvedev, Roy. *A Question of Madness.* New York: Alfred A. Knopf, 1971.

Mendenhall, George E. "Law and Covenant in Israel and the Ancient Near East." In *The Biblical Archaeologist* 17 (May 1954):26–46; (September 1954):49–76.

Menon, I. A., and Habman, H. F. "The Medical Students' Oath of Ancient India." *Medical History* 14(1970):295–96.

Menzel, Paul J. "Are Killing and Letting Die Morally Different in Medical Contexts?" *Journal of Medicine and Philosophy* 4(1979):269–93.

————. "Cash or In-Kind Aid?" In *Costworthy Health Care,* edited by Paul J. Menzel. Unpublished.

Meyer, Bernard. "Truth and the Physician." In *Ethical Issues in Medicine,* edited by E. Fuller Torrey, p. 172. Boston: Little Brown, 1968.

Milcinski, Janey. "Abortion and Infanticide in Yugoslavia." In *International Symposium on Society, Medicine and Law,* edited by Heinrich Karplus, pp. 163–71. Amsterdam: Elsevier, 1973.

Milgram, Stanley, *Obedience to Authority.* New York: Harper and Row, 1974.

Mill, John Stuart. *On Liberty.* 1859. New York: The Liberal Arts Press, 1956.

————. *Utilitarianism.* 1863. Edited by Oskar Priest. New York: Bobbs-Merrill, 1957.

Moore, G. E. *Principia Ethica.* 1903. Reprint. Cambridge: At the University Press, 1966.

Morison, Robert S. "Rights and Responsibilities: Redressing the Uneasy Balance." *Hastings Center Report* 4(April 1974):1–4.

Murthy, K. R. Srikanta. "Professional Ethics in Ancient Indian Medicine." *Indian Journal of the History of Medicine* 18(1978):45–49.

Musallam, Basim. "Population Ethics: Religious Traditions, Islamic." In *Encyclopedia of Bioethics,* vol. 3, edited by Warren T. Reich, pp. 1264–69. New York: The Free Press, 1978.

Nakamura, Hajime. "Buddhism." In *Encyclopedia of Bioethics,* vol. 1, edited by Warren T. Reich, pp. 134–37. New York: The Free Press, 1978.

Nakane, Chie. *Japanese Society.* Berkeley and Los Angeles: University of California Press, 1970.

National Commission for the Protection of Human Subjects of Biomedical and Behavioral Research. *The Belmont Report.* Washington, D.C.: DHEW Publication No. (OS) 78–0012.

Navarro, Vincente. "Health, Health Services, and Health Planning in Cuba." *International Journal of Health Services* 2(1972):397–432.

Nelson, James B. *Human Medicine.* Minnesota: Augsburg Publishing House, 1973.

Nemic, Jaroslav. "Legal Medicine in the Soviet Union: A Brief History of its Origins,

Organization, and Teaching." In *International Symposium on Society, Medicine, and Law*, edited by Heinrich Karplus, pp. 135–48. New York: Elsevier Scientific Publishing Co., 1973.

Neuhauser, Duncan, and Lewicki, Ann M. "What Do We Gain from the Sixth Stool Guaiac?" *New England Journal of Medicine* 293(1975):226–28.

"New Ethical Principles for Nation's Physicians Voted by AMA House." *American Medical News* (August 1–8, 1980):1–9.

Ninomiya, Rikuo. "Medical Ethics, History of: Contemporary Japan, Medical Ethics and Legal Practice." In *Encyclopedia of Bioethics*, vol. 3, edited by Warren T. Reich, pp. 926–29. New York: The Free Press, 1978.

Novack, Dennis H., et al. "Changes in Physicians' Attitudes toward Telling the Cancer Patient." *Journal of the American Medical Association* 241 (1979):897–900.

Nowell-Smith, Patrick H. "Free Will and Moral Responsibility." *Mind* 57 (1948):45–61.

Noyes, Russell Jr., and Travis, Terry A. "The Care of Terminally Ill Patients." *Archives of Internal Medicine* 132(1973):607–11.

Noyes, Russell, Jr.; Jochimsen, Peter R.; and Travis, Terry A. "The Changing Attitudes of Physicians Toward Prolonging Life." *Journal of the American Geriatrics Society* 25(1977): 470–74.

Nozick, Robert. *Anarchy, State, and Utopia.* New York: Basic Books, 1974.

O'Donnell, Thomas J. *Medicine and Christian Morality.* New York: Alba House, 1976.

_____. *Morals in Medicine.* Westminster, Md.: The Newman Press, 1956.

Oken, Donald. "What to Tell Cancer Patients: A Study of Medical Attitudes." *Journal of the American Medical Association* 175 (1961):1120–28.

Oldham, J. H. "The Function of the Church in Society." In *The Church and its Function in Society*, edited by W. A. Visser't Hooft and J. H. Oldham, pp. 101–254. London: George Allen and Unwin, 1937.

Outka, Gene. "Social Justice and Equal Access to Health Care." *Journal of Religious Ethics* 2(1974):11–32.

Outka, Gene, and Ramsey, Paul. *Norm and Context in Christian Ethics.* New York: Scribner's, 1968.

Page, Benjamin B. "Medical Ethics, History of: Eastern Europe in the Twentieth Century." In *Encyclopedia of Bioethics*, vol. 3, edited by Warren T. Reich, pp. 977–81. New York: The Free Press, 1978.

Park, Lee C., and Covi, Lino. "Nonblind Placebo Trial: An Exploration of Neurotic Outpatients' Responses to Placebo When Its Inert Content is Disclosed." *Archives of General Psychiatry* 12(1965):336–45.

Parsons, Talcott. *The Social System.* Glenview, Ill.: The Free Press, 1951.

Parsons, Talcott; Fox, Renée C.; and Lidz, Victor M. "The 'Gift of Life' and Its Reciprocation." *Social Research* 39(1972):367–415.

Patient's Bill of Rights. American Hospital Association, 1972.

Pellegrino, Edmund D. "Toward an Expanded Medical Ethics: The Hippocratic Ethic Revisited." In *Hippocrates Revisited: A Search for Meaning*, edited by Roger J. Bulger, pp. 133–47. New York: Medcom Press, 1973.

Percival, Thomas. *Percival's Medical Ethics*, 1803. Reprint. Edited by Chauncey D. Leake. Baltimore: Williams and Wilkins, 1927.

Perry, J. Christopher, and Chapman, Carleton B. "Medical Participation in Capital Punishment." *New England Journal of Medicine* 302(1980):971.

Piatt, L. M. "Physician and the Cancer Patient." *Ohio State Medical Journal* 42(1946):371–72.

Pickhall, Mohammed Marmaduke, trans. Meaning of the Glorious Koran: An Explanatory Translation. New York: Mentor Books, 1953.

Powledge, Tabitha M. "A Report from the Del Zio Trial." *The Hastings Center Report* 8(October 1978):15–17.

Rachels, James. "Active and Passive Euthanasia." *New England Journal of Medicine* 292(1975):78–80.

_____. "Killing and Starving to Death." *Philosophy* 54 (1979):159–71.

Ramsey, Paul. *Basic Christian Ethics.* New York: Scribner's, 1950.

_____. *Deeds and Rules in Christian Ethics.* New York: Scribner's, 1967.

_____. *Ethics at the Edges of Life.* New Haven: Yale University Press, 1978.

Bibliography

————— . *Fabricated Man*. New Haven: Yale University Press, 1970.

————— . *The Ethics of Fetal Research*. New Haven: Yale University Press, 1975.

————— . *The Patient as Person*. New Haven: Yale University Press, 1970.

Rao, K. L. Seshagiri. "Population Ethics: Religious Traditions, a Hindu Perspective." In *Encyclopedia of Bioethics*, vol. 3, edited by Warren T. Reich, pp. 1269–72. New York: The Free Press, 1978.

Rawls, John. *A Theory of Justice*. Cambridge, Mass: Harvard University Press, 1971.

————— . "Two Concepts of Rules." *The Philosophical Review*, 44(1955):3–32.

Regan, Tom, and Singer, Peter. *Animal Rights and Human Obligations*. Englewood Cliffs, N.J.: Prentice-Hall, 1976.

Reich, Warren T. "Medical Ethics in a Catholic Perspective: Some Present-Day Trends." In *Pastoral Care of the Sick: A Practical Guide for the Catholic Chaplain*, edited by National Association of Catholic Chaplains, pp. 171–84. Washington, D.C.: United States Catholic Conference, 1974.

Rensberger, Boyce. "Amphetamines Used by a Physician To Lift Moods of Famous Patients." *New York Times* (December 4, 1972):1, 34.

The Revolutionary Committee, Hua Shan Hospital, Shanghai First Medical College, Shanghai. "Hospital-Run Medical Colleges are Fine." *Chinese Medical Journal* 1(1975):315–24.

Reynolds, Frank. "Death: Eastern Thought." In *Encyclopedia of Bioethics*, vol. 1, edited by Warren T. Reich, pp. 229–35. New York: The Free Press, 1978.

————— . "Natural Death: A History of Religious Perspective." In *Life Span: Values and Life-Extending Technologies*, edited by Robert M. Veatch, pp. 145–75. New York: Harper and Row, 1979.

Risse, Guenter. "Medical Ethics, History of: Central Europe in the Nineteenth Century." In *Encyclopedia of Bioethics*, vol. 3, edited by Warren T. Reich, pp. 968–70. New York: The Free Press, 1978.

Robitscher, Jonas. *The Powers of Psychiatry*. Boston: Houghton Mifflin, 1980.

Roemer, Milton I. *Comparative National Policies on Health Care*. New York: Marcel Dekker, 1977.

Roemer, Milton I., and Roemer, Ruth. *Health Manpower in the Socialist Health Care System of Poland*. Washington, D.C.: US Department of Health, Education, and Welfare, 1977.

Rosner, Fred. "Autopsy in Jewish Law and the Israeli Autopsy Controversy." In *Jewish Bioethics*, edited by Fred Rosner and J. David Bleich, pp. 331–48. New York: Sanhedrin Press, 1979.

————— . "The Jewish Attitude Toward Euthanasia." In *Jewish Bioethics*, edited by Fred Rosner and J. David Bleich, pp. 253–65. New York: Sanhedrin Press, 1979.

————— . *Modern Medicine and Jewish Law*. Edited by Leon D. Stitkin. New York: Yeshiva University Department of Special Publications, 1972.

Rosner, Fred, and Bleich, David J., eds. *Jewish Bioethics*. New York: Sanhedrin Press, 1979.

Ross, W. David. *Foundations of Ethics*. Oxford: Oxford University Press, 1939.

————— . *The Right and the Good*. Oxford: Oxford University Press, 1930.

Roth, Russell B. "Medicine's Ethical Responsibilities." *Journal of The American Medical Association* 215(1971):1956–58.

Rousseau, Jean Jacques. *The Social Contract*. 1762. Reprint. London: Everyman's Library. 1947.

Ryan, Michael. "Aspects of Ethics." *British Medical Journal* 2(1979):585–86.

Saddhatissa, H. *Buddhist Ethics*. New York: George Braziller, 1970.

Sade, Robert M. "Concept of Rights: Philosophy and Application to Health Care." *Linacre Quarterly* 46(1979):330–44.

————— . "Medical Care as a Right: A Refutation." *New England Journal of Medicine* 285(1971):1288–92.

Sandulescu, C. "*Primum non nocere*: Philological Commentaries on a Medical Aphorism." *Acta Antiqua Hungarica* 13(1965):359–68.

Saunders, Cecily M. "A Death in the Family: A Professional View." *British Medical Journal* (January 6, 1973):30–31.

————— . "The Treatment of Intractable Pain in Terminal Cancer." *Proceedings of the Royal Society of Medicine* 56(1963):195.

Schwarzschild, Henry. "Lethal Injection and the Death Penalty." *Hastings Center Report* 10(February 1980):4.

Seigel, Seymour. "Medical Ethics, History of: Contemporary Israel." In *Encyclopedia of Bioethics*, vol. 2, edited by Warren T. Reich, pp. 895-96. New York: The Free Press, 1978.

Shannon, Thomas A. "The Tradition of a Tradition: An Evaluation of Roman Catholic Medical Ethics." In *Bioethics: Basic Writings on the Key Ethical Questions*, edited by Thomas A. Shannon, pp. 3-10. New York: Paulist Press, 1976.

Shaw, Anthony; Randolph, Judson G.; and Manard, Barbara. "Ethical Issues in Pediatric Surgery: A National Survey of Pediatricians and Pediatric Surgeons." *Pediatrics* 60(1977):588-99.

Shenker, Israel. "Test of Samaritan Parable: Who Helps the Helpless?" *New York Times* (April 10, 1971):L-25.

Shimm, David S.; Logue, Gerald L.; Maltbie, Allan A.; and Dugan, Sally. "Medical Management of Chronic Cancer Pain." *Journal of the American Medical Association* 241(1979):2408-12.

Shklar, Judith, *Legalism*. Cambridge, Mass: Harvard University Press, 1964.

Sidgwick, Henry. *The Methods of Ethics*. 1874. Reprint. New York: Dover Publications, 1966.

Siegler, Mark. "Pascal's Wager and the Hanging of Crepe." *New England Journal of Medicine* 293(1975):853-57.

Sigerist, Henry E. *A History of Medicine: Early Greek, Hindu and Persian Medicine*, vol. 2. New York: Oxford University Press, 1961.

————. *On the History of Medicine*, edited by Felix Marti-Ibaney. New York: MD Publications, 1960.

————. *On the Sociology of Medicine*, edited by Milton I. Roemer. New York: MD Publications, 1960.

Silberman, Barry D. "The Right of a Patient to Refuse Blood Transfusions: A Dilemma of Conscience and Law for Patient, Physician and Hospital." *San Fernando Valley Law Review* 3(1974):91-104.

Simmons, Beth. "Problems in Deceptive Medical Procedures: An Ethical and Legal Analysis of the Administration of Placebos." *Journal of Medical Ethics*, 4(1978):172-81.

Singer, Peter. *Animal Liberation: A New Ethics for Our Treatment of Animals*. New York: Random House, a New York Review Book, 1975.

————. "Utilitarianism and Vegetarianism." *Philosophy and Public Affairs* 9(1980):325-37.

Smart, J. J. C., and Williams, Bernard. *Utilitarianism: For and Against*. Cambridge: At the University Press, 1973.

Smith, Harmon L. *Ethics and the New Medicine*. New York: Abingdon Press, 1970.

Smith, Huston. *The Religions of Man*. New York: Harper & Row, 1958.

Smith, Robert M. "FTC Charges Illegality in Curbs on Doctors' Ads." *New York Times* (December 23, 1975): 1.

Smith, Wesley D. *The Hippocratic Tradition*. Ithaca, N.Y.: Cornell University Press, 1971.

Smith, Wilfred Cantwell. *The Faith of Other Men*. New York: Mentor Books, 1962.

————. *The Meaning and End of Religion*. NY: Mentor Books, 1962.

Soble, Alan. "Deception in Social Science Research: Is Informed Consent Possible:" *Hastings Center Report* 8(October 1978):40-46.

Somers, Anne R., and Hayden, Mary C. "Rights and Responsibilities in Prevention." *Health Education* 9(1978):37-39.

"So You Think You Know What's Ethical." *Medical Economics* (July 23, 1973):90-95.

Sparer, Edward V. "The Legal Right to Health Care: Public Policy and Equal Access." *Hastings Center Report* 6(October 1976):39-47.

Sperry, Willard L. *The Ethical Basis of Medical Practice*. New York: Paul B. Haeber, 1950.

Steinfels, Peter, and Veatch, Robert M. "Who Should Pay for Smokers' Medical Care?" *Hastings Center Report* 4(November 1974):9-10.

Sumner, William Graham. *Folkways*. Boston: Ginn, 1906.

Syme, Leonard, and Beckman, Ira. "Social Class, Susceptibility and Sickness." *American Journal of Epidemiology* 104(1976):1-8.

Takemi, Taro. "Medical Ethics, History of: Traditional Professional Ethics in Japanese

Medicine." In *Encyclopedia of Bioethics,* vol 3, edited by Warren T. Reich, pp. 924–26. New York: The Free Press, 1978.

Tarasoff v. Regents of University of California. Supreme Court of California Sup., 131 Cal. Rptr. 14.

Taylor, Paul W. *Principles of Ethics: An Introduction.* Encino, Calif.: Dickenson, 1975.

Temkin, Owsei. "Geschichte des Hippokratismus in ausgehenden Altertum." *Kyklos* 4(1932):1–80.

————— . "Medicine and the Problem of Moral Responsibility." *Bulletin of the History of Medicine* 23(1949):1–20.

Tendler, Rabbi Moses D. *Medical Ethics.* 5th ed. New York: Committee on Religious Affairs, Federation of Jewish Philanthropies of New York, 1975.

"New Principles of Ethics." *American Medical News* 23(August 1–8, 1980):9.

Thomson, Judith Jarvis. "A Defense of Abortion." *Philosophy and Public Affairs* 1(1971):47–66.

————— . "Killing, Letting Die and the Trolley Problem." *The Monist* 59(1976):204–17.

Tillich, Paul. *Systematic Theology.* Vol. 1. Chicago: University of Chicago Press, 1951.

Tooley, Michael. "Abortion and Infanticide." *Philosophy and Public Affairs* 2(1972):37–65.

————— . "Decision to Terminate Life and the Concept of Person." In *Ethical Issues Relating to Life and Death.* Edited by John Ladd, pp. 62–93. New York: Oxford University Press, 1979.

Toufexis, Anastasia. "Execution-by-Injection Laws: Moral Challenge to Doctors." *Medical Tribune* (January 11, 1978):1.

————— . "Injection-Death Laws Pose Ethical Problems." *Medical Tribune* (January 18, 1978):1.

Troeltsch, Ernst. "Das stoische-christliche Naturrecht und die moderne profane Naturrecht." In *Gesammelte Schriften* 4, pp. 156–66. Tübingen: Verlag von J.C.B. Mohr (Paul Siebeck), 1925.

————— . "The Ideas of Natural Law and Humanity in World Politics." 1925. In *Natural Law and the Theory of Society: 1500 to 1800,* edited by Otto Gierke, pp. 201–22. Boston: Beacon Press, 1960.

Twycross, Robert C. "Diseases of the Central Nervous System: Relief of Terminal Pain." *British Medical Journal* 4(1975):212–14.

Ullman, Manfred. *Islamic Medicine.* Edinburgh: Edinburgh University Press, 1978.

Unschuld, Paul U. "Confucianism." In *Encyclopedia of Bioethics,* vol. 1, edited by Warren T. Reich, pp. 200–4. New York: The Free Press, 1978.

————— . "Medical Ethics, History of: Prerepublican China." In *Encyclopedia of Bioethics,* vol. 3, edited by Warren T. Reich, pp. 911–16. New York: The Free Press, 1978.

————— . "Medical Ethics, History of: South East Asia, General Historical Survey." In *Encyclopedia of Bioethics,* vol. 3, edited by Warren T. Reich, pp. 901–6. New York: The Free Press, 1978.

————— . *Medical Ethics in Imperial China: A Study in Historical Anthropology.* Berkeley and Los Angeles: University of California Press, 1979.

Vakil, Rastom Jal. *Our Glorious Heritage.* Bombay: The Times of India Press, 1966.

Vaughan, Ted R. "Governmental Intervention in Social Research: Political and Ethical Dimensions in Wichita Jury Recordings." In *Ethics, Politics, and Social Research,* edited by Gideon Sjoberg, pp. 50–77. Cambridge, Mass.: Schenkman, 1971.

Vaux, Kenneth. *Who Shall Live?* Philadelphia: Fortress Press, 1970.

Veatch, Robert M. *Case Studies in Medical Ethics.* Cambridge, Mass.: Harvard University Press, 1977.

————— . "Courts, Committees, and Caring." *American Medical News* 23(May 23, 1980):1.

————— . *Death, Dying, and the Biological Revolution.* New Haven: Yale University Press, 1976.

————— . "Ethical Principles in Medical Experimentation." In *Ethical and Legal Issues of Social Experimentation,* edited by Alice M. Rivlin and P. Michael Timpane, pp. 21–59. Washington, D.C.: The Brookings Institution, 1975.

————— . "Generalization of Expertise: Scientific Expertise and Value Judgments." *Hastings Center Studies* 1(May 1973):29–40.

————— . "The Hippocratic Ethic: Consequentialism, Individualism, and Paternalism."

In *No Rush to Judgment: Essays on Medical Ethics,* edited by David H. Smith and Linda M. Bernstein, pp. 238–64. Bloomington, Ind.: The Poynter Center, 1978.

———. "Justice and Valuing Lives." In *Life Span: Values and Life-Extending Technologies,* pp. 197–224. New York: Harper and Row, 1979.

———. "Medical Ethics: Professional or Universal?" *Harvard Theological Review* 65(1972):531–59.

———. "Models for Ethical Medicine in a Revolutionary Age." *Hastings Center Report* 2(June 1972):5–7.

———. "Three Theories of Informed Consent: Philosophical Foundations and Policy Implications." *The Belmont Report,* pp. 26–1 through 26–66. Washington, D.C.: DHEW Publication No. (OS) 78–0014.

———. "The Unexpected Chromosome . . . A Counselor's Dilemma." *Hastings Center Report* 2(February, 1972):8–9.

———. *Value-Freedom in Science and Technology.* Missoula, Montana: Scholar's Press, 1976.

———. "Voluntary Risks to Health: The Ethical Issues." *Journal of the American Association* 243(1980):50–55.

———. "The Whole-Brain-Oriented Concept of Death: An Outmoded Philosophical Formulation." *Journal of Thanatology* 3(1975):13–30.

———. "Why Get Consent?" *Hospital Physician* 11(December 1975):30–31.

Veatch, Robert M., and Tai, Ernest. "Talking About Death: Patterns of Lay and Professional Change." *Annals of the American Academy of Political and Social Science* 447(1980):29–45.

Waddington, Ivan. "The Development of Medical Ethics—A Sociological Analysis." *Medical History* 19(1975):36–51.

Watson, Liselotte B. "Status of Medical and Religious Personnel in International Law." *JAG Journal* 20(1965):41–59.

Welborn, Mary. "The Long Tradition: A Study in Fourteenth-Century Medical Deontology." In *Medieval and Historiographical Essays in Honor of James Westfall Thompson,* edited by James Cate and Eugene Anderson, pp. 204–17. Chicago: University of Chicago Press, 1938.

Westermarck, Edward Alexander. *Ethical Relativity.* 1932. Reprint. Paterson, New Jersey: Littlefield Adams, 1960.

———. "The Killing of Parents, Sick Persons, Children—Feticide." In *The Origin and Development of Moral Ideas,* vol. 1, pp. 393–413. London: Macmillan & Co., 1906.

Williams, Bernard. "The Idea of Equality." In *Justice and Equality,* edited by Hugo A. Bedau, pp. 116–37. Englewood Cliffs, N.J.: Prentice-Hall, 1971.

Winer, Richard; Veatch, Robert M.; Sidel, Victor W.; and Spivack, Morton. "Informed Consent: The Use of Lay Surrogates to Determine How Much Information Should Be Transmitted." Submitted for publication 1981.

Winget, Carolyn; Knapps, Frederic T.; and Yeaworth, Rosalee C. "Attitudes Toward Euthansia." *Journal of Medical Ethics* 3(March 1977):18–25.

Yeo, Clayton. "Psychiatry, The Law, and Dissent in the Soviet Union." *Review of the International Commission of Jurists* 14(1975):34–41.

Zachary, R. B. "Life with Spina Bifida." *British Medical Journal* (December 3, 1977): 1460–62.

Zaehner, R. C. *Hinduism.* London: Oxford University Press, 1962.

Zimmer, Henry R. *Hindu Medicine.* Baltimore: Johns Hopkins University Press, 1948.

Index

Barry, Brian, and lexical ordering of non-consequential principles, 301

Barth, Karl, 41; and natural law, 115

basic principles, *see* moral principles

basic social contract, 110–27; and analysis of medical ethical problems, 281; and autonomy, 192–97; honesty in, 214–16; and just health care, 269; and justice, 262, 269–81; and killing avoidance, 229–37; and promise keeping, 179–83; and professional relationships, 144; *see also* social contract

basic social relationship, of a moral community, 126

Bates case and professional advertising, 81

behavioral control, ethical issue of, 5

Belmont Report, 46

ben Berachyahu, Asaph, and Jewish medical oath, 29

beneficence, principle of, 145–49, 214; and autonomy, 149, 201, 210, 211, 212; and breaking confidentiality, 141–43, 186, 188; in Catholic medical ethics, 36–37; consent and conflict with, 201; distributional adjustment for, 354n38; and egalitarian distribution of health care, 301; harm avoidance and conflict with, 160; and health risk behavior, 277; and Hippocratic tradition, 22, 147–69, 312; and honesty, 216; individualism versus aggregate good, 156; and Japanese medical ethics, 68; and killing, 227; and lexical ordering of moral principles, 298–99, 302, 303; and medical execution, 296; modification of, 146, 152; as an overarching principle, 297; and paternalism, 149–54, 195–96; to physician autonomy, 149; and patient's rights, 46, 151; and preservation of life; 165, 167; and promise keeping, 181; and utilitarianism, 170–74, 326

beneficent euthanasia, 231

benefit-cost ratio, and health care, 258

benefit-harm judgments, and individual cases, 311–15

benefits, distribution of, in maximin theory, 261; individual/community balance of, 267

"benefit the patient," and Hippocratic medical ethics, 4, 10; *see also* beneficence

Bennett, John, on omission and commission, 348n29

Bentham, Jeremy: and utilitarianism, 146, 147–48, 155, 258, 259

Bhagavad Gita, and Hindu ethics, 61

biblical history, and covenant relationships, 122

biological function, and death, 242–43

Birmingham Brook Advisory Centre, and confidentiality case, 142

birth control, 4, 40, 58

Blaurock, George, 44

Bleich, David, 28

Board of Medical Quality Assurance: *Physician Responsibility,* 104

bodily function, irreversibility of, 245

bodily harm, and confidentiality exception, 189

bombing, and killing avoidance, 236

Bondareva, Galina Petrova, and Soviet psychiatry, 54

brain function, irreversibility of, and death, 245; and moral standing, 243

brain-injured, organs from, 241

Brandt, Richard, on currency utility, 352n12

British Medical Association (BMA): and beneficence, 147; on confidentiality, 142, 143, 144, 153, 186; *Ethical Handbook,* 89; General Medical Council of, 102; *Medical Ethics,* 101–2; and opposition to medical execution, 294

Brock, (Lord), on physicians' knowledge of professional ethics, 98

Brody, Howard, on medical ethics, 7

Brunner, and natural law, 115

Buddhism: and Chinese medical ethics, 62; equality and, 65; and harm avoidance, 160; and Hindu medical ethics, 60; and Japanese morality, 69–73 (*see also* Japanese medical ethics); preservation of life and, 164; and suffering, 70

Butler, Bishop, 304

California, adjudication of medical misconduct in, 104

Calvinist tradition, and covenant theory, 41, 123

Calvin, John, and natural law, 115

capital punishment: and beneficence/killing avoidance conflict, 305; and Catholic ethical tradition, 37–38; and killing avoidance, 234, 295; *see also* medical execution

Caraka Samhita, and Indian medical ethics, 59–60

case-by-case decision making, 306–323

cash grants, and free market health care, 273

casuistry, 35–36

Catholic community/professional relationship, 111

Catholic medical ethics, 4, 33–40; and preservation of life, 30; *see also* double effect principle